THE AVIATORS

★ ★ ★ ★ ★

THE AVIATORS

★ ★ ★ ★ ★

EDDIE RICKENBACKER, JIMMY DOOLITTLE,
CHARLES LINDBERGH, *and the* EPIC AGE OF FLIGHT

★ ★ ★ ★ ★

WINSTON GROOM

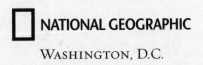

NATIONAL GEOGRAPHIC
WASHINGTON, D.C.

Published by the National Geographic Society
1145 17th Street N.W., Washington, D.C. 20036

For illustrations credits and map credits see pp. 455 and 464.

First paperback printing 2015
ISBN 978-1-4262-1369-4

The Library of Congress has cataloged the hardcover edition as follows:
Groom, Winston, 1944-
The aviators : Eddie Rickenbacker, Jimmy Doolittle, Charles Lindbergh, and the epic age of flight / Winston Groom.
p. cm.
Includes bibliographical references and index.
ISBN 978-1-4262-1156-0 (hardback : alkaline paper)
1. Rickenbacker, Eddie, 1890-1973. 2. Doolittle, James Harold, 1896-1993. 3. Lindbergh, Charles A. (Charles Augustus), 1902-1974. 4. Air pilots--United States--Biography. 5. Air pilots, Military--United States--Biography. 6. Heroes--United States--Biography. 7. Adventure and adventurers--United States--Biography. 8. Aeronautics--United States--History--20th century. 9. Aeronautics, Military--United States--History--20th century. 10. United States--History, Military--20th century. I. Title.
TL539.G73 2013
629.13092'273--dc23

2013015171

The National Geographic Society is one of the world's largest nonprofit scientific and educational organizations. Founded in 1888 to "increase and diffuse geographic knowledge," the Society's mission is to inspire people to care about the planet. It reaches more than 400 million people worldwide each month through its official journal, *National Geographic,* and other magazines; National Geographic Channel; television documentaries; music; radio; films; books; DVDs; maps; exhibitions; live events; school publishing programs; interactive media; and merchandise. National Geographic has funded more than 10,000 scientific research, conservation, and exploration projects and supports an education program promoting geographic literacy.

For more information, visit www.nationalgeographic.com.

National Geographic Society
1145 17th Street N.W.
Washington, D.C. 20036-4688 U.S.A.

For information about special discounts for bulk purchases, please contact National Geographic Books Special Sales: ngspecsales@ngs.org

For rights or permissions inquiries, please contact National Geographic Books Subsidiary Rights: ngbookrights@ngs.org

Interior design: Melissa Farris

Printed in the United States of America

15/QGF-CML/1 (paperback)
15/QGF-CML/3 (hardcover)

For Theron Raines (1925–2012),
author's representative.
For thirty-five years, a mentor, confidant,
business partner, and friend: Well done.

Oh Captain! my Captain! our fearful trip is done;
The ship has weathered every rack, the prize we sought is won.

—WALT WHITMAN (1865)

For I dipt into the future, far as human eye could see,
Saw the Vision of the world, and all the wonder that would be;
Saw the heavens fill with commerce, argosies of magic sails,
Pilots of the purple twilight dropping down with costly bales;
Heard the heavens fill with shouting, and there rain'd a ghastly dew
From the nations' airy navies grappling in the central blue;
Far along the world-wide whisper of the south-wind rushing warm,
With the standards of the peoples plunging thro' the thunder-storm

—ALFRED, LORD TENNYSON (1809–1892)

We loop in the purple twilight
We spin in the silvery dawn
With a trail of smoke behind us
To show where our comrades have gone.

So stand to your glasses steady,
This world is a world full of lies.
Here's a toast to those dead already,
And here's to the next man to die.

—WORLD WAR I–ERA AVIATOR'S TOAST

In flying's Hall of Fame
There's a special breed of men,
The Old Gray Eagle
Is among the best of them.

You see him totter on his cane
As he goes walking to his plane
So old you wouldn't think they'd let him fly.

But when he gets into the air,
And if you ever meet him there
You'll know that he's a master of the sky.

His snowy hair is so much whiter
Than all the rest of them,
The Old Gray Eagle
Among the best of men.

—COMBAT PILOT'S DRINKING SONG
(SUNG TO THE TUNE OF "THE OLD LAMPLIGHTER")

★ CONTENTS ★

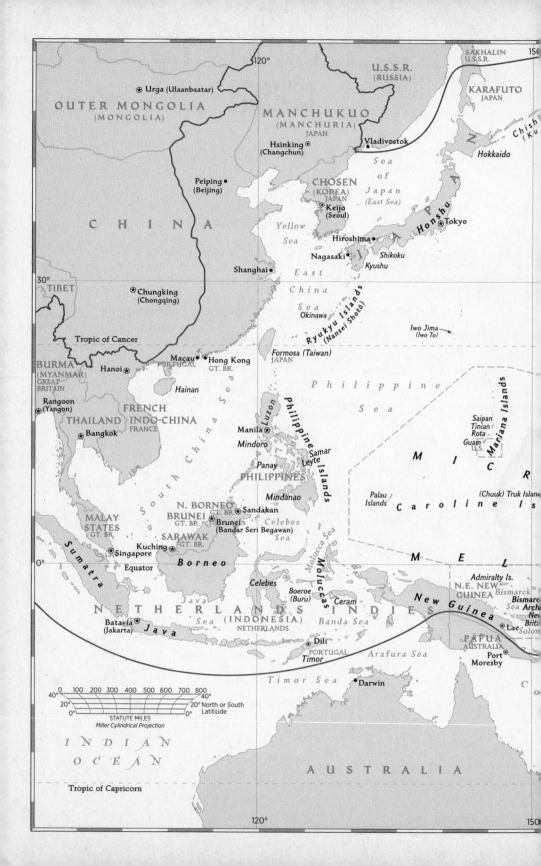

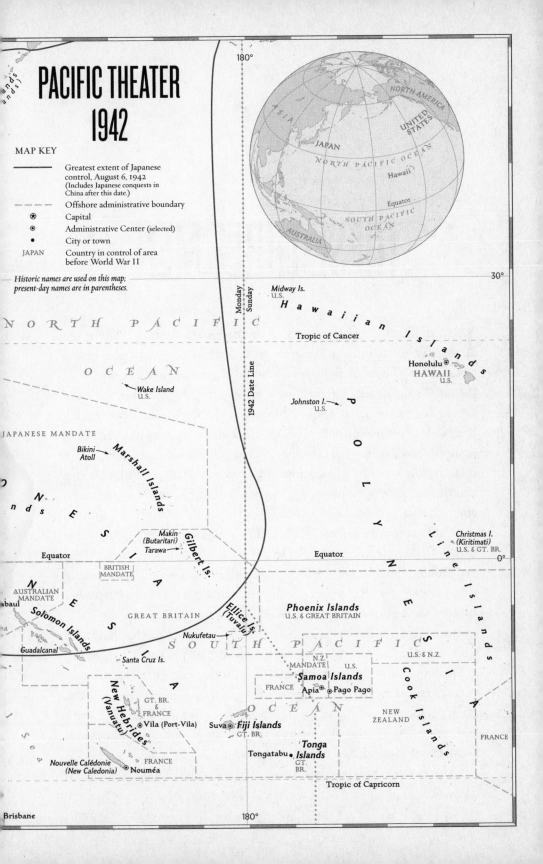

PACIFIC THEATER 1942

MAP KEY

———— Greatest extent of Japanese control, August 6, 1942 (Includes Japanese conquests in China after this date.)

- - - - Offshore administrative boundary

⊛ Capital

⊚ Administrative Center (selected)

• City or town

JAPAN Country in control of area before World War II

Historic names are used on this map; present-day names are in parentheses.

30°

NORTH AMERICA

ASIA

UNITED STATES

JAPAN

NORTH PACIFIC OCEAN

Hawaii

Equator

SOUTH PACIFIC OCEAN

AUSTRALIA

180°

Monday Sunday

Midway Is.
U.S.

H a w a i i a n   I s l a n d s

Tropic of Cancer

Honolulu ⊚
HAWAII
U.S.

N O R T H   P A C I F I C

O C E A N

Wake Island
U.S.

1942 Date Line

Johnston I.
U.S.

P
O
L
Y

JAPANESE MANDATE

Bikini Atoll

Marshall Islands

M
I
C
R
O
N
E
S
I
A

Christmas I.
(Kiritimati)
U.S. & GT. BR.

Makin
(Butaritari)
Tarawa

Gilbert Is.

Equator   Equator   0°

BRITISH MANDATE

N
E
S
I
A

L
i
n
e
   I
s
l
a
n
d
s

AUSTRALIAN MANDATE

abaul

Solomon Islands

GREAT BRITAIN

Ellice Is.
(Tuvalu)

Phoenix Islands
U.S. & GREAT BRITAIN

Guadalcanal

Santa Cruz Is.

Nukufetau

S O U T H   S E A   P A C I F I C

N.Z.
MANDATE

U.S. & N.Z.

New Hebrides
(Vanuatu)

GT. BR. & FRANCE

FRANCE

Samoa Islands
Apia ⊚ ⊚ Pago Pago

Cook Islands

U.S.

Vila (Port-Vila)

Suva ⊚ Fiji Islands
GT. BR.

O C E A N

NEW ZEALAND

FRANCE

Nouvelle Calédonie
(New Caledonia) ⊚ Nouméa

FRANCE

Tonga
Tongatabu • Islands
GT. BR.

Tropic of Capricorn

Brisbane

180°

CHAPTER 1

★ ★ ★ ★ ★

THESE THREE MEN

IN THE MURKY, EARLY YEARS of the twentieth century, when flight was still in its infancy, Americans flocked to air shows and "flying circuses" to marvel at flying machines and ponder man's conquest of the air. To the deafening, thrilling roar of racing engines they gaped in awe at displays of aerial dexterity: loops, rolls, dives, and zooms and the stunts of barnstorming daredevils that included wing walking, parachute jumping, and balancing acts in the sky. The pilots were dashing figures in their aviator's caps, goggles, white silk scarves, and high polished boots, and their airplanes, barely more than wooden frames held together with glue and cotton canvas, were wonders of the modern world.

In the years immediately after the Wright brothers' remarkable flights at Kitty Hawk in 1903, a frenzy of airplane makers cropped up, experimenting with different styles of planes: biplanes with two sets of wings, triplanes with three sets, and even quadra-planes. So-called pusher engines, with propellers located behind the wings, gave way to forward-mounted engines, and by the end of the decade contraptions had advanced from the Wrights' measly 12 horsepower to as much as 100 horsepower.

There was, however, before World War I, little practical use for aviation beyond curiosity. Early daredevils set records for nearly every flight, often competing for trophies and prize money put forth by businessmen and civic organizations. But flying remained an exceptionally dangerous occupation. Take the case of Cal Rodgers.

Rodgers was a daredevil bon vivant with only sixty flying hours to his name. On September 17, 1911, the ex–University of Virginia football star attempted a coast-to-coast flight in quest of a $50,000 prize offered by the newspaper owner William Randolph Hearst to the first person to fly from New York to California in thirty days or less. Wearing a business suit and tie, and with a cigar clamped between his teeth, the handsome thirty-two-year-old Rodgers climbed into the bucket seat on the forward edge of the wings and took off from the infield of a horse track in Sheepshead Bay, Brooklyn. Most people thought he was mad and the line from the New York bookies said he wouldn't make it past the Hudson River.

Backed by the scion of the Chicago Armour meatpacking house, Rodgers named his 35-horsepower, cloth-covered biplane *Vin Fiz,* for a grape soda manufactured by an Armour subsidiary, and plastered the name all over the wings and tail—thus becoming America's first flying billboard. Airports did not exist in those days, and pilots landed in farmers' fields. There were no fueling stations or navigational aids either, so flying was strictly seat of the pants.

Rodgers planned to follow railroad tracks (what pilots of the day called the "iron compass") to California. To improve his chances, he persuaded Armour to arrange for a special three-car train to accompany the *Vin Fiz,* complete with a Pullman for sleeping, a dining and lounge car, and a special shop car, with two mechanics, which carried fuel and spare parts for everything. The entourage included Rodgers's wife and mother.

After successfully flying a hundred miles on the first day, next morning Rodgers caught a wing on a tree while taking off and crashed into a chicken coop, sheering off the wing and lacerating his skull. The following day he was forced down in Binghamton, New York, trying to avoid a flock of crows. Over Elmira he was nearly killed in a lightning storm, and while he was trying to locate Akron, Ohio, strong winds blew him into a cow pasture, where he spent the night fending off cows that wanted to lick the glue off his plane's fabric.

In Huntington, Indiana, he crashed into a fence, smashing both propellers, a wing, and the landing gear. After a week's repair he flew on to Chicago, where he performed aerial stunts for inmates gathered in the yard of the Joliet penitentiary. At Kansas City, he flew southwest to avoid the Rocky Mountains, taking fourteen days and twenty-three landings—half of them unplanned—just to get out of the state of Texas.

By then his thirty-day window for the prize was exhausted but he flew on anyway to prove a point.

On his arrival in Arizona, Rodgers crashed and broke a leg. After it was set in a cast he flew on over the California desert, but when *Vin Fiz* exploded a cylinder and sent hot steel shrapnel tearing into his arm and boiling oil spraying in his face he managed a controlled crash in a dry lake bed. Flying through the six-thousand-foot San Gorgonio Pass into coastal California the radiator sprung a leak and wires of the magneto began to unravel. He put down in a plowed field, but by now the only parts remaining from the original flying machine were the vertical rudder, the oil drip pan, and a single wing strut.

At last, on November 5, 1911, forty-nine days out of New York City, Rodgers landed *Vin Fiz* on a racetrack in Pasadena to the delight of a crowd of twenty thousand alerted to his arrival by the Hearst press. They hauled him from the plane, wrapped him in an American flag, and paraded him through the streets. Three days afterward he flew on to the Pacific shore where his engine failed and he crashed on the beach, breaking both legs, several ribs, and his collarbone. Five months later, in April 1912, he decided to chase a flock of seagulls over Long Beach when one got stuck in his rudder, disabling it and throwing *Vin Fiz* out of control. In the ensuing crash Rodgers's neck was broken, killing him.

Some might argue that Cal Rodgers's case was an exception but they would be wrong. Pilots were killed somewhere every day in crashes caused by mechanical or structural failure and pilot error. Airmen—and a few airwomen—were just then learning what the airplane could and could not do, and about the only way to learn it was through trial and sometimes fatal error.[*]

The successes—and failures—of these early aviators were front-page news. Pilots featured especially prominently in boys' magazines and

---

[*] Rodgers's successor for the bottling company's sponsorship was a woman flier, handsome thirty-seven-year-old Harriet Quimby, who had been the first woman to fly across the English Channel. In 1912 she was killed after being ejected from her open-cockpit Blériot monoplane, lately christened the new *Vin Fiz*, over Boston Harbor. She was not wearing a seat belt as there were arguments at the time against wearing one. Her death settled the argument.

comics, fueling young imaginations at a time when America and the world had awakened to the awesome changes happening as automobiles replaced horses, electricity spread into homes, the new motion pictures vied with vaudeville, and the telephone came into widespread use.

But the airplanes of the early days had no flying instruments to speak of, which probably would have been superfluous anyway because so many pilots took to the air with precious few hours of training under their belts. More than one flew into a cloud, spun out the bottom, and crashed and burned without ever understanding the causes of vertigo. Nor was there weather forecasting worthy of the name. If a pilot saw a storm he tried to fly around it; if that proved impossible he found a farm field to land in—or tried to. Luckily, the relatively slow aircraft speeds of the day allowed many pilots to survive crashes.

There was no aeronautics board to investigate the causes of accidents and regulate improvements. Nevertheless, every experience of danger or crashing, or aerial uncertainty, was passed on from pilot to pilot or from mechanic to pilot. The accident rate, however, remained such that the actuarial life of an aviator was depressingly short.

In these early years three American boys would be among the many thousands who marveled at the spectacle of flight. They almost certainly would have followed the day-to-day flying travails of Cal Rodgers, as his cross-country flight was big news in most papers. They could not have known, as crowds cheered to stunts like the barrel roll or figure-eight loop, that one day crowds would roar for them, catapulting them to the highest levels of aviation proficiency in the twentieth century, to a point where they weren't merely great pilots but visionaries, gurus, entrepreneurs, and ultimately heroes of the highest order. They would become masters of the sky and hold a place in history that was never before and may never again be equaled.

Their names were James H. Doolittle, Edward V. Rickenbacker, and Charles A. Lindbergh. In their time no one received the sort of frenzied admiration bestowed on these three men. In 1918 Rickenbacker was America's number one World War I airman—known as the Ace of Aces; Lindbergh, a captain in the U.S. Army, electrified the world in 1927 when he flew alone nonstop across the Atlantic; Doolittle, then a lieutenant in the army, paved the way for modern airpower in 1929 by flying a plane completely "blind"—on instruments alone. In addition to their other accolades each was awarded the Medal of Honor.

This story is about those worthy feats and how these men affected America, but their stories do not end there. When World War II erupted all three were middle-aged, married with families, rich, and highly accomplished, having earned the right to rest on their laurels. The amazing thing is that instead they volunteered to put their lives on the line once more and took to the air on what would be their most dangerous missions ever.

They had vastly different personalities, these three, but strikingly similar backgrounds. Each was raised on the edge of poverty (Lindbergh's family, the most well-off, was middle class at best). Each was estranged from his father early on and each formed a lifelong attachment to his mother. All were attracted at a young age to the notion of flight, and each in his own way became a pioneer of aeronautical science.

All three visited Hitler's Germany during the late 1930s and warned American military authorities of the menacing buildup of German airpower. As experienced military pilots they were acutely aware of the growing danger from Nazi Germany's air superiority. Yet their admonitions seemed to fall on deaf ears. Airpower had not been a significant factor in the First World War, and most people, including world leaders and politicians, saw no reason why it should present a threat in the escalating crisis between Germany and the Western democracies.

England, for instance, was particularly vulnerable, but these American experts were unable to convince British leaders that, even though they lived on an island protected by the world's most powerful navy, long-range enemy aircraft—unlike anything seen in the First World War—could now destroy their cities and industrial complexes. It was nearly as difficult to persuade American politicians. The nation remained at the time in the throes of the Great Depression, and in Washington, Congress and the bureaucracy were in no mood to spend money to keep up with Germany's growing dominance in airpower.

The definitive shift toward aviation, both military and civilian in the first part of the twentieth century, and its tremendous expansion and development of capabilities in the second part, is a powerful, important story whose impact can hardly be overstated. From the flimsy crate the

Wright brothers flew in 1903, to the B-29 that erased Hiroshima with an atomic bomb in 1945, to the sleek jet aircraft of today, men of the air have braved the dangerous skies the way early seafaring explorers braved uncharted oceans. They flew, saw planes crash and men die, and flew on. No one has left in his wake a greater example of devotion to the concept of flight, critical aviation knowledge, and sheer raw courage than Rickenbacker, Doolittle, and Lindbergh.

CHAPTER 2

★ ★ ★ ★ ★

THE KING OF DIRT

Shortly after sunrise on September 25, 1918, Captain Edward V. Rickenbacker of the U.S. Army Air Service, 94th Aero Pursuit Squadron, was flying solo along the Meuse River above the grisly boneyard that was Verdun, France.

It was Rickenbacker's first day as commander of the 94th, the notorious "Hat in the Ring" gang of American Expeditionary Force pilots, and he had gone up alone that morning, to sort things out, get a grip on himself, to see how things had changed, "for the better or the worse."

The squadron had been organized six months earlier as American troops began to pour into France. Now there were just three of the original twenty-four pilots left. Rickenbacker's experience led him to conclude that air squadron leaders could not command from behind a desk; it was imperative that the commander lead personally, by example, in the air.[1]

September 25 was a critical day on the Western Front. Below, in the valley of the Meuse, nearly 250,000 American soldiers of the U.S. First Army were steadily moving into the frontline trenches between the Meuse and the Argonne Forest for the first great American offensive of the war. Suspecting that an attack was imminent, the Germans had been launching large observation balloons and sending up photographic air reconnaissance patrols in an effort to comprehend the Allied buildup.

Rickenbacker's job was to see that the German missions failed. Ten days earlier, by default, so to speak, he had been named America's "Ace of Aces" in aerial combat, an honorary title that he considered dubious, at best.

Not that the title of top American ace wasn't flattering. After all, Rickenbacker had shot down seven enemy planes in as many months. It was just that all of the former recipients of the honor had all been killed, and he could not help but ruminate over what he called "the unavoidable doom that had overtaken its previous holders."

Rickenbacker was tooling along at about 3,000 feet in his French-built Spad XIII, a new compact, rugged single-seat fighter with a 220-horsepower engine and armed with two Vickers .303-caliber machine guns. Beneath him he could see both the German and Allied trench lines snaking into the distance with the desolated, evil-looking muck of no-man's-land in between. Seven hundred thousand men had been killed there two years earlier, during the Battle of Verdun in 1916.

The day was clear and cool, with no clouds to hide in, when out of the blue two enemy planes appeared, at first far off, as specks. They soon proved to be a pair of German LVGs of the photographic reconnaissance variety, two-seater biplanes with 7.92mm Spandau machine guns in front and rear, and so they would be fairly dangerous to attack, coming out of Germany from the direction of Metz for a picture-taking expedition over Allied lines.

With the big push scheduled for early next day Rickenbacker did not hesitate, for they would have discovered the preparations for the attack. He had just begun to push his stick over to engage when a sudden glimpse of a piece of sky revealed some sinister company. Five Fokker machines were flying escort above the photographic planes.

The Fokkers were a menacing presence: top-of-the-line German bi-winged fighters, highly maneuverable and deadly, favored by the so-called Flying Circus of the late Manfred von Richthofen, the Red Baron, which continued to operate opposite the American lines despite the death of its leader. Its new leader, Lieutenant Hermann Göring, would become infamous two decades later.

Immediately Rickenbacker reversed himself and climbed for the sun to put himself out of view. As luck would have it, neither the Fokkers nor the German photo planes noticed until he got in the rear of them, a black, batlike object, angling in, and backlit by the sun—a perfect position from which to attack—above and behind. It did not seem to register on Rickenbacker that he was taking on seven enemy combat planes completely alone. He made a beeline for the nearest Fokker.

By the time the Germans spotted him it was too late. Rickenbacker tore into the formation, pressed his thumbs on the triggers, and a blast of bullets from the Spad ripped through the enemy fuselage front to rear. Simultaneously the pilot tried to pull away but he must have been killed almost instantly, Rickenbacker thought, since his plane burst into flames and crashed just south of Étain.

Rickenbacker had first intended to zoom upward and protect himself against the four remaining Fokkers, but their pilots were so dumbfounded at the sudden appearance of the fierce little Spad that, instead of rounding up for an attack, they continued in their tight formation just long enough for Rickenbacker to plummet straight through it to get at the photographing planes just ahead. This tactic so horrified the Fokkers that they immediately peeled off and turned tail in all directions "to save their own skins," as Rickenbacker put it later.

That gave him enough airspace to dive on the LVGs, whose pilots had already seen his attack on the Fokkers and were diving to escape.

The Spad plunged after the nearest two-seater, taking him in the gun sights as the two German planes began to split up. The gunners in the rear seats began firing on Rickenbacker as he glanced over his shoulder to see the four Fokkers circling above in an effort to get back into a new formation in order to attack.

Rickenbacker dived his Spad full out and plunged below the rear LVG, zooming up on the other side ready to turn in for the kill. The German pilot, however, "kicked his tail around, giving his gunner another shot at me," Rickenbacker said. "I had to postpone shooting . . . and in the meantime I saw tracer bullets go whizzing and streaking past my face." The second two-seater, it seemed, had somehow sneaked up in Rickenbacker's rear and was trying to blow him apart.

Rickenbacker peeled off out of range and performed a *renversement**— a change of direction—that put him back directly on his original target. But the German copycatted the maneuver, and Rickenbacker was compelled to perform another *renversement,* at the same time keeping a

---

* (re-vers-moh) "Suddenly zooming up, then throwing the airplane over on to one wing, and kicking the tail around to the rear," i.e., reversing direction.

weather eye on the four Fokker fighters that were wrangling themselves into formation. He also took ominous note that all the while they were all drifting deeper into Germany.

This was a dogfight, one man now against six, with *renversements, piques, zooms, chandelles, Immelmanns*—all the maneuvers that Rickenbacker had learned at his first French flying school. Push the stick—dive; pull up—zoom; working feet correcting ailerons, elevators, rudder, and hands on the triggers like a one-man band—kill or be killed—and all of it dainty as a French minuet. Below, men in the trenches were looking up, cheering, cursing. Both sides knew the difference between friendly and enemy planes. If the planes got low enough the soldiers would shoot.

Rickenbacker understood that time was short; he saw his chance and took it. The LVGs had created an opening between themselves, flying parallel to each other about fifty yards apart. He sideslipped downward until he was between the two German planes, leveled out, and then eased off the gas and began firing as he dropped back. The closest German passed right through Rickenbacker's machine-gun pattern, and just as he released the trigger buttons Rickenbacker had the satisfaction of watching him burst into flames.

The blazing enemy reconnaissance plane began to tumble until it was completely engulfed in fire and then plunged headlong toward earth. Over his shoulder Rickenbacker noticed that the Fokkers had at last reorganized themselves and were now rushing toward him from various angles, a development that led him to conclude enough had been accomplished for the day. He "put on the gas" and escaped toward his own lines. The whole thing hadn't taken five minutes.

For this action—taking on seven enemy planes and shooting down two of them—Rickenbacker was later awarded the Medal of Honor. He remained the Ace of Aces until war's end and returned home as America's hero of World War I.

EDWARD RICKENBACHER WAS BORN October 8, 1890, the year of the massacre at Wounded Knee. He was the third of eight children of impoverished immigrants from the ancient population of Swiss-Germans who had fled the old country and settled in Columbus, Ohio, and other cities of the Midwest. (After World War I broke out Eddie personally changed the Teutonic spelling of his name to the more anglicized Rickenbacker.)[2]

His father, William Richenbacher, had come over in 1879 at the age of twenty-two from the outlands of the Swiss canton Basel to escape the enduring poverty that gripped Europe's lower classes. Elizabeth Basler (Liesl, or Lizzie), Eddie's mother-to-be, arrived three years later, for the same reasons, with a note pinned on her in German saying who she was and where she wanted to go. She was eighteen. Her family had been so poor when she was thirteen that they had had to give her away, and when, five years later, she boarded the ship to America, all she had to eat during the seven-day voyage was "a round of cheese in her apron," which "she ate . . . with hard rolls that she softened with seawater."[3]

William worked at a brewery for a time but was mainly a day laborer. By 1893 the couple had saved and borrowed enough to buy a lot and build a small frame house on the wrong side of the railroad tracks in a subdivision amid factories and warehouses near the Columbus city limits.

Eddie, who was often called Rick, was pugnacious and indifferent as a student, but he enjoyed daring things. He once jumped on the back of a moving coal car in the rail yards and had to be rescued by one of his brothers. Later, he fell into a cistern headfirst when curiosity about its contents got the better of him, and another time he went too far out on a limb picking walnuts and suffered a concussion.

In 1898 he witnessed a dirigible floating over a field near his home in Columbus, which inspired him, at the age of eight, to construct a flying device consisting of a bicycle and an umbrella that he hauled to the roof of a nearby barn. Then, with the umbrella attached to the bicycle and a push from behind by an assisting friend, he flew down the steep tin barn roof and into thin air, hoping to glide at least long enough to experience the sensation of flight. The umbrella, however, immediately "turned inside out," and the only sensation Rickenbacker felt was of plunging toward earth in a promiscuous heap—bike, umbrella, and self—into a pile of sand that lay beside the barn.

The Rickenbacher home was without running water, unelectrified, unplumbed, unheated except by the kitchen stove. The children slept in a lightless loft under the eves that was freezing in winter, broiling in summer, and the family raised practically all its food. On the quarter-acre lot that wasn't occupied by the house itself they kept a large vegetable garden—potatoes, carrots, cabbage, turnips—and a handful of small barnyard animals, including pigs, goats, and chickens. Eddie wore hand-me-downs, including shoes that his father rebuilt by sewing tears and cobbling on new heels and soles. He was particularly humiliated once when fellow students poked fun at him because his shoes didn't match—in either color or style—and he fought every boy who teased him about it.

Eddie's father was old-fashioned, a firm believer that beatings were a part of a boy's education. These were administered with such regularity that Eddie was once thrashed, following the assassination of President William McKinley in 1901, merely because he questioned the notion of his own mortality and eternity. In particular, Eddie became suddenly dismayed by the thought that if he died the world would simply go on without him, and he would be forgotten, and that would be the end of it and of him. William Richenbacher's reasoning for beating him was that abstract concepts such as these were better left to him and other adults rather than occupy important time in a ten-year-old's mind.

His mother, Lizzie, was a practicing Christian who saw that the children attended Sunday services at a German-speaking Protestant church, read them the Bible daily, and insisted they kneel to say prayers before bedtime. History does not give us Eddie's reaction to such fervent religiosity—especially Lizzie's allegiance to the ominous Twenty-third Psalm—but it served him well in later life, as we shall see.

All the while Eddie's parents were keen to instill in the children how lucky they were to be Americans, born in the land of freedom and opportunity. They told stories of life back in Europe, where opportunities were rare and rules were strict and countries were almost always at war; where if you were not born of wealth there was scant chance you could ever acquire it in your lifetime. Most men toiled in the fields or factories, while women were hired help, basically little better than serfs. They weren't just preaching sunshine patriotism either. In 1898 when the Spanish-American War broke out, Eddie's father tried to enlist as a private in the army but was declared ineligible because of the size of his family. Eddie was only eight then, but he never forgot how his father would pound into the children that they had to "fight for their freedom."

By mid-century Columbus, Ohio, was a bustling manufacturing city teeming with 125,000 citizens, a large number of them immigrants, a city of smoking factories and clanking rails, chemicals, fertilizers, livestock, and above all breweries. At an early age Eddie became a newsboy, rising before dawn to hawk copies of the *Columbus Dispatch* on street corners. He and his brothers scavenged for coal lumps by the railroad tracks and brought them home for fuel for the kitchen stove or sold them for precious pennies. They likewise foraged for animal bones that they would then sell to the local rag and bone man, who'd pay by the pound and grind them up for fertilizer.

"Occasionally, somebody would shoot a horse," Rickenbacker said. In those days they ate horse meat, and for a boy the bones were worth a small fortune. A cow's carcass was even better.

The rag and bone man, Rickenbacker claimed, had crooked scales, and so Eddie's remedy for this was to soak the bones in muddy water before handing them in. Because bones are porous, his bones always weighed more than the other kids', he informed an interviewer, with profound satisfaction sixty years afterward, parlaying the occasion into a disquisition on the value of a penny. At that point Rickenbacker had been, for nearly forty years, president and CEO of Eastern Air Lines, one of the nation's premier businesses.

When he was eight, at a gravel quarry near his home, young Eddie Rickenbacker had one of his many brushes with death that involved an infatuation with speed. He'd become the leader of a crew of borderline juvenile delinquents known as the Horsehead Gang. The quarry was closed for Saturday when the gang entered the premises and spied a hundred feet down at the bottom of the pit the small metal cart on rail tracks that was used to haul the gravel to the top.

The pit was as deep as a ten-story building, but somehow the boys managed to drag the cart to the top themselves and secured it with chocks of wood, right at the lip of the pit. "It was like a ski jump," Rickenbacker later said, "except there was no landing place."

The gang climbed into the cart. Eddie knocked the chocks from under the front wheels before scrambling aboard and they began their descent into the pit. Gravity took over and the cart lurched down the incline, faster and faster, until it wobbled out of control and flipped over.

The rest of the gang was thrown clear but Eddie, being in front, was mauled by the cart, which ran him over as he was being thrown out, then bounced down along the tracks until it crashed at the bottom of the pit. Eddie was "a mess," bloody and bruised and his leg laid open to the bone, a scar he carried to the grave. One wrong bounce and it might have been his skull or his neck but it wasn't. The Rickenbacker luck was just beginning.

He built a racing car of the Soap Box Derby variety out of wood and baby carriage wheels. But there were no hills in Columbus as there were in Akron where the official Soap Box Derby was held, at least not in Eddie's neighborhood, and so the car became what he called a "pushmobile," in which a second boy would run behind with his hands on the driver's shoulders to propel the vehicle. They would race these contraptions down paved streets, drivers and pushers alternating and, barring breakdowns and accidents, the winner was nearly always the strongest and fastest team. Eddie, who had described himself as "puny" as a youngster, began to fill out in adolescence, becoming wiry and muscular.

When Eddie was thirteen his father died. Newspaper accounts say William Rickenbacher succumbed several weeks after being struck on the head by a blunt instrument during a fight with a fellow worker at a construction site in Columbus.

The night of the funeral Eddie couldn't sleep and went into the kitchen, where he found his mother at the table with her head in her hands, crying. Sitting beside his mother (in his father's chair, he suddenly realized), Eddie promised that he would abandon his wild behavior and be a burden to her no longer. True to his word, next morning instead of going to school he went out and found a job.

He would have been in the seventh grade, but instead Eddie Rickenbacker found employment on the twelve-hour night shift of the Federal Glass factory, marching freshly blown glass tumblers to the tempering ovens for three dollars and fifty cents a week.* Working twelve hours a shift six days a week was not only disagreeable for a thirteen-year-old but also deadly.† One night he quit in mid-shift, but by seven

---

* In today's money, worth $91.20.

† Glass blowers had an exceptionally high mortality rate, the causes of which were not well understood at the time. It was later attributed to toxic chemicals in the glass, especially colored glass.

that same morning he had found another job in a steel-casting company for twice the pay. Three months later he found work capping bottles in a brewery, while setting pins in a bowling alley on the side. In time, the hops used in brewing gave him headaches, and so his next employment found Eddie working in a stone yard. After a few months of cutting marble he became so proficient that he cut a headstone for his own father's grave, an accomplishment that he remained proud of all his life.

Around the time Eddie turned fifteen he was enveloped by an epiphany. A man appeared in Columbus with a brand-new two-passenger Ford turtleback roadster. Eddie had seen horseless carriages before but nothing like the sleek, polished little speedster—all for $500.

Eddie asked for a ride and with it acquired a lifetime infatuation with all things mechanical. The internal combustion engine began to exert "an irresistible pull" on the teenaged Eddie, and a desire to look under the hood of that Ford and find out what made it tick.

Not far from home was a small bicycle shop that was in the process of converting into a garage and repair works for the newfangled automobile. Eddie accepted a job as cleanup boy at reduced wages of seventy-five cents a day. Back then, "horseless carriages," as they were called, were powered by three types of engines—steam, which could be explosive; electric, which required constantly charged batteries; and the gasoline engine.

Eddie learned to drive by parking the cars customers kept in the garage, which led to his first personal encounter with the vagaries of the internal combustion engine. One afternoon he was driving somebody's one-cylinder Packard around the garage and neglected to check the oil. Suddenly the engine completely seized up. Eddie panicked, thinking he had ruined the automobile. He gingerly opened the hood, stared at the weird things inside, and deduced that the piston had stuck. He unbolted the crankshaft and, sure enough, the piston was stuck tight in the cylinder casing, which was dry as a bone. Eddie took a big gamble: he put a crowbar behind the connecting rod and levered with all his might. Instead of bending or breaking the connecting rod, to Eddie's immense relief the piston finally broke loose. He poured a can of motor oil into the cylinder, turned the hand crank to work it around, reassembled the casing, and, presto, the car ran fine.

Thus began what Rickenbacker described much later as some of his "happiest days." His obsession with engines led him to an institution of higher learning, namely the International Correspondence School in Scranton, Pennsylvania, which offered a mail-order course in mechanical engineering, with emphasis on the automobile and the internal combustion engine. It was a tough curriculum presented at college level, and the first lesson nearly did him in. He had to learn how to study and, moreover, learn how to think.

The bicycle-auto garage job lasted only eight or nine months before Eddie was ready to move on. He wanted to go where automobiles were actually made, and that turned out to be the Frayer Automotive Company, owned by Lee Frayer.

In the days of the burgeoning automobile business after the turn of the century there were car manufacturing companies on nearly every city block—Columbus alone had more than forty. Each company made practically everything itself—frames, bodies, and engines and all their accoutrements: carburetors, cams, pins, axles, valves, rings, flywheels, rods, pistons, blowers, tanks, and so forth. Eddie's first job at Frayer, like his previous one at the bicycle shop, was cleaning up the place, but that did not last for long.[4]

It soon became apparent to workmen, and then to their supervisors, that they had something special in young Eddie Rickenbacker, who had a gift, almost a prescient way with engines. An old Dutchman taught him how to build a carburetor, and Lee Frayer began to move him through the process. After carburetors, it was engine assembly, bearings, all the phases up to and including assembly of the chassis. One morning, months later, Frayer said to him, "Eddie, I want you to go into the engineering department now." That was his brave new world—designing and setting specifications for automobiles.

By the early 1900s there had arisen a great national interest in automobiles, and with them automobile racing. Americans were obsessed with speed (by 1906 the automobile record was approaching 100 miles per hour) and also morbidly fixated on the gruesome wrecks, which were all too frequent, and hardly a week went by during racing season that some young man's life wasn't snuffed out on the track. In that sense auto racing in the early twentieth century was not too far removed from the Roman arena and its gladiatorial combat.

The greatest of all these early races in the United States was the Vanderbilt Cup with an estimated 250,000 spectators, a grueling three-hundred-mile, five-hour grind in Nassau County, Long Island, and the borough of Queens, New York. First prize was the fabulous Vanderbilt Cup itself, an enormous sterling silver goblet weighing thirty pounds, and $10,000 in prize money.*

Winning this prestigious event had become more than Lee Frayer's dream; it was his lifeline. Frayer's company was in financial trouble, and only a miracle such as the prize money from the Vanderbilt event could save him. Frayer intended to enter three cars in the race, which was to be held October 16, 1906. One of the cars he would drive himself, and he had found two other race car drivers. A month before the race, the three cars and a team of Frayer mechanics were loaded on the train to New York. Eddie had been there to help, and as the last car was being put on board Frayer said to him, "Eddie, how long would it take you to run home and get your bag?"

He didn't need to be asked twice, hightailing it back to the depot with his father's ragged old duffel "traveling bag." It was going to be quite an adventure for a fifteen-year-old boy who'd never been out of Columbus, Ohio, and it only got better the morning after they arrived when Frayer handed him a leather driving helmet and a pair of fancy Zeiss goggles. "I want you to be my riding mechanic," Frayer said, and began instructing him in his duties.

The driver, Frayer explained, has to pay full attention to the road and the race. Eddie, as the mechanic, was to monitor the oil and gasoline pressure, pumping them up if pressure got low, as well as watching the tires. Tires frequently came apart during races; none would last more than a hundred miles and Eddie was to keep a close watch for telltale signs. In addition, Eddie was to keep an eye to the rear and bang Frayer once on the knee with his fist if a car was coming up to pass. The tapping system was developed because they would be unable to hear each other over the roar of the mufflerless engine. Two bangs meant a passing car.

---

* Roughly $250,000 in today's money.

On the second day of practice they had a wreck. The brakes failed and they missed a curve and hit a ditch, bounced out of it, and hit a sand dune. The car turned over and threw both of them clear, aghast but unhurt except for cuts and bruises.

Next day doing seventy down a stretch they flew through a flock of guinea hens crossing the road. Feathers and fowl burst everywhere. One bird was sucked into the large blower in front and the Frayer race car became a one-man poultry processing plant: "We picked him up, killed him, feathered him, broiled him, and carved him up all in a split second," Rickenbacker said.

On September 22 the elimination race was held.

As they entered a curve Frayer pushed the car too hard and a rear tire exploded; they fishtailed before control was regained and stopped to change the tire. No sooner had they gotten under way than Rickenbacker saw the engine temperature was in the red zone. He noticed a faint knocking that steadily grew and the car began losing speed. He had squeezed the oil pressure up, but the knocking grew louder and other cars began to pass. Through some leak, the engine oil was gone, as well as the race, the money, the cup, and Frayer's auto racing enterprise. Frayer pulled to the side of the road and turned off the ignition. "We're through" was all he said.

Frayer may have been out of the racing business but he soon landed on his feet as chief engineer of Clinton DeWitt Firestone's* Columbus Buggy Company, with a thousand-man workforce, one of the largest in the country, which had started putting out electric-powered horse buggies and now wished to build a full-fledged automobile. Frayer brought the now seventeen-year-old Eddie Rickenbacker with him as chief of design at $20 a week, with a dozen grown men under him.

Eddie had shown himself to be a mechanical genius, and he was so personable at smoothing over problems that Firestone made him a sales manager, opening dealerships throughout Texas, at the princely sum of $125 a month. The new job not only allowed Eddie to contribute significantly to his family's support, but it also helped him pay off the mortgage on their home. He continued moving up in the company,

---

* A cousin to the Firestone who started the motor tire empire.

becoming a branch manager in Omaha, with another hefty raise in salary. Satisfying as this was, though, no amount of money or power could slake Eddie Rickenbacker's lust for speed.

By 1910 he was nineteen years old, a strapping six feet, two inches tall, and ruggedly handsome with a head of rich black hair, a square jaw, conspicuous dimples, a prominent nose, and dark penetrating eyes. In small midwestern towns of the day, dirt track auto racing was immensely popular. Lee Frayer had produced a sleek little Firestone roadster that Eddie determined would be perfect for such events and add to the luster of the Firestone brand if he began winning races.[5]

He stripped one of the roadsters down to its essentials, removing its body and fenders, and installed an extra gas tank in the rear. He had the car painted white, which would become his racing trademark, and had a pair of white coveralls made to match.

The first event Rickenbacker entered was a twenty-five-mile county fair contest in Red Oak, Iowa. Most of his competitors were fellow car salesmen and dealers, trying to promote their products and win some prize money at the same time. The day before the race Eddie arrived in Red Oak and drove alone on the track, round and round, until he had memorized the dimensions of every curve and calculated the fastest safe speed at which it could be taken. When he was finished, Eddie knew when to brake, when to accelerate, and when to coast or float along the entire track, a practice that would set him apart during his entire racing career.

Eddie lost at Red Oak but he quickly strung together victories at Omaha and Columbus.

In the weeks before each of his races Eddie practiced at the track so many times he could take the curves "blindfolded." Not only was he consistently a winner in these races, but people would come up to him afterward and say, "I want that car," which made him doubly successful.

BY 1911 THE INDIANAPOLIS 500 had become the foremost automotive event in the world and featured some of the greatest drivers of the day: Ray Harroun, Bob Burman, Louis Chevrolet, Barney Oldfield, and Art Greiner. With Rickenbacker and Frayer alternating as drivers in Frayer's powerful new Red Wing Special, Eddie was driving about halfway through the race when just ahead of him Greiner's wheel disintegrated and the car pitched, sending Greiner's mechanic through the air to his death and breaking Greiner's arm. Harroun won with an average speed of 74.69 miles per hour* and the Frayer-Rickenbacker Red Wing placed eleventh—just out of the money but not a bad start for beginners in a big-time race.

It was the first time Rickenbacker had come face-to-face with death on the racetrack, but if he was unnerved he didn't show it. It was also the first time that Rickenbacker fully absorbed the sordid bloodlust of the crowd. There was no mistaking the fervent, electrified exhortations for "More speed! More speed!" and "Faster! Faster!" As one observer put it, here was the "ugliest animal sound in all nature: the frenzied screaming, yelling, howling of men and women who in their lust for thrills and blood had torn their garments of human dignity to shreds."[6] The drivers knew this, but auto racing was a big-time sport, with major paydays, which made front-page news.

After Indianapolis, Eddie found it difficult no matter how much money he was making to go back to selling cars and dirt track racing in the sticks. After another year he resigned from Firestone's company and purchased a one-way ticket to Des Moines and the Maytag-Mason Motor Company, whose chief engineer was a thirty-six-year-old automotive genius named Fred Duesenberg.

At the newly prestigious Sioux City 300 on July 4, 1914, the Duesenberg team was so broke it couldn't afford a garage for the cars, so Eddie drove the Duesenbergs under the grandstand, where the mechanics slept on cots and ate on credit from a local diner after promising the proprietor a share of the prize money they said they were sure to win. Even their cat, whose name was Lady Luck, deserted them.

At some point Rickenbacker remembered a story from Swiss folklore that his mother once told him about being down on your luck: get a bat, cut its heart out, and tie it to your middle finger with red silk thread. This would make things go well. Ever since he was a small boy Rickenbacker

---

* Harroun eschewed having a mechanic ride with him—a first for this race—and in his place installed a gadget that proved to be a rearview mirror, according to Eddie, "The first one ever seen."

had been superstitious and kept a collection of rabbits' feet, buckeyes, and other charms to ward off bad luck. But the bat heart was supposed to *bring good luck,* a desperate move for desperate times. Rickenbacker was boarding with a local farmer (also on credit) and offered the man's children a silver dollar for the first one who brought him a live bat. The night before the race, just as he was preparing for bed, one of the youngsters produced "a mean-looking mouse-like creature." Early next morning Rickenbacker drove to town for a spool of red silk string and, in secret, murdered the bat, cut out what he thought was its heart, tied it to his middle finger, and assumed he was invincible.

The Sioux City Speedway was wretched. A two-mile oval racecourse was built across the Missouri River from the city, so it was actually in Nebraska, cut out of a large cornfield, and instead of using boards, concrete, or bricks as they did at Indianapolis, the Sioux City promoters tried to create a track out of dirt and thirty thousand gallons of crude oil, which was supposed to solidify into a smooth racing surface. It did no such thing. When it was dry the cars broke up the congealed overlay into rock-hard chunks that often flew back at the drivers with terrific force. The drivers called it "gumbo." Rickenbacker had fabricated a wire-mesh screen to protect himself and his drivers and mechanics from it, but it wasn't foolproof, as he soon found out.

The Sioux City Race Week began on an ominous note. On June 28 in far-off Sarajevo, Bosnia, a Serbian assassin shot and killed Archduke Franz Ferdinand of Austria. The event was scarcely noticed in the American press but would have a profound effect on the life and career of then twenty-three-year-old Eddie Rickenbacker.

Promoters of the Sioux City race had forecast as many as ten thousand spectators would show up, but when fully fifty thousand unruly race fans arrived neither the sponsors nor the city were prepared for the influx. The weather was firecracker hot when high rollers from Chicago disembarked from their private railcars and headed for the nearest saloons, which were crammed with everyone from royalty to riffraff. The Iowa Anti-Saloon League and a host of indignant evangelists set up an enormous tent to convert the sinners and buttress the faithful. But all good intentions were swamped by the hard-drinking, hard-gambling mob, which included cardsharps, prostitutes, reporters, pickpockets, and the morbidly curious, as well as the aforesaid swells, many of whom slept a dozen to a room, or in hotel lobbies, or as a last resort on sidewalks or in the woods, like hoboes.

By day and by night, along with the boozing, they laid odds on the racing field, which included such stellar drivers as "Wild Bob" Burman*— whom the bookies were giving odds of 5 to 1—Howdy Wilcox,† Spencer Wishart,‡ Billy Chandler,§ and the ubiquitous Barney Oldfield. The relatively little-known Rickenbacker was supremely confident in what he called "a golden period" in his life, while the gamblers put his chances of winning at 8 to 1.

Soon after the gun went off Rickenbacker and his mechanic Eddie O'Donnell◖ were proceeding as planned, armed with the dried-out bat heart. Their car was not as fast as some of the others, but Eddie made up for it on the turns, which he had thoroughly mapped out in his mind, as usual.

Toward the end of the race Rickenbacker was in a two-man duel for the lead with his friend Wishart, who was driving one of the cars that was faster than the Duesenberg on the straightaways. As Wishart pulled ahead he created a virulent stream of gumbo that spattered the Duesenberg from grille to windscreen and often bounced lethally overhead, causing the drivers to duck.

With five laps to go, Rickenbacker regained a slight lead, but when he looked at the oil gauge he noticed the pressure had fallen. He nudged O'Donnell as they went into a curve, but when they came out on the straightaway the pressure was even lower. "What in the hell is the matter with Eddie?" Rickenbacker thought, but when he managed to glance over his heart sank. The mechanic was sprawled in his seat, either dead or unconscious from a big chunk of gumbo that had struck him in the forehead.

Rickenbacker made a decision not to stop, and on the next stretch he leaned over himself and made a few pumps of the oil bulb, which was

---

* Burman was killed in a racing accident in 1916.

† Wilcox did not survive a race car crash in 1923.

‡ Wishart died in a crash the following September.

§ Chandler was killed on the racetrack in 1924.

◖ O'Donnell died in a racing wreck in 1920.

good enough until O'Donnell at last came to and was able to resume his duties. They won the race by forty-eight seconds, and with the $10,000 Eddie won plus $2,500 from a third-place win by another Duesenberg racer the team checked into first-class rooms in the best hotel in town and dined on meals fit for a king.

Rickenbacker had now broken into the big-time race car circuit as a serious player, and his photograph, grinning and mud-spattered, was flashed on sports pages from coast to coast and foreign lands as well. Also, as was the custom of the day, sportswriters gave Rickenbacker half a dozen sobriquets, most of them a nod to his Germanic-sounding name: "The Dutch Demon," "Baron Von Rickenbacher," the "Big Teuton," and so forth. A racing writer even published a two-stanza poem about Eddie in the magazine *Motor Age* in which he referred to him as "That Deutscher, Rickenbacher"—all of which would cause Eddie a good deal of trouble before long.

RICKENBACKER PLACED IN THE MONEY in two other major races that season, and two minor ones as well, and was rated the sixth best driver in the country. This accolade was tempered by the death of Spencer Wishart, who was killed a few weeks after the Sioux City event when he smashed into a tree on the fourteenth lap of a race in Elgin, Illinois.

When the season was done Rickenbacker looked to his immediate future. He liked the Duesenberg team but had lost confidence in the company's ability to build a car that could withstand the rigors of a long race. After Sioux City, on several occasions he was forced to drop out of races because of mechanical troubles. Also there was the constant worry of financing.

Eddie left Maytag-Mason Motors in November 1914 and took one of the big Peugeot racers he had come to admire to California to drive in the three-hundred-mile Point Loma race in San Diego on Thanksgiving Day. He remained in California and in January 1915 he won the Los Angeles Grand Prize and the Vanderbilt Cup—which was held in San Francisco that year—and established new records in winning at Providence, Sioux City, and Omaha, where his average speed was 93 miles per hour. He continued to rely on the superstition of tying a dead bat's heart to his finger, the bats being supplied by his brother Albert, who would ship them to him in a cigar box via rail express.

Eddie went on to win a second championship at the Sioux City Speedway, but tragedy struck halfway through the race. Eddie was attempting to pass Charlie Cox, who moved over as required, but then swerved back to avoid another car, causing Rickenbacker's Duesenberg to slightly strike Cox's left rear wheel. It was enough to send Cox's Ogden Special rocketing out of control, smashing through the fence, flipping over, and bouncing high in the air before coming down to crush both Cox and his mechanic, killing them instantly.

After that incident, Eddie took stock. He woke up one night in his hotel room with a terrible dream that he was in the midst of a crash from which there was "no possible escape." Nothing he'd ever experienced was so terrifying, and as he sat up in bed shaking he began to recount and relive his many brushes with death. Then it began to dawn on him just how fortunate he was that although he had come within an eyelash of death more times than he could count he was still alive.

This led to another epiphany, a revelation that the Lord had somehow saved him for "some special purpose," though he knew not what. Nevertheless he decided that he must prepare himself both spiritually and physically for the challenge.[7]

That night, Rickenbacker said sixty years later, and every night thereafter, when he was able, he got down on his knees to pray, as his mother had taught him. To strengthen his body, Rickenbacker swore off cigarettes and alcohol (a pledge that was not long maintained) and developed a special physical exercise regimen performed for fifteen minutes every morning when he woke and every night before he went to bed. He kept this up, he claimed, well into his seventies.

He also designed a strict self-improvement program, starting with the practice of carrying with him every day a pocket dictionary to look up words gleaned from men in "higher positions," whom he had begun to meet as he worked his way up the race car circuit. For some reason, he also gave himself a middle name—which his parents had somehow neglected to bestow upon him—"Vernon," because he liked the sound of it and the way it looked on paper. And he drew up a whole "booklet of rules," a sort of life guide he swore to abide by, beginning with: "Always conduct yourself as a gentleman."

These were fairly reasonable resolutions, and they reflected the one overarching feature of Rickenbacker's character to this point, which was an almost superhuman determination to succeed at whatever he decided to do. Armed with all this positive new philosophy, Rickenbacker now set out to become the best race car driver in the world.

IN 1916 EDDIE TORE UP THE TRACKS, and one of his specialties was the somewhat dubious tactic of purposely skidding into sharp turns on dirt courses in order to stir up an impenetrable cloud of track dust that temporarily blinded the drivers behind him and caused them to slow down. Barney Oldfield was particularly indignant over this ploy, but Rickenbacker remained self-possessed and wore with pride the additional moniker "King of Dirt," making jokes with newspaper reporters about "leaving 'em in my dust."

He had so far been faithful to his resolutions; after work or a race, instead of carousing in the saloons with the other drivers, Eddie went back to his hotel and generally ordered supper from room service with some of his crew. Unlike many of his comrades he did not go for loud clothing. Instead, he was soft-spoken and courteous, and off track he wore conservative business suits. He kept away from crowds, avoided publicity and women, wanting no distractions from his racing. Nevertheless, he was a target for hundreds of mash notes from female fans and was constantly dogged by "engagement" rumors. For example, he received this telegram from a Miss Irene Tams, a movie actress whose latest hit, *Lola,* was described thusly: "With the help of an electric ray machine a scientist brings back to life his daughter killed in a car crash, but fails to revive her soul." From the Seminole Hotel in Jacksonville, Florida, she telegraphed Rickenbacker proposing a "leap year marriage" to him.*

Eddie replied with a profusely flattering letter that ended this way, however: "A women is only a woman, but my soul mate is a racing car."[8]

Eddie changed race cars again that year—to Maxwells—in his quest to find an automobile that would run consistently through an entire race

---

* It was a custom of the times that in leap years women were permitted to propose to men.

without breaking down. For $25,000 he bought four race cars and set up a syndicate consisting of the owners of the Indianapolis 500 racetrack.

He streamlined the Maxwells from the tires up; engines were overhauled and all extra weight removed, giving the cars an extra 10 to 12 miles per hour. Eddie designed a special cowl to protect drivers in rollovers. He paid the mechanics and other team members on an incentive basis from the net winnings. Days were long and tedious—seven a.m. till after dark—and Eddie introduced a phonograph to the garage so that every time work began to drag he would put on a stirring march or other fast-time music.

Out of thirteen major races that Eddie's team entered in 1916, his Maxwells won seven. Counting revenues from sponsors and exhibitions the profit after expenses was $78,000;[*] that total was not counting $60,000 Eddie had personally won. Late in the season Eddie decided to go to California to race with the Duesenberg team in Santa Monica for the American Grand Prize. There he had two fateful encounters that would change his life forever.

The first occurred a few days before the race when he was driving through Riverside, in the Moreno Valley about halfway between Los Angeles and Palm Springs, and he spotted a flying machine parked beside a hangar. On an impulse, Eddie turned in because he'd never seen an airplane up close. As he was peering into the cockpit, the plane's owner, a man about his own age, emerged from the hangar and immediately recognized him from the newspapers. He introduced himself as Glenn Martin.[†] The plane, Martin said, was a two-seat "bomber" he had designed for the U.S. Navy, and he said to Eddie, "Would you like to take a ride?"

Death-defying race car driver that he was, Rickenbacker had a fear of heights tracing back to the flying umbrella bicycle fiasco of his childhood. Even looking down from tall buildings made him dizzy. Also, at that

---

[*] About $1.5 million today.

[†] Glenn L. Martin was president of the newly formed Wright-Martin Aircraft Company, founded with Wilbur and Orville Wright. Over the years it would merge into the giant Martin Marietta and eventually the Lockheed Martin aeronautics and aerospace conglomerate.

point, Eddie held the airplane in low esteem. Barnstormers and stunt fliers were crashing and dying with such gruesome regularity that most Americans considered the flying machine "a deathtrap." One would almost automatically have expected him to say no.

Instead, he said, "Sure," and thus began his lifelong affair with aviation.[9]

Once they were airborne Eddie had to screw up the courage to look down from the cockpit. The sensations of dizziness and fear were gone. Fascinated, Eddie marveled at being aloft, floating high above the roads and fields of the valley, while Martin hollered back, pointing out sights and landmarks above the engine's roar. The landing unnerved Rickenbacker, because the ground had seemed to come up so swiftly, but he quickly got over it. They had been up for about thirty minutes and Eddie was so excited over the experience he couldn't resist telling Martin about his vertigo, and wondering why it hadn't occurred on the flight.

"It's because there's nothing to judge height by," Martin told him. "There's no edge to look over."

The encounter with Glenn Martin was quickly followed by another chance meeting freighted with possibilities. Again, Eddie was driving through the countryside near Los Angeles when he passed by a cow pasture in which sat a single-seat U.S. Army biplane with a pilot standing beside it despondently staring at the engine. Eddie pulled over to see what could be done.

The pilot was a Major T. F. Dodd of the Army Air Service, which was then so lowly regarded by the military army brass that it was part of the Signal Corps. Dodd explained that he'd had to put the plane down in the pasture because its engine had lost power. "It runs," Dodd said unhappily, "but does not deliver enough power to keep aloft."

He asked Eddie if he knew anything about engines.

Eddie said he did.

Dodd spun the prop and the engine caught. Eddie quickly determined that the problem lay in the ignition system; upon further inspection he saw that a coupling had slipped off the magneto, which powered the plane's electrical system. Eddie reinstalled the coupling and the engine performed splendidly. Rickenbacker didn't know it but he'd made a friend who would change his fortunes at a most opportune moment.

★ ★ ★ ★ ★

CHAPTER 3

THE MAN WITH THE OUTSIDE LOOP

O N THE FOGGY MORNING of September 24, 1929, at Mitchel Field on New York's Long Island, U.S. Army First Lieutenant James H. "Jimmy" Doolittle, already one of the world's most famed aviators, strapped himself into the seat of a Consolidated NY-2 U.S. Navy training plane, stuck his head under a canvas hood, and, with no view whatsoever of the outside world, taxied, took off, flew around, and landed, using nothing but the crude navigational instruments beneath his shroud. By this singular, decisive feat Doolittle advanced aviation into the modern age, in which weather would no longer be a controlling factor in flying.

Doolittle started a colossal revolution; previously, pilots had been taught to mistrust instruments and fly by their instincts, to get the "feel of the plane"—in other words, to fly by seat of the pants. Pilots invariably let bravado get the better of them, and thousands of aviators worldwide perished in fog, rainstorms, blizzards, cloud banks, and dark of night during the nearly quarter century after the Wright brothers' historic first flight.

Those were the days when flying was among the most dangerous of occupations. For example, thirty-one of the forty pilots hired by the U.S. Postal Service to deliver airmail between 1919 and 1926 were killed in crashes. "It was pretty much a suicide club," one of them remarked later. Charles Lindbergh was one of these airmail pilots, but somehow he escaped death or serious injury, though he had to bail out of a crashing plane more than once. The most perilous aerial affliction was vertigo, which often comes on when a pilot cannot see the ground, usually because of fog or clouds. It confuses the senses, leading the flier to mistrust his instincts and his instruments (if he has them) and become unbalanced, sometimes thinking he is turning right when he is turning left, or climbing when he is actually losing altitude or stalling.* By 1929 a handful of farsighted flight pioneers had concluded that "aviation could not progress until planes could fly safely day or night in almost any kind of weather." Foremost among these was Dr. Jimmy Doolittle, recently armed with a PhD in aeronautical engineering from the Massachusetts Institute of Technology.

In 1928, already world famous as a test pilot and aerial racer, Doolittle was lent by the army to head up a group of fliers and scientists financed by Guggenheim money at Mitchel Field† near Hempstead, Long Island, to investigate and provide solutions for "blind flying conditions" and "aircraft spin control."

The day after Doolittle made his flight, the story's headline in the *New York Times* read, "Blind Plane Flies 15 Miles and Lands: Fog Peril Overcome." That was a bit of a stretch, but it would not be off the mark to say that Doolittle's feat was a giant leap forward for the viability of commercial aviation.

JAMES HAROLD DOOLITTLE WAS BORN in Alameda, California, on December 14, 1896.[1] His father, Frank Henry Doolittle, a carpenter, was descended from protestant Huguenots who fled religious persecution in France and settled in New England in the late 1700s or early 1800s. In the mid-1890s he married Doolittle's mother, Rosa Cerenah Shephard,

---

* This is the condition thought to be responsible for the strange flying death of John F. Kennedy Jr. and his wife and sister-in-law, whose plane dived into the ocean off Martha's Vineyard in 1999.

† Now home of the Cradle of Aviation Museum, the Nassau Coliseum, and Hofstra University.

a strong-willed, twenty-six-year-old beauty of "sturdy pioneer stock." James was their only child and their means were modest.

Frank Doolittle turned out to be one of the dreamers and wanderers who were constantly on the make for adventure and fortune. Less than six months after James Doolittle was born his father joined the frantic stampede known as the Klondike Gold Rush. Bad luck overtook him from the start when he lost all of his carpenter's tools in a shipwreck on his way to the Yukon. He then made his way to Nome, Alaska, an Eskimo fishing village on a vast and treeless plain, bound by the bleakness of the Bering Sea.

Flakes of gold had been discovered along oceanfront beaches and the banks of the river that washed out of the distant mountains, and—much to the amazement and dismay of the Eskimos—an immense tent city soon materialized around Nome as thousands arrived to sift the sands for gold. Frank Doolittle prospected among them and put his carpentry skills to use as well, and in due time he sent for James and his mother, who arrived by steamer, after a trip of eight days and three thousand miles, in the summer of 1900.

Nome quickly became a typical gold-rush town, with an overabundance of gamblers and prostitutes. There was carpentry work for James's father to perform; by the time James was five the town boasted a bank, three churches, six whorehouses, and twenty saloons. The next year a schoolhouse was added, which was where James—now known as Jimmy, learned to fight. Being the shortest boy in his class, Jimmy was subjected to teasing and provocations by his older, taller mates, and soon he gained a reputation for defending himself from insults.

In 1908, when he was eleven, Jimmy and his mother boarded a steamer for Los Angeles, while his father remained in Nome. By then relations between father and son had become strained, and they would meet only once more. After finishing elementary school, Jimmy enrolled at the Los Angeles Manual Arts High School, a trade school where among his classmates were, curiously enough, the future Metropolitan Opera star and Hollywood actor Lawrence Tibbett; Goodwin Knight, who became governor of California; and Frank Capra, who went on to direct *It's a Wonderful Life* and *Mr. Smith Goes to Washington,* among many other popular Hollywood movies. For sports, Doolittle took up tumbling and joined the school team.

Around this time one of Doolittle's English teachers offered to teach him scientific boxing after witnessing him in a school yard brawl, which—contentious, like Eddie Rickenbacker—the fifteen-year-old happily accepted. Before long Jimmy was winning amateur boxing matches along the Pacific coast, first in the flyweight, then bantamweight classes. At five-foot-four he was as tall as he was going to get. That same year, 1912, he won the Pacific Coast amateur championship, held at the Los Angeles Athletic Club, and appeared to be on his way to a career in boxing.

Not all of Doolittle's pugilism was confined to the ring, however. From time to time he would engage in street brawls, which scandalized his mother, who was trying to steer him toward a respectable life. He was cured of his pugnaciousness once and for all after landing in jail for fighting a truck driver who had insulted a girl. Rosa Doolittle let him sweat it out in a cell for the rest of the weekend. "I'll be around Monday morning and get him out in time for school," she told the desk sergeant when he called. After getting a good look at the inside of a hoosegow, Jimmy decided that street fighting was a dead-end form of recreation.

It was also about this time that Doolittle met the love of his life, Josephine Daniels, an attractive A-student classmate with a biting humor and seductive smile whom everyone called "Joe." One of Jimmy's friends described Joe as a "Sunday girl," meaning that you could have your Friday and Saturday night flings, but the girl you took out on Sunday was one of those types to be treated special.

At first Joe Daniels wanted little to do with the motorcycle-riding, C-student brawler, but in time she apparently saw something in him, and he, in turn, started combing his hair, dressing up with a necktie, and minding his language around her. By the end of high school they were talking about marriage, but both wanted to go to college. Jimmy had no money and turned pro in his boxing career in order to earn his tuition. Fighting under the name "Jimmy Pierce" so his mother and the amateur authorities wouldn't know, he motorcycled up and down the Pacific coast to fight clubs on the weekends, earning about thirty dollars a bout—all either wins or draws.

Because Joe had no desire to marry someone whose only skill was fighting, Doolittle entered Los Angeles Junior College in 1914, where he studied mining engineering. In 1916 he transferred to the Engineering School at the University of California, Berkeley, where he joined the boxing team and never lost a match. He joined the college varsity gymnastics team as well and received high praise for his acrobatics.

His boxing career came to an end the following year when a tough promoter overmatched him against a seasoned pro named "Spider" Reilly, who danced all over the ring with Jimmy chasing and never laying a glove on him. After that Doolittle concluded that he had best stick to engineering.

By the spring of 1917 Doolittle was well on his way to a degree at the University of California when the United States declared war on Germany. That autumn, when he returned to Berkeley for his senior year, Doolittle was caught up in war fever and instead enrolled for pilot training in the U.S. Signal Corps aviation section.

JOE HAD GONE TO WORK for a large insurance company and became expert in a type of filing system that was a forerunner to computerized filing. By the time World War I came along she had moved to work in a shipyard and, employing the revolutionary filing system, had several hundred girls under her. The two were married, over the objections of Joe's mother, on Christmas Eve, 1917.

Jimmy was still awaiting the army orders that would send him to ground school and didn't have a cent, so Joe had to pay for the marriage license. They honeymooned in San Diego on her last twenty dollars, eating in cafeterias where servicemen were given free meals.

After graduating ground school in January of 1918, Jimmy went to San Diego for flight training at Rockwell Field. On the first day, as he and his instructor taxied out in a Curtiss JN-4 "Jenny," they heard the shocking boom of wood and metal followed by an eerie quiet. Two of the trainers had crashed and the wreckage fell only yards from Jimmy's plane. He and his instructor rushed over to the nearest Jenny, which was being flown solo by a student. He was dead. The other plane contained a student and his instructor, both mangled but alive. Jimmy helped pull them from the wreckage as the ambulance arrived. Jimmy's instructor gave him a look and motioned for him to get back in the plane.

"I was shaken by what I had seen but nodded in agreement," Jimmy said, then he went up for his first lesson. "If there is such a thing as love at first sight, my love for flying began on that day at that hour." After seven flying hours he soloed and, after that, the class practiced cross-country flying, aerobatics, and formation flying.

At graduation Doolittle was commissioned as a second lieutenant and military aviator. At the time, crashes were frequent and many were fatal. An army report noted that "teaching men to fly is probably the most dangerous occupation in the world," which is precisely what Jimmy Doolittle was assigned to do after he received some advanced training in the S-4C Scout, a much unloved plane. As an instructor himself, whenever there was a crash Doolittle immediately asked for volunteers to go flying. Anyone not volunteering was usually washed out of the program.

The war ended before Doolittle could get into it, despite his repeated attempts for an overseas transfer. He thought about returning to finish his engineering degree but he had caught the flying bug. Fortuitously, the Army Air Service had decided at about the same time that it needed publicity to keep up a visible public presence to avoid downsizing after the war. To that end, the service began offering its crack pilots for aerobatic exhibitions and demonstrations, known as flying circuses, in towns and cities throughout America. Doolittle was tapped as one of the stunt fliers.

The army aerobatic circus that Doolittle belonged to traveled more than nineteen thousand miles in the month of April 1919 alone, making one-day stands in eighty-eight cities and forty-five states using eighteen different planes, including French, British, and captured German Fokkers.

Talented as an aviator, Doolittle was also something of a prankster and a daredevil. He was grounded and confined to the post for wing walking and axle sitting, considered stunts by the army brass. Once he buzzed a couple of army privates walking down a country road and almost decapitated one of them, wrecking his plane in the bargain. On another occasion he wrecked one of the Jennys after chasing a flock of flying ducks down into what turned out to be a box canyon.

Jimmy's schedule left him and Joe apart for long periods, as he moved about the country and she remained home at her job in California. One day while she was at work, Joe got a phone call from a reporter saying that Jimmy had been killed in a crash in Buffalo. Her reply was, "I don't believe it," and she didn't, but after she hung up she sent a telegram to the post commander at Gerstner Field in Louisiana, where Jimmy was supposed to be stationed. As it turned out, the army had two James Doolittles listed as aviators, and the one whose middle initial was "R" had in fact been killed that day. Jimmy's middle name was Harold.

In another instance, Joe was riding on a streetcar when she glanced at the headline of a newspaper being read by the passenger sitting in front of her, which read "Flier Killed in Crash," and with the subhead, "Lt. James Doolittle . . ." She could not see the rest because the passenger turned the page. Too shocked to ask to see the paper, Joe got off at the next stop and purchased a paper, only to learn to her immense relief that it was yet another Doolittle.

The couple decided that Joe would join Jimmy in his army life and she moved to Ream flying field near San Diego. They paid a rent of $55 per month, leaving them exactly $2.83 a day to live out of his second lieutenant's pay.

One time Doolittle decided to surprise her by growing a beard and wearing it when she got off the train, but instead of acting shocked or remarking on the beard she began describing her trip and chatting about this and that, all the while Doolittle was driving her to their new home on the post, until finally he could stand it no longer and said, "Can't you even see I've grown a beard!"

To which she replied, looking him up and down, "You know, Doolittle, I did feel that you looked a bit different. I guess it is the beard."[2]

In the spring of 1921 Jimmy went to parachute school. In those days it was optional whether or not you actually jumped, and Jimmy chose to jump in a chute he himself had packed. He noted that at the time most pilots didn't wear parachutes because they were considered "sissified."

Many fliers changed their minds, however, after one of the army's top test pilots, Lieutenant Harold R. Harris, became the first man in the U.S. Army to save his life with a parachute. Harris was performing a stress test at altitude with a Loening aircraft when the stick began to vibrate uncontrollably. One of his ailerons—the hinged part of the wing that controls aircraft movement—had failed, and the wing fabric was tearing off. Harris unbuckled his seat belt, stood up, "and was plucked out of the Loening like a cork out of a bottle." At the last moment he managed to pull the rip cord on his chute and he floated down unharmed into somebody's grape arbor.

After that a sign was posted in the pilots' room that read:

DON'T FORGET YOUR PARACHUTE. IF YOU NEED IT
AND HAVEN'T GOT IT, YOU'LL NEVER NEED IT AGAIN.

AN ASSIGNMENT AT LANGLEY FIELD, Virginia, in 1921 put Doolittle in the company of General William L. "Billy" Mitchell, a tireless aviation advocate who had been second in command of the U.S. Army Air Service in World War I.

By the early 1920s a rivalry of sorts had developed between the traditional army branches and the newfangled flying-machine corps. There was even talk that the airplane would one day replace the infantry, artillery, and cavalry* by being able to bomb enemies into submission— to destroy entire cities and whole armies and navies from the air. This alarmed the conventional military establishment, which reacted defensively by giving the flying corps short shrift in appropriations and shunting it aside to remote bases—or so it was charged.

No one was more vocal during this period than Billy Mitchell.[3] Ever since the war ended, Mitchell had been a tireless promoter of U.S. airpower. In particular he believed that the air arms of the various services should be concentrated in one separate air corps, and he was positively incensed that nonflying officers were making the big decisions in the air corps. He insisted that in the next war—and there would be a next war, he predicted—the airplane would be paramount. He made the extravagant claim that airplanes could sink battleships, prompting then secretary of the navy Josephus Daniels to ridicule Mitchell, exclaiming that he would gladly "stand on the deck" of any such a ship "with my hat off" while Mitchell tried to bomb it.

In July of 1921, with former navy secretary Daniels in attendance along with army and navy brass aboard an observation vessel, a flight

---

* Cavalry, whose principal mission was reconnaissance, was only then beginning to employ motorized vehicles and armored tanks.

of Mitchell's army bombers flew over the captured German battleship *Ostfriesland* and released their loads of one-thousand- and two-thousand-pound bombs. One explosion occurred when a bomb bounced off into the water and blew the battleship's hull inward. To the delight of the army observers and the dismay of the navy—especially Josephus Daniels—within minutes the big German warship rolled over and sank. Despite the fact that the battleship was standing still and not furiously maneuvering at sea, let alone firing antiaircraft guns, the demonstration was considered a milestone for the future of U.S. military aviation. Neither was its significance lost on the Japanese, who were just then beginning to develop fighter bomber–style warplanes.

Doolittle had been posted to Mitchell's command during this period and was an assistant squadron commander during the *Ostfriesland* bombing missions, as well as a personal aide to Mitchell for one hectic day. During that period Doolittle came to admire Mitchell, and the two became friends.

Mitchell was a great showman and tramped all over the country speaking to anybody who would listen, from Congress to business groups, state legislatures, and Rotary Clubs; it was even said that he buttonholed men in the street to preach the benefits of airpower.

After a trip to Japan Mitchell famously predicted that the next war would be fought in the Pacific after a Japanese sneak attack on a Sunday morning in Hawaii. Eddie Rickenbacker, who had served as Mitchell's driver before becoming an ace combat pilot, wryly quipped that "the only people who paid any attention to him were the Japanese."

Most of the young fliers in the Air Service idolized Mitchell, not only because they agreed with him but because they felt he had their interests and the interests of the country at heart. Yet Mitchell's zealotry would soon get him into trouble and lead to his infamous court-martial. For his part, Doolittle thought that Mitchell's almost fanatical promotion of airpower was causing him to lose sight of his objective, which, ultimately, was the creation of a separate air force.

IN 1922, AFTER A PREVIOUS ATTEMPT to cross the United States by airplane in under twenty-four hours had ended in the death of the pilot, Doolittle decided to give it a go himself. The army was agreeable because setting those kinds of records attracted serious public interest. Each success seemed to lift a veil of uncertainty about exactly what the airplane could accomplish.

Doolittle's first attempt at a cross-country flight ended in disaster, and was nearly a catastrophe, when he tried to take off from a beach south of Jacksonville, Florida, en route to San Diego. He had made a significant modification to the plane that addressed one problem of being in the air for long periods of time. He fabricated a funnel with a tube that went out a small hole in the bottom of the plane, with the tube facing aft. When the plane was airborne and the pilot needed to relieve himself the airflow outside evacuated the tube. This arrangement became standard equipment on all military fighter aircraft for decades to come.

Doolittle had heard that Florida's sandy beaches were hard-packed enough for automobile races and, hoping to make it an ocean-to-ocean event, saw no reason why an airplane could not take off from one. On August 4, 1922, a throng of well-wishers gathered on a beach south of Jacksonville. He found out in short order when, nearing takeoff speed, one of his wheels caught a patch of mushy sand and sent the plane careening off the beach and into the water, where an incoming wave capsized it.

Doolittle emerged from the wreckage and began to clamber up on the fuselage as the crowd rushed toward him to help, some laughing when they saw he was alive and well. One woman asked if he was hurt, and Doolittle courteously replied, "No, but my feelings are."

A month later he tried again. At 9:52 p.m. on September 4, after carefully checking the consistency of the sand, Doolittle took off from Pablo Beach near Jacksonville, Florida, headed west. For the first few hours he had the advantage of a full moon but then ran into terrific electrical storms with lightning bolts that cracked so close he could smell the ozone.

Trusting his compass and other instruments Doolittle plunged into the maelstrom, using a Rand McNally road map to check for landmarks below as they were lit up by the flashes. Over New Orleans the rain became so fierce it stung his face and blurred his vision, but west of the Mississippi the storm abated. He landed for refueling and breakfast at Kelly Field in San Antonio with nothing but sunshine and a cheer that rose up from a crowd that had assembled before dawn as he came into sight.

At 8:30 a.m. Doolittle took off for San Diego, flying across the desolate mountains and deserts of the Southwest. By the time he reached the Arizona border he had been in the air close to fifteen hours and the monotonous drone of the engine was lulling him to sleep. Then, out of an otherwise clear sky, a light rain began to fall, which the prop wash threw over the top wing in a steady icy stream that dripped down the back of Doolittle's neck, annoying him to the point that he stayed awake.

Late that afternoon he landed in San Diego on the Pacific, twenty-two hours and thirty minutes after he had taken off from Pablo Beach on the Atlantic, becoming the first person ever to cross the continental United States in less than a day. Accolades great and small issued from the national press and the popular new medium of radio.

This was Doolittle's first brush with national fame. He received congratulatory letters not only from the chief of the Army Air Service but, more important to him, from General Billy Mitchell, whom he greatly admired. It also earned him his first Distinguished Flying Cross, for demonstrating "the possibility of moving Air Corps units to any portion of the United States in less than 24 hours."

MEANWHILE, THE DOOLITTLES had started a family, beginning with James Jr., born October 2, 1920, then John, who came along June 29, 1922, both at the post hospital at Fort Sam Houston, Texas. When Joe wasn't looking after the boys she had a Chinese cook teach her how to prepare Mexican food and acquired some odd pieces of furniture to make a home. In time, the Doolittles' residence, humble as it was, routinely became a kind of center of gravity for the best and brightest on the posts where they were stationed. There was always food, drink, and laughter, and serious, intellectual conversations as well, and a warmth that grew out of lasting friendships formed amid the gray trials of army life.

Following a year of service as a test pilot and performer in aerobatic exhibitions, Doolittle took advantage of an army program to study for a master's degree in aeronautical engineering at the Massachusetts Institute of Technology.

In the fall of 1923 he, Joe, and the two boys moved into an apartment near Cambridge. As a master's thesis Doolittle planned to compute the aeronautical stresses and forces it would take to break up a plane in the air—with himself as guinea pig.

He took planes for test flights and pushed them to their outermost limits, diving at speeds often exceeding 200 miles per hour, inducing cracks in the structural frame and other components just short of having the plane come apart with him in it. It was an extremely dangerous way to find out a plane's limitations, but the only way. Using delicate instruments he found, for instance, that the habit of some pilots to tighten the bracing wires running along the wings in fact promoted wing failure.

Doolittle also investigated pilot blackouts induced by these speeds and maneuvers. Again, flying alone, he used himself as a guinea pig. He found that any extended acceleration of 4.5 G* resulted in a complete loss of consciousness, and further he concluded that if such acceleration continued for more than ten to twelve seconds it would be fatal.

The thesis was such a success that a paper developed from it was translated into a dozen languages and circulated abroad, earning Doolittle international fame as well as his second Distinguished Flying Cross. He applied for, and was granted, the opportunity to study for his doctorate at MIT.

The subject of his study was the effect that wind velocity had on flying an airplane. Doolittle chose this as a theme because he knew experienced pilots held differing opinions about it, and he wrote the paper so as "to be understood by the average pilot." But when he turned in a draft of his doctoral dissertation his advisers rejected it.

On further inquiry, Doolittle was told his paper wasn't studious-enough looking, that it needed more mathematical calculations, graphs, charts, etc.; in other words, it needed to be tarted up so as to look more scholarly. He went back to the drawing board, and in June 1925 the Massachusetts Institute of Technology awarded him a doctorate in

---

* A "G" or g-force is a force of acceleration in excess of the normal force of gravity (or free fall).

aeronautical sciences, one of the first of its kind. Doolittle was proud of that, but for the rest of his life he regretted that he had rewritten the paper so it would "be locked away and never read by anyone." He thought it could have saved lives.[4]

BY THE MID-1920S AIRCRAFT ENGINES had become increasingly powerful and public fascination with flying led to the great popularity of air racing competitions—which had come a long way and were a far cry from the days of the flying circuses. Since the end of the First World War the speed of aircraft had increased past 250 miles per hour and flying clubs throughout the world held races and offered silver loving cups as trophies and often handsome cash prizes to the winners. As with the setting of speed or distance records, the military services encouraged their pilots to enter these competitions as a way of publicizing themselves, if not actually justifying their existence. Jimmy Doolittle finished on top in many of these events, and his national reputation as a flying ace continued to grow. Air racing competition between the army and the navy pilots had become almost frenzied. Doolittle's first crack at a championship came in October 1925, when the army entered him in the prestigious Schneider Cup, a seaplane race in Baltimore. The problem was that Doolittle had never flown a seaplane before.

In less than a week he was obliged to learn the techniques of flying a plane with an entirely new configuration and center of balance from anything he had ever flown before—not to mention taking off and landing on water. He had had to put pontoons on his sleek and powerful 610-horsepower Curtiss R3C racer, while the navy pilots had flown with them since their first days at flight school.

After the elimination in qualifying rounds of more than half the entrants in various crashes and malfunctions, the racing field now consisted of four planes: two navy pilots, an Italian pilot, and Doolittle. The racecourse was laid out as a 31.7-mile triangle in the Chesapeake Bay, marked off by tall pylons. The racers had to fly around the course seven times, for a total of about 220 miles. After observing qualification tests, Doolittle thought he saw a way to shave a little time by banking steeply past the pylons and gunning out of the turn, but he mentioned none of this to the navy pilots, whose entourage included most of the U.S. Naval Academy at Annapolis as well as various admirals, Washington naval attachés, and a squadron of navy planes that flew in formation over the spectators. Also present was Orville Wright, who had started it all back in 1903. It was a sunny but choppy autumn day on the Chesapeake. To compete with the navy's flying squadron the army had sent a blimp that cruised out over the bay "like a majestic silver fish," according to a report in *Aviation* magazine.

Doolittle drew first position. His plan was to climb rapidly, then dive sharply as he passed the pylons, banking steeply to get a speed advantage. Once Doolittle had the lead he kept it; the Italian plane dropped out and it became a race between the army and the navy.

Then one of the navy pilots developed engine trouble and had to land on the bay, and on the final lap the other found his plane engulfed in flames from an engine fire (somehow he brought the aircraft safely down on the water). U.S. Army Lieutenant Jimmy Doolittle won the day at a record-setting average speed of 232.573 miles per hour, while the two planes entered by the U.S. Navy had to be ignominiously towed back to shore in full view of the navy brass and the corps of midshipmen from the United States Naval Academy.

Doolittle's grease-smeared smile was featured prominently in the sports pages at home and abroad, including the *New York Times,* which, in noting that Doolittle had won "the world's premier seaplane trophy," observed cattily that "the Army men never seem to take tows in Neptune's realm."

BY THE MID-1920S BILLY MITCHELL'S attacks against politicians and the army brass had become more strident and relentless, as he accused them of ignorance and even willful collaboration in the deaths of military pilots as the result of a lack of funding and oversight. At first the commander of the Air Corps tried to silence Mitchell by reducing his rank and banishing him to duty in San Antonio instead of making him permanent second in command, slotted for the future top spot.

This only made Mitchell more outspoken and caused him to publish an accusatory book lambasting the Navy and War Departments, Congress, and even the president. In 1925 he used the occasion of several fatal air crashes to charge that the administration of the national defense was "incompetent, criminally negligent, and almost treasonable." President Calvin Coolidge convened a board of business and military men to construct some coherent national policy regarding aviation, headed by the Morgan & Co. banker Dwight W. Morrow (the future father-in-law of Charles Lindbergh).

Called to testify before the Morrow commission, Mitchell lashed out with the same caustic verbiage he had been using to condemn the administration, naming names, which of course filled the press columns day after sensational day. That was enough for Coolidge who, using his powers under the articles of war, preferred court-martial charges through the War Department against Mitchell for insubordination. The specific allegation was that Mitchell's conduct was "prejudicial to good order and military discipline" and "of a nature to bring discredit upon the military service."

The case quickly developed a circus atmosphere. The trial, begun in October 1925, was held in a decrepit warehouse near the Capitol in Washington, D.C. The court was composed of U.S. Army generals—including the young major general Douglas MacArthur—none of whom were fliers or had any experience with aviation.

The military judge in the case straightaway agreed with the prosecutor that Mitchell's guilt or innocence was not dependent on the truth of his accusations against the higher authorities, only whether they were prejudicial to good martial order and whether they discredited the military organization, a legal confinement that severely hamstrung Mitchell's planned defense and limited him from making the trial a cause célèbre for the promotion of airpower.

Public sentiment was on the side of Billy Mitchell, and the press slanted their reporting toward him, too, since he always provided good copy. Among the throng of spectators was the humorist Will Rogers, who had taken his first plane ride with Mitchell. It was reported that hundreds of spectators mobbed the sidewalks trying to get into the courtroom, including mink-draped society matrons "in luxuriously equipped limousines," who had to compete for seats with the military, the press, and hoi polloi.

Doolittle and his fellow flying officers continued to agree with much of what Mitchell said, but Jimmy again opined that Mitchell "had gone overboard in his criticisms." Eddie Rickenbacker, however, was under no such constraints as Doolittle and the other active duty servicemen; he was free to speak his mind and did so with acerbic gusto when it came his time to testify about his former boss.

IN 1926 THE CURTISS-WRIGHT CORPORATION asked the army to grant Doolittle extended leave to help in its effort to market the Curtiss P-1 Hawk fighter in South America. Doolittle would become, in effect, a "flying salesman, [to] demonstrate the plane's capabilities in flight, and prove that it was the finest pursuit airplane in the world." It was a smart move on Curtiss-Wright's part. Ever anxious in peacetime to unburden itself of another salary to pay, the army promptly acceded to the request. For Doolittle it was a dream assignment. The money was good and he got extra for doing trick maneuvers—his specialty.

Doolittle's first assignment was the government of Chile, and in April of 1926 he boarded a freighter and steamed through the Panama Canal with a crated P-1 Hawk in the hold and a skilled Curtiss mechanic as his traveling companion.

Doolittle did not have a captive audience when he reached Santiago, a dirty, sprawling metropolis in the foothills of the Andes. Pilots from England, Italy, and Germany had already arrived to peddle their wares. "I wasn't worried about the British or Italian models," he said. "It was the German Dornier flown by Karl A. von Schoenebeck that was the greatest threat."

Schoenebeck, it seems, had been an ace in Richthofen's famous Flying Circus that had clashed so often with Eddie Rickenbacker's Hat in the Ring squadron on the Western Front. The flying shows would begin in June at the *aerodromo* El Bosque, on the outskirts of town.

Ten days before the aerial demonstrations the Chilean aviators threw a party for the foreign fliers at their officers' club, a handsome stone building in downtown Santiago dating to colonial times. As the party gathered steam, the visiting officers were introduced to the *pisco* sour, "a delightful specialty of the fun-loving Chileans," which combines three ounces of *pisco,* a clear brandy of Spanish origin, with sugar, lemon juice, and ice (note: three ounces of alcohol in a single drink is more than *twice* the dose of a usual American cocktail). Let Jimmy Doolittle pick up the story from here.

At some point the name of the silent film actor Douglas Fairbanks was raised, whose "balcony-leaping, sword-playing swashbuckling roles" had excited the fancy of the Chilean pilots.

As the evening wore on, and after swigging several or more of the *pisco* sours, Doolittle announced that Fairbanks's stunts weren't particularly unusual. In fact, said he, *all* American children learn to do those things. Doolittle's command of Spanish was not as good as he thought, but when that statement was finally translated the Chileans' "eyebrows raised in doubt."

"Inspired by the *pisco* sours," Doolittle said, "I upended into a handstand, and 'walked' a few paces." This polished gymnastic exhibition delighted the Chilean hosts, who clapped and shouted *ole!* Doolittle then entertained them with a series of flips, which electrified the crowd and elicited even more handclapping and shouting.

One of the Chilean pilots offered that he had seen Fairbanks perform a handstand on a windowsill, which struck Doolittle as "reasonable," so he went to an open window, climbed through, and did a two-hand stand on the two-foot-wide ledge. This led to a one-hand stand, which, after more ovation, prompted the agile former boxer and gymnast to overextend himself, as it were, with a stunt from his tumbling days.

"Grasping the inside of the ledge with one hand," Doolittle said, "I extended my legs and body parallel with the courtyard, one story below. This isn't difficult. Just requires a little practice and knowledge of body leverage." Otherwise known as a one-armed body lever, this was an extremely difficult stunt, especially when "practice" was nonexistent.

Reveling in the applause from his hosts, Doolittle held his precarious position for a few seconds until, to his dismay, he felt the sandstone of the ancient ledge he was holding begin to crumble beneath his fingers and break off. There was nothing to be done. The laws of gravity took over.

Doolittle plunged about twenty feet from the second story to a stone courtyard, luckily landing feet first—if you can call breaking both your ankles lucky. That was the verdict when they got him to the hospital and X-rayed the damage. It was a sobering experience in more ways than one, as Doolittle quickly realized the foolhardiness of what he had done. A minimum of six weeks, the doctors told him, would have to pass before the bones healed. What was he to say to the people at Curtiss-Wright? Or to his superiors in the army? A drunken stunt had put him hors de combat at a time when he might have sold planes and enhanced the army's reputation immensely. Instead, he feared he would become a laughingstock. To complicate things further, the Chilean doctors misread the X-rays and his plaster casts were put on the wrong feet, each fracture being different, resulting in the bones being improperly set.

Doolittle had no intention of lying in a hospital bed while others sold their planes to the Chilean air force. After nine days in traction he had his mechanic come with a hacksaw and cut him out of the plaster at the ankles, whereupon he escaped to the airfield, clattering across the runway on crutches to be lifted aboard his plane.

With metal clips bolted on his flying shoes by the mechanic to hold his feet on the pedals, on June 24, 1926, Doolittle did a practice demonstration with the Curtiss P-1 Hawk. He flew all of his snap rolls to the right that afternoon and his right cast broke.

That night he went back to the hospital to have the cast replaced and next day went out and flew a demonstration with all his snap rolls to the left.

The left cast broke.

Back at the hospital the doctors called him a "crazy Yankee" and blackballed him, so Doolittle found a German cast maker in town who fixed him up with extra heavy-duty prostheses that were reinforced by, of all things, women's steel corset stays. These worked fine, but he still had to hobble around on crutches.

By the day of the big airplane demonstration, word of Doolittle's gallant persistence had gotten out, and crowds at the air show increased tenfold. Chileans are fond of underdogs and apparently viewed Doolittle in the same way as they might a one-legged bullfighter.

He was driven to the flying field and assisted into the cockpit. The president of Chile, Carlos Ibáñez del Campo, was there, along with his cabinet and a large contingent of army and navy officers. Von Schoenebeck was already aloft, demonstrating his aerobatic routine in the Dornier. Doolittle decided he needed some competition, "So I took off, and climbed to meet him," he said.

Doolittle flew up beside a surprised von Schoenebeck and wagged his wings, the sign for a mock dogfight. The German saluted and the fight was on. Try as he might, it turned out there was no maneuver von Schoenebeck could perform to keep Doolittle off his tail, and he went through them all—barrel rolls, dives, Immelmanns, sideslips—but every time the German looked back there was the Curtiss Hawk, dogging him like a pesky horsefly.

Doolittle was enjoying himself immensely. He knew his P-1 was faster (400 horsepower to the Dornier's 260) and more maneuverable, and he whipped all around the German with close passes, then zoomed to show the Curtiss's superior speed. After enough of this humiliation, von Schoenebeck broke off the engagement. As he began to descend, Doolittle saw that the fabric covering the Dornier's upper wing was coming apart.* Doolittle then went through his aerobatic routine and as a finale sped across the field in front of the spectators, flying upside down at treetop level. The audience clapped, cheered, and threw hats into the air as Doolittle was lifted out of his cockpit, and several of the Hawks were sold that day.

Doolittle's next destination was Bolivia, and he flew the Hawk due south between the mountains and the Pacific coast, setting a new record of 11 hours, 23 minutes between Santiago and La Paz. Unbeknownst to Doolittle, however, Bolivia and Chile were having one of their perennial border disputes and he arrived to find his residence, the Stranger's Club, surrounded by a thousand-man mob of angry and arson-minded Bolivians shouting anti-Chilean and anti-American slogans, including the stock insult "Gringo go home!" Newspapers had reported that Doolittle was in fact a spy for Chile, and he was presently being denounced from the streets to the halls of the Bolivian parliament.

---

* Some of the spectators thought that Doolittle might have struck von Schoenebeck's plane with his own and caused the damage, but this was incorrect, as the German himself admitted. The unraveling of the wing fabric was a structural failure of the Dornier.

The Bolivian army arrived and dispersed the mob but authorities suggested that Doolittle leave town as soon as possible, advice he took to heart, since talk had begun of a firing squad. Airplane sales under present conditions were less than promising.

His next stop was Buenos Aires, which would require flying over the Andes, a hazardous adventure in 1926. He would be flying at roughly 18,000 feet, and as high as 20,000 feet at some points, meaning that the air would be awfully thin, and extreme turbulence was not uncommon at those altitudes. On top of all this was the matter of his broken ankles. If he ran into trouble he would have no choice but to try to set the plane down.

Nevertheless, on September 3, 1926, Jimmy Doolittle set another record by becoming the first American to fly over the Andes range (several Argentinians had done it, but more had perished in the attempt), and he broke the present speed record at that, making the trip from Santiago to Buenos Aires in 6 hours, 45 minutes. He was also, he pointed out, "the only man ever to fly over [the Andes] with two broken ankles."

In Argentina Doolittle gave the requisite aerial performances—minus von Schoenebeck as his foil—and managed to sell several more Curtiss Hawks, and following this he sailed for home.

WHEN HE REACHED THE UNITED STATES in October 1926 Doolittle checked himself into Walter Reed Hospital because his ankles were still painful and not healing properly. The doctors were "shocked" when they read the X-rays. The healing was abnormal, but because of the length of time that had passed since Doolittle's fall it was decided to let the healing continue without refracturing the bones. When his ankles were put in new casts he was sentenced to immobilization in the hospital for an indeterminate period of time.

It was during this interlude that Doolittle ginned up the notion of performing the notorious "outside loop," an aircraft maneuver that puts such enormous stress on both the pilot and the aircraft that many aviators believed it was impossible. Not Doolittle.

Flying an inside loop is relatively easy because the pilot is on the vertical inside of the loop, where centrifugal forces hold him in place and his blood is not rushed to the head. In an outside loop, however, this is reversed and the pilot's feet, rather than his head, are pointed toward the center of the circle. The body is subjected to mighty strains, including an ever increasing centrifugal force that pushes the blood to the brain with tremendous pressure. In addition, there was the question among aviators of what it might do to the pilot's internal organs. And would he "red out" and become unconscious when he attempted to push the plane around on the second half of the loop? Let alone, the effects of all that strain on the aircraft.

Only such a man as Doolittle could ask these questions with the apparent intention of testing them on himself.

In April 1927, shortly after he was released from the hospital, Doolittle secretly began practicing the outside loop in the Curtiss Hawk. He took it one stage at a time, going through the bottom half, then going around and under, a sensation that was disagreeable at first, similar to hanging upside down for a long time on the horizontal gymnastics bar. The second half of the loop was the tricky part, because when the plane reached the bottom the pilot had to remain alert enough to put on sufficient speed and push the plane out the top.

On May 25, 1927—four days after Lindbergh had soloed across the Atlantic—Jimmy Doolittle asked six of his fellow test pilots to "watch a patch of sky" about 10,000 feet up while he went into his stunt. At about 350 miles per hour Doolittle shoved the stick forward and began the loop. He saw red as the blood rushed into his brain. The g-force pressure was so great that it burst the blood vessels in his eyes, but other than that, and a great deal of "discomfort," he had, that day, in fact achieved the seemingly impossible.

His buddies got word to the newspapers and next day headlines had Doolittle as "the first man in history to perform the outside loop." Reporters wrote that his eyes were completely bloodshot and that he had a ruptured lung (this last was untrue). When one reporter wanted to know how he did it, Doolittle replied with characteristic self-effacement. "Don't know. I just thought it up on the spur of the moment."

When army brass got wind of Doolittle's stunt many were horrified that now other, less experienced pilots would try it and wreck their planes. Orders were quickly posted banning anyone from attempting an outside loop.

Soon the Curtiss-Wright Corporation came calling again. The company asked the army if it could reprise last year's South American sales tour, again featuring Doolittle. Again the army acceded, probably in some measure glad to be rid of him, thus providing a new set of opportunities for Doolittle's growing repertoire of adventures and misadventures.

THIS TIME DOOLITTLE had two planes to show off. Besides the Curtiss Hawk there was a two-seat observation plane, the Curtiss O-1, a civilian test pilot, William McMullen, and, lastly, two Curtiss mechanics, who assembled both planes when they reached Lima, Peru.

When the Doolittle air show arrived in Bolivia, this time Doolittle was welcomed with open arms, the border dispute having blown over.

In between demonstrations of the planes, the Doolittle team met an American gold mine manager named Charles Wallen who had just arrived in La Paz with a strange story to tell after a nine-day trek by burro from his mine a hundred miles into the jungle. He had come for medical supplies, he said, for some native mine workers* who, while drunk on their day off, enjoyed playing a dangerous game called *probando la suerte* ("trying your luck"). It worked this way: forty or so men would stand in a circle with their arms outstretched barely touching hands with those on either side of them. A quarter of a stick of dynamite with a long fuse would then be lit and passed from man to man. The man holding it when it blew up was considered *sin suerte* ("without luck"). Back at the mine, Wallen said, were a dozen or so Indians still alive from the last game but horribly mangled and tended to by the mine doctor, who had run out of everything but whiskey and quinine.

Wallen needed to return with the medical supplies as soon as possible and Doolittle volunteered to fly him back. In the O-1 with Wallen in the passenger seat, they flew above the jungle and dropped the supplies in a clearing near the mine. During the remainder of his stay in Bolivia, Doolittle continued to volunteer to fly emergency supplies out to the

---

* These people were known locally as "bad Indians" because of their penchant for murdering government tax collectors.

country's many mines, and for this, before he left, President Hernando Siles Reyes presented him with the National Order of the Condor of the Andes, Bolivia's highest decoration for foreigners.*

Still merely an army first lieutenant, Doolittle for the remainder of the tour was wined and dined by prominent South American politicians and military officers—presidents, ministers, and generals—and he spread goodwill for his company and the United States, too, by setting every new flying record he could think of—record times flying between cities, over mountains, over jungles—connecting the continent by air.†

WHEN HE RETURNED FROM SOUTH AMERICA on August 15, 1928, Doolittle had already begun to experience what might be characterized as an "organized midlife crisis."

He was thirty-one years old and still a first lieutenant; in those days promotions came with such glacial slowness that Doolittle couldn't even contemplate when he might make captain. As it was, he had to support Joe and the boys, as well as his and Joe's mothers, on his lieutenant's pay. He was equipped with a doctoral degree in aeronautical engineering, as well as thousands of hours of flying time, but what did the world hold? Flying was his life, but what if there were no flying jobs outside the army? Flying was still perceived by the public as risky, and viable commercial passenger airlines were a decade into the future.‡ As he and Joe wrestled with these things, a prospect came his way that he considered the opportunity of a lifetime.

It came via Harry F. Guggenheim,[5] the handsome, dapper, fabulously wealthy scion of the Guggenheim Mexican mining empire, who had

---

* Wallen was so impressed by the airplane ride that he bought a Curtiss himself and later started a Bolivian airline.

† For being the first pilot to fly over the infamous Mato Grosso, a remote and uncharted sea of vegetation some 350,000 miles square, Doolittle was elected to membership in the eminent Explorers Club.

‡ In May 1928, the Guggenheim foundation began an experimental airline between San Francisco and Los Angeles using a Fokker trimotor that seated eight. It was called Western Air Express.

developed a love of flying. After graduating college at Cambridge University in 1913, Guggenheim bought a Curtiss seaplane and joined the U.S. Navy as a reserve officer. When America entered World War I he served as a combat flier on the Western Front and in Italy.

In 1924 Guggenheim convinced his parents to set up a fund through their foundation, capitalized initially with $3 million, that was devoted to promoting air travel and making air travel safer. They made Harry a director and, later, president. Among the fund's many projects was something called the Full Flight Laboratory at Mitchel Field, Long Island. Its goal was to develop instruments that would allow pilots to take off, fly, and land blind—using only the instruments as their guide. The concept was almost unheard of since the flying instruments of the day were so few and crude, and it was basically contrary to the customary practice of stressing that the pilot should simply develop good instincts and fly by them.

Now with Guggenheim there was an organization, backed by big money, that was set up entirely to conquer the problem of low visibility or "fog flying," because among the visibility issues—darkness, rain, snow—fog was by far the greatest killer. The answer of course was finding a way of flying blind. Would Doolittle join the team, Guggenheim wanted to know?

If anyone understood the problems that were holding up progress in aviation, it was Jimmy Doolittle; he flew with them every day. He had been to the outer limits many times and seen the shadow of death. At the time there was nothing he'd rather do than find solutions to these problems.

CHAPTER 4

★ ★ ★ ★ ★

CAN THOSE BE STARS?

For more than an hour Charles Lindbergh had been waiting for the moon to rise.[1] Squeezed as he was into the tiny cockpit of the *Spirit of St. Louis,* he might well have been the loneliest man in the world, flying alone in the inky dark somewhere high above the North Atlantic while all around him towering thunderheads were pulsating and growling with pinkish-yellow lightning flashes. It was May 20, 1927. The meteorologist's report that morning had indicated clearing skies. It was wrong. For the first time, he thought of turning back.

Years afterward, Lindbergh mused about it in his book *The Spirit of St. Louis.* "Great cliffs tower over me," he said, as he threaded his way among the giant clouds boiling with electricity, "[they] ward me off with icy walls. There'd be no rending crash if my wing struck one of them," he said. "They carry a subtler death. To plunge into these mountains . . . would be like stepping in quicksand."

It was the sixteenth hour since he'd left Long Island's Roosevelt Field; he'd soared across the Long Island Sound, over New England, Nova Scotia, Newfoundland, and Labrador, where he'd turned east across the great ocean. It had been four long hours since he lost both land and light, a final glance backward at sunset, past huge icebergs 10,000 feet below to the sun's last rays on the silhouette of the mountains that stood out against the western sky. It was the last he would see of America for a while, and he felt almost as if he were traveling through outer space—displaced, unconnected. There was nothing now before him but thousands of miles of ocean. He was twenty-five years old.

That had been four hours ago—the last of America—but now he wavered. It was nearly eleven p.m., and ahead the storm clouds piled up in great columns while Lindbergh maneuvered to wiggle through the valleys between them, which wasn't always possible.

The *Spirit of St. Louis* shuddered as it entered a turbulent cumulus and Lindbergh was sensitive to each jerk and spasm. It felt at times that some violent invisible hand had seized his aircraft and was determined to shake it to pieces. Inside the cloud was all black darkness, with no clouds below to judge for distance, no stars above to guide by. Nothing but the burning flash of his engine's exhaust on the mist inside the cloud and the greenish-yellow radium of the glowing instrument dials saved him from utter blindness. He was in fact flying blind by the standards of the day—altimeter, compass, turn and bank indicator—these were all he had in the world to make the aircraft fly straight and level, along with every ounce of concentration he could muster to keep them in precarious harmony. No one had tried this before and lived to tell about it. That, too, was on his mind.

It was cold and Lindbergh zipped his flight jacket tight and put on his leather mittens, but not his flying boots. That would come later, if necessary. He didn't need to get too warm, too comfortable right now; it made him sleepy. He kicked himself for last night, when he had the chance to catch a few hours of sleep but didn't, then couldn't when the idiot "aide" his army reserve unit sent out kept disturbing him. Lindbergh had been awake now for thirty-eight hours, and his mind wandered back to home, to autumn in the Minnesota woods. It was still cold and he checked the altimeter—10,500 feet.

A moment of panic: "Good Lord! How could I forget!"

He snatched off a mitten and stuck his arm out the window, where a needlelike sting filled the palm of his hand. Ice. His flashlight revealed a shiny coating on the leading edge of the plane's struts and wires. He must exit the cloud immediately and find open, drier air. But not too fast; many a pilot in such a situation has lost his life to vertigo. Watch the instruments, Lindbergh worried, before they, too, iced up and froze. Flying blind contradicts all of a pilot's natural instincts and Lindbergh had to wrestle with himself to go slow. Turning too fast could fling you out of control. The airspeed indicator showed him slowing down, but too much and the plane would stall. Was it the ice on the wings slowing him? Another look with the flashlight told him yes, there was more ice, and then, abruptly, he found his way out of the cloud.

"My eyes sense a change in the blackness of the cockpit," Lindbergh wrote. "I look through the window. Can those be stars? Is this the same sky? How bright! How clear! Here's something I never saw before—the brilliant light of a black night."

He decided to climb another five or six thousand feet, where the valleys between the mountainous thunderheads might be wider and easier to navigate. If he couldn't find a pass to the east or south he'd have to turn back, he decided, back over Newfoundland, Nova Scotia, New England, right back to where he'd started on the mud-soaked runway of the airfield. He calculated that by the time he actually got back he would have been in the air at least long enough to reach Ireland. That would be something at least—New York to Ireland had never been done. It was worth a shot. Lindbergh steered on eastward; do it or die trying. In the passes between the thunderheads, occasionally he saw the stars that let him plot his course.

The incessant thrum and vibration of the engine was lulling his senses. The instruments weren't behaving right. Lindbergh had an earth-inductor compass, a complicated and finicky apparatus that was now gyrating so wildly its magnetic field seemed affected by the electrical storms. Likewise, the liquid compass overhead appeared to be out of order. If both compasses failed he'd have nothing but the stars, and if the storms blotted out the stars he wouldn't know if he was flying north, south, east, west, or around in circles until he ran out of gas. He flew on.

Imperceptibly, the sky seemed brighter and the edges of the clouds sharper. He had nearly forgotten the moon, but suddenly there it was in a valley in the clouds. Forming ahead and above, however, was an ominous layer, pierced by thick spiral columns from a second bank of clouds several thousand feet below, so that it appeared to Lindbergh that he was flying into some colossal temple in the sky. It was unnerving, as though he were entering the maw of a gigantic beast.

His fatigue was now appalling; he wanted to walk around and shake it off but he was strapped into a narrow wicker chair in the cramped cockpit of the plane. He put his hand out the window to direct a stream of cold air on his face. That helped.

His eyelids sagged and he couldn't stop them. The walls of the temple began to close in and fog enveloped the *Spirit of St. Louis*. The ocean began to draw him like a siren's call. He thought about crashing into it, wondering what it would be like. His muscles ached and his legs were cramped. There was barely room to stretch. He had the impression he was going nowhere, just hanging in the air. He needed to get out of the fog.

Again he considered turning back, but he worried the fog had by now overtaken the coast of Newfoundland. Using instruments of the day, pilots could fly in fog and clouds, but landing on instruments alone remained impossible—Jimmy Doolittle's fabulous experiment in blind flying was still two years in the future. He might have been able to fly back and jump, if necessary, except Lindbergh carried no parachute because of weight. It was like working a circus high wire without the net. There would be no more questions of jumping or of turning back.

The fog seemed worse higher up, so Lindbergh nosed down, down, down; at last, at 200 feet, it had dissolved and the sea appeared. The waves were gigantic, sweeping eastward. He dropped down until he could smell the salt spray whipped up by the high wind. A light drizzle flashed past his windows and some of the drops spattered in, splashing on his face, a welcome experience as it helped keep him awake. Everything was staying awake; every second he fought against sleep. The waves were frighteningly high, forty to fifty feet, he estimated, and the howling wind blew their tops off, making huge foamy whitecaps.

Then, something uncanny happened. In his half consciousness, Lindbergh began to experience the presence of some sort of phantoms in the back of the fuselage. They were "friendly, vapor-like shapes, without substance, able to vanish or appear at will," he wrote later. At times they were all crowded in behind him; sometimes there were only one or two.

These spirits, or apparitions, would come forward one at a time to speak to Lindbergh, offering advice on his flight, giving tips on navigation, discussion, reassurance, chitchat. Suddenly Lindbergh wasn't alone; there were companions here in the little plane clawing its way across the North Atlantic.

They were familiar, friendly—not strangers. He wasn't sure when they came aboard. He felt he had known them before and was pleased to have some company.

Fatigue was the enemy now, more even than faulty navigation or fog. Sleep was death, and Lindbergh knew it. It should be dawn soon and he decided to turn his thoughts toward sunrise, watching for any sign of brightening in the east. It would be easier to stay awake in the daytime, he thought, especially flying into that red ball of fire that would rise out of the ocean. He began counting the minutes as they ticked past. "I never wanted so badly—to sleep," he said.

CHARLES AUGUSTUS LINDBERGH JR. was born in Detroit on February 4, 1902, a year before the Wright brothers made their famous flight at Kitty Hawk. He was delivered by Dr. Edwin Lodge, his great-uncle from his mother's family of prominent physicians. Six weeks later, mother and child journeyed nearly eight hundred miles northwest to the town of Little Falls, Minnesota, where her husband, the baby's father, had his law practice, his real estate business, and his farm.

His father, Charles Lindbergh Sr., was a Swede by birth, the bastard son of Ola Mansson, who had once been an important man in Sweden—an eloquent, self-educated farmer who in the 1850s rose to leadership in the Riksdag, the Swedish parliament, and was close friends with the soon-to-be-king Crown Prince Carl XV. But after a series of scandals, including his wife's discovery of an extramarital affair with a twenty-year-old waitress who birthed his child, a son, and charges of embezzlement, Mansson decided to flee with his mistress, Lovisa, to America. As a parting note, before leaving the witness stand, in an act of breathtaking cheek he wiped his buttocks with one of the prosecution's evidentiary documents.

Now in disgrace, he changed his name to August Lindberg* and named the baby Charles August Lindberg. The family settled in a tiny hamlet named Melrose in the deep woods on the edge of the Minnesota lakes region, which, in 1859, constituted the American frontier, complete with tribes of often hostile Indians.

August Lindbergh carved out a living from the land under the Homestead Act, in turn building a sod hut, a log cabin, and a frame

---

* He later added the *h*.

house around it with multiple stories—the aspirational Valhalla for all immigrant Scandinavian farmers. In time he fathered six more children by Lovisa (whose name by then had become anglicized to "Louisa"). In 1870 he became sworn as a U.S. citizen and joined the Republican Party. In 1885 he at long last officially married Louisa.

Over time August became such a respectable presence in the small village of Melrose that he was selected as town clerk and village recorder, postmaster, justice of the peace, and member of the school board. He instilled in all of his children the firm Scandinavian work ethic, but none more strictly than his new family's firstborn, Charles August, who grew into the most handsome young man in Stearns County—maybe in all of Minnesota. He stood about six feet tall in the erect posture of a soldier, was slender and well made, with blue eyes and blond hair and a high forehead, patrician nose, and dimpled chin. Early on, Charles, or C.A. as he came to be called, had learned the mysteries of the forest from his father and soon became the Lindbergh family's designated hunter. He never darkened the doors of a school until he was twelve years old, but when he turned eighteen, his father sent C.A. to the Grove Park Academy, run by a Catholic priest, which prepared him for law school at the University of Michigan, where he graduated in 1883. At last something besides a farmer had come out of the Mansson/Lindbergh family line.

C.A. hung his shingle in Little Falls, a town of several thousand on the Mississippi River in a part of the state that was thriving with the giant Weyerhaeuser lumber company, McCormick Harvester, and several large sawmills and brickyards, all of which became C.A.'s clients.

Shortly after moving to Little Falls C.A. married Mary LaFond, with whom he had two daughters. His clientele and prestige continued to increase but in 1898 Mary's life was lost in childbirth. He soon sent his daughters to boarding school and moved from their substantial home into a hotel room near his office downtown. But there he met, and soon married, Evangeline Lodge Land, who would become the mother of Charles A. Lindbergh Jr.

She was the beautiful and high-strung twenty-four-year-old daughter of two prominent Detroit families; her mother was one of the Lodges, a family of physicians, and her father was Dr. Charles Henry Land, a cantankerous but famous dentist who invented, among other things, the porcelain jacket crown.

At first, everything seemed to go swimmingly for the Lindbergh family. Evangeline ensconced herself and baby Charles in the dream house on the Mississippi River that C.A. had built for her. Also in the home were C.A.'s two daughters from his previous marriage, Lillian, fourteen, and Eva, ten, now reunited in the new home. C.A. stayed busier than ever, and domestic life was made comfortable with a cook, housekeeper, and coach driver who doubled as the farmer tending C.A.'s crops, orchards, and livestock.

Those were bucolic days in the American century, as if from a Currier & Ives engraving. A few automobiles had begun to appear on the streets of Little Falls but most travel was by carriage, wagon, or horse. Baseball was the nation's pastime, and on Sundays bandstands in local parks were graced with musicians playing brass instruments.

Charles Lindbergh's earliest memories were of his toys: lead and tin soldiers and Indians with bows and arrows; a toy steam train with a whistle. And there were views of the Mississippi, clear and fast running and nearly a quarter mile wide at that point. The family had three dogs roaming the premises, including a Great Dane who used to beat Charles about the head with his tail.

When Charles was three and a half, he vividly remembered, he heard "a sudden shouting—women's voices. I was picked up quickly and taken across the road to a place behind the barn. I got to a corner of the barn and looked around it to see a huge column of smoke billowing skyward from our house. Then I was taken back and told I mustn't look."[2]

By the time the fire was out the house had collapsed into the basement, a charred and total wreck. A saving grace was that the blaze had started upstairs, giving servants and farmhands time to salvage much of the furniture, tableware, and other valuables. At last Charles was taken to the scene, and fifty years later he clearly remembered what he'd seen: a lone chimney with a small red clay Mexican idol on the stone fireplace shelf.

While the house was being rebuilt, the Lindberghs moved into a hotel in town, which seemed to young Charles a "dreary" place with nothing to do but look out the window at the dirt street below, bustling with people and horses. It was around this time that C.A. decided to run for

Congress. In the staunch Republican district the previous congressman was in disgrace from accusations of graft, and C.A. not only had a lily-white reputation, he was known as something of a crusader in matters of public honesty. At this stage of the twentieth century a growing disharmony was taking shape between yeoman farmers of the West and the big money of the East, embodied most famously in the perennial presidential candidate William Jennings Bryan and his legendary "Cross of Gold" speech. The farmers of Minnesota's Sixth District were receptive to C.A.'s bid for Washington; after all, he was one of them and a favorite son to boot.

The suggestion has been made by at least one historian that there were ulterior motives for C.A.'s decision to run for office, namely, that he wanted to get away from his wife without the scandal of having to divorce her, which in those times likely would have put a quick end to his political career. In any case, beneath all the outward perceptions of homespun harmony, the Lindbergh marriage seethed.

In fact we now know there was a strain of insanity in Evangeline's family—her grandmother was possibly schizophrenic[*] and various other parents or grandparents turned out to be peculiar, dotty, or addicted to alcohol. In that period the appellation "high spirited," often applied in connection with Evangeline, had several meanings, one of which was "crazy." Documents suggest that she did not get along well with the other women in Little Falls, perhaps because of the age difference between her and the wives of C.A.'s friends. And there were tales by staff of disharmony at home. Antagonism had also festered between Evangeline and her two stepdaughters, the oldest of whom was only a few years younger than she was. It was also clear that some trouble had occurred between Evangeline and C.A., for he had moved from their bedroom even before the house burned.

On top of all that, C.A.'s storied business success had turned into a financial house of cards. He had encumbered himself with so many property loans that he was "land poor," meaning he held property but his cash flow was dried up. Since 1904 the country had been in recession,

---

[*] See A. Scott Berg's masterful biography *Lindbergh*.

followed by the Panic of 1907, in which banks collapsed, money suddenly became tight, and real estate values plummeted. Adjusted to today's values, C.A. held title to more than $5 million worth of real estate but owed more than $1 million of debt on it, plus taxes. There was an immediate need to slash the family budget in half, and the new house on the bluff above the river would suffer a commensurate scaling back.

After C.A.'s election Evangeline took Charles to Washington to be near his father, but she rented an apartment instead of living with her husband. He had convinced her that divorce would cost him his political office and bring on intolerable financial strain.

In summers, when Congress was not in session, she either took Charles to visit his grandparents in Detroit or returned to the rebuilt house on the river, which was roughly half the size of the original and so rustically finished that Evangeline called it "the camp." Gone were the cook, the nurse, the housekeeper, and the coach driver, and Evangeline herself kept both the flower and vegetable gardens. Whatever their living arrangements, C.A. remained in close contact with Evangeline and spent as much time as possible with young Charles, teaching him to swim in the local creeks and in the river and later how to hunt, fish, and live off the land.

Charles's favorite spot in the new house was the screened porch overlooking the river, which he appropriated for his bedroom, summer and winter—weather permitting—"in close contact with sun, wind, rain and stars." He most preferred stormy nights. He kept a succession of dogs, played with the neighboring children, kept collections of rocks, arrowheads, coins, stamps, marbles, baseball trading cards, and most everything else under the sun. He also made himself a pair of stilts with which to startle his mother and others by suddenly appearing at their windows.

In winters, when Congress was in session, Evangeline would take Charles back to the capital to be near his father, while the two stepdaughters attended first boarding school and then college. On one of these occasions, in 1912, when Charles was ten, Evangeline took him to an air show at Fort Myer in Virginia. There, he witnessed close up a race between an airplane and an automobile around an oval track. "You could see the pilot clearly, out in front," he wrote years afterward, "pants' legs flapping, and cap visor pointed backwards to streamline the wind. It was so intense and fascinating that I wanted to fly myself."

C.A. would have Evangeline and Charles to lunch in the congressional dining room and arranged for them to sit in the House gallery, especially if he was making a speech. Charles was introduced to a number of political luminaries of the day; he got to shake hands with President Woodrow Wilson and roll Easter eggs on the White House lawn, a tradition that dated back to the administration of Andrew Johnson.

In public, the Lindberghs presented a congenial family picture, but their private lives were marred by antipathy and harsh words, usually over money. Evangeline resented what C.A. spent on his daughters, believing that it was at her expense; she was unmoved when he explained that it was because they were motherless and had been shipped away from home. How all of this affected Charles is difficult to judge, since he was reticent to speak of it, even much later in life, but it should be understood that he was subjected to the psychological damage of being raised by parents in an unhappy marriage.

Charles sporadically attended schools in the Washington area, but only for a few months at a time while he and his mother were residing in town. For two sessions, he attended the Sidwell Friends School,* a Quaker institution, where among his classmates were Quentin and Kermit Roosevelt, sons of the former president.

From about the age of ten on, Charles demonstrated an aptitude for complex mechanical projects. For instance, he built a Rube Goldberg–type device for hauling big cakes of river ice from the icehouse by the water's edge up the hill and into the family icebox in the kitchen pantry. Also as Charles became older he helped Evangeline with the chores, such as splitting and stacking firewood, planting, weeding, and cleaning, as well as the aforementioned ice moving.

In 1912 C.A. bought a black Ford Model T that they named Maria (with a long *i*). It was a four-cylinder, folding-top, hand-cranked Tourabout with carbide headlamps and a squeeze rubber-bulb horn, and it represented a major purchase for the Lindbergh family. When C.A. wasn't using Maria for campaigning it was put to work on the farm.

---

* The institution attended by the two daughters of President Barack Obama.

Evangeline was rather afraid of the thing and, according to Charles, when she took it into town for groceries she drove it only in low gear, which took a lot of time and strained the engine to the boiling point. In due time Charles was taught to drive Maria, and thus began, like Rickenbacker and Doolittle before him, Lindbergh's lifelong thrall with the internal combustion engine.

The roads around Little Falls in 1912 left much to be desired and most of the time a horse was far more useful than an automobile, but during the next few years Charles, who had grown unusually close to his mother, would drive Evangeline and himself on picnic visits to nearby towns and attractions such as the many lakes in the area. Later, Charles would accompany his father on campaign trips, usually doing the driving and distributing campaign literature.

In 1916, when Charles was fourteen, Maria was sold and a new automobile acquired, a big six-cylinder Saxon with an electric starter, which cost twice as much as a Model T and could outrun a railroad train. At Charles's suggestion C.A. had a portion of the basement converted into a garage, where Charles serviced the Saxon Six, including a complete engine overhaul with new piston rings and valves. He also utilized the garage space to build himself a boat, a twelve-foot flat-bottom skiff that was light enough to carry through the woods.

Throughout her son's youth, Evangeline arranged educational trips to broaden his horizons. They motored to Philadelphia, New York, and other cities on the East Coast and in the Middle West. In 1913 one of the congressional committees C.A. sat on planned a visit to the Panama Canal and Charles and Evangeline went along, by ship, to see this marvelous "wonder of the world," then under construction. There they saw the great steam shovels chewing through the isthmus. In 1916 they traveled from Little Falls to California, with Charles driving on some of the worst roads imaginable. The trip took forty days.

By 1913 C.A.'s political career had played out. From the day he arrived in Washington C.A. had been a "progressive liberal," meaning that he sought radical reform of the economic system. These were the years of the Bull Moose Party, of trust busting, and antibanking tirades, to which C.A. Lindbergh was no stranger. He railed on behalf of the farmers of Minnesota against what he called the financial parasites and speculators of the East. He was furious when, two days before Christmas 1913, Wilson signed the Federal Reserve Act, creating the U.S. central banking system, which C.A. deemed "the worst legislative crime of the ages [that] establishes the greatest trust on earth!"

As the war raged in Europe and calls came for American intervention, C.A. nearly became unhinged, charging that the whole affair was instigated by the big monied interests, namely, J. P. Morgan, Andrew Carnegie, John D. Rockefeller, and other financial giants of the day. He actually issued a bill of impeachment against the five members of the Federal Reserve Board, on grounds of "high crimes and misdemeanors."

When America did enter World War I C.A., much as he was against intervention, decided it was his patriotic duty to utilize the farm for production of food, which he knew was going to be in short supply as the nation went on war footing and the sons of farmers were taken into the army. C.A. put Charles, now fifteen, in charge of this enterprise.

It was probably a good thing because Charles's grades at the Little Falls high school had fallen so low that he himself doubted he could pass the final exams. His schooling had grown spottier over the years, interspersed with the frequent and often lengthy trips that Evangeline had arranged. As luck would have it, the principal announced in the fall of 1917 that, because of the shortage of food, any student who went to work on a farm would "get full academic credit, just as though he had attended his classes and taken examinations."

Charles was ecstatic. He spent his days building and mending fences, plowing fields, felling trees, herding livestock, dynamiting rocks, driving the tractor, operating the milking machine and the incubator in the chicken coop, and tending to the thousand and one other "endless tasks that arise from day to day" on a farm. By then he had sprouted to nearly six feet tall and was slim and trim. With his father's blond mane of hair, his blue eyes, high cheekbones, and dimpled chin, and a magnetic smile, he was on the way to becoming a fitting heir for the title of most handsome man in Minnesota.

In Washington, C.A. was in the process of committing political suicide. He was so irate at Wilson's sending "American farm boys" to be killed in the war that he decided his presence was called for in a more influential venue, namely the governorship of Minnesota. As a congressman he had sided with a die-hard minority of politicians to oppose the war, and even after the U.S. entry he continued to preach so vehemently against the "Money Trust" and the evils of war that the press began to portray him as pro-German and disloyal.

Instead of countering this, C.A. redoubled his antiwar rants. As a gubernatorial candidate C.A. ran on the slate of the Nonpartisan League, a midwestern socialist-isolationist organization, and soon he began to vent socialist bombast along with the antiwar rhetoric in his stump speeches. This led to mobs pelting him with rotten eggs and to insinuations of tar and feathers. The distinguished *New York Times* reporter Harrison Salisbury, who grew up in Minneapolis, wrote: "He was arrested on charges of conspiracy along with the Nonpartisan Leaguers; a rally at Madison, Minnesota, was broken up with fire hoses; he was hanged in effigy in Red Wing, dragged from the speaking platform, threatened with lynching, and he escaped from one town amid a volley of shots."*

C.A. lost the election by a wide margin, and following this sorry pass he quit politics for a while and began publishing a magazine that soon failed. For his remaining years C.A. had no real fixed address but moved about in various ventures and misadventures, some involving postwar Florida real estate, the marketing of which even today remains the butt of bitter humor. At one point he told Charles, "You are living in an extraordinary time. Great changes are going to happen. I may not live to see them, but you will."

Charles remained on the farm, trying to make a go of it. C.A. had taken the Saxon Six with him when he left, so Charles bought a two-cylinder Excelsior motorcycle that he rode around at breakneck speeds. When purchases needed to be made C.A. "sent what he could, when he could," but essentially, Charles was on his own, while Evangeline cooked, cleaned, sewed, and relentlessly dunned C.A. for money.

One day the quiet of the woods around the farm was broken by the sound of a motor. As it came closer Charles recognized it was the drone of an airplane engine. He rushed out to see the machine soaring above the treetops; it was so slow it seemed to hang in the sky and an eternity

---

* See Harrison Salisbury's memoir *A Journey for Our Times.*

passed before it flew across the river. "I dreamed often of having a plane of my own," he said later, "and I searched the newspapers for accounts of aerial combats—articles about Fonck, Mannock, Bishop, Richthofen and Rickenbacker." Since the beginning of the war Charles had looked forward to a new monthly edition of *Everybody's Magazine* for the latest installment of "Tam o' the Scoots," the serialized adventures of a fictional scout plane–flying Scotsman on the Western Front. To Lindbergh, these knights of the air were as chivalrous as anything dreamed up by Sir Walter Scott. He decided that when he was old enough he would join the army and become a fighter pilot.[3]

On November 11, 1918, the war ended and the troops would be coming home. There was no patriotic need to farm anymore, and the Lindberghs' operation was barely breaking even as it was. Like many teenagers, Charles was torn as to what direction to take in life, and the end of the war forced decisions upon him. He liked Little Falls but he was aware that there was a bigger world he'd never seen—and he still had dreams of flying. The farming went on for a while longer, but with Evangeline's urging soon he was planning to go to college to study mechanical engineering. In the end he picked the University of Wisconsin, "more because of its nearby lakes" he wrote, "than because of its high engineering standards."

LINDBERGH'S ASSESSMENT OF WHY he chose the University of Wisconsin was telling, for he was not prepared for college in any way whatever. Academic subjects defeated him entirely and by midway through his first semester Lindbergh was placed on probation for failing English and receiving D's in math and chemistry. He developed a hatred for the rules of English and refused to understand that conformity imposed on the language was what made it manageable.

Not only was he not much of a student, Lindbergh was a loner who didn't partake of traditional college life at the dawn of the Jazz Age: beer parties, fraternities, flappers, bathtub gin, pep rallies, bonfires, "On Wisconsin!" and other rah, rah. By all accounts he didn't even partake of girls; no one ever mentioned seeing him with a female other than his mother, who had moved to Madison and found work teaching as a substitute in the public schools. This in itself seems peculiar, since Lindbergh by now had grown to his full six-foot-two height and resembled, if anything, a lean Greek god.

One would think the girls would have thrown themselves at him, and maybe they did, but Lindbergh had become strangely stoic when it came to women—an intellectual prude, almost. In his opinion women were silly. It had to be explained to him by a fellow student that the intellectual approach to girls was good only so far; then, Lindbergh's acquaintance informed him, one should physically seduce them. If not shocked, Lindbergh was at least firm in his convictions. "I could not understand why you should want to overcome resistance until you found a girl you really loved," he said. Until the end of his life, all through the many years that women swooned at the mere mention of his name, the term ladies' man (even with respect to his ultimate infidelities) was never applied to Charles Lindbergh.

He had few friends in college. The lone exceptions were two fellow motorcycle enthusiasts with whom he would tear around the town and the countryside, tormenting residents with the machines' obnoxious roar. An often told story has Lindbergh becoming a daredevil during this period, risking his neck to make a 90-degree turn at high speed on a dead-end street. The first time he tried it he cracked up; the bike skidded from under him, bounced over a curb, and wound up on a lawn. Lindbergh miraculously was unhurt and upon dusting himself off declared he was going to try it again—which he did until he finally got it right.

The one college activity Lindbergh seemed to enjoy was army training. He entered Wisconsin's Reserve Officers' Training Corps and discovered—quite strangely, for he was essentially a nonconformist—that he adapted well to military life. As a member of Wisconsin's rifle and pistol teams he was an expert marksman and in fact won first prize in the competition for the school's best shooter and received a brand-new Colt .45.

He barely scraped by his first semester academically and remained on probation. When his freshman year ended he began six weeks of ROTC summer camp at Fort Knox, Kentucky, training for the field artillery.

After camp he took off for Florida on the Excelsior motorcycle to see his father, but by some failure of communication the two did not connect and Charles toured much of the Southeast the rest of the summer. He arrived back in Madison to be greeted by his grades from the previous semester and a letter from C.A., neither of which carried much promise for his prospects as a student. The grades were awful—including F's in math and chemistry—and except for good marks in shop and ROTC Lindbergh would enter his third and final probationary period in the fall. His father poured more cold water on Lindbergh's college future by informing Charles that he was broke and could send no more money for tuition.

C.A. had suggested to Evangeline that they mortgage the house but she wouldn't hear of it. Charles scraped up enough cash for one more semester but it soon became apparent his heart wasn't in it. He realized he was failing, letting his parents down, but the more he sat in class the more he realized it was flying that engaged his soul.

About that time one of Lindbergh's motorcycle riding friends showed him some literature and brochures that he had requested from flying schools. Lindbergh was most definitely intrigued. The friend had ordered the material only on a lark, he said—not seriously—pointing out the dangers of flying and that the life expectancy of an aviator in war was measured in hours. But Lindbergh saw in this a way out of the "life of drawing boards, meetings, and conformity" he had come to dread. He had never been in a flying machine, but somewhere in the back of his mind, ever since he'd watched the plane race the automobile at ten years old, there was an excitement, a rush of derring-do—his teachers always said his head was in the clouds and didn't know how right they were.

IN FEBRUARY 1922, LINDBERGH was informed that he had been dropped from the rolls of the University of Wisconsin for academic deficiency. The feeling was mutual. He put himself and the Excelsior on a railroad train and headed for Lincoln, Nebraska, where the Nebraska Aircraft Corporation and Ray Page's Flying School awaited him. After trying every argument to dissuade his son from flying, C.A. had somehow been able to cough up the $500 tuition for several weeks of work in the airplane factory, followed by several weeks of actual flying. The school, though, was basically a scam.

Lindbergh got his first week in the factory, learning beside trained technicians how to recondition army surplus training planes, the famous "flying Jennys," as they were affectionately known, left over from the First World War. The most significant change the factory made was to replace the Jennys' 150-horsepower motors with the more powerful 220 Hispano-Suiza engines. Otherwise he found himself doping wing fabric, replacing struts and guys, and all the other tasks associated with converting military aircraft into commercial planes. However, between the time Lindbergh received the Nebraska Aircraft Corporation brochure and his arrival in Lincoln, the company not only had changed its name to Lincoln Standard Aircraft, it also had more or less dropped the idea of a flying school—one reason being that Charles A. Lindbergh was the only student to show up. Nevertheless, Ray Page accepted Lindbergh's money and put him to work. At the end of the week, Sunday, April 9, 1922, he was given his first plane ride. Well into old age, Lindbergh remembered the exhilaration of every moment, the plane hauled out from the factory the day before, wings not yet attached to the fuselage.

"I stood on the field all morning," Lindbergh said, "watching riggers attach wings and 'hook up' ailerons, flippers, and rudder; watching mechanics strain in fuel, drain the sediment bulb, tune up the engine, watching the engineer test cable tautness with his fingers and measure wing droop with his knowing eye. Behind every movement, word and detail, one felt the strength of life, the presence of death."

The mechanic jerked the propeller and the engine sputtered to life.

"Wings begin to tremble—the roar becomes deafening—the plane lurches forward—the ground recedes—over treetops—across a ravine like a hawk—a hidden, topsy-turvy stage with height to draw its curtains."

Lindbergh wrote these dramatic words in 1952—thirty years after he first took off in an airplane—so it is easy to conclude that the experience of flight left him almost in shock.

"Trees become bushes; barns, toys as we climb. I live only in the moment in this strange, unmortal place, crowded with beauty, pierced with danger."

It was around this time that Lindbergh picked up the nickname "Slim," apt enough, since there were only 168 pounds on his lanky frame. His flying instructor was Ira "Biff" Biffle, an ex–Army Air Corps man—querulous, salty, profane, cynical. He had apparently seen one too many crack-up or, as Lindbergh put it, "lost the love of his art," for when

Charles looked eagerly for the flying lessons he'd paid for Biffle was generally nowhere to be found.

In the meantime, Lindbergh hung around the factory, absorbing the hundreds of details necessary to care for a plane, since a pilot in those times also needed to be a mechanic, tailor, carpenter, and rigger. There was always talk of crashes at the factory, of who had died, and why. One of Biffle's close friends had "spun in" recently, they said. "Slim" Lindbergh had received only eight hours of flying time when Biffle told him he was ready to solo.

There was a hitch, though. Ray Page refused to let him solo in one of his planes unless he posted a bond to cover the possibility of crash. At that point Lindbergh was down to his last dollars and in May he departed Lincoln Standard Aircraft to become the flunky of a barnstorming pilot named Erold Bahl. At first he was consigned to spin the prop, clean the plane, and repair canvas but soon he graduated to the exalted position of "wing walker," to please the barnstorming crowds.

One day a parachute maker appeared in Lincoln to demonstrate his product, which he did by jumping out of a perfectly good airplane from two thousand feet in the air. Lindbergh was so impressed that he had to try it himself. He made the jump next day, a life-changing event, at least for Lindbergh. In fact, he made a "double jump," in which halfway through the fall he collapses his first chute, free falls to give the crowd a thrill, then opens a second chute. If flying was a daredevil's avocation, Lindbergh had just become a double daredevil and discovered that he liked it.

FOR CIVILIAN PILOTS AT THE BEGINNING of the 1920s there were few moneymaking opportunities aside from barnstorming, that is, doing tricks or stunts for money at county fairs or taking passengers up for five dollars a ride. Commercial airlines were still somewhere in the future, even flying the post by airmail was in the future. Lindbergh knew he needed more flying lessons before he could solo. He'd saved up money over the years to buy his own plane and, not wanting to spend it, he bought himself a silk chute and began offering wing walking and parachute jumps and mechanical help to pilots in exchange for lessons.

Flying, by then, had become an almost mystical experience for Lindbergh, a sort of holy grail, which he explained philosophically—and somewhat arrogantly: "In flying, I tasted the wine of the gods of which [the earthbound] could know nothing. Who valued life more highly, the aviators who spent it on the art they loved, or these misers who doled it out like pennies through their antlike days? I decided that if I could fly for ten years before I was killed in a crash, it would be a worthwhile trade for an ordinary lifetime."

Thus Slim entered the world of barnstorming where, it was said, "if flying was considered dangerous, wing walking and parachuting were regarded as suicidal." Lindbergh practiced exhaustively, though, and he didn't consider it daredevil because he'd worked out every technicality beforehand on the theory that "most accidents were caused by errors which could be avoided."

Others, however, claimed to be unconvinced. On posters throughout the rural Midwest he was featured prominently as DAREDEVIL LINDBERGH. Exhilarating as it was, however, barnstorming as a daredevil, with its circus-like atmosphere, seemed to be a dead end so far as Lindbergh's aspirations for becoming a pilot were concerned. He got some flying lessons but, as airplanes were uninsurable in those days, no one would let him use his plane to solo. Then he heard tell from his father that the army had auctioned off a number of surplus war aircraft down in Americus, Georgia, and word was out they could be bought cheap. Upon further investigation, Lindbergh discovered he could purchase a used, twin-seat Jenny with a brand-new eight-cylinder Curtiss OX-5 engine for a mere five hundred dollars.

In Americus, however, Slim was confronted with an awkward predicament—namely, how to fly the plane off the airfield. He tried taxiing around for a while to get the feel of it. Once, he accidently left the ground and sailed along about four feet above the grass before he managed to bounce down on one wheel. A knot of pilots who happened to be loafing around a hangar witnessed this embarrassing demonstration, and one of them, named Henderson, generously offered to help Lindbergh do some takeoffs and landings. Fortunately the dual controls on the Jenny were still in place, and Slim and Henderson spent the better part of an hour doing takeoffs and touchdowns. Right before sundown, Slim

Lindbergh made his first solo flight, and he slept that night under the wing of his airplane, peaceful as a baby.

LINDBERGH SPENT A WEEK at the Americus field practicing more takeoffs and landings before he felt comfortable enough to fly off on his own. When he did, it was a long, overland hop across Alabama and into Mississippi where, at Meridian, he found his first paying passenger. Slim had landed in a farmer's field, where he spent the night under the plane, and next day as he was preparing to leave a fat man waddled up and, claiming to have been a pilot during the war, produced a five-dollar bill if Lindbergh would take him for a ride.

It was a tough haul. First, the OX-5 developed only about 80 or 90 horsepower, which meant the plane was essentially underpowered; secondly, Lindbergh had not accounted for the weight of his passenger, said to have been some three hundred pounds. The plane barely got off the ground on an uphill takeoff but, "in true Jenny style," escaped a crash and Slim kept his passenger in the air for twenty minutes, chasing a buzzard.

After that, Lindbergh took off for Texas. It was indeed seat-of-the-pants flying. There were numerous storms. Lindbergh had purchased a compass but failed to install it on the dashboard. The only chart he owned was an oil company map of the entire United States, which naturally contained few ground reference points. He became lost almost immediately and stayed lost until dusk, when he put down in a friendly-looking farm field. The landing went well, but as he was taxiing to a fence corner a large ditch suddenly appeared in front of him.

He hit it fairly hard. As the plane nosed in the prop splintered. Then as the landing gear rolled down the tail reared up until Lindbergh feared the plane might flip. Instead, it settled back down. Now he could add to his list of "firsts" his first crack-up.

The nearest town to the field where he'd crashed was Maben, Mississippi. He wired Americus for a new prop and made so many friends waiting for it that he had hundreds of dollars' worth of paying customers by the time he got the plane fixed. At this point in his life Lindbergh was perfectly comfortable around admiring spectators and anxious to educate them about aviation. Puddle hopping northward through Texas and Nebraska, Slim stopped off at the old factory to show his new plane to the guys, then headed home to Minnesota.

C.A., it seemed, had decided to run for an open seat in the U.S. Senate, and so Charles offered to fly him around the state. Unfortunately, no sooner had he arrived within its boundaries than he cracked up again, landing in a swamp and splintering another propeller to matchsticks.

Despite the novelty of a candidate flying into his stump speeches, C.A.'s political career was over, and he finished a distant third. He had not been himself recently either; he had extreme reactions toward heat and cold and memory loss as well. Slim stayed in the area, barnstorming in Minnesota and Iowa, and he was earning a respectable living. One day a car drove up to the airfield with several young officers who had recently graduated from the army flight training school. They were snappy-looking in their silver wings, polished boots, and Sam Browne belts.

One of them suggested to Lindbergh that he come into the army as a military aviator. After thinking it over Slim decided it wasn't a bad idea; he had always wanted to fly powerful, modern planes, and perhaps become a fighter pilot, and the only way he could do any of that was via the U.S. Army. That night, in his hotel room, he wrote a letter to the chief of Air Service at the War Department in Washington, D.C., and the upshot was that on March 16, 1924, he reported, as ordered, to the army pilot training school at Brooks Field, near San Antonio, Texas.

★ ★ ★ ★ ★

CHAPTER 5

AIR COMBAT IS NOT SPORT, IT IS SCIENTIFIC MURDER

Dᴜʀɪɴɢ ᴛʜᴇ ʟᴀsᴛ ᴍᴏɴᴛʜ ᴏғ 1916 Eddie Rickenbacker had another epiphany. He was riding east on the Santa Fe Railway's *Super Chief* from California, headed for Wolverhampton, England, to join the Sunbeam Automotive Company as an engineering and design adviser at the behest of its president, Louis Coatalen, who had approached him in California. Actually, he had been working up to this moment for several months, so perhaps it wasn't an epiphany after all, but it was still a very big decision. Rickenbacker was through with automobile racing.

In his private compartment on the train, Rickenbacker emptied out his coat and pants pockets of all the amulets, talismans, jujus, and other good-luck charms he'd collected over the years and laid them by the washbasin. What good had they done him, anyway, he thought? Only recently, a falling object had nearly brained him as he avoided walking under a ladder. It was superstition versus religion—and religion was the real thing from now on, he decided.[1] He was still holding good to his abstinence pledge of no liquor and no cigarettes; he didn't need those "lucky" crutches either.

During his decade-long racing career he had seen his friends and competitors one by one killed or horribly injured. Car racing was far and away the world's most dangerous sport, with something of a Roman circus aura about it.

As the train rolled across the cold Southwest desert, Eddie lifted the lid of the commode and dropped his lucky charms into the bowl—rabbits' feet, dried four-leaf clovers, a rattlesnake's rattles, miniature Billiken dolls,* buckeyes, wishbones, and bear claws; also included were several tiny, shriveled-up bats' hearts—"the weirdest collection of charms ever carried in the clothing of one person"—and pulled the chain, watching as they were flushed out onto the bare gravel and cross ties rushing by below.

That year the American Automobile Association championship list ranked him the third best driver in the nation, an extraordinary achievement, and that year also he had netted nearly $40,000.† Rickenbacker would always be connected with car racing, he felt, as a backer or even an owner, but no longer a driver.

When the train reached Indianapolis he stopped to pick up some documents at the Motor Speedway, then continued on to Washington where he applied for a passport, using officially for the first time the new spelling of his name, substituting the more anglicized k for the Germanic h.

At the time, the Germans had not yet begun unrestricted sea warfare, but U-boat commanders were known to stop ships on the ocean and check their cargo and passenger lists, so the voyage took on an edgy mood. In New York Rickenbacker boarded the ocean liner St. Louis, bound for Liverpool. Among the passengers aboard was William Thaw II, from the prominent Pittsburgh family, who had learned to fly at Yale. In 1914, despite poor vision, defective hearing, and a bad knee, Thaw had volunteered himself, and his plane, to fight the Germans in what became the Lafayette Escadrille, a fighter squadron in the French army consisting of mostly American pilots. Eddie and Major Thaw found that they had engines and speed in common, and Thaw suggested to Rickenbacker that because of his racing experience he would be a good candidate for the Escadrille. For the first time Eddie actually began to consider the dimensions and consequences of the war that was tearing much of the

---

* Billiken dolls, quite popular in their time, were plump Buddha-like creatures with elfin ears and a mischievous smile, the 1908 creation of a Missouri art teacher who said the image came to her in a dream.

† Upwards of $1 million in today's dollars.

world apart but had not yet affected America. Yet he wasn't ready to jump out of the racing kettle and into a shooting fire.

Others aboard were a pair named Goodyear and Immermann (Rickenbacker took them for Canadians), who said they were in the wheat business. All across the bleak North Atlantic the passengers engaged in small talk, but the Canadian wheat salesmen seemed to take a particular interest in Rickenbacker and joked about how he would be received in England with his German-sounding name.

When the *St. Louis* arrived in Liverpool a few days before Christmas, Eddie discovered that the men weren't joking at all. Instead of debarking, when Rickenbacker produced his passport, a British official with a drooping mustache shouted in his face, "What's your name?"

"Rickenbacker," he answered. "You can read it right there on the passport."

"What's your purpose in England?" the official demanded. And before Eddie could answer he added, "Don't you know there's a war on?"

Suddenly, a big long-nosed Scotland Yard detective wearing a bowler hat materialized and escorted Rickenbacker into ship's cabin A, and who should be sitting there but Goodyear and Immermann, who promptly revealed themselves as inspectors from Scotland Yard and accused Rickenbacker of being a German spy!

Immermann said to Rickenbacker, "You might as well own up. You'll be executed anyway. But it will save a lot of trouble."

They had been sarcastically calling him "Baron von Rickenbacher," and Eddie asked, "What is all this 'Baron' stuff about?"

They proudly produced a dossier they said had been kept on Eddie, going back some years. It was filled with old newspaper clippings from his racing days.

It seems that at the 1913 Santa Monica races an inventive sports reporter, in an act that would make the *National Enquirer* blush, wrote a story claiming that Eddie was in fact a man named Edwart von Rickenbacher, long-lost scion of a colonel in the German army who was also a Prussian baron. The story claimed that he had been expelled from the Vienna Military Academy for the offense of "speeding" after he outraced Germany's most famous race car driver, the Mercedes engineer Max Sailer, in a car full of drunken cadets. The story went on to say that the disgrace caused his father to disinherit "Baron von Rickenbacher," which drove him to exile in the United States, where he changed the spelling of his name and the only calling he could think of was racing cars.

Eddie hadn't denied the story at the time, either because he didn't see the original or because he thought the publicity might do him some good. In any event the fiction was consequently reprinted as true and produced such nicknames for him in the press as the "Wild Teuton," the "Happy Heinie," and the "Daredevil Dutchman," and all this in time became part of auto-racing lore. To Eddie, it had been a joke, but judging by the demeanor of these British policemen, it was no longer a joking matter.

They strip-searched him, Eddie said, going so far as to remove the heels of his shoes to see if there was anything hidden inside, and rubbed lemon juice and acids on his skin to detect secret writing. They sifted through his luggage and cut open the seams of his suit jackets—all the while questioning him relentlessly and refusing his pleas to contact his sponsor Louis Coatalen at the Sunbeam factory.

Nothing criminal was found but nevertheless they confined Rickenbacker to the ship until it sailed, banishing him from setting foot on British soil. When he protested, the long-nosed sergeant threatened to throw him into the Tower of London.

On Christmas Eve, with the help of the ship's captain, Eddie persuaded his tormentors to at least let him go ashore and spend the night in a hotel in Liverpool, where he could get some Christmas dinner. They agreed but took rooms next to his and refused to let him out of their sight. From the hotel he repeatedly phoned Coatalen, who was neither at home nor at work, but on Christmas morning his luck changed. Coatalen at last was contacted and immediately interceded with Scotland Yard. By that afternoon Eddie was on a train for London, bound for the fabulous Savoy Hotel.[2]

AT THE CRACK OF DAWN next day Eddie was awakened by the roar of many engines as British fighter and bomber squadrons flew low over the Thames River on training maneuvers. "On hearing the engines he would hop out of bed, rush to the window, watch the formations with eager eyes, and decided that it would not be such a bad idea to join up."[3] Meantime, there was work to do at the Sunbeam factory.

Sunbeam's facility was located in the Midlands and Rickenbacker spent the workweek there, designing and streamlining Sunbeam racers for the upcoming season. But on the weekends he returned to the Savoy and the flights of warplanes every morning. Everything in England seemed to involve the war, and with so many young men on the streets in khaki Eddie began to feel self-conscious. He was then twenty-seven years old and decided that if the United States became involved in the war he wanted to be a fighter pilot. What he didn't know was that twenty-seven was too old to become a fighter pilot, according to U.S. Army regulations. He also decided that he *wanted* the United States to get involved in the war, which turned out to be sooner than he thought.

Rickenbacker had been in England less than two months when Germany announced it would begin unrestricted submarine warfare against all ships in British waters. At this the United States broke off diplomatic relations, and the Germans gave Americans living in England a five-day grace period in which to sail home. That was the end of the Sunbeam racing team. Eddie decided to go home but reservations were tight. He managed to share an upper berth on, of all ships, the *St. Louis,* where his old nemesis the long-nosed sergeant from Scotland Yard awaited him. Again he was marched to cabin A, and once again he was greeted by Inspectors Goodyear and Immermann, who began their interrogations anew. They searched all of his baggage and papers and confiscated drawings and plans of race cars he was working on. At long last they left him be, and once they had gone he went into the ship's salon where he encountered an old friend, the noted playwright and artist Gene Buck, drinking tea and eating bonbons, who told him, "Say, Eddie, have you heard the news? There's a big German spy on board. That's why the boat is delayed!"

ON THE VOYAGE HOME to the United States Eddie had an idea. He remembered the conversation he'd had on the trip over with Major Thaw, who had tried to recruit him into the Lafayette Escadrille by suggesting that his race driving experience would be an asset as a pilot. It made perfect sense. Drivers were also good mechanics, who knew how to get the most out of their engines; they had excellent reflexes and instincts (or they would not be alive); they were used to making instantaneous decisions and were brave and accustomed to putting themselves in harm's way. If he could recruit fifty—even a hundred—drivers, the cream of the professional race car circuit, to become U.S. Army aviators, it would certainly be a formidable bunch. He even thought up a name for such a group: the Aero Reserves of America.

When the *St. Louis* docked in New York the usual gaggle of newsmen awaited, including a reporter for the *New York Times,* which carried a story in next day's paper headlined, "Plans to Enlist Race Drivers for Aviation," with Eddie quoted as promising a nationwide tour, signing up the drivers.

Before leaving New York, Eddie contacted Captain Walter G. Kilner who ran the army aviation school at Mineola, Long Island, who referred him to a Brigadier General Squier, commander of the Signal Corps in Washington, under which the Army Air Service languished. Militarily, the army had found practically no use for its air arm, which in 1917 was barely six years old and possessed fewer than fifty planes and no more than forty pilots. No one on the general staff had any aviation training, or much interest in it either.

Despite the American brass's ambivalence over the airplane as a weapon, by 1917 aerial warfare had become an integral part of the war in Europe, which sealed its future as a critical element in any wars to come as well. At first planes were used for scouting, as mounted cavalry had performed in previous conflicts. From heights, planes could pick up troop and artillery movements or the construction of fortifications. Opposing forces quickly began to arm pilots to attack these intruding scouts—at first with rifles, pistols, even shotguns, but soon with machine guns, which had become ubiquitous during the war. Initially the machine guns had to be mounted above the propeller if it was front-mounted, which made firing them awkward, but by 1915 the Germans had found a way to synchronize the timing of the machine-gun fire to the revolutions of the propeller so that the bullets fired in between the spinning blades of the prop, which made aerial battle all the more accurate and deadly.

Photographic aircraft also soon appeared in enemy territory, with a cameraman/observer/machine gunner taking pictures of the battlefield for interpretation by intelligence officers and also for mapmaking purposes. These, too, developed counterparts in "pursuit" or fighter planes, whose job it was to shoot down the interlopers before they could complete their mission. Likewise, bombers appeared on both sides, with ever heavier explosive loads commensurate with their increase in size, power, and sophistication. They also had to contend with the pursuit fighters.

In late 1915 there appeared on the Western Front a German flier named Manfred von Richthofen, known as the Red Baron, after his royal title and a penchant for painting his squadron's Fokker triwing fighters red. He was a natural born killer who shot down more than eighty enemy aircraft before himself being fatally brought down by ground fire from a trench containing Australian infantry while battling a British plane at low altitude. He was so vainglorious that each time he shot down a plane Richthofen ordered a Berlin jeweler to produce a specially engraved silver goblet with the date and type of airplane that was his "kill."

It was Richthofen and others like him on both sides who gave rise to the term "ace," the appellation applied to pilots who shot down a certain number of enemy planes—usually, at least five. In the process, these men invented the elaborate flying maneuvers used in what were known as dogfights—brief, bloody, and often fatal encounters among two or more enemy planes. Many of these aerial ploys were named after the pilots who perfected them—the Immelmann turn, the Lufbery loop, Dicta Boelcke, and so forth—which in turn triggered rapid improvements in speed, maneuverability, and firepower of the aircraft they flew.

Undaunted by his putdown by the U.S. Army brass, Eddie used his celebrity to make pro-intervention speeches to men's clubs in such cities as Cleveland, Detroit, and Chicago. West of the Alleghenies, however, he found that interest in the ongoing war in Europe had waned. Also, at some point, he began to have a sensation that someone was following him. Everywhere he went, it seemed, a certain tall blond man would appear—in his hotel lobby, at speeches, in restaurants. When Eddie tried to confront the man it was as if he'd vanished into thin air.

Rickenbacker had reached Los Angeles in mid-March 1917 when the infamous Zimmermann Telegram was revealed. The British, it seemed, had intercepted a wire from Germany's foreign minister Arthur Zimmermann to Heinrich von Eckardt, the German ambassador to Mexico, offering to return to the Mexicans the provinces lost to the United States in the 1846–48 Mexican-American War in exchange for Mexican support against England, France, and the Allies. Newspapers played up the presumptuous German clandestine offer in major headlines and a surge of furious indignation swept across California, which had been free from Mexican rule only sixty-six years at that point. Eddie's speeches suddenly began attracting large crowds.

He was standing in the lobby of L.A.'s Alexandria Hotel one morning when the tall blond stranger materialized in an archway, approached, and introduced himself to the startled Rickenbacker with a strong British accent. "I just want to tell you," said the man, "that my government and I are now fully satisfied as to your status as a loyal and patriotic American." Before Rickenbacker could react, the man added, "But I do want to thank you for the wonderful trip I've had, following you about this interesting country." He then turned with a nod and seemed to vanish as mysteriously as he had appeared.[4]

ON APRIL 2, 1917, WOODROW WILSON asked Congress for a declaration of war against Germany, which was approved four days later, on April 6. Eddie got on a train for Washington with the list of racing car drivers he had recruited, including, among others, world champions Ralph DePalma, Earl Cooper, Eddie Pullen, and Ray Harroun.

As Rickenbacker enthusiastically unfolded his plan to the army brass, he noticed many of the officers looking at him askance. Eddie Rickenbacker, famous race car driver or not: what they wanted to know was whether or not he had a college degree. When he told them about the correspondence course he had taken in mechanical engineering they mocked him, and when they found out he was twenty-seven they told him he was too old, that the Air Service accepted only college graduates twenty-five years of age or under. One officer even went so far as to explain that the army didn't want fliers who understood engines because there was *always* something wrong with airplane engines, and men who were accomplished mechanics would use that as an excuse not to fly missions.

Eddie was frustrated but he wasn't crushed. He never let a setback get him down. The war was big, and he sensed he was still somehow going to be a part of it.

A few weeks later, while in Cincinnati, he received a phone call from an army major named Lewis Burgess, an old friend and racing enthusiast, who told him there was a top secret ship sailing out of New York for France and that if he wanted to go he'd better be at the dock the next morning. Major Burgess said that it involved some important people who needed drivers. The position carried the rank of staff sergeant. Still itching to fly in combat, Eddie considered that, if he accepted, being among the first U.S. soldiers in France he just might be able to circumvent the age and education restrictions for army pilots. It was one of those opportunities he felt he simply had to take, for it might not come his way again.

The secret mission turned out to be the departure of the U.S. Army commander General John J. "Black Jack" Pershing, and his staff, including headquarters chief Captain George S. Patton Jr. and Pershing's air officer Colonel T. F. Dodd, the same man whose airplane motor Eddie had fixed in the cow pasture near Los Angeles the previous year.

Next morning Rickenbacker was sworn in as a sergeant in the army and given his uniform and gear. The advance party shipped out on the White Star Line's RMS *Baltic,* with Eddie consigned to a hammock in the steerage, which, he complained, was grubby and the mess hall was grubby too. Up on deck he ran into a friendly fellow sergeant and was amazed to learn that this man had been installed in a comfortable second-class cabin.

"It's because I'm a sergeant first class," the man told him, pointing out that Eddie was just a staff sergeant. Rickenbacker hadn't known there were different kinds of sergeants. Immediately he sought out his old pal Colonel Dodd, who he figured owed him a favor. When Eddie said he wanted to be promoted, Dodd replied that "promotions come through meritorious service, Eddie. How do you intend to go about that?"

"I don't know, Colonel," Eddie told him. "That's why I brought you along."

Dodd burst out laughing and Rickenbacker got his promotion—as well as a bump up to second-class accommodations.

Once in France Rickenbacker began driving for the great air pioneer Colonel William "Billy" Mitchell, who took to Eddie's homespun humor and frank honesty—and of course to his driving. Mitchell liked to go fast. The war soon convinced Mitchell, who became chief of the U.S. Air Service in France, that airplanes were warfare's wave of the future, and he became deeply concerned that the United States was lagging behind.

One day in Paris while walking the Champs-Élysées the Rickenbacker luck struck again. He ran into an acquaintance, yet another racing enthusiast, who was a New York banker in civilian life but now the officer in charge of setting up an American school for pilots in France. He immediately offered Rickenbacker the job of chief engineer, with the rank of second lieutenant. Eddie accepted, with the provision that because he could hardly serve as engineer for a flying school unless he himself was a pilot, he must first learn to fly a plane.

He'd had to ask Billy Mitchell's permission, of course, and Mitchell gave it, even though it would cost him his driver and his confidant. He simply looked his protégé in the eye and asked, "Eddie, do you really want to fly?" When the answer was "yessir," Mitchell said, "I'll see what I can do." In fact, Mitchell pulled some rigid strings to get Eddie past regulations and into pilot training.

Soon Rickenbacker was practicing takeoffs and landings at a flying school in Tours, conducted entirely by the French. There was a little practice plane to start with, he said, that had no wings to speak of, so it would not take off, but the students hop-skipped it over grass fields to get the hang of flying and learn the coordination of steering with both hands and feet.

His first solo, like Lindbergh's, was a hair-raising experience. It was in an old nine-cylinder Caudron, a "pusher," with its propeller behind the pilot. He was nearly frightened to death. First off, his six-foot-two frame barely fit in the small flying compartment. There was a crosswind; he overcompensated on the rudder and the plane left the runway and took off right for the hangar. He missed the hangar by about five feet and bumped along the grassy field until the thing finally became airborne. He did some banks and turns and then it was time to land. Again he was frightened nearly out of his wits. Eddie's first attempt left him about fifty feet above the field, but gradually he made lower and lower passes until he worked himself to the ground.

After seventeen days of flying school he could now call himself a pilot. After putting in twenty-five hours of flying time, he was commissioned a first lieutenant in the U.S. Army.

WHEN HE REPORTED TO HIS ASSIGNMENT as engineer at the American flying school he found it was run by five officers whose names, ironically, were Spaatz, Wiedenbach, Tittel, Spiegel, and himself, Rickenbacker. Behind their backs they were known snidely as "the five German spies."

As engineering officer, Rickenbacker was burdened with duties. There was no time for him to take ground school flying instruction, but armed with what little he had learned from the French he managed to get into the air every day after work and try out maneuvers he'd heard the flying students talking about—stalls, rolls, loops, spins, and Immelmanns. Sometimes he managed to duck into an instruction class and then try it later for himself. It was risky business, and he had to sneak an airplane out without benefit of an instructor. There was a graveyard right there on the field for those who did not learn their lessons well.

Soon Rickenbacker developed a relationship with Colonel Carl "Tooey" Spaatz that could be described as troubled. One time Eddie was flying back from a trip to Tours when he saw the Ivy League pilots in training playing a football game on the flying field below. For some reason this inspired him to perform a spin right above the field, which went awry until he was able to regain control and pull out at less than fifty feet above the ground, scattering terrified players and spectators. For this, an infuriated Spaatz grounded Rickenbacker for thirty days.

More than once his self-instruction nearly killed him, but soon Rickenbacker talked his way into a French gunnery school. Spaatz at first refused to let him go because he was needed as an engineer, but like Billy Mitchell before him, he finally relented with a smile and a handshake, declaring, "If your heart's set on going to Cazaux, you're no damn good to me around here, so good luck."*

For Rickenbacker the gunnery school at Cazaux was a trial. For one thing, classes were conducted in French, with a translator. Right off, Eddie was put in a boat in the middle of a lake where, day after day, he was supposed to shoot at targets with a .30-caliber rifle. Next he was sent up in a plane armed with machine guns to fire at a moving target— in this case a ten-foot-long, four-foot-wide sock, "towed by two

---

* During World War II Spaatz would take command of the renowned Eighth Air Force, based in England, and later air operations in the European theater. Afterward, he served as chief of staff of the U.S. Air Force.

Frenchmen in a beat-up old Caudron." The first time Rickenbacker pulled the triggers he cut the tow rope in two. The Frenchmen dove straight down and landed on the airfield and Eddie followed. They came running up to him, shouting, "Tirez la! Tirez la!" nodding their heads and pointing to the sock, which had floated down onto the field. Then, pointing to their plane, they began shaking their heads and shouting, "Pas la! Pas la!"[5]

In the early spring of 1918 Rickenbacker was assigned to the first All-American air squadron to go into action on the Western Front, the 94th Aero Pursuit Squadron—the soon-to-be-famous Hat in the Ring gang.

It was commanded by Major John W.F.M. Huffer, a former Lafayette Escadrille flier who had been born in Paris and lived all of his life in France, where his father was an American tobacco executive. But its most famous member was the celebrated Ace of Aces Major Raoul Lufbery, who had brought down sixteen German planes, had won the Legion d'Honneur and the Croix de Guerre, and was idolized on both sides of the Atlantic.

Lufbery was a French expatriate who had immigrated to America when he was seventeen, but he retained the eccentricities of his native land, including an addiction to Gauloises cigarettes and a taste for fine wines. He returned to France, of course, when war broke out and joined the Lafayette Escadrille, where he was acknowledged as the most proficient pilot of them all. When he wasn't flying or raising hell, "he was, incongruously, picking mushrooms, for which he had an inordinate passion."[6] To the airmen in France, Lufbery was a character larger than life. He was short and stocky, with a bull neck, square jaw, aquiline nose, and soulful Gallic eyes. He had a wide, toothy smile and little or no use for picayune army regulations, which endeared him to his American-raised comrades once they got past his heavy French accent. He was also brave as the lions he once owned when he flew with the Escadrille.*

---

* Whiskey, a male lion, so named because he once drank a saucer of it, and Soda, a female, were originally acquired as cubs for mascots by some Escadrille fliers, but Lufbery raised them, and as they grew large they followed him everywhere around the aerodrome. When the Lafayette Escadrille was broken up the lions were sent to the Paris zoo.

THE LAFAYETTE ESCADRILLE, organized in France before the United States entered the war, was composed of American volunteers and some Frenchmen. It now provided the backbone of the U.S. air effort, with many of its pilots joining the ranks of the new American pursuit squadrons, where their combat experience was invaluable. They brought with them also a certain joie de vivre that was not always appreciated by the high command.

For example, following the Battle of Verdun, when the Escadrille returned to its base in Luxeuil, according to information obtained by the author Quentin Reynolds: "They took over the Hotel Lion d'Or and tossed a party during the course of which every dish, cup, saucer and bit of furniture was hilariously broken. At the height of the party, shots were heard outside. A dozen pilots rushed to investigate, only to find they had been fired by a former Canadian Mountie."

The Mountie, it seemed, had gotten into a discussion with Lufbery about shooting, and Lufbery proposed that they stage a target practice. He was holding a book of British drill instructions at arm's length, and from thirty paces the Canadian was riddling it splendidly. Lufbery was forced to admit it was the best shooting he had ever seen in view of the fact that it was nighttime and, because he'd been drinking wine all day, he presented an extremely unsteady target to aim at.

In Paris they would take over such haunts as Harry's New York Bar, where someone of their number would play the piano and they would drink and sing:

> The trip was long, the boys arrived
> They ripped off shirts and collars.
> The pretty maid who welcomed them
> Made thirty thousand dollars.

Until they became drunk and, upon those frequent occasions, would further sing (to the tune of "My Bonnie Lies Over the Ocean"):

> The young aviator went stunting,
> And as 'neath the wreckage he lay,
> To the mechanics assembled around him
> These last parting words did he say.

Take the cylinders out of my kidneys
The connecting rod out of my brain
From the small of my back take the crankshaft
And assemble the engine again.

The song continues in the same vein, with ever more vulgar verses, which accompanied the Escadrille volunteers to the 94th Aero Pursuit Squadron, and pervaded it still when Eddie Rickenbacker and his fellow death-defying flying school graduates came aboard.

Lufbery was older—an old man, actually—at thirty-three, and with his experience he was named operations officer. Rickenbacker was also older, and more or less an odd man out among these Ivy League pilots. The two men naturally gravitated toward each other.

Despite a strong appetite for levity among the men of the 94th Aero, when the workday began before sunrise, and the pilots pulled on their flying suits and filed in for the day's briefing, while outside the armorers were loading machine-gun belts into the planes that the mechanics had worked on all night and were now warming up in the grass on the side of the runway—in the chill of the dawn and the unceasing roar of the big rotary engines—the business got very serious indeed.

It had taken the squadron a few days to get organized, giving the pilots time to personalize and decorate their planes. The most immediate task became finding a name and insignia to give the 94th. Major Huffer suggested a stovepipe hat like the one Uncle Sam wore, with a hatband of stars and stripes. The squadron surgeon recommended putting a ring around the hat, after the old frontier custom by pugilists of throwing their hat in a ring, signifying they were ready to fight. Everyone was delighted and the squadron artist got to work. Forever after they were known as the Hat in the Ring gang, the most decorated air corps squadron in France.[7]

ON MARCH 21, 1918, Rickenbacker had the honor of being chosen by Major Lufbery—who was disgusted because the squadron's machine guns hadn't arrived—as one of two new pilots to fly the 94th Aero's first combat patrol, only he had to do it without weapons.

The plane that Rickenbacker flew was the Nieuport 28, a sleek French-built single-seat biplane fighter with twin Vickers machine guns and a 160-horsepower, Gnome nine-cylinder rotary engine—"rotary" meaning that the entire engine spun with the speed of the propeller around the stationary crankshaft, which produced a "gyroscopic effect that permitted the plane to turn on a dime."[8] There were twenty-five of these in the squadron.

The reason they were flying French-made planes was, to the great annoyance of Billy Mitchell as well as General Pershing, that the U.S. Army had no American planes. A large appropriation had been made by Congress but so far nothing had come off the U.S. assembly lines and arrangements had to be made to buy combat aircraft from the French, of which Pershing had purchased five thousand. But that was a tall order to fill, and before these could be built American aviators were obliged to fly whatever the French had left over for them.

Even though the Nieuport was secondhand, it probably wasn't so bad as a fighting craft. Aviation had undergone a terrific evolution since the start of the war, and by this time, after nearly four years of fighting, both planes and tactics had become comparatively sophisticated. The best plane that the French produced was the Spad XIII, but the Nieuport 28 wasn't far behind it, and in most cases it was superior to what the Germans had on this part of the Western Front, which made every difference.

It could climb faster than any German fighter and turn and bank more tightly, though these characteristics had grown somewhat obsolete: by late 1918 there were so many planes available that pilots had figured out there was safety in numbers, mitigating the need for the complicated maneuvers practiced by Richthofen, Oswald Boelcke, Billy Bishop, Lufbery, and other aces.

One unfortunate characteristic of the Nieuport was the tendency of its engine to catch fire in combat because of the way the copper fuel tubes were attached. Fire was an aviator's most dreaded fear, and "crash and burn" stories preoccupied many a pilot's mind.

So far as fire safety went the typical World War I plane was little more than a flying matchstick—the frames were made of wood covered by fabric stretched by applying highly flammable glue, or "dope," and the tiniest fire could quickly become an inferno. Another unhappy feature was that in some cases cheap or shoddy glue had been used to stretch the fabric on the Nieuport's wings, which resulted in its sometimes tearing away on fast, steep dives—a frightening prospect.[*]

There were lengthy discussions among aviators about whether to jump out or to try and ride a burning plane down. Both were problematic because the American air forces were not supplied with parachutes at that time. Lufbery's advice was to stay with the plane and sideslip in order to fan the flames away from oneself. Some suggested it might be possible to jump at the last moment into water or the soft mud of no-man's-land, but the consensus was against it. In any case the Nieuport 28—like the de Havilland, another biplane whose rear fuel tank earned its reputation as the "flaming coffin"—had its detractors.

THE MORNING THAT MAJOR LUFBERY, Rickenbacker, and Lieutenant Douglas Campbell took off—unarmed—on the 94th's first patrol coincided precisely with the great German offensive of 1918. The Allies had been expecting a major offensive since the advent of the Russian Revolution when subsequent communist capitulation the year before took Russia out of the war and resulted in freeing a million German soldiers to relocate to the Western Front.

For Germany it was a desperate move. After four years of war, with its population at home starving because of the British blockade and Americans entering the war against them by the millions, the German army was terribly jaded. The German commander Field Marshal Erich Ludendorff hoped to catch the Allies off guard, including the newly arrived First U.S. Army, under Major General Hunter Liggett. He did.

To the rumble of thousands of pieces of artillery, a quarter million Germans swarmed out of their trenches toward Allied lines in the St. Mihiel–Pont-à-Mousson sector on the French–German border, as

---

[*] Lieutenant James Meissner, after such a dive, was horrified to find that he had lost almost the entire fabric covering his upper wing. He bumped home on the bottom wing, but if that, too, had lost its fabric his plane would have assumed the aerodynamic characteristics of a stone.

Major Lufbery and his little dawn patrol went up for a look-see. Lufbery had told them to stay close to him and, if there was any trouble, to do what he did.

They flew east picking up the Moselle River valley and were tooling along toward the Rhine when they were assailed by huge black bursts of enemy antiaircraft fire, commonly known as flak but then called archie.* Eighteen-pound artillery shells jerked and buffeted their fragile cloth-covered aircraft so violently that it felt as if the planes would be thrown out of the sky.

Experience had shown that antiaircraft fire was seldom accurate, so they proceeded on to Pont-à-Mousson, checkpoint of the first thirty-mile-long leg of the big isosceles triangle that defined their patrol sector. From thence they steered northeast toward St.-Mihiel, the second checkpoint, and from there along the valley of the Meuse, then westward to Toul and home. Whenever Rickenbacker fell behind, Lufbery would make a *virage*—a bank, or circle, in the air—and come up reassuringly beside him. They made the triangle four times before completing the patrol.

When they returned, all the other pilots and mechanics gathered around waiting breathlessly to know how it was. Lufbery let Rickenbacker do the talking. He told them they had seen no other planes, friend or foe, and that the archie was simply wasting ammo.

While the others absorbed Rickenbacker's and also Campbell's account, the silence was broken by a chuckle from Lufbery.

"Sure there weren't any other planes around, Rick?" he asked.

"Dead sure," Rickenbacker said.

Lufbery then explained that there had been at least fifteen planes, both friendly and enemy, which had come within a mile of them and admonished everyone to "learn to look around."

As if this humiliation wasn't enough, a grinning Lufbery led them over to their planes. On Rickenbacker's plane Lufbery stuck his finger through shrapnel holes in both tail and wing and another a foot away from the cockpit. Rickenbacker was flabbergasted. He could have been

---

* Because of the type of powder used, German antiaircraft fire burst with black puffs; French burst with white puffs.

killed! He decided then and there he had a lot to learn, and not much time to learn it, if he didn't want to get shot out of the sky.[9]

From that day on, whenever he had spare time, Rickenbacker took a plane up and practiced things that Lufbery had taught him, in particular, a kind of corkscrew maneuver Lufbery had invented to quickly look 360 degrees all around the sky—almost as if he had eyes in the back of his head. The violent twists of this contorted exercise made Rickenbacker airsick, and he threw up in his cockpit more than once, he admitted, until one day the airsickness simply disappeared and never returned. Since gun jams were a major problem, Eddie also began to emulate Luf's practice of individually polishing each of his machine-gun bullets the night before a mission. A mere speck of dirt or grime could lock the weapon tight—not a good thing in the middle of a dogfight.[10]

APRIL 14, 1918, marked the 94th Aero's first combat mission with guns and live ammo, and Rickenbacker was again chosen as part of the first three-plane patrol. The fighting on the ground was as heavy as ever and the Germans continued to send up reconnaissance planes and fighter escorts to protect them.

There was a heavy fog but the 94th inadvisably took off anyway. The operation almost immediately became a shambles. In Rickenbacker's flight the leader turned back because the fog was so thick, but Rickenbacker assumed it was because of engine trouble and continued on. Then he and his companion became separated and Rickenbacker flew on alone. Upon his return Rickenbacker was informed that two enemy planes, which, unbeknownst to him, had been chasing him, had mistakenly wandered over the 94th's airfield and were brought down in flames by two other squadron members. Not bad for the first day on the job.*

Bad weather socked them in for a week but, on April 23, responding to a report that an enemy plane had been sighted between St.-Mihiel and Pont-à-Mousson, Rickenbacker took off in pursuit. Instead of an enemy

---

* The German pilots of both planes escaped serious injury.

he found only a French Spad humming along at 8,000 feet. Returning empty-handed, he found himself swarmed with congratulations owing to a report that a German plane had been shot down in the sector where he'd been patrolling. Rickenbacker thought it was a pity having to tell them the truth—but he did.

On the evening of April 23 a report came in from a French artillery battery that an enemy plane had crossed the lines. Eddie Rickenbacker had been waiting around the hangar on call, along with the Lafayette Escadrille veteran Captain James N. "Jimmy" Hall, a promising poet and all-around nice guy. The two were already wearing their flying suits and immediately took off.

Right where the German was supposed to be headed Eddie spied an airplane, and he rose, preparing for an attack, but on closer inspection it turned out to be a French plane. Meanwhile Captain Hall was having a "delightful time" above the German lines. Amid a perfect fountain of archie flak, Hall was baiting the German gunners with a variety of loops and barrel rolls as the black puffs of smoke burst around him.

When the Germans had just about expended their ammunition, Hall suddenly wiggled his wings and headed west to Pont-à-Mousson, where a lone enemy plane was rising and coming straight toward them. It was a new Pfalz fighter, and Hall and Eddie put themselves between it and the sun and began their climb. When Hall peeled off toward the German, Eddie reasoned that if the Pfalz saw them he would dive back into Germany, and he maneuvered into a position so as to cut him off.

Sure enough, the German pilot spotted Eddie but, instead of diving, he began to climb to get above him. But he had not seen Hall, who was coming down behind him hell for leather.

Hall gave the Pfalz a burst and the startled German pilot banked and dived back for home just as Eddie predicted he would. Rickenbacker put his Nieuport on the tail of the Pfalz and swooped down with full throttle open. With every passing second Eddie gained on the German, who must have been terrified at that point, seeing an enemy fighter closing directly on him.

Eddie kept the cockpit of the Pfalz dead center in his gun sights and at 150 yards he let off a burst. With every fourth bullet a tracer, there was a living stream of fire coming from the barrels of his guns right into the tail of the enemy plane. When Rickenbacker raised the nose of his plane ever so slightly it was like lifting a fiery stream of water from a hose. He could actually see the stream of his bullets climbing up the German's fuselage and into the pilot's seat.

The Pfalz settled into a long spiraling curve, like a wounded dove. It did not simply fall out of the sky but, as Eddie pulled out of his dive, curled on its wide, graceful, dead-man's glide until it crashed near the German lines several thousand feet below.

When Hall and Rickenbacker returned to the aerodrome pilots, mechanics, clerks, cooks, and bottle washers poured out of living quarters, hangars, mess halls, and lounges and swarmed across the field to greet them. Word of the kill had preceded them by telephone from a French outpost in the front lines.

Word of Eddie's first kill quickly spread and because of his celebrity it was carried by the papers and radio as big news, prompting a flood of congratulatory telegrams and letters. This first hard brush with life and death might have shaken or at least been sobering for many men, but Rickenbacker had already adopted a stoic warrior ethos. "I had no regrets about killing a fellow human being," he said later, in response to a newspaperman's question. "I do not believe that at that moment I even considered the matter. I never thought about killing an individual, but of shooting down an enemy plane. . . . The best way to shoot down a plane was to put a burst of bullets in the pilot's back, [but] there was never, at least in my mind, any personal animosity. I would have been delighted to learn that the pilot of the Pfalz or any other pilot I shot down had escaped with his life."

THE WEATHER CLOSED IN intermittently all spring and what else was there to do but explore the countryside. They found the villages as dismal as the weather. That corner of northeast France is coal and mining country, not as picturesque as elsewhere in the tourist books, and marred by unsightly quarries and slag heaps. By this time Eddie had started smoking cigarettes again, and drinking, too, like most of the others, to help cope with the eternal strain of knowing that almost any moment a call could come to joust with death. Most men don't have to face that in a lifetime, but in France, in the spring of 1918, the twenty-something-year-olds of the 94th Aero faced it every day it didn't rain, even if they weren't in the mood.

On the first of May, for example, Lufbery suddenly put down the phone in the hangar and began pulling on his flying suit. Eddie asked him what was up. A German plane was reported near St.-Mihiel, he said. Eddie asked if he could come along.

"Come ahead," said Lufbery.

The air was misty, thick, and layered, and the visibility terrible; they searched for an hour but saw nothing but empty sky. Lufbery signaled to head for home and as they passed over Pont-à-Mousson at about 2,000 feet Rickenbacker saw Luf suddenly dive down. Eddie pushed his stick forward and followed, thinking the major was attacking, but he quickly saw that his friend was in terrible trouble. Luf's propeller had stopped and Eddie, helpless, could see him looking frantically below for a place to land. They were less than three miles from enemy lines.

Following behind, Eddie watched as Lufbery glided down onto a plowed field south of Pont-à-Mousson. He made a perfectly smooth landing before the mud caught the Nieuport's landing gear and tipped its nose into the mud, so that the tail pointed skyward like a phone pole. Then, to Rickenbacker's astonishment, as he passed about a hundred feet overhead, the tail continued its roll until Lufbery was turned completely upside down—a condition known to French pilots as a *panne.*

Eddie banked and circled back to see Luf crawling out from beneath the wreckage covered in mud from head to toe. He waved to indicate he was unhurt as Eddie hurried home to get help.[11]

That was the way it was, day in and day out. In this case the mishap turned out all right. Lufbery had blown a cylinder and had just enough altitude to glide toward a usable landing field. If he'd been any lower the accident might have turned tragic.

Tragedy did, inevitably, strike the 94th Aero Squadron. Since their first combat patrol April 14 the pilots had enjoyed a string of five aerial victories over the Germans with no losses to themselves. But on May 8 Captain David Peterson returned from a flight and, with everyone gathered around his plane, told how, after sending an enemy Pfalz down in flames, one of the Nieuports in his command "pass[ed] swiftly by him, ablaze from stem to stern." Other pilots later filled in the details. The burning plane belonged to Second Lieutenant Charles W. Chapman, of Waterloo, Iowa, one of the squadron's most popular pilots. It was sobering news. Everyone knew they couldn't go through the war without some being killed, but this understanding did not help. Old soldiers say the first casualty is usually the most difficult, but it's not necessarily so.

FOUR DAYS AFTER CHAPMAN WAS KILLED word came from a frontline outpost that four Pfalz fighting machines had taken off from a German aerodrome and crossed into Allied lines. Led by Jimmy Hall, Rickenbacker and Edward Green went up to intercept them.

The German archie suddenly fired well before they crossed the line— and then an observation plane appeared, almost a sitting duck. Eddie's first impulse was to go after the two-seater but then he recalled Luf's continued remonstrations against falling into enemy traps, a German specialty. Sure enough, four Pfalzs materialized below, in formation, climbing for altitude and cutting off escape to the west. The decoy two-seater fled behind enemy lines. They were already three or four miles into Germany, and now the serious fighting would begin.

Rickenbacker wiggled his wings to signal the danger and Hall responded by diving to attack while the Germans were still below them. Eddie nosed over toward the Pfalz formation and let the throttle out but noticed that Hall had suddenly wandered off farther behind the lines. He turned back to his target, which was the rearmost enemy fighter, and pressed the gun triggers at two hundred yards. He kept pressing to fifty yards as the German pilot rolled over and began a fatal spin to the ground. Zooming straight up until his tail was vertical, Rickenbacker looked around and to his relief there was no enemy after him, but off to his right, at less than a hundred yards, was an American plane diving sharply, and diving right behind him was a Pfalz, which was pouring streams of tracer bullets into the Nieuport's fuselage and cockpit.

Rickenbacker was horrified. It had to be either Hall or Green, but whoever it was suddenly turned the tables by looping over and exiting the loop right behind his antagonist. Now the Nieuport let off a long burst that caused the twisting Pfalz to drop from the sky like a shot goose. And to Eddie's astonishment, when he drew up to the Nieuport, he saw it was

Green—not Jimmy Hall—in the pilot seat. But where was Hall? They were deep behind German lines and had already overstayed their welcome; Eddie gave the signal to head for home. When they landed, Eddie ran over to Green's plane to find out if he knew anything about Hall.

"Went down in a tailspin with his upper wing gone!" Green hollered even before Eddie could reach him. Hall had dived on a German, Green said, but the next time he saw him he was in a spin with a Pfalz on top firing into his cockpit, and he went down in the woods.

Rickenbacker's head hung low at this horrible news that could not be mitigated even in the least by the fact they'd shot down two enemy planes. Jimmy Hall had been one of Eddie's mentors and friends. A native of Iowa, a Harvard man, and an accomplished poet, Hall had been a social worker in Boston before he posed as a Canadian to get into the British army when the war broke out, and he had distinguished himself with the Lafayette Escadrille before coming to the 94th.

The news spread quickly around the aerodrome and presently Lufbery appeared in a murderous frame of mind, with his jaw set and wearing his flying suit. He got into his plane. Hall had been one of Luf's closest friends, and woe betide the first German to meet him in the air.

Just before dark Lufbery returned. Having flown deep into German territory without seeing any enemy in the air he was about out of gas when, north of St.-Mihiel, there appeared three German machines that he attacked with such ferocity two pilots fled for their lives while the third failed to escape and was shot to rags in his cockpit. Even this vengeance did little to assuage the loss of Jimmy Hall.[12]

A FEW DAYS AFTERWARD ON A "DUD" (rainy) day, Billy Mitchell arrived at the aerodrome and invited Rickenbacker, Huffer, and a few other pilots to an afternoon tea with a French countess. It was at her magnificent estate called Château Sirur, which had not—or not yet—been touched by the war. The place included many thousands of acres of woods and lawns kept beautifully manicured, with a babbling stream crossed by old stone bridges, fish ponds, and forests stocked with wild game such as boar and pheasant. The home itself was enormous, parts of it dating to the time of the Romans.

Even after the height of his celebrity in America Eddie had never seen such opulence and the incongruity of it all—tucked away here so close to the horrid fighting lines—was staggering.

On May 15, General Paul Gerard, commander of the Eighth French Army Corps, arrived with three companies of infantry and a band of musicians to decorate Rickenbacker, Jimmy Meissner, and David Peterson with the Croix de Guerre for their feats. The medal would also be presented posthumously to Charles Chapman and to Jimmy Hall, listed as "missing." Prior to the ceremony there was much teasing within the ranks of the 94th Aero about the French custom of kissing the cheeks of the honoree after pinning the medal on him. The recipients were said to have shaved their faces carefully and powdered their cheeks with talc in anticipation of this practice, but General Gerard was short, and Rickenbacker intended to stand on his tiptoes to avoid the kiss. However, to everyone's surprise, Gerard presented the medals with a handshake and a proper salute.[13]

By this time the international press had begun to immortalize Allied pilots throughout the world, doubtless to the detriment of the many brave infantry officers and others in the combat arms who endured almost unbelievably frightful conditions on the front lines. But the pilots were novel—"knights of the air" was an expression often used to describe them. Besides, they were available for interviews and photographs in relatively comfortable quarters, in contrast to the grimy infantrymen, who lived day and night at the very dangerous front.

The day after Hall's disappearance, Eddie was named to replace him as commander of Number 1 Flight, a position for which he felt completely inadequate but knew he'd somehow have to measure up.

On May 19 Rickenbacker, in his role as flight leader, was instructing a new man, Lieutenant Walter Smythe of New York. They made a full patrol along the front lines and, finding no action, crossed over into Germany. Near Verdun Rickenbacker spotted a German Albatros below and pounced, but he missed his shots and the two-seater fled.

Fuming at himself, Rickenbacker made for home, but just as they crossed the front lines the Albatros appeared again, headed into Allied territory to take pictures. Incensed by the German's insolence, Rickenbacker prepared to cut him off, but the German pilot was alerted and began his escape for a second time. When Rickenbacker looked around for Smythe he was nowhere to be found. Aghast that he might have lost his young charge, Rickenbacker glumly headed for home, where he would receive perhaps the hardest blow of his entire experience in the war. Much of the squadron was standing outside the hangar, talking in low tones, as he came in to land.

Raoul Lufbery had just been killed.

Smythe, it turned out, was safe and sound after an emergency landing at an aerodrome not far away, having developed engine problems while Rickenbacker was chasing the Albatros. But earlier that morning, not long after Eddie and Smythe had taken off, a large enemy observation aircraft appeared over the field from the direction of St.-Mihiel.

The plane, which was said to have been armored, and with multiple machine guns, was possibly a Gotha twin-engine bomber.[*] The only 94th Aero Squadron aviators available as the enemy plane lumbered brazenly over the airfield were Major Huffer, the commander, and a pilot named Oscar J. Gude, a wealthy New York–born, Viennese-trained pianist, widely thought to be a coward. Huffer and Gude took off in pursuit of the German, but Huffer was forced to return with engine trouble. Gude rose to the German's altitude of approximately 2,000 feet and attacked but, much to the dismay of the spectators below, he shied so far away from the enemy machine as to be ineffective, at the same time expending all of his ammunition. The enemy pilot then began a long, wide turn and started a shambling retreat back toward Germany.

Watching this irresolute show with mounting disgust, Lufbery jumped on a motorcycle parked in front of his barracks and sped to the hangars, where he found that his own plane was down for maintenance. However,

---

[*] Controversy over the type of German plane will probably never be resolved. Rickenbacker thought it was an Albatros but didn't actually see it. Junkers armored some of its planes to protect crew but did not make a biplane. Gotha, which also armored for crew, did make a biplane, but it was a bomber, not an observation machine. Others insist that it was a Rumpler, but that company did not make a twin-engine plane. The only thing most parties agree on is that the German machine was large and crew served.

another Nieuport, belonging to Lieutenant Phillip W. Davis, was lined up on the runway, armed and fit to go. With no further ado, Lufbery climbed into the machine and took off.

When he caught up with the German he immediately closed and attacked, but then he quickly broke off, evidently because of a gun jam. When he had cleared the jam Lufbery renewed his assault, firing short bursts, but as he dived closer to the German he suddenly veered off sharply. Flames were shooting from his machine, which seemed almost to hover on its tail for a moment before spiraling straight down.

Somewhere about 1,500 feet above the village of Maron, Lufbery rose up out of the cockpit toward the tail and leaped away from the flaming inferno that now engulfed most of his aircraft. When he landed he was violently impaled on a picket fence in the backyard rose garden of a peasant woman. One of her daughters heard a noise and went out to see and recognized Luf from newspaper photos. He had become a colossal hero to the French. Inconsolable, and having nothing else, she quickly strewed his crumpled body with rose petals and other blossoms to cover the sad heap.

Lufbery's plane landed less than a quarter mile away in a field across the Moselle River, a charred, smoldering wreckage.* Soon other villagers arrived and they carried his remains to a bier in the ancient town hall, where as was the custom they shrouded his broken, still-warm corpse in the flowers of the French countryside in May. Even as Rickenbacker was being told the first details of the incident at the field, the telephone in the hangar rang with news from a French officer as to the exact spot where Lufbery had fallen. Eddie, Huffer, Campbell, and other of Luf's friends jumped into a car and arrived at the cottage less than thirty minutes after the mishap occurred, only to find, as Eddie remembered later, that "loving hands had removed his body."

The pilots asked the French authorities to send the body to the American hospital near their aerodrome and sadly made their way back home. There they were met by a Captain DeRode, a French Escadrille

---

* It was speculated that part or all of Lufbery's mishap was due to his flying a plane with which he was not completely familiar. Ironically, Lieutenant Davis, whose plane Lufbery had borrowed, was killed less than two weeks later, flying Lufbery's plane.

flier, who informed them that his leading ace had witnessed the Lufbery affair and immediately pursued the German plane but was shot dead through the heart, crashing only a mile from where Lufbery had gone down. Another French pilot, however, at last downed the miserable thing within French lines, and soldiers made prisoners of its crew. Nothing, though, could offset the black grief that hovered like a pall over the 94th Aero Squadron. Somebody once asked Lufbery what he planned to do after the war, and he laughed and replied, "There won't be any after the war for a fighter pilot." Luf had been their mentor, inspiration, guiding spirit, and friend.

Lufbery's funeral was conducted next afternoon. The fliers of the 94th Aero Squadron spent the morning in spit-and-polish, because they wanted to look their very best. Among the hundreds of mourners would be the generals Gerard, Liggett, Edwards, and of course Billy Mitchell—Lufbery had been one of his favorites. A grave had been prepared in a small corner of a cemetery near the base hospital. Known as the Aviators Cemetery, it already contained the remains of half a dozen fliers of the First Pursuit Group. Flowers surrounded the grave, as well as a large pyramid of floral wreaths sent by a number of military commands.

The mourners gathered on the airfield, and as the procession carrying the casket made its way up a hill to the graveside Lieutenant Kenneth P. Culbert, a marine detached to the army as an aerial observer and mapmaker, described the scene in a letter to his former history professor at Harvard. "As we marched to the grave the sun was sinking behind the mountain that rises so abruptly in front of Toul. The sky was faultless blue and the air heavy with the scent of blossoms. An American and a French general led the procession, followed by a band which played the funeral march and 'Nearer My God to Thee' so beautifully that I for one could hardly keep my eyes dry. We passed before crowds of American nurses in their clean white uniforms and a throng of patients and French civilians. He was given a full military burial with the salutes of the firing squad and the repetition of taps, one echoing the other from the west. I have never heard 'Taps' blown as beautifully as on that afternoon. Even some of the officers joined the women at dabbing at their eyes with white handkerchiefs. My only prayer is that somehow, by some means, I may do as much as he for my country before I too go west [get killed]—if in that direction I am to travel."*

At a precisely synchronized moment during the service, Eddie Rickenbacker and four other pilots of I-Flight throttled down their engines and glided quietly above the funeral cortege, which had gathered around with hats off as Luf was being lowered into his grave. Each pilot cast out sprays of flower petals that floated down like snow upon the mourners, then they flew back to the 94th Aero field, which was starkly empty. U.S. Army Major Gervais Raoul Lufbery had been the first American Ace of Aces, credited with shooting down eighteen German planes. Afterward, someone wrote of him, "Luf belonged to the balladiers and the boulevards—he was out of another age, and he would face death as he faced life."[14]

WITH THE DEATH OF LUFBERY, Rickenbacker's war became personal. No longer did he see it, as others did, as some kind of game of medieval-style jousting, or a competition to see whose skills were greater in stunts and maneuvers. He captured it well, and darkly, by saying, "Fighting in the air is not sport, it is scientific murder."

The squadron had arrived at Toul aerodrome barely six weeks earlier, but by now the grind of war was taking its toll on Rickenbacker and the other pilots. Day after day they played cat and mouse with the crafty Germans who, except for their observation planes and their escorts, rarely crossed the front into Allied lines. Instead they were content to set traps behind German lines for the American pilots—who by now had become wary of them—and when confronted the Germans would usually retreat unless they were flying in large groups. Rickenbacker considered this "pure yellowness."

On May 28, Eddie and Doug Campbell sprang one of these traps near Pont-à-Mousson when the Germans used an Albatros as bait while they waited above with four Pfalz fighting machines. Rickenbacker and Campbell

---

* Lieutenant Culbert was killed next day while mapping enemy positions, in the crash of an observation plane piloted by Lieutenant Walter Barneby, near Toul.

smelled the rat. They scared off the Pfalzs, then fell on the Albatros, which went into a spin and broke to pieces near the edge of the town of Flirey.

A few days later the gloom that lingered over Lufbery's death was lifted somewhat by receipt of a letter from behind German lines. Jimmy Hall was alive, taken as a prisoner of war in a Bavarian castle!

During the melee Hall had gone into a steep screaming dive against one of the Pfalzs when poor wing fabric glue—the old bugaboo of the Nieuport—did him in. As the fabric began to tear away, suddenly his upper right wing broke off from the struts, which unbalanced him and threw him into a spin. He managed to pull out of the spin, and turn back more or less toward American lines, but was barely above stall speed when there came an unexpected lurch forward in the engine. Whatever it was caused the propeller to stop, and Hall began sinking tailfirst toward the ground. If this was not bad enough, the Pfalz he had been attacking now came down on him with a vengeance, spraying bullets at his cockpit.

Hall jammed the rudder over, which finally set the plane on an even keel, but the ground was coming up fast and he was flat out of options. He crashed through a copse of trees that ripped off the wings and shot the fuselage out into a field where it came to an abrupt halt that broke Hall's ankle, and his nose, as his face smashed into the windscreen.*

German soldiers quickly captured him, and before his broken ankle was set Hall was invited to lunch at the German fliers' dining hall, where he learned that the Pfalz Rickenbacker had engaged had crashed in flames and all aboard were dead. The Germans also determined that the "lurch" Hall had felt in the nose of his plane was an unexploded antiaircraft shell, which had lodged solidly in his engine. If it had gone off he would have been blown to smithereens.

Two days after the funeral service for Luf, Rickenbacker, Reed Chambers, and a new pilot named Paul Kurtz encountered three Albatros

---

* A photograph exists of a sour-looking, bare-headed Hall glaring out of a German staff car with a handkerchief tied at the back of his head as a bandage for his nose. After the war, Hall located in Tahiti and went on to cowrite the novel *Mutiny on the Bounty,* from which several motion pictures were made.

fighters near St.-Mihiel and moved in to attack. Eddie blasted one and it began to spiral down, but before he could see if it crashed he caught a glimpse of two planes above him. Terrified, he fled for home, but the two aircraft followed right behind him and seemed to be catching up. Seeing no other choice, Rickenbacker skidded his plane into a vicious turn to face his pursuers, but something made him stop just short of pressing the trigger. A moment later he saw the big red, white, and blue circle—the American insignia—on Reed Chambers's wings. He had been a finger twitch away from blowing his best friend out of the sky.

The delay had put Kurtz ahead of Rickenbacker and Chambers, and they found him circling the aerodrome, waiting to land. Kurtz was making his final turn when, to Rickenbacker's astonishment and horror, Kurtz's Nieuport dropped into a spin and crashed straight to the ground and burst into flame with Kurtz inside amidst a tangle of barbwire and trenchworks. Next day, once more, Rickenbacker and the rest of the 94th found themselves at the Aviators Cemetery for a sad and unsettling funeral. They discovered that Kurtz had confided to one of his fellow pilots that he sometimes suffered dizzy or fainting spells in the air. Evidently his death had been caused by such a spell; there seemed no other explanation. Eddie somehow found himself furious at Kurtz for not telling him this. Eddie would have grounded him, and they would not be standing here today by his grave.

When Eddie returned to the base that afternoon, official word arrived from the front that an infantry officer had witnessed the crash of the German Albatros that Eddie had engaged. Another kill raised Eddie's standing even higher in the 94th, which also put him within a victory of becoming an ace.

THERE WERE MORE WING-FABRIC FAILURES with the Nieuport, including a hair-raising incident in which Eddie was diving on an Albatros when to his horror the fabric began peeling back from his upper wing, throwing him into a spin and nearly doing him in. He managed to recover and land safely but it was both maddening and disheartening at the same time. No one yet understood it was faulty glue, but everyone knew that real danger lay in diving a Nieuport too fast.

Just as the 94th Aero Squadron was on the verge of despair that they were flying a death trap, General Benjamin Foulois, then chief of the U.S. Air Service, who had heard other complaints, announced that the Nieuports would be replaced by the new Spad XIII in the fighting squadrons. Everyone breathed a sigh of relief, but then collectively drew in their breaths again after learning that until the Spads could be delivered they would have to continue flying Nieuports.

IN EARLY JUNE EDDIE took his first short leave and went to Paris, where he was stunned by the throngs of miserable refugees. Germany's last, desperate attack in March had been checked, but hundreds of thousands of people from the French countryside had been dislocated by the German gains. They had come to Paris in search of food and shelter, when there was little of either.

Eddie returned to learn that his fifth victory had been confirmed by high command and he was now the second American Ace of the war, behind his friend Doug Campbell. He also learned that the squadron was about to be moved to a busier section of the front, namely the Marne, where Pershing was preparing to make his "big push" with the American army. Everyone in 94th Aero seemed delighted by this news because the hunting was said to be far better around the Marne; anyone who wasn't so pleased kept it to himself.

On June 27, 1918, the four American fighting squadrons, including the 94th, were ordered to the Château-Thierry sector and based at an aerodrome near the "miserable" village of Touquin.

They arrived, however, without their highly regarded commander Major John W.F.M. Huffer, who had fallen victim to a power struggle between General Foulois and Billy Mitchell. Major Davenport Johnson, who commanded the 95th Squadron and was allied with Foulois, had pressed charges against Huffer (assumed to be allied with Mitchell) for "conduct unbecoming an officer and a gentleman," and Foulois relieved Huffer from command.*

---

* Specifically, Johnson accused Huffer of appearing at a party in public with a "notorious prostitute." At the court-martial Billy Mitchell testified that Huffer had

Everybody knew that Huffer was too good a leader to waste, and within a week he was made commander of the new 93rd Pursuit Squadron. Also transferred to that outfit was Oscar Gude. His arrant and open cowardice had been more or less tolerated, and even treated as a joke, until his craven performance against the enemy plane that killed Lufbery. After that, he became persona non grata within the Hat in the Ring squadron.

The 94th's operational area was another isosceles triangle beginning at Touquin—a thirty-mile leg to Reims, another thirty-mile leg to Soissons, and back to Touquin. The airfield itself was in fine condition, smooth and with adequate hangars, but there were no provisions for the pilots. In a stroke of luck they appropriated an abandoned but intact château a few miles south of the aerodrome. It was furnished splendidly and surrounded by sumptuous grounds.

But their luxurious accommodations would do them little good when they got into the air, for the German opposition they faced included Richthofen's infamous Flying Circus, filled with enemy aces and now led by none other than Ober Lieutenant Hermann Göring. The three German Jagdstaffels in this sector contained no less than eighty planes— most of them the menacing Fokker triwings, which patrolled in tight five- to seven-plane formations, making them extremely difficult to get at.

There was one thing in the 94th's favor, though. After a Fourth of July leave in Paris—celebrated in biblical proportion—Rickenbacker took a taxi to the big American aerodrome at Orly to find out something about the Hat in the Ring's Spad XIIIs. Turning on the charm, he introduced himself to the major who ran the supply depot and soon learned that not only were the Spads already in transit, but the first three of them were sitting on the runway at that very moment.

Delighted, Eddie rushed to the field where the Spads were lined up. The nearest one had the numeral "I" painted on its side, and Eddie asked the head mechanic if that plane had been tested.

---

come to the American service "from the French" where, he implied, sexual mores were somewhat more relaxed, and therefore Huffer didn't know any better. In the end the prosecution was apparently unable to disprove the virtue—or lack of—of the lady in question, and Huffer was acquitted.

"Yes, sir! All ready to go to the front!" the man replied.

Eddie explained that he was from the 94th Aero Squadron and asked if there was any reason the plane could not be taken there today. "None that I know of," answered the mechanic.

Within ten minutes Eddie was strapped and ready to take off in "the finest little Spad that ever flew French skies." Whatever violation of regulations this may have constituted, all was forgiven when Eddie landed at the airfield at Touquin and taxied up to the Hat in the Ring headquarters.[15]

Everyone rushed out and gathered around the neat little replacement for the temperamental Nieuport. Its 220-horsepower Hispano-Suiza eight-cylinder engine gave it a top speed of 135 miles per hour—10 miles per hour faster than the Fokker. It was stubby but strong, durable though not always a joy to fly until you were used to it.

DURING ITS TWO MONTHS in the Château-Thierry sector the First Pursuit Group had lost thirty-six pilots killed or captured. (Among the dead was twenty-year-old Quentin Roosevelt, youngest son of TR and onetime classmate of Charles Lindbergh at the Sidwell Friends School, who had dropped out of Harvard to join the flying service.)[*] During the same period the group inflicted thirty-eight aerial victories over the Germans, a slim margin of success.

The Battle of Château-Thierry was over and the Americans had won. But the Battle of the Meuse-Argonne was about to begin. The Hat in the Ring group, along with the rest of the First Pursuit Squadron, was transferred back to the St.-Mihiel sector, where the German army was pushed out in a huge salient, or bulge. Pershing, with 650,000 men and 3,300 guns, was preparing to drive them back into Germany.

German observation and photographic planes had catalogued the American buildup and the German high command had moved to St.-Mihiel several squadrons of the same aerial aces the Americans had faced during the Château-Thierry campaign.

---

[*] Harvard conferred a bachelor of arts degree on Quentin Roosevelt posthumously.

During the next thirty-five days, until the war ended, Eddie Rickenbacker passed into legend. His attack on the Germans was so ferocious and unrelenting that he personally shot down the equivalent of nearly an entire German squadron.

On September 14, 1918, Rickenbacker was promoted to captain and made deputy commander of the squadron. That same day he went out alone (as deputy commander he no longer had to ask for permission) and was flying at about 10,000 feet over Villey Waiville when below he spied a formation of four Fokkers with the red and white markings of Richthofen's Flying Circus. He piqued* hawklike upon the last plane and let off several bursts. The triplane turned over into an uncontrollable spin that ended in a fiery crash, then Rickenbacker turned tail and ran for his life before the other three pilots could collect themselves.

Next day he pulled off the same stunt, downing another enemy plane—another Fokker—his seventh, which made him the new American Ace of Aces. The longevity of Aces of Aces, however, was depressingly short. Twenty-two-year-old Frank Bayliss, of New Bedford, Massachusetts, was shot down and killed on June 17 after downing twelve enemy planes—most of them while serving with the French. The honor of Ace of Aces then passed to Lufbery. Lufbery's successor lasted only two days before being shot down, wounded, and made a prisoner, whereupon the mantle went to the late Lieutenant David Putnam.

Somehow by now Rickenbacker had learned to manage fear. It was one of the main reasons for his success. All of the pilots had their methods of doing this—some more successful than others—but Eddie had acclimated himself to that great numbing terror of flying into a fray where it was nearly certain someone would be killed.

Through a kind of strange cerebral transference, Rickenbacker was able to postpone fear until after he landed; even he couldn't quite understand how he did it, though he had done it in auto racing too. In a spasm of self-analysis he pointedly asked himself, "Was I in that strange class of men who have plumbed the possibilities of danger in the air—who have mastered to the limits the powers of airplanes and airplane

---

* Went into a steep dive.

guns, who know that they are personally superior to their antagonists for this very reason—who are therefore superior in truth because of the self-confidence that this knowledge brings them?"

Whatever the answer, when he got into the air Rickenbacker seemed to have felt he was bulletproof. It didn't mean he had no fear. "Courage is doing what you're afraid to do," he famously said. "There can't be courage unless you're scared." Rickenbacker simply waited until the plane touched down on the runway and then the shaking began. That was how he dealt with it.

SEPTEMBER 26 WAS THE BIG AMERICAN PUSH at the Battle of the Meuse-Argonne, and the squadron received orders to attack the German observation balloons that were run up all along the front each day about fifteen miles apart and two miles behind the lines. The observation balloon, used by both sides, was an extremely useful tool for gathering immediate intelligence of enemy movement. They were enormous blimp-size bags filled with highly flammable hydrogen gas, winched up on cable to a height of about 1,500 feet, from which an observer with a telescope or field glasses had a remarkable and immediate view of enemy positions and activity for up to twenty miles in all directions.

These apparatuses were vulnerable to enemy fighter planes whose every fourth bullet was an incendiary tracer, liable to ignite the hydrogen balloons. But often it took many, many bullets to bring them down in flames, perhaps because of early morning moisture. Suspended in the basket below the balloon, the observer stood or sat with a parachute strapped around his stomach, and at the first sign of trouble he leaped over the side of his gondola to the safety of the ground. If, however, an enemy pilot cut his engine and glided silently in to shoot the balloon, it could explode before the observer was able to escape.

After four years of trial and error on the Western Front, elaborate defense arrangements had been established to protect the *Drachen* or gas bags. Antiaircraft cannons were dug in all around the balloon, and if the archie was ineffective at high altitudes, at 1,500 feet it was deadly. The balloons were also surrounded by machine guns, which were highly accurate at that range. Eddie had already been foiled on a balloon-hunting expedition about a month earlier. This time he was taking no chances.

Hat in the Ring had been assigned to take out two balloons on the morning of the big American attack. Eddie summoned five of his best fliers and took off at 5:20 a.m., before daylight, timed to arrive behind the front just as the day broke and the Germans were getting their balloons in the air. As the pilots climbed there began to unfold from Rickenbacker's perspective the entire panorama of the battle in progress. The horizon was lit up with a continuous flashing from thousands of Allied guns and the rolling barrage exploded in front of hundreds of thousands of American doughboys moving forward to attack the German positions.

Flying over the dreadful no-man's-land Eddie saw ahead in the just-breaking dawn several vertical streams of machine-gun tracer bullets, indicating that the enemy balloon was being attacked by his men. A moment later came a gigantic burst of flame, then another huge flare to the north as the second balloon was destroyed. Delighted at the success, Eddie was nevertheless frustrated that he'd missed the action and turned east where he knew there lay another German gas bag. No sooner had he leveled out than a sudden great conflagration ahead announced that that balloon, too, had gone up in flames.

While Rickenbacker watched the fiery tumult light the sky and landscape and slowly fade away, he suddenly had a feeling that he was not alone. Lo and behold, when he looked to his left, there was a German Fokker flying right alongside him. Eddie turned to face him but the Fokker pilot must have seen Rickenbacker just a moment earlier, because he had already turned into Eddie and begun firing. As they headed directly toward each other the two planes seemed to be connected by "ropes of fire" as the tracers of each plane's two guns seemed to make a solid line in the dim morning light. Before they could collide the German dived and Eddie made a *renversement,* coming up on the Fokker's tail, whereupon he pressed the triggers and the Fokker spun and crashed to the earth. As he watched it falling, Eddie suddenly felt a big jerk, followed by intense vibration in the plane, and he turned back toward Allied lines. The vibration threatened to wreck the plane and Rickenbacker considered himself lucky to make it to the first aerodrome he saw, which was that of the new 27th Squadron. After he landed Eddie discovered the source of the vibration. One or more bullets from the Fokker had severed his propeller blade nearly in half. Again, he was lucky to be alive. Next morning Eddie shot down a balloon of his own.

AS THE ALLIED ATTACKS CONTINUED to push the Germans farther back, particularly in the American sector, the air war over the Meuse River and Argonne Forest became more ferocious. The Germans, desperate for timely intelligence on the American advance, were constantly sending up balloons and aerial observation planes. It was the First Pursuit Group's job to knock these down and, as usual, the 94th's Hat in the Ring gang was in the thick of the fighting.

It was about this time that Rickenbacker acquired a captured Alsatian, or German shepherd dog. From whom is unclear, but probably someone in the front lines. He named him Spad, and from then on the animal became the mascot of the Hat in the Ring squadron, and Eddie Rickenbacker's devoted follower.

The army was increasingly concerned that the Germans were replacing their balloons as fast as the airplanes could shoot them down, so Billy Mitchell ordered the entire group out to remedy the situation. Rickenbacker devised a technique in which two pilots would attack a balloon while the rest of the squadron hovered above to protect them. On the afternoon of October 10 he selected Hamilton Coolidge and his pal Reed Chambers to attack two particularly obnoxious balloons near Aincreville.

When they arrived the balloon wasn't up, but Rickenbacker spotted eleven Fokkers flying in beautiful formation below and instantly sicced himself on the last in line, setting the enemy's fuel tank on fire with incendiary tracer bullets. Circling to follow the plane as it dropped, Rickenbacker saw the German pilot bring his flaming plane level and, to Eddie's astonishment, suddenly leaped overboard into space. Attached to the German's seat was a "dainty parachute" and the man floated gently to earth while the amazed Rickenbacker watched from above.

On the way home Eddie recognized his friend Jimmy Meissner being attacked by two Fokkers. He jumped into the fray and sent one of the brutes down out of control, while the other fled for his life. It would have made for a good day except the group lost two pilots killed in the action, one of them turned into a blazing inferno by archie as he attacked a balloon.

On October 11, Rickenbacker got a Fokker and one of his two favorite balloon busters, Reed Chambers, got two. His balloon-busting partner and second ranking ace in the 94th, Captain Coolidge, who had dropped out of Harvard to join the Air Service, wasn't so lucky. He had come to the aid of some American de Havilland bombers under attack by a squadron of Fokkers when he inadvertently flew into a barrage of archie intended for the bombers and was killed.*

As the American bombers crossed over into Allied territory one fell behind and began to lose altitude. A Fokker with the red-painted nose of Richthofen's Flying Circus swooped down for what the pilot must have thought would be an easy kill. Rickenbacker was on him like a hawk. Desperate, the Fokker pilot tried to loop up and over to get behind the Spad, but at the apex of his loop he stalled and his engine quit. The pilot attempted to glide back to German territory but Eddie, hoping to keep him within Allied lines and capture his plane intact, began herding him like a prized sheep, nipping at his nose with tracer bullets to head him off toward an American airstrip.

He just about had the Fokker forced down when "an unknown idiot in a Spad" suddenly flew in and attacked it. Furious, Rickenbacker ran the Spad off but it was too late; in trying to avoid the Spad the Fokker was forced to land short of the American runway and crashed on hard terrain, demolishing the aircraft. The pilot climbed out of the wreckage and waved at Rickenbacker as an American officer mounted on horseback arrived to arrest him.

Next morning Rickenbacker and several of Ham Coolidge's friends drove a staff car up to the front lines to look for Coolidge's body. An infantry lieutenant who had witnessed the crash led them to the wreckage and provided a squad of gravediggers. Under constant shellfire, the chaplain of the infantry regiment conducted burial services as they laid the mangled corpse into the grave, over which was placed a cross and a wreath of flowers, also courtesy of the infantry regiment. Eddie, using a borrowed Kodak camera, took a photograph of the grave to send to the family.

On October 22, Lieutenant Oscar Gude, who had been cashiered from the 94th Hat in the Ring to the 93rd Indian Head Squadron after his disgraceful performance against the German aircraft that killed

---

* "Ham" Coolidge was the great-great-great-grandson of Thomas Jefferson and the best friend of Quentin Roosevelt, who had been killed three months earlier. Like Roosevelt, Coolidge received his degree with the Harvard Class of 1919 posthumously.

Raoul Lufbery, performed his final deed of treachery. He deserted to the Germans. Not only that, he did it in the Spad XIII belonging to Major John Huffer, formerly the commanding officer of the 94th before he was forced to transfer to the 93rd following his court-martial.

Gude was flying Huffer's plane on patrol in the rain when he suddenly vanished from the back of a pack of eight American fighter planes. His fellow pilots could not account for him, and he was carried as "missing in action."

According to the official history of the 93rd[16]: "Gude landed on the German airfield at Metz [Mars la Tour] after circling the field twice, taxied up to the line and got out smiling, rather weakly, and said, 'Fini la Guerre.'" The history shows a photograph of German pilots surrounding Huffer's perfectly intact Spad. In prison camp, Gude told the story of having shot down two German planes before running out of gas, but upon making this assertion he was attacked and severely beaten by a British pilot who had seen the entire sorry episode.*

October 30 was a big day over the Argonne. The Germans were convulsed in a death spasm and throwing everything they had into the air. That afternoon Rickenbacker jumped two Fokkers, both red nosers from the Richthofen bunch, who were stalking a Spad, hoping to ambush it. Instead Eddie sent one down in flames while the other ingloriously fled for home. He didn't know it then but this, his twenty-sixth victory, would also be his last.

The next day it began to rain and Eddie received a pass to Paris, which he described as a changed city from the careworn place he'd last visited. Turkey had just surrendered and Austria-Hungary was that day expected to do the same. Everyone knew the end was near. Eddie bought up several stacks of English-language newspapers and, next day, took off for the front lines where he passed out copies to the infantrymen in their trenches.

---

* Upon his release after the war, Gude was not court-martialed, apparently for lack of evidence—or lack of interest—and he went on to distinguish himself (and become fabulously wealthy) as a pioneer in the electrical sign business, especially in the lighting up of Broadway, for which he is said to have coined the phrase "the Great White Way."

In the pilot's mess the evening of November 10, Eddie answered the phone and was informed that an order to cease firing would be invoked at eleven o'clock next morning. He put down the phone and said, "The war is over!"

At first there was silence in the room, and then pandemonium erupted. Men began to shout and whoop and rushed to their rooms to get pistols to shoot off in celebration. As word quickly spread, archie up and down the lines began firing promiscuously. Outside, mortars sent up star shells and flares and rockets were also fired. Somebody took out all the liquor from the whiskey locker and emptied it into a large tub, from which orderlies served it, without ice, in coffee cups, themselves included. Rickenbacker caught a group of pilots rolling out tanks of gasoline from the hangar. Instead of stopping them, he joined them, striking the match that set it off and dancing around the bonfire like everybody else, slapping one another on the back.

Some men jumped into mud holes and rolled around like swine. Others broke up furniture and dishes. One pilot, an ace, swooped up to Eddie flapping his arms and shouted incredulously, *We won't be shot at anymore!*

Next morning broke muggy and foggy. Even though the orders said for pilots to stay on the ground, Rickenbacker got in his plane about ten a.m. and took off for the front, where for four years millions of men had been trying to kill each other along a five-hundred-mile line (and millions had succeeded). Flying low—around 500 feet—he arrived over Verdun where he saw both Germans and Americans hunkering in their trenches. At exactly the eleventh hour of the eleventh day of the eleventh month, men on both sides began clambering out of their trenches and into no-man's-land, casting away their guns, flinging their helmets into the air. In other parts of the line it was more subdued, and men gingerly poked their heads up and looked around, amazed that they were not shot at. In some places, field larks wheeled in the sky. French, British, and American regimental bands played their country's national anthem. At last the storms were over. Away from the front, the archie and mortars again began their triumphal celebrations and Rickenbacker figured he'd best get back on the ground before somebody accidently blew him away.

CHAPTER 6

★ ★ ★ ★ ★

NEW YORK TO PARIS

No flying machine will ever fly from New York to Paris.

—ORVILLE WRIGHT

CHARLES LINDBERGH TOOK SURPRISINGLY WELL to the U.S. Army's stern regimentation. In March of 1924, age twenty-two, he reported along with 104 other cadets to the U.S. Army Flying School at Brooks Field, near San Antonio, Texas. When the courses of instruction and the weeding-out process were over a year later, only nineteen of these would be left to graduate as officers, and Lindbergh would stand at the top of the class.

With the lessons of World War I firmly entrenched in its curriculum, the school was perhaps the finest of its type in the world. The first half year of instruction included twenty-five courses, among them aerodynamics, field service regulations, engines, mapmaking, ratio theory, aerial photography, and military law. This was on top of ground school and actual flying.

The flying was done in the morning because there was less wind. The instructors were war-hardened veterans, and the training plane was the Curtiss Jenny, such as Lindbergh had once owned but with a more powerful Hispano-Suiza 150-horsepower engine and a top speed of 125 miles per hour, compared with his Jenny's 90 miles per hour.* Other courses were conducted in observation, meteorology, gunnery, navigation, formation flying, bombing, combat attack and pursuit—this last was the most difficult and dangerous and the branch Lindbergh aspired to.

When he first arrived, though, Lindbergh seemed to slip into his old sloppy studying habits, and his first grades were low C's—barely passing, when two failing marks constituted a washout. This time, he took stock and realized that this was something he really wanted to do and that there would be no second chances. It was an epiphany of sorts, and a good one. He studied until taps and then often made his way to the latrine to study under the lights till midnight. For once in his life he was scared of failure.

It was all the more remarkable that Lindbergh was able to achieve his academic and practical success because he received a most severe emotional blow. He had not been at Brooks Field more than three weeks when a telegram arrived from his half sister informing him that his father, C.A., was in the hospital ill with a "bad breakdown." Two weeks later a second, more urgent, telegram arrived, saying Lindbergh's father was "very low."

C.A. had been taken to the hospital founded by the two Mayo brothers in Rochester, Minnesota, after his behavior became increasingly unstable. He was confused, had lost his sense of taste, repeatedly asked the same questions, and had motor-physical difficulty. Charles arranged for a short furlough, but by the time he arrived in Rochester the doctors had diagnosed an inoperable brain tumor. Charles spent as much time as possible with C.A. and at first the sixty-five-year-old brightened to see his son, only to drift back into confusion and stupor minutes later. Before Charles's eyes, C.A. was losing his senses, and after a week it became clear that death was only a matter of time.

When it was apparent that C.A. could no longer recognize him, Charles decided to return to Brooks Field; if he pushed his furlough longer he could be washed out of flying school. On May 24, 1924, C.A. died.

---

* The Jenny is the plane featured on the famous 1918 "inverted Jenny" airmail stamp, in which a printing error caused the plane to appear upside down. Only a handful of these stamps exist today and an example brings near $1 million.

The service was held three days later at the First Unitarian Church in Minneapolis, attended by family and many old political associates, after which the body was cremated. It had been C.A.'s wish that Charles "throw his ashes to the winds" from a plane over the old farm at Little Falls. It would take him ten years to do it.

After his father died, Charles's personality seemed to open up somewhat. Where before he had been an introspective loner he now engaged in practical jokes with the other cadets, was friendly with everyone (but close to no one), and kept a smiling disposition. He still abstained from alcohol, tobacco, caffeine, and women but nobody seemed to mind.[1]

After graduation in September the thirty-two remaining cadets were taken to Kelly Field a dozen or so miles away for advanced training. Here they flew the de Havilland DH-4B observation plane, which had a 400-horsepower engine and an unfortunate tendency for the wings to fall off if pushed too hard. They also flew the SE-5 Sopwith pursuit fighter.

Lindbergh almost didn't make it out of flight school, or anyplace else, due to a midair accident during a dogfight exercise barely a week before graduation. He and a Lieutenant McAllister were in fighters at 8,000 feet and instructed to dive and mock fight a DH-4B "enemy" flying below at 5,000 feet. They came at the enemy from different angles and Lindbergh ducked under the de Havilland, expecting to come up on the other side into empty air. Instead he felt a jolt, and then a crash, and to his shock and amazement, when he'd recovered from banging his head on the cowling, he discovered that McAllister's plane and his had not only collided but were locked in a wing-to-wing, fuselage-to-fuselage dance of death— a slow, unrecoverable spin, revolving toward earth "like a windmill."

Lindbergh looked over and saw McAllister, not four feet away, who had climbed out of his cockpit and was preparing to jump. Lindbergh did the same, crawling out on the engine cowling, which at that point was almost vertical, he said.* Jumping from an airplane was old hat for Lindbergh, but this was the first time he'd ever been *forced* to jump. He and McAllister thus became, respectively, the twelfth and thirteenth

---

* Fortunately, the Air Service had recently adopted parachutes as standard equipment for its fliers; in fact, the class of 1925, Lindbergh's class, was the first to use them.

members of the so-called Caterpillar Club, a select fraternity including, later, Jimmy Doolittle, who had parachuted out of airplanes to save their lives.*

On March 14, 1925, Lindbergh graduated from the army's Advanced Flying School at the head of his class and was commissioned as a second lieutenant in the Air Service Reserve Corps.

HE HAD ALSO, HOWEVER, graduated at the absolute nadir of military aviation. At the end of World War I there had been nearly two hundred thousand men and eight thousand aircraft in the U.S. Army Air Service. By 1925 there were fewer than ten thousand men and fifteen hundred aircraft on active duty. At that point the only person of any consequence hustling for a strong air corps was Billy Mitchell, and he was about to find himself sacrificed on the altar of internecine rivalry.

Lindbergh applied, without much hope, for a slot in the regular army. While he waited to hear he resumed his barnstorming career, but he realized that, ultimately, it was a dead end. The only other possibility lay in getting involved with airmail. In 1918 the federal government began a scheduled airmail service between New York, Philadelphia, and Washington, D.C., expanding in 1920 to California on a route laid out by Eddie Rickenbacker, who had recently returned from the war and entered the aviation business. But in 1925 the government decided to get out of flying its own airmail and let contracts to private enterprises, a godsend to small aviation companies struggling for income. Lindbergh applied to one of these companies, Robertson Aircraft of St. Louis, to become an airmail pilot, and he was accepted pending confirmation of the Robertson company's airmail contract with the U.S. Postal Service.

Action on both his request for a regular army commission and the airmail contract were agonizingly slow, so that summer he took a job with Captain Wray Vaughn's Mil-Hi Airways and Flying Circus in Denver, Colorado—mainly to study the behavior of updrafts, downdrafts, and

---

* The club was formed in 1922 by a parachute maker. To date it can claim an estimated one hundred thousand current or former members.

other turbulence in the mountain canyons. It was dangerous business involving many unknowns and unpredictables, but Lindbergh had by now developed—at least in the beginning stages—the curious mind of a scientific intellectual, wanting to sop up knowledge for its own sake, no matter what the cost.

In Denver all that summer and into the fall, for $400 a month, Lindbergh was a wing walker, parachute jumper, all-around stuntman, and mechanic as the little flying circus made the rounds of small country fairs in Colorado, Kansas, Montana, and Wyoming. At some point he acquired a dog that enjoyed seeing the sights from the front cockpit of the plane, and was strapped in when Lindbergh was doing stunts, and people came from miles around to see them. "Ranchers, cowboys, storekeepers in town, followed with their eyes as I walked by," Lindbergh said. "Had I been the ghost of 'Liver-Eating Johnson' I could hardly have been accorded more prestige. Shooting and gunplay those people understood. But a man who'd willingly jump off an airplane's wing was beyond them."[2]

At last the Robertson brothers' airmail contract was confirmed, and the winter of 1926 found Lindbergh back in St. Louis as chief pilot, mapping the mail route, going over aircraft, and hiring pilots. They had five planes, army surplus de Havillands—the old "flaming coffins," whose fuel tanks were located behind the pilot—and the pilots that he hired were pals from army flying school Phil Love and Thomas Nelson. Lindbergh surveyed nine landing fields along the three-hundred-mile route from St. Louis to Chicago, which were little more than spacious farm fields where a pilot could put down near a small storage of gasoline and a nearby telephone. A majority of the flying would be at night, and if a pilot got in trouble his only landing lighting was by parachute flare, which he would throw out over the field and then circle back to and come down as quickly as possible. If fog moved in, or fierce rainstorms, or a low ceiling, the pilot was basically out of luck. There were no aeronautical instruments tested as yet to permit blind landings.

The Robertson company had agreed to fly five round-trips a week, and Lindbergh inaugurated the first of them at 3:30 on the afternoon of April 15, 1926. The occasion was especially festive, and all the town fathers, pols, and hoity-toity folks of St. Louis turned out with speeches and ribbon cuttings captured on motion picture film. The highlight of the affair was when Myrtle Lambert, the thirteen-year-old daughter of the airfield owner, strewed flowers on the wings of Lindbergh's plane and said, "I christen you 'St. Louis.' May your wings never be clipped!" whereupon Slim Lindbergh roared off northward toward Springfield to pick up fifteen thousand pieces of mail bound for Chicago.

The airmail service saved a day over regular scheduled trains, which to some people—such as bankers—was important.[3] But it was frightfully dangerous work. Navigation was visual only except for a compass, especially at night. A pilot could only estimate his position by counting the "glow" of towns and cities along the route. Planes tended to break down at inconvenient times—such as when they were in the air—and often involved things the pilot couldn't fix once he landed. In those cases the mail was put on the nearest train.

Around seven o'clock on the night of September 16, 1926, fog closed in somewhere over Peoria; Lindbergh turned away from Chicago into open country, hoping to find a hole in the fog. He tossed out a flare but it failed to ignite. He kept on flying, right on through his regular and reserve gas tanks when, at 5,000 feet, the engine died. Lindbergh rolled out over the right side of the cockpit, pulled the rip cord, and was sinking down toward the fog bank with nothing but the wind whistling in his ears when he heard a chilling sound. The engine of the plane had sputtered back to life, apparently because its angle had shifted with his bail-out and whatever gas was left ran back into the carburetor. He hadn't bothered to turn off the ignition because he thought the fuel was all gone.

He could hear the plane spiraling around him with its engine roaring, threatening to mow him down in midair. But soon the plane veered off and Lindbergh landed safely in a cornfield. With the help of a nearby farmer he located the aircraft, which was smashed into a pile. But with no gas there was no fire, and they managed to get the mail on the 3:30 milk train to Chicago.

A few weeks later it happened again. On November 3, Lindbergh took off in good, clear weather but was soon fighting rain, sleet, snow, and dark of night—all at once. Again he turned away toward open country, but when he couldn't find any hole in the clouds and gas was about gone, he flung himself over the left side, pulled the rip cord, and came down on a barbwire fence. Next day he found the plane and got the mail to the railroad depot, but Lindbergh knew he was due for a change. One day the odds were going to catch up with him and the odds weren't good. It seemed as if every month an airmail pilot was killed. He gave the Robertsons a few weeks' notice.

Flying the mail was a solitary business with a lot of time for thinking. As with most pilots, Lindbergh's calculations were about how to improve his flying conditions—things like speed, capacity, and navigation. The aircraft industry was undergoing a stupendous era of change in the 1920s. From only a handful of enthusiasts before 1918, thousands of pilots had been created by the war, and new inventions and designs were being produced at a furious rate. On one of his seemingly endless trips over Peoria Lindbergh began to wonder how far a plane could fly if it was loaded with as much fuel as it could carry.

It was a moonlit night, with no sign of fog. He tried performing mathematical calculations of how much fuel could be loaded into a plane and still get airborne. He'd heard of a long-range monoplane the Wright Aeronautical company was offering that had less drag and an engine able to lift heavy loads. Monoplanes—with only one pair of wings—were relatively innovative at that point. Most pilots felt the dual wings of a biplane gave greater lift and stability. It had been asserted, however, that this plane could fly nonstop from St. Louis to New York—but the aircraft was expensive, between ten and fifteen thousand dollars.[*]

This was the Wright-Bellanca, named for its designer Giuseppe M. Bellanca, an Italian immigrant; its engine, the Wright J-5 Whirlwind, was a 220-horsepower, air-cooled radial, which allowed the plane to reach speeds upwards of 200 miles per hour. The Wright-Bellanca was designed as a general aviation plane to carry four passengers and their luggage. But what if, Lindbergh mused, those passenger seats and freight compartments were instead filled with fuel tanks? How far could the plane then travel? Lindbergh knew the J-5 Whirlwind had the reputation of being the first wholly reliable and fuel-efficient aircraft engine. Weight of passengers and freight must be about a thousand pounds, he figured. What would the range be with an additional thousand pounds of fuel? Enough to cross the Atlantic? Enough to get to Paris?

---

[*] Roughly $200,000 today.

He was aware of the Orteig Prize that had been outstanding since 1919—all serious pilots coveted it—which was $25,000 offered by the French-born New York hotelier Raymond Orteig for the first nonstop flight between New York and Paris, either way. The Atlantic had been crossed successfully before, in 1919 by two British fliers, but they took off from Newfoundland and (crash) landed in an Irish bog, slightly less than two thousand miles. New York to Paris was a full thirty-six hundred miles. Others had died trying. At the time that Orteig had first announced the prize, Orville Wright weighed in this way: "No flying machine will ever fly from New York to Paris . . . [because] no known motor can run at the required speed for four days without stopping."

Lindbergh was within a few days of quitting the airmail business, wondering why fuel needed to be so heavy. He was flying the night leg of a mail run, droning tediously over some little burg north of Peoria, where the ground was marked only by faint glowing light—beer halls, churches, houses. Gasoline weighed six pounds per gallon. If a gallon of gas weighed only a pound you could fly practically anywhere, so long as the engine kept running. How much fuel *could* a plane carry if its fuselage was filled with tanks? But hadn't René Fonck, the famous French aviator, tried that out in his big Sikorsky biplane only a few days ago and crashed into flames on takeoff on a New York field?*

If he had the Bellanca, Lindbergh calculated, he could "fly on all night—like the moon." What if every available bit of space on the plane was used to store gasoline? The plane could stay aloft through daylight and darkness. Lindbergh suddenly thought he saw the way, if the thing could only get off the ground, to make a flight between New York and Paris. This is how some great deeds begin—with simple daydreams in a flight of fancy.

Now it was time to convince himself. One thing for certain was that Slim Lindbergh did not have the money to buy a Bellanca, but he did have four years of aviation experience and nearly two thousand hours' flying time. He had barnstormed, stunted, wing-walked, dog-fought,

---

* René Fonck was an Allied Ace of Aces in World War I with seventy-five victories. Fonck's attempt at the Orteig Prize ended on September 21, 1926, in a fiery crash that killed two crew members, though he survived.

crashed, parachuted, and flown day and night through fierce storms, fog, and baffling wind currents—sometimes with paying passengers, sometimes with other people's mail, and sometimes with a dog riding in the front seat. He was twenty-five years old, in the prime of life and the picture of health—plus, he had just been promoted to the rank of captain in the 110th Observation Squadron of Missouri's National Guard. The notion, of its own, was breathtaking. Why the hell *not* fly to Paris![4]

IMMEDIATELY HE BEGAN STUDYING the problem in earnest—or problems, for there were many. The first one was how to acquire and pay for a proper plane. While he was working on that, Lindbergh began to rough out the actual flight itself: the fuel needed, navigation, safety procedures; it was much more complicated than he'd thought. At the time, nobody in aviation but Lindbergh believed the cross-ocean flight could be made with less than a three-engine aircraft, let alone a monoplane. But Lindbergh thought that was what caused Fonck his trouble: Fonck had commissioned Igor Sikorsky to build him a huge three-engine flying club car with leather seats, a bed, two enormous radios, and a crew of four with hors d'oeuvres and croissants, and look what happened. It couldn't even get off the ground.

A Lindbergh ship would be different. For one thing, it would require a crew of one, himself, and be stripped of absolutely everything not vital to the exploit. His one concession to both weight and comfort would be a wicker pilot's seat, which was less than a third the weight of leather. Crossing the Atlantic would be a calculated risk, and Lindbergh had calculated that the odds were in his favor.

He polished off his plan, or proposal, and in late September took it to the St. Louis insurance executive Earl Thompson, who was also a flier. Lindbergh emphasized that a successful crossing would be a terrific boost for St. Louis, let alone aviation in general, whose stature would shine with a nonstop transatlantic flight. Lindbergh told Thompson he was seeking backers among wealthy St. Louis businessmen and wanted his advice as to the $25,000-prize flight.

Thompson was skeptical when he found that Lindbergh was proposing a monoplane for the flight. Lindbergh countered that a triplane would cost "a huge amount of money,[5] and in this he was correct. It happened that a representative of the Fokker company was in St. Louis to see about opening up a sales agency and Lindbergh approached him about building a plane to fly to Paris. The man had been extolling Fokker's safety record and the reliability of multiengine craft. It was already under consideration, the man said, and would cost nearly $100,000, provided the order was put in immediately. If that wasn't enough to stun Lindbergh, Fokker's man added that the company would have to approve the pilot and crew, the implication being that only highly experienced and well-known fliers would be considered. Building a single-engine plane for that purpose was out of the question, he said. Fokker didn't want blood on its hands if such a plane failed to make it.

More discouraging news was received when Lindbergh approached Wright about the Bellanca—the company had already sold it to a New Yorker named Charles Lavine, of the Lavine Aircraft Corporation, who intended to enter it in the Paris contest. Then word came that the explorer Commander Richard E. Byrd, of North Pole (and later South Pole) fame, might try for the prize in a Fokker.

Meantime, Lindbergh set about acquiring backers. He went to see his friend Harry Knight, a prosperous stockbroker and president of the St. Louis Flying Club. Knight was receptive and rounded up some friends who were interested. By the time it was over, Lindbergh had eight backers, including Major Albert Lambert of the Lambert Flying Field and Major William Robertson, owner of the airmail service that he flew for. The arrangement was that they would get their money back, with interest, from the $25,000 prize. Banker Harold Bixby, who was head of the St. Louis Chamber of Commerce, suggested naming the plane the *Spirit of St. Louis* and Lindbergh liked the ring of it.

Then there was an encouraging telegram from Giuseppe Bellanca saying that Lavine might be willing to sell the Bellanca. Lindbergh put on his best suit and caught a train to New York, only to be told the plane would now cost fifteen thousand dollars and Lavine reserved the right to say who flew it.

If all this sounds odd, it must be remembered that enormous prestige would attach to any company owning the plane that won the New York to Paris contest—but a corresponding discredit would result if the plane failed to make it. And so Lavine jerked Lindbergh around outrageously over the next several weeks, with phony offers to sell the plane only to continue to insist that he reserved the right to choose who flew it.

There were only two other companies that made planes comparable to the Bellanca—one was Travel Air in Kansas and the other was Ryan Aeronautical Company in San Diego. Travel Air turned Lindbergh down almost immediately but Ryan responded that it could build a plane similar to the Bellanca, and with a Wright Whirlwind engine, for six thousand dollars minus motor and instruments. It was Lindbergh's twenty-fifth birthday and his best present ever; immediately he wired for the aircraft's specifications and asked if it could be built in quicker than three months. Word came back that the plane would cruise at a hundred miles per hour and carry 2,280 pounds of gasoline—380 gallons—enough to fly him from New York to Paris. Furthermore, Ryan guaranteed finishing the work in two months, upon receipt of a deposit of half the cost of the machine.

On February 23, 1927, Lindbergh left St. Louis in a sleet storm. Two days later he arrived in San Diego amid waving palms and pristine Pacific beaches to see the Ryan people about the project.[6] Despite its somewhat lofty name, Ryan Aeronautical's factory was a dingy low-slung building with no hangar or runway, permeated by the odor of a sardine canning plant next door and the pungent aroma of "dope" from drying fabric material. There were no great experimental engines roaring; instead a couple of dozen workers were absorbed in various tasks: grinding, welding, splicing cables, sawing, measuring, and cutting, while in the drafting room, bent studiously over their drawing boards, were several engineers, chief among them Donald Hall, who would shepherd the *Spirit of St. Louis* project from beginning to end. Lindbergh immediately took a shine to the place.

Ryan had been formed a few years earlier by Benjamin Franklin Mahoney, a financial trader who had taken a few flying lessons and then bought the Claude Ryan Flying School, which he turned into a factory turning out airplanes from war surplus craft.

Hall, a handsome, tanned, well-made man who stood a foot shorter than Lindbergh, quickly got around to discussing technical particulars. Lindbergh listed what he needed in the way of performance and instruments. Hall said they would have to design a new fuselage from the standard Ryan pattern. All of Ryan's fuselages, Hall said, were constructed of tubular metal frames. While Hall sketched out a form, lengthening the wingspan and fuselage and drawing in heavier landing gear, Mahoney discussed money. He said he'd be unable to come up with an exact figure for the Wright J-5 Whirlwind engine and instruments but offered to charge only what they cost him, which struck Lindbergh as more than fair.

Hall said the main fuel tank would have to go in front of the cockpit for balance, then looked up and asked, "Now where are you going to put the cockpits for you and the navigator?"

"I only want one cockpit," Lindbergh replied. "I'll do the navigating myself."

There was a stony silence. Clearly startled, Hall looked at Mahoney, then back to Lindbergh.

"You don't plan to make this flight alone, do you?"

Unfazed, Lindbergh explained that he had considered it at length and decided he'd do much better alone. "I'd rather have the gasoline than an extra man," he said.

Hall wrestled with this new concept a few moments before he grasped it. Then his mind shifted back into gear. "Well, of course that would be a big help from the standpoint of weight and performance," he said. With just one pilot the fuselage would not have to be lengthened or widened after all; the weight saving would probably total three hundred and fifty pounds—about fifty extra gallons of gas.*

Then Hall asked Lindbergh if he was sure he could fly that distance by himself—perhaps forty hours in the air with no sleep, he guessed. "Say, exactly how far is it between New York and Paris by the route you're going to follow?" he asked.

Lindbergh replied it was about thirty-five hundred miles. "We could get a pretty close check by scaling it off a globe," he offered. "Do you know where there is one?"

Minutes later they were in Hall's 1923 Buick convertible heading for the San Diego library, where Lindbergh, hovering over a large globe, used a piece of grocery store string to measure off the miles along the great northern route, which turned out to be thirty-*six* hundred, give or take a mile or two.

---

* Including the weight of the tank.

They discussed contingencies—tailwinds or, God forbid, headwinds; fuel reserves, wing tensions; would Lindbergh follow the shipping lanes? No, "I'll fly straight," he said. "What's the use of flying extra hours over water just to follow the ship lanes?"* Hall was scribbling all this on the back of an envelope. He said he'd figure to load the plane with enough gas to give Lindbergh a four-thousand-mile range. If he flew the thirty-six hundred miles from New York to Paris at cruising speed, in still air, Hall said, Lindbergh should have some four hundred miles of fuel left over. If he deviated from the route, got lost, ran into headwinds or weather, he was on his own.

Back at the factory they hashed it out with Mahoney and his number cruncher and it was agreed that Ryan would deliver a finished plane, with engine, in sixty days, for $10,580, instruments extra. This was telegraphed back to St. Louis and the deposit was wired into the Ryan company's account. It was a risky decision for Lindbergh and his backers, because Ryan was not nearly as well established as Wright or some of the other aircraft makers. But he felt himself a good judge of character, and he liked what he saw in Hall and Mahoney. In this instance Lindbergh judged well.

Lindbergh stayed in San Diego to supervise the building of the *Spirit of St. Louis*. He was a man of few worldly wants and needs other than food, shelter, and a respectable latrine. Otherwise, he was to be found at the Ryan Aeronautical factory from opening to well after official closing time. This job, for everyone involved, was going to require overtime every day, Sundays included.

One of the first design questions Hall had was where to put the cockpit. Lindbergh told him to put it behind the fuel tank.

"But then you couldn't see straight ahead," Hall said incredulously. He didn't call Lindbergh "Slim"; he called him "Charlie."

"You know we always look out at an angle when we take off," Lindbergh said. "The nose of the fuselage blocks the view straight ahead, anyway."

Hall replied that he wasn't talking about takeoff, but of flying forward at altitude. Lindbergh repeated he didn't need to see ahead. Where he was

---

* In 1919 the U.S. Navy attempted an Atlantic crossing from New York City to the Azores using three seaplanes and stationing destroyers every sixty miles along the proposed route. Two planes crashed or gave out, one made the Azores.

going, he wouldn't be in any danger of hitting another plane, and when it came time to land he could size up the situation by banking and looking out of the side windows. Hall began to rough in a single-seat cockpit with no forward view. Next he asked about safety equipment. Lindbergh wanted a parachute, night-flying gear, a radio. Too much weight, was the reply. He would take a small inflatable life raft, though, in case he had to put down in the ocean. At least that would give him a fighting chance.

About this time a San Diego paper carried a story about the New York to Paris race, with headlines stating that Rodman Wanamaker, the Philadelphia department store magnate, had put up $100,000 to sponsor Commander Byrd's attempt at the Orteig Prize, and that he would probably be racing against Fonck, who was back in the game after his crack-up, with a big Fokker trimotor. The story reported that these men were preparing to take off sometime in May. It went on about how Byrd would be carrying "the most advanced instruments and navigational devices known to science." At the very bottom, more or less as an "added starter," or even an "also ran," the article mentioned that Charles Lindbergh, who was identified as a "St. Louis mail pilot," had likewise filed an entry in the competition.

NOW LINDBERGH HAD A MAJOR HURDLE to contend with—specifically, how to navigate over thousands of miles of empty ocean. They'd never taught him that in flying school, because the army fought its battles over land where there were identifying features that could be put on maps such as towns, lakes, rivers, railroad tracks, and so on. Over water the compass would be his only reference. Because the Earth is round, long-distance pilots have to fly what is known as a great circle route; if you tried flying a straight line from New York to Paris, you'd probably wind up in Portugal, or even Africa. Lindbergh hadn't the foggiest notion of how to lay out a great circle route. Instead of approaching some of the many naval officers stationed in San Diego, who would be experienced in such things, he decided to do it on his own. His reasoning was that there was so much skepticism about his adventure that he didn't wish to add to it. People now looked at him "askance," he said, after they learned what he planned to do—alone and in a monoplane. They would shake their heads and tell him he was too young to know what he was doing.

Lindbergh found a ship chandlery on the San Diego waterfront but they carried only charts of the Pacific. At San Pedro, however, he found a chandler who pulled out "two oblong sheets" of Mercator projections that covered the North Atlantic, including New York and Paris. He also found there a trove of useful tools—world time zone chart, gnomonic projection,* magnetic variation chart, prevailing winds chart. Back at Ryan Aeronautical, Hall cleared off a table in the drafting room for Lindbergh to spread out his charts and compasses. First he drew a straight line on the gnomonic projection, and then with a compass divider he measured thirty-six intervals of a hundred miles each, which he transferred to the Mercator projection, connected with straight lines. In this way, he was able to ink in his magnetic compass course to be checked and corrected every hour or every hundred miles, assuming he was able to cruise consistently at 100 miles per hour.

Lindbergh was so cheap about weight that he sliced the edges off his charts, and he eschewed bringing along a sextant to check his celestial positions because it weighed too much. Instead he would take two different compasses and compare readings between them; everything else when he got over water would be stars and dead reckoning.[7]

The way Lindbergh saw it, navigation was not so tricky but having a sizable reserve of fuel was. He concluded that even if he was off course a little on some of his intervals, and if he just kept heading east, at some point he was going to run into Europe—assuming the plane didn't conk out on him. If he navigated poorly he might wind up in Norway, but at least he'd be over land and with enough fuel could find his way to Paris. So everything came down to weight. Lindbergh became so weight obsessed that he considered having Ryan build a landing gear, which weighed several hundred pounds, that could be discarded once the plane took off. It would mean he'd have to crash-land in Paris, but the prize rules said nothing about having to come in on a three-point landing.

Ryan was building the plane at a pace one stop short of frantic. Hall arrived at five every morning to check on the work. Everyone at the factory seemed to take a personal interest in its progress. Many workmen

---

* A chart that shows all the circle lines on a globe as imaginary straight lines.

even volunteered for overtime. Construction on other planes practically ceased, and all energy went into the mighty effort to construct the *Spirit of St. Louis,* which had begun to take shape with tubular skeletons of the fuselage and wings. But even Lindbergh knew you could not build a sound plane frantically, so he took charge and told Hall he needed to stop working so hard and get some sleep.

Around this time a stamp collector offered Lindbergh a thousand dollars to carry one pound of airmail letters with him—this would be of course the first cross-Atlantic airmail and invaluable as such. It was a temptation almost too rich to resist. But then, in typical Lindbergh fashion, his conscience gave him second thoughts. It was "the principle involved," he said. "If I start compromising, I won't know where to stop." A single pound of airmail for a thousand dollars, he marveled. "I'll write my partners about it," but in the end he turned the offer down.

In late March the J-5 Whirlwind engine arrived from Wright. "We gather around the wooden crate as though some statue was about to be unveiled," he wrote later. "It's like a huge jewel, lying there set in its wrappings. We marvel at the quality of its cosmoline-painted parts. Here is the ultimate in lightness of weight and power . . . On this intricate perfection, I am to trust my life across the Atlantic Ocean."

News of Lindbergh's bid for the prize began to stir up interest. Aviators dropped by the factory to see the plane, as did several reporters, who wrote stories in the local papers. Imagine his chagrin when at one point a naval aviator arrived to ask Lindbergh if he would come to the air station and give a talk on long-distance aerial navigation! Imagine his trepidation when, caught off guard and not knowing what else to do, he accepted.

The race for the Orteig Prize was seriously heating up. In addition to Commander Byrd and René Fonck, another navy officer, Lieutenant Commander Noel Davis, sponsored by the American Legion to the tune of $100,000, planned to take off in June in a Keystone Pathfinder biplane powered by three of Wright's big Whirlwind engines. A few days later the papers carried this headline: "French Ace Announces Paris to New York Flight." This was the legendary Captain Charles Nungesser, former ace fighter pilot of the Lafayette Escadrille, who planned to enter the race in a two-man French-built monoplane carrying 800 gallons of fuel and powered by a 450-horsepower engine.

IT WAS BEGINNING TO LOOK AS THOUGH Lindbergh would end up on the short end of the race, so to speak, for the Orteig Prize. Several contestants had got their planes to New York before him. But then a string of calamities ensued. On April 16 Commander Byrd's Fokker trimotor crashed on takeoff, injuring three of the four crew members and seriously damaging the plane. On the twenty-fourth Clarence D. Chamberlin, a former army flier, wrecked his landing gear on takeoff and then, after he got mixed up with Lindbergh's old nemesis the duplicitous Charles Lavine, he became embroiled in a legal dispute that kept the plane on the ground. On April 26, navy commander Noel Davis and his navigator Stanton Wooster were killed in a crash trying to take off in their big Keystone trimotor. Oddsmaker Lloyd's of London was forecasting 10 to 1 odds against a successful crossing by anybody.

Lindbergh remained undeterred, though certainly he took no joy in the misfortune of his competition. "Crashed planes and flyers in hospitals," he wrote, noting that his friend Floyd Bennett's leg had been crushed in the Byrd disaster, "impair all of aviation, and destroy the joy of flight." In fact, Lindbergh's self-image at this point was not as a seeker of prizes and fame but, as he wrote much later, "When I became convinced that man had a great destiny in the air—that planes would some day cross continents and oceans with their cargoes of people, mail and freight, I believed that America should lead the world in the development of flight. I devoted my life to planes and engines, to surveying airlines, to preaching, whenever men would listen, the limitless future of the sky."[8] Although he didn't know it at the time, Lindbergh was already becoming exceptional.

ON APRIL 24, AT NEARLY two o'clock in the morning, work on the *Spirit* was finished. Lindbergh wired his backers in St. Louis. Next morning the workmen at Ryan faced a situation similar to the apocryphal story of the man who builds a boat in his basement, only to find he has made it too large to get it out. The wings and fuselage of *Spirit* were constructed separately in an old fish cannery, but they had to remove the landing gear from the plane so as to get it through the doors. Constant design changes to the wings had left them ten feet longer than originally planned and, with a fraction of an inch to spare, they managed to slide them out the second-floor windows onto the top of a railroad boxcar and from there onto a truck, which hauled the *Spirit of St. Louis* to the flying field hangar in several parts, with the fuselage on a trailer bringing up the rear.

At nearby Dutch Flats, on the San Diego Bay, the plane was completely assembled. All the workmen lined up and signed their names to the fabric covering the wing, "to ride along on the flight for good luck." It was nearly half again as wide as it was long—twenty-seven feet from prop to rudder, while the wings spanned forty-six feet. On April 28 Lindbergh went on his initial test flight. Other than noting a few needed adjustments, he was thoroughly satisfied with the plane, but more testing was in order.

On May 8 the newspapers screamed: NUNGESSER OVER THE ATLANTIC— DUE IN NEW YORK TOMORROW. The great French aviator had taken off. Lindbergh was deflated but not defeated. He began examining charts for a cross-Pacific flight instead. On May 9 the world waited for news of Nungesser and his navigator and wartime colleague François Coli. Early press editions began with a report that the plane had been sighted over Cape Race, at the southernmost tip of Newfoundland. But as the day wore on headlines became grimmer, until the late editions carried stories saying, "Nungesser and Coli lost—Paris Fears Worst."

In the midst of this, Slim Lindbergh was making ready to depart. The first leg of the trip was San Diego to St. Louis, which would be easy because he had friends in both places and along the route. But on the second and third legs he knew no one he could count on, either in New York or in Paris. The weather bureau was forecasting a low-pressure system in the mountains, limited visibility, clouds, rain, ice, hail, fog. Of these, fog was, of course, the worst. As Lindbergh said, "Aviation will never amount to much until we learn to free ourselves from mist," adding that the gyroscopic turn indicator was "a step in the right direction, but it will take much more than that." Just how much more, Jimmy Doolittle would prove in a few short years.

On the morning of May 10 Lindbergh packed a light bag with a few personal items and went to the airfield. His friends had advised him against trying to fly through the mountains at night in the deteriorating weather but, as usual, he was impossible.

A small crowd of well-wishers was there to see him off: Hall, Mahoney, and many of the work crew from Ryan, plus officers from the naval base.

He donned his heavy flying suit and took a five-minute flight to North Island airfield to avoid the trees and telephone wires at Dutch Flats. Just before four p.m. the *Spirit of St. Louis* was again airborne, bound fifteen hundred miles east for St. Louis.

The trip went surprisingly well, all things considered. He ran into some ice problems over Arizona but by sunrise Lindbergh was flying over his old barnstorming haunts in Colorado. At 8:20 a.m. Central Time he landed at Lambert Field in St. Louis in time for a breakfast of ham and eggs at Louie's shack, a celebrated diner, with his old pals from the Robertsons' mail-flying enterprise. Owner Louie DeHatre had assembled a collection of photographs of fliers that he hung on his walls—aviators still living were on one wall and those who'd been killed were on another. Lindbergh checked the pictures to make sure he was on the right wall. Once in a while some joker would switch them around. Around here, in the "suicide club," they still called him Slim.

Harry Knight and several of Lindbergh's St. Louis partners arrived with excitement. It seems Lindbergh's San Diego–St. Louis flight had broken a cross-country flying record. They were duly impressed when he showed them the plane and asked him how long he was staying around— there were numerous dinner invitations dangling in front of him.

He'd stay for as long as they wanted, he told them, then said, "But I think I ought to go right on to New York. If I don't, somebody else will beat us to the takeoff."

He flew out of St. Louis a little after eight the following morning into a clear sky headed straight to New York City. Three hours out, over Columbus, Ohio, the weather became overcast. Lindbergh had caught up with the tail of the storm that had been raging over the Sierras when he'd left San Diego. The Alleghenies were always a challenge in this kind of weather. Lindbergh picked his way through passes and valleys, emerging into Pennsylvania, riding the edge of the bad weather. If it stuck around for a few days the storm would keep his competitors grounded.

After surveying several flying fields from the air halfway out on New York's Long Island, Lindbergh chose Curtiss Field because it had the longest runway. The choice was critical. All of the crack-ups so far had been on takeoffs, and with his heavy load of fuel it would take Lindbergh a long time to become airborne.

Word of his pending arrival had traveled fast; as Lindbergh circled to land he saw a mob of several hundred spectators. As he made his approach they closed in on the runway, and some of them actually got out onto the runway. He veered to avoid them and hit the ground at 4:30 p.m., then looped around to taxi as the crowd, led by dozens of photographers and reporters, quickly surrounded the plane. "Get clear of the propeller!" he shouted. Someone was grinding away at a big Fox Movietone camera on a tripod; flash pans exploded around the plane; some of the photographers began to climb onto the wings to get close-ups. Mechanics came to the rescue. Rushing from the hangars, they burst through the throng, drove people back from the prop, shooed the newsmen off the wings, and cleared a way to lead Lindbergh as he taxied the *Spirit of St. Louis* toward a hangar.

An excitement coursed through the air as the handsome young aviator stepped down from his plane. A phalanx of photographers had arrived beside him and somebody asked Lindbergh if he'd mind posing with his plane, as some had deadlines. Lindbergh agreed but felt uncomfortable at their shoving and cursing and jostling one another for position. They ordered him around like a servant—"Look this way!" "Smile!" "Say something!"—as dozens of flash pans snapped and popped, nearly blinding him with the light, while reporters shouted questions. "Hold it!" "Just one more!"

This was Lindbergh's introduction to the infamous New York press corps, which, for the most part, were as competitive as piranha and ethical as ghouls. It was the start of a long and trying relationship. All the recent crashes and deaths associated with the Orteig Prize had created a frenzy over this race to cross the Atlantic, which the press people were pumping up with tornado-like intensity. Some editors were calling it the "story of the year"— maybe even the century. Reporters took out their notepads and scribbled away as Lindbergh attempted patiently to answer their questions, but he drew the line at "Do you have a sweetheart?" and "What's your favorite pie?"

When at last these people had been sent away, Lindbergh was besieged yet again. A representative from the distinguished Pioneer Instrument Company had brought Lindbergh the earth-inductor compass he had requested, so as to compare its readings against those of his magnetic compass. An oil company man was there to sell him the best gas, the airport offered him its best mechanic, Wright's best engineer was on his way, and so forth.

Next morning the weather was still bad. Commander Byrd's plane had been repaired and Byrd was still planning to make the attempt. He came to Lindbergh's hangar to wish him well and offer him the use of his runway at Roosevelt Field, which he had under lease. So did Chamberlin, who still expected to fly the Bellanca. The Roosevelt's runway was better than the Curtiss's for a heavy-load takeoff, Byrd said. After walking over both fields, Lindbergh gratefully accepted the offer.

The day's newspapers were strewn about the office in the hangar. Lindbergh was startled to find his picture featured prominently on page one. One of the tabloids dubbed him the "Flying Fool." He became further distressed after reading some of the stories. Everything he had told them the evening before was either ignored or twisted beyond recognition. Papers insisted he was from Michigan instead of Minnesota; that he had learned to fly in Omaha instead of St. Louis; that his plane had periscopes to look through for takeoffs and landings. When he returned to his hotel he found the lobby clogged with newspapermen wanting him to answer more questions. It was the same when he returned to his hangar—they mobbed about outside and shouted at him as he got out of the car. All this did not take long to wear on Lindbergh's nerves. Then a bellhop knocked on his door with a telegram:

ARRIVE NEW YORK TOMORROW MORNING—MOTHER.

True to her word, Lindbergh's mother arrived on May 14, spent one day with him, and left. "She felt she had to have that day," Lindbergh said later. Lindbergh's disgust with the tabloid press reached new lows when, after he and his mother refused to embrace each other for the cameras as she was leaving the train station, several editors, in an early version of Photoshop, created a fake photo by having two people hug each other and then substituting old headshots of Lindbergh and his mother.

By the sixteenth the weather was still too bad along the route of flight to try a takeoff and Lindbergh was getting antsy. With each passing hour, it seemed, interest in the race to Paris increased. Wire services had spread Lindbergh's story to every city and village on both sides of the Atlantic. Telegrams of encouragement were coming in by the hundreds, as well as sales pitches, offers of marriage, and threats by cranks.

Similarly, the mail brought autograph seekers, advice givers, religious nuts, and inventors with projects to offer. Seventy-five hundred people showed up at the airport on Saturday to see if anyone was taking off. By Sunday, according to the *New York Times,* the crowd had reached thirty thousand.

The weather persistently refused to clear, and all sorts of aviation pioneers arrived to see Lindbergh, including the head of the Curtiss Corporation and Anthony Fokker, the Dutchman who had created the infamous fighter planes for Richthofen's Flying Circus, as well as the debonair and unfortunate René Fonck, who'd dashed his hopes beyond repair eight months earlier when he'd crashed his Fokker trimotor. Lindbergh was also touched when the philanthropist Harry Guggenheim and his handsome wife Caroline, who were to be such good friends with Jimmy Doolittle, dropped in to wish him well.

A week had passed and still the weather refused to cooperate—rain, fog, and a low-pressure system clung stubbornly to the eastern seaboard. Lindbergh now had an official aide, courtesy of his National Guard flying squadron back in St. Louis, which sent out a young spiffed-up lieutenant to handle Slim's mundane chores. Harry Knight phoned from St. Louis to say they had sold the exclusive rights to Lindbergh's story to the *New York Times* for national syndication.

Lindbergh made friends with the U.S. Weather Service's New York bureau chief Dr. James Kimball, who in turn kept him advised on conditions locally and along his route of flight. Like most things scientific, weather forecasting in the 1920s was crude by today's standards, with no radar or scout planes, let alone satellites. Weathermen relied on the barometer, overseas cable, and radio reports from land stations and ships at sea. For Lindbergh this meant there would be spotty coverage of any weather he might encounter across the Atlantic.

Word got around that Commander Byrd was stocking his plane and preparing to take off, but Lindbergh put no substance in it. There was also a rumor Chamberlin would depart, but the afternoon's newspapers carried stories that the Bellanca was tied up by three separate court injunctions. To Lindbergh's mortification, a headline read, "Flying Fool Adopts Mystery Air, Indicating Quick Takeoff." It seemed there was nothing in the newspapers, here or abroad, but the cross-Atlantic contest, and Slim Lindbergh had risen from added starter to house favorite in the eyes of the press.

That night a group of Lindbergh's aviation contingent went into the city to watch the new stage musical *Río Rita* from backstage, courtesy of an aviation publicist. It was damp and foggy as they drove down Forty-second Street but Lindbergh insisted they stop and call Dr. Kimball about the weather. Word came back, "Weather over the ocean is clearing." The low-pressure system, it seemed, was moving out, but it would take another day for the skies to clear entirely. In modern times the decision would likely be made by a committee or at least some kind of headman, but in those times pilots were their own headman, and Lindbergh told the driver to go back to the airfield. The time had come, he said. He would take off in the morning.

The *Spirit* was ready, but there were details to attend to: fueling, moving the plane from Curtiss to Roosevelt Field, double-checking everything from water canteens to flares to charts. They ordered extra sandwiches. All these things the crews accomplished in a state of highest agitation disguised as utmost calm, under the supervision of twenty-five-year-old Charles Lindbergh, who remained composure personified.

He was surprised upon his return to the airfield that in his competitors' camps nothing was stirring. Lindbergh was the lone contestant that day. Going on midnight, several autograph hounds appeared out of nowhere in his hangar, and there was a man who thrust a movie contract at Lindbergh, promising him $250,000. Another, talking similarly high figures, wanted him to agree to appearances on the stage. He dismissed them politely, saying that he was not making any future plans "until after I reach Paris." He returned to the hotel, only to find he couldn't sleep, in part because the spiffy lieutenant from his National Guard unit kept waking him up for all those people making fantastic money offers.

It was three in the morning when he returned to the flying field, and it was still drizzling. It wasn't much better at daybreak but he pulled on his flying suit and entered the cockpit. The mechanics spun the prop, the engine caught, but revs were thirty revolutions low—when each revolution counted. "It's this weather," said the mechanic. More ominous, the wind had shifted from head to tail. Not good for a takeoff.

The runway was soggy, with occasional pools of water. A mile down at the end lay a tangle of telephone and telegraph wires that spanned the field like a high fence. The mechanics stood outside as if frozen in time; they knew the plane was ready and understood the problems now arisen. The air seemed to pancake down heavily.

LINDBERGH LEANED OUT THE LEFT SIDE window and sighted down the runway, then pushed the throttle wide open. Men behind were shoving against the wing struts. The *Spirit of St. Louis* lurched forward more like a truck than an airplane. Lindbergh began lumbering down the soggy runway at a maddeningly low speed. He had to reach at least 60 miles per hour for takeoff—maybe more, with no headwind—but he felt as if he were being pressed down by the five thousand extra pounds he was trying to lift off the runway.

The grass began to blur and he felt the controls tighten up—good signs; then he felt the tail skid lift up off the runway, causing a wobble as the load shifted its balance. At the halfway mark a huge decision had to be made—whether to continue or abort—and in an instant Lindbergh made it. Pulling the stick he felt the wheels lift off, and just as quickly they bounced back into a puddle that sprayed mud and water everywhere. This unsteadied the plane for a moment as Lindbergh fought for control, regained it, and bounced again, and then tension in the controls shivered up from wing and strut and tail and rudder. He was airborne!

Ahead the phone wires, snarled on their poles thirty feet high, loomed at the end of the runway. He had a glimpse of them out the side of the cockpit: he pulled his chin up, as if to lift the plane, and then they were below and behind him! Barely hanging in the sky, there was a moment, Lindbergh said, when the *Spirit of St. Louis* "seems balanced on a pin point, as though the slightest movement of controls would cause it to topple over and fall."

Slowly, still she climbed, clawing at the heavy air; more than flying, it felt as if the prop was merely dragging him along. He cleared a hill with trees and, confident now, eased off on the throttle—1,875 rpm—1,800 rpm—1,775 rpm—he was flying 100 miles per hour at 1,775 rpm, cruising speed. Below were the grand Long Island estates of New York's wealthy, including Falaise, the fabulous French Norman manor house of

Harry Guggenheim, where Lindbergh was destined to spend so much time in future years. He glanced at his watch—it was 7:54 a.m., May 20, 1927; he'd had no sleep in twenty-three hours and there were thirty-six hundred miles to go.

Spirit seemed to get its "air legs," flying low at 150 feet, just beneath the cloud ceiling. Lindbergh set his compass course at 65 degrees for the first hundred-mile leg of the great circle route. The Long Island Sound loomed out of the mist and the plane began to buck and shake but Lindbergh knew there was often turbulence where air and water meet. At Port Jefferson he turned northeast out over the Sound toward the Connecticut River, thirty-five miles away. A plane full of newspaper photographers that had been following him dipped a wing and turned back. Good riddance, he thought. The air began to smooth out and Lindbergh settled in. He could touch both sides of the fuselage with his elbows—the "little box with fabric walls," he called it. "My cockpit has been tailored to me like a suit of clothes."

As he reached the north shore he worried about the cloud ceiling dropping. There are hills in Connecticut, so if the ceiling dropped another hundred feet he'd have to turn back. Above him were the switches for the various fuel tanks in the wings and fuselage. He turned off the center wing fuel tank and switched on the nose tank. He'll have to do this every fifteen minutes during the entire trip—switch from tank to tank—to keep the plane in trim. There was a little periscope in the cockpit that allowed Lindbergh to look out the left side to check for hills, tall factory chimneys, or high radio towers.

At New London the mist began to lift. He climbed up to 600 feet. He'd reached the first hundred-mile leg of the great circle route, not far off course, and a hundred pounds lighter—just thirty-five legs left to go. It was 8:54 a.m. Suddenly he was over Rhode Island, astonished at how compact New England was. Below were farms along the rivers with pastures of cattle and sheep—and stone; great boulders of it were everywhere, and there would be no field in New England where he could put down without smashing up.[9]

Presently he came to Narragansett Bay and entered Massachusetts airspace. He'd been through four U.S. states in the time it took to walk a single mile. The sky was changing; there were patches of blue. He put aside his New England maps and reached for the Mercator projection of the Atlantic that he'd spent so many hours calculating a course on back in San Diego. Once he left the coast, this strange-looking chart, his compass, and the sun and stars would be the only things to guide him.

Now he was over the Atlantic, where the skies were clear. He dropped down to ride the ocean air, just twenty feet above the waves, and savor the smell of saltwater. The next land he'd see was Nova Scotia, about 250 miles NNE, which would also be the first big test of his over-ocean navigation skills.

A fishing schooner appeared, probably headed to the Grand Banks. Lindbergh gave the fishermen a thrill by flying past at mast-top level. He took the plane up a hundred feet where, on both sides, cumulus clouds billowed, which could electrify and turn dangerously stormy without much warning. He climbed higher, worrying about the clouds. The wind was blowing fairly steady from the northwest, not what he wanted, or needed—it could mean that a storm was making up ahead. What he wanted was the opposite, a southwest wind to push him along.

His legs felt cramped and the sun was hot in the cockpit. He began to feel tired but caught himself—he was less than a tenth of the way to Paris with a long way to go. Out on the bottom of the left wing he spied a clump of mud that the wheel had thrown up during takeoff. It bothered him. He wanted to reach out and scrape it off but it was too far out. He considered that he had torn pages from his notebooks and sliced the margins off his charts, only to be weighted down now by a clump of mud that he'd have to look at all the way to Paris. That bothered him more. He pulled the periscope into the cockpit, on grounds that eliminating its resistance to the wind would compensate for the mud. Before he knew it he was half asleep; he put a hand out the side to direct a stream of air to his face and saw the mud again. He couldn't help looking at it. Suddenly he became afraid it might drive him batty.

LAND HO! The green of Nova Scotia appeared ahead, streaked with rays of sunshine. It was just past noon. Even from 200 feet (the height of a twenty-story building) Lindbergh could take it all in—the Bay of Fundy, New Brunswick to the west, and the verdant forests and fields of Nova

Scotia (New Scotland) stretching back to a line of mountainous hills to the northwest. There were towns below, with bays filled with fishing boats. He climbed to 1,000 feet and took readings from his compasses— only six miles off course, not bad, considering. He calculated that if this margin of error held, the worst he could do would be fifty miles off course when he hit Ireland, and Ireland was hard to miss. Lindbergh was now on the fifth leg of his great circle route.

It took Lindbergh an hour to fly up the Nova Scotian coast. It was one o'clock—lunchtime in New York City, and lunchtime aboard the *Spirit of St. Louis* too. He reached in his sandwich bag but then changed his mind. He wasn't starved. Might need them for later, might make him sleepy. He flew on.

Along the north coast of Nova Scotia he could see clouds forming in the east, and the air became bumpy. Accidentally he nudged his Mercator chart and the wind from the open window caught an edge. In a sudden panic he quickly snatched it back. A fine kettle of fish it would be to have his only cross-Atlantic guide sucked out the window.

The big cumuli ahead were crowding out the sunlight now, a gathering storm. And to the north the sky was bulging enormously in a sinister gray. Below, he could see whitecaps and wind streaks on the water. Newfoundland, his last landmass, was up in the darkness ahead. The air was becoming violent, jerking Lindbergh around like a carnival ride. He tightened his safety harness and worried about the safety of the plane, in particular that a wing might fail. He'd burned some five hundred pounds worth of gas but the aircraft was still dangerously overloaded. The turbulence increased, "gathering my plane in its teeth," he said, "like a dog picks up a rabbit." He slowed airspeed and had an argument with himself over not bringing a parachute.

A squall hit with blinding rain and even more turbulence, soaking Lindbergh and his charts in the cockpit. He gave up his course to avoid the worst storms, flying due east. At 1:52 p.m. he was six legs out, with thirty more to go. The storm abated. On the ground below was old snow; it was late May and he was in the northern climes. Then, on the horizon, he saw a thin, white band of fog along the coast.

How far the fog bank extended was Lindbergh's next great concern. Was it all the way to Newfoundland? He knew not. As luck would have it, the fog bank was merely a thin strip right along the coast, and as he crossed the strait to Cape Breton Island the sky opened up in brilliant sunshine. He checked his earth-inductor compass. The cockpit was so tight that the mechanic had had to install it above and behind Lindbergh's head, and so he'd have to read the compass with a mirror.

At midafternoon Lindbergh guided the *Spirit* past Cape Breton toward Newfoundland, two hundred miles northeast over the sea. The sunshine held; there was no turbulence; the engine vibrated evenly. He marveled at the thin fabric covering the plane inside and out. "I understand how the giant Gulliver was tied so firmly to the ground," he wrote afterward. "As he was bound to earth, I am held in the air—by the strength of threads." The sky at these latitudes seemed enormous, and he was a mere pinprick moving across it. Rarely had a hundred miles per hour seemed so slow.

Over the open sea once more he checked the Mercator projection resting on his knees and reset his course. Suddenly he became conscious of being very tired, and he decided it must be the monotony of flying over nothing but endless water. He blinked his eyes hard, making sure each time to remember not to leave them closed. He was so far north the sun was already sinking. He fought the impulse to close his eyes but felt that sleep was gaining.

In a moment of panic he jerked back on the stick and pulled the *Spirit* up two hundred feet above the waves, shaking his head and tensing his muscles in a deadly fight against sleep. He was surprised at how soon it had come but ought not to have been, for he'd been awake for almost thirty hours and in the plane for nearly eight. He was stuck in the cramped cockpit like a hand in a glove, without room even to bend or stretch. He decided to concentrate on navigation to exercise his mind. He was on the eighth leg—one quarter of the way to Paris! That at least was something, and right on schedule too.

Lindbergh knew the wind was blowing him slightly off course—a good twenty knots from the west, a quartering tailwind. He knew it by the crude but efficient method of flying low and checking wind streaks on the surface of the water. He knew what a twenty-knot streak looked like; if there weren't clouds, after moonrise he planned to check his drift that way as often as possible. Before he left he'd memorized the topography of Ireland, Scotland, England, and France, and it rolled around in his mind as he continued the losing battle against sleep. As the engine droned on, his eyes dropped to the compass needle and it read that he was ten degrees off course. He corrected, and then from below came a godsend, a huge white something brilliant and dazzling in the setting sun as far as he could see—an ice field. Something new to look at! He was awake once more.

Entering his tenth hour aloft, Lindbergh began to feel the lightness in the plane, and quickness in the controls, now that he'd burned off eight hundred pounds of gasoline. He glided down for a closer look at the ice and began to ruminate on what would happen if he was forced to land on it—a fool's errand—because nobody would ever find him and he'd starve to death after his sandwiches were eaten up, if a polar bear didn't get him first.

He flew over Newfoundland in semidarkness with mountain ridges and Conception Bay barely visible. In the bay were outlines of fishing boats. The town of St. John's came into view. In the twilight Lindbergh dropped down low to let them have a good look at him. He could see workers at the docks and wharves stop and stare up. People came out of houses at the sound of his engine. Enough people saw him that he knew the telegrams would soon go out, wires humming via the cable to Nova Scotia, and the one to Land's End, in England, reporting that Lindbergh was coming, that he was sighted at dusk passing over St. John's, Newfoundland. He looked back at the long finger of land projecting into the dark Atlantic and wondered if he would ever see America again. And behind that, this longest day was now merely a faint pink glow in the western sky.

His thoughts became gloomy and filled with doom: bobbing in his rubber raft in freezing empty seas, stranded in the wilderness, plunging headlong into the water, eaten by polar bears on the ice . . . He flew on.

A gigantic iceberg appeared below, then another, and another, seemingly connected by wisps of fog that soon galvanized into patches, which sooner still became a solid bank—fog, that deadliest of enemies— but luckily he was able to climb above it so that the fog passed below like a soft, white blanket. Inside the cockpit, with his hand controlling the stick, Lindbergh was snug as could be, secure for the moment, as the *Spirit* throbbed eastward into the night.

He was flying at 5,000 feet, barely skimming over the top of the fog blanket. Above there were stars. He knew the constellations since childhood and at least they told him he was still flying in the right direction. If he'd brought a sextant, and had three hands to use it, he could have shot a reading from the stars and fixed his exact location on the chart. But without the three hands he would have to make do with his compasses and Mercator.

The fog bank seem to be growing higher, threatening to cut Lindbergh off from the stars. There was danger in it, because flying blind in fog by instruments alone would be exceedingly tedious, and his battle with sleep was just beginning. Again black thoughts filled his brain. He worried about engine failure, about ice clogging the instruments so they couldn't be trusted. He thought of crashing, dying: "Do you really meet your God, or does blank nothingness replace your being?"

HE'D BEEN SKIMMING THE CLOUDS but the altimeter kept climbing, telling him the big cumuli were boiling with trouble. How high can a storm climb? Higher than your plane can fly. "If a storm gets so bad you can't stay under it, you had better find a field and land." That was the conventional wisdom. The latter option being unavailable, however, he climbed to 15,000 feet but could go no higher; the air was too light and he didn't have an oxygen tank. If the storm exceeded that height, then he and the storm were just going to have to fight it out.

And that's what they did.

It took until nearly midnight to outfly the storm. At one point Lindbergh looked out the window and saw lights below, thinking perhaps they were from a ship and that he wasn't so alone. But a glance at the gauges told him otherwise. In the darkness he'd become disoriented and was flying wing low; the lights he saw were stars.

As he fought his way through the storm, sleep returned as Lindbergh's greatest enemy. "There's no alternative [to staying awake] but death and failure." He repeated that truism over and over to keep from going to sleep. Like starvation, sleep deprivation is a cruel punishment. And then to make things worse he flew straight into a blanket of fog.

He tried to climb out of it but above the fog was such turbulence it was as if a huge hand had seized the plane and was jerking it around in the sky; it slammed Lindbergh from one side of his safety harness to the other and jiggled the instruments so that the needles made no sense. He decided the turbulence was worse than the fog and dove back into it, hoping for the best.

The sleep danger returned in a pernicious form—he fell asleep with his eyes open. When he woke up—jerked himself awake actually—the *Spirit* was all over the sky: into a steep left turn, wing down, losing altitude fast, rpms dropping, nose down. He had to bring it under control, but not too fast. Jerking back on the stick could make the plane uncontrollable. He got it back on course but it was a close call. He was down to fifteen hundred feet above the ocean. It was 4:20 a.m., his twenty-first hour aloft and still in the fog, but he was better than halfway to Paris.

SOON THE PHANTOMS BEGAN TO APPEAR. They were just as real to Lindbergh as if he were chatting with them over a dinner table. They stepped into the fuselage "as though no walls were there," and provided friendly, reassuring advice on navigation and other difficulties of the flight that were "unattainable in ordinary life." He didn't write about or mention the spirits for twenty years after his flight, maybe because he worried that people would think he was nuts. But when he finally did write about them it was a lucid account about the spiritual world. He wondered, in his exhaustion, whether he was actually entering the realm of the dead.

It was hour twenty-three, the twenty-third leg, 6:05 a.m. Lindbergh's log had been nearly bare for the past several hours except to record the switching of the fuel tanks. That was critical: he had to keep a record of which was full and which was empty. With unheralded suddenness he erupted through a band of clouds and mist into a clear, blue, boundless morning sky. He had at last passed through most of the great storm that began five hours earlier. Its angry remnants splashed across the sky on all sides but glorious, sunny patches of blue lay ahead and above. He figured to strike the coast of Ireland in eight hours, a workingman's day.

Below, upon the mountainous sea, the endless breakers rolled but their whitecaps were fewer, meaning there would be less wind drift. There were also patches of fog above the waves, and patches of clouds in the sky, but he could pick his way in between them.

Fatigue returned in the form of mirages. A green, rocky coast appeared—an island where none was supposed to be. An entire coastline came into view, complete with spruce trees lining its bluffs. It was so realistic Lindbergh even dived down to investigate, but then it all went *poof* in his face. If these hallucinations continued, how was he to recognize the real thing when he came upon it? He kept shaking his head and sticking it out the window and stamping his feet to keep awake, but that wasn't working as well as it had before. He tried playing mind games, calculating the math of how far he had flown, and how far was left, which resulted only in paroxysms of confusion.

Lindbergh's mind began to drift between unconsciousness and a sort of living stupor; he was staying awake only moment by moment now. Small tasks broke this phase: spreading the chart on his knees, checking navigation, cupping a hand out the window to direct a flow of cool air on his face. After a period of complex calculation he came up with the disagreeable possibility that he could be some 440 miles south of his intended landfall in Ireland.

The morning turned to afternoon as Lindbergh and *Spirit* droned on. The skies were fairly clear now, and he had become remarkably accustomed to the fatigue, the terrible sleepiness, almost automatically catching himself whenever he drifted off. In the water below he saw porpoises, then gulls wheeling above them—signs of the coast? Sunbeams danced in the cockpit and he began to expect to see the coastline any time. He needed to make landfall before dark, otherwise he wouldn't know where he struck the coast, or where to look for mountains. It would be difficult to tell the cities in the dark only by their lights—he thought he could tell London, though, because of its size. One thing for sure, he was a long way from Peoria.

Suddenly, in the distance, a small, black dot. A boat! More than one, actually. He dropped down and flew toward them. The fishing boats seemed to blanket him in security for he wasn't alone anymore. But when Lindbergh circled the first boat about fifty feet above no humans appeared. Maybe they were afraid of him, he thought. He went to the next boat and circled but no one came on deck there either.

Then, bizarrely, a man stuck his head through a porthole and gawked up at him. The man's face was pale—or at least it seemed so to Lindbergh. He circled the boat three times and each time the man's head remained motionless through the porthole, discombobulated, peering up at him, as in a tableau.

Lindbergh shut down his throttle and shouted: "WHICH WAY IS IRELAND?"

He received no response to this from the head in the porthole. It might be he speaks no English. But if this was the Irish coast, then it stood to reason the man was likely Irish. Maybe he was too stupefied to answer. Or maybe he was a Portuguese fisherman, or Norwegian. He flew on. If he'd navigated himself this far across the Atlantic, Lindbergh figured, he didn't need to stop and ask for directions.

The skies clouded up again. About three o'clock in the afternoon he saw a long shape ahead. He was flying only a hundred feet above the water but it looked like a coastline. After so many illusions Lindbergh took it with a grain of salt, but he climbed a thousand feet for a better look. Slowly, like a time-lapse photograph, the coastline materialized before him—barren islands, bays, rocky fingers of land, inlets, low rounded mountains, green fields. He checked the map on his knees. Dingle Bay and Valentia fit snugly, as in a jigsaw puzzle. Lindbergh had struck the southwest coast of Ireland where, as usual, it was raining. But he was right where he wanted to be, and two hours ahead of schedule! Through all the storms, the spoiling winds and fog, the crude instruments of navigation, sleep deprivation, uncertainties, fears, phantoms, mirages, and haunted heads, if this wasn't a miracle it ought to be.

THERE WERE VILLAGES BETWEEN the rock-ledged fields where sheep and cattle grazed. People rushed out of their houses at the first buzz of his plane, waving up at him. Lindbergh began to experience some kind of epiphany, brought on by the knowledge that he had crossed the Atlantic Ocean. He suddenly realized, and felt ashamed, at all the things he'd taken for granted in life. The mass of waving, friendly, welcoming people below had caused him to repent that. This, in turn, created such mental turmoil that he actually found himself flying once more over the ocean and believed he was having another hallucination—until he realized that in the excitement he'd completely turned around and was going exactly the wrong way, back in the direction he'd come from. He reversed his course and flew on.

He passed over the St. George's Channel to strike the English coast along the great cliffs at Cornwall, his mind swelling at the prospects of aviation now that the Atlantic has been crossed. Larger, faster, safer planes will soon come, carrying loads of passengers, freight, and mail between continents, opening up new vistas, new opportunities, new alliances. The possibilities seemed limitless. It's just a matter of time. He calculated that because of the tailwind that had carried him a full two hours ahead of schedule, he might even have enough fuel left over to reach Rome instead of Paris! What a coup that would be, he thought. Imagine their faces back in St. Louis when he wired them from Rome! Rome! And then . . . *crump!* A sinister shudder in the engine spelled trouble, freezing Lindbergh in place—a great *cough* as the engine strained against its motor mounts, and then another . . . He was out of gas! The nose dropped down, he began losing altitude, the engine wheezed and knocked. He'd forgotten to switch over from the nose tank, which ran dry. A quick turn of the switch to the right wing tank and a few pulls on the hand pump got the engine running smoothly again and put him back on course. It seemed there was always some little thing like that to stir up excitement.

Lindbergh's first sensation about England was how *small* it seemed. He was across the southern part in no time, he thought, and then over the English Channel, which at that point was eighty-five miles wide to the coast of France. He struck it in the last rosy gleam of sunset, at the same place near where the unfortunate Nungesser and Coli had crossed over on their fatal flight two weeks earlier. Having experienced the trial of the Atlantic firsthand, Lindbergh couldn't help but wonder how they died.

He folded the Mercator projection for the final time and put it away. There was no more water to cross. Below was Cherbourg, and the Norman coast, and Lindbergh felt he could relax somewhat. The worst was certainly over. With no more fog angst, phantoms, navigation nightmares, crosswinds, storms, or mirages to bedevil him, his mind drifted to practical matters, such as what would he actually *do* once he landed in Paris at Le Bourget airport. He wondered if there would be anyone there to meet him since he was two hours ahead of schedule. He didn't speak a *mot* of French and had even neglected to get a visa, which could mean trouble with the authorities. Where would he *sleep?* Where would he *eat?* Would anything be open?

Tomorrow, for one thing, he would need to buy a suit of clothes; there would be reporters to contend with, and photographers. They would want to see

the *Spirit of St. Louis.* "That will be fun," he said. "I like showing off the plane."
For another, he'd have to find a telegraph office where someone spoke English
and send a wire informing his people back in St. Louis that he'd arrived.

What he didn't know, couldn't know, was that after tonight, for the rest of
his life, he would *never* have to inform anyone that Lindbergh had arrived.

THE FRENCH FARM FIELDS, Lindbergh reported with some relief, were
larger than those of Ireland and England, with plenty of places "where I
could land in emergency without cracking up." Otherwise, his reception
was the same: people rushing out of their houses in the dim twilight and
waving up at him, "looking as though they had jumped up from the supper
table." Which reminded him, it was 9:20 p.m., Paris time, and he was
hungry and grabbed a sandwich. He started to fling the paper wrapping
out the window but stopped himself. "I don't want the litter from a
sandwich to symbolize my first contact with France," Lindbergh said.

He flew on toward Paris, a hundred miles ahead, following the Seine,
over the winking lights of villages, towns, and cities, until he spied one of
the bright air navigation beacons set up by the French to guide aircraft
after dark. He followed the beacons right into Paris, which appeared,
he said, as "a patch of starlit earth under a starlit sky." Soon the city
itself took shape, with buildings, parks, and avenues seeming to radiate
from a gigantic pillar lit by thousands of electric lights, which Lindbergh
recognized immediately as the Eiffel Tower. All sense of sleepiness had
vanished now. He felt as if he could fly another three thousand miles.

Le Bourget airport was just northeast of the city, so he circled the Eiffel
Tower once and headed that way. There were no beacons or searchlights
but he did see a large semidarkened space that could have been an airport,
yet it seemed surrounded by a factory with hundreds of lighted windows.
He dropped down to investigate, only to discover it wasn't a factory but
thousands of automobiles that appeared stuck in some kind of traffic jam.
Only half of the grass runway was lit, Lindbergh noted—at least he *hoped*
that was the case; if it weren't, it wouldn't be long enough to land on.
Spiraling down three times, he sized up the field and began his approach—
there were no visible obstructions—and he cut his speed at half throttle,
still worried about what might lie in the unlit part of the runway.

The airspeed indicator read 90 miles per hour—way too fast—but the plane felt as if it might stall. He closed the throttle, which set the engine to idling, and timed his descent to touch down not far beyond the hangars. He'd never landed *Spirit* at night before and was arrested by conflicting instincts—too high, too fast; too low, too slow. He started to do a touch-and-go and reached for the throttle, then just as quickly decided against it, and in another instant he was on the ground, just like that. After thirty-four hours and thirty-six hundred miles in the air, Lindbergh was bumping along toward he knew not what in the darkened part of the runway. "What" turned out to be perfectly good grass, and Lindbergh let himself roll to a solid stop on terra firma before turning to taxi back toward the hangars. That was when he saw the crowd, or mob, and they saw him, more than a hundred thousand of them, men, women, and children, rushing toward him screaming things in French, of which the only thing he understood was his name.

It was suddenly startling, then terrifying, not the least because these people seemed to be rushing toward certain decapitation by his spinning propeller. Now, wouldn't that be a fine spectacle upon his arrival in Paris? Lindbergh's flight had been tracked from Nova Scotia to Ireland, to England, and across the French coast. By the time he put down in Paris the media had turned his arrival into a frenzied carnival of celebration and adulation. The police and aviation authorities, fearing such a demonstration, had contained the crowd behind steel fences, but they broke through them anyway and rushed the field.

Lindbergh, still inside the cockpit, could feel the stiff fabric skin of the plane begin to crack as the mob surged against the fuselage. He opened the door and was immediately seized by frantic hands and carried around and around on people's shoulders, who were all the while shouting and screaming in an incomprehensible babble. It went on that way nearly half an hour, with Lindbergh at times fearing for his life—that he might be smothered or trampled to death. He shouted in English if there were any mechanics around but his pleas were consumed by the din.

Someone suddenly jerked his leather flying helmet off, and just as suddenly he found himself on his feet—on French soil at last! Friendly, firm hands gripped his arms and steered him out of the crowd. It turned out that two savvy French pilots had seen his distress and intervened. It had been they who took his flying helmet and jammed it on the head of an unsuspecting bystander, shouting and pointing, "Here is Lindbergh!" And soon enough that hapless man was hoisted up and trundled around the field as Lindbergh had been before him.

They took Lindbergh to a hangar where there was a private room and asked what he needed—food, drink, doctor, bathroom? Lindbergh told them he was fine but embarrassed that he had neglected to bring a visa. Would there be trouble? They only laughed at him. He asked if there was any news of Nungesser and Coli. The pilots shook their heads sadly.

Presently the proud U.S. ambassador to France, Myron T. Herrick, appeared with congratulations and offers of assistance. He would have come sooner, he said, but had been delayed when the bystander wearing Lindbergh's flying helmet had been presented to him as the real McCoy, and by the time that was straightened out the crowd had once more gone berserk.

The ambassador wanted Lindbergh to come with him to stay at the American embassy, but Lindbergh wanted to see his plane. He feared for the damage it had suffered. Reluctantly, they took him to the hangar in which the *Spirit of St. Louis* had been placed under lock and key and guarded by armed soldiers. Lindbergh was appalled at the sight. The crowd had gouged holes in the fuselage fabric and jerked small parts off of the engine as souvenirs, but on closer examination it appeared that no serious damage had been done. It was mostly cosmetic and the plane would be good as new by tomorrow afternoon. The French would gladly see to that.

The pilots drove Lindbergh to the embassy by side roads to avoid the traffic but turned back down the Champs-Élysées and came to a halt beneath the Arc de Triomphe, which contained the Tomb of the Unknown Soldier of France in the Great War. Lindbergh did not know this, and didn't understand what the pilots were saying, but he did recognize that this place was important to them.

It was after three a.m. before Ambassador Herrick, having himself been caught up in the wild traffic jams outside the airport, returned to his residence. He arrived to find Lindbergh munching on a fine nocturnal repast, courtesy of his kitchen staff. At the ambassador's suggestion, Captain Charles Lindbergh took a few minutes to speak with reporters, and then, in pajamas borrowed from the ambassador, he turned in for the night.

CHAPTER 7

★ ★ ★ ★ ★

MAN'S GREATEST ENEMY IN THE AIR

Man's greatest enemy in the air, fog, was conquered yesterday . . .

—*NEW YORK TIMES*
SEPTEMBER 25, 1929

I N THE AUTUMN OF 1928 Jimmy Doolittle was entirely in his element when he went to work for Harry Guggenheim at the Full Flight Laboratory at Mitchel Field, Long Island, New York. He lived with Joe and the boys—Jim, eight, and John, six—in "a long termite-ridden building built in World War I," and Doolittle enjoyed every moment of it. At the age of thirty-one, the man and the hour had met. Doolittle's outstanding qualities as a pilot and his professional knowledge as a Phd in aeronautical engineering would now be put to use in tandem to solve the dilemma his friend Slim Lindbergh had alluded to when he declared before his famous Atlantic flight that "aviation will never amount to much until we learn to free ourselves from mist."[1]

It was too true. Since the inception of flight, aviation had been used for war, to carry mail, and for barnstorming performances and sport racing. But for ordinary civilians airplanes remained, basically, a novelty. Even though airplane cockpits were beginning to be enclosed to make more comfortable cabins, mass transportation was left to ships, trains, and automobiles, because without the ability to fly in fog, blizzards, and other heavy weather—flying "blind" was the expression—airlines could guarantee no regular schedules, and without dependable schedules, as Lindbergh pointed out, they were not attractive for either freight or passengers.

Lindbergh found out the hard way during one of his mail runs to Chicago. Both St. Louis and Springfield were fogged in and night had closed around him and his de Havilland mail plane. He'd been trying to find a hole in the cloud ceiling when suddenly he saw a blur of treetops less than a hundred feet below and jerked up hard on the stick, forced to rely on his "untrusted" instruments in the black nothingness. He went up too fast, however, lost control, and began dropping down, but he caught the plane and leveled it out. Then the controls went loose, the engine lost power, the wings began to tremble, and the nose dropped again. He was in a stall because he had failed to keep the turn indicator centered and the airspeed needle high. Instead, he'd been flying seat-of-the-pants—controlling the plane the way he *thought* it ought to be controlled, instead of relying on his instruments to warn him of danger. Lindbergh fought the stall with stick, pedals, and throttle and was preparing to jump but luckily he reclaimed control after the second whip. As the plane slowly climbed, he vowed to teach himself to fly by instruments in the future.

Many other pilots weren't so lucky. Too many tried to tough it out against the weather; through some sort of misguided machismo they actually held the weather in contempt. Thousands of accidents and deaths and injuries could be directly attributed to pilots who either couldn't fly by instruments or refused to believe them.

The way Doolittle saw the problem, if scientific advances in airplane design, navigation instruments, and radio communication "could be merged, I thought flying in weather could be mastered." That was a big, bold statement but, like Lindbergh and Rickenbacker, Jimmy Doolittle thought big and bold. He was not a boaster. He was a serious, competent pilot and scientist, and he set about his quest for supremacy over the weather with persistence and ferocity.

With the help of U.S. Navy Captain Emory "Jerry" Land, the vice president of the Guggenheim Fund for the Promotion of Aeronautics, as well as Slim Lindbergh's first cousin, Doolittle procured two modern planes with which to conduct experiments. One was a Consolidated NY-2 Husky, a sturdy two-seater with a Wright J-5 Whirlwind engine, that was to be used in instruments testing for blind flying. To that end, a special canvas hood was put over the pilot's cockpit so he saw nothing before him of the outside world—only his instrument panel. The second plane was a navy Vought O2U-1 Corsair, a fast-flying aircraft that the team used for cross-country flying and transportation to locations they might need to visit in the course of the project. Doolittle, the famous aviation racer, was quite fond of the Corsair, but he had little use for the Husky, whose slowness he complained of in a letter to the president of Consolidated Aircraft, saying, among other things, "On one occasion, while we were flying low over a road and into a head wind, a green automobile overtook and passed us. It hurt my pride."

The first thing Doolittle realized as he studied the problem was that the instruments fliers were presently using—the magnetic compass, earth inductor compass, altimeter, airspeed indicator, turn-and-bank indicator, and artificial horizon—were too crude to be trusted in a blind landing when a pilot had to know his exact position, speed, altitude, attitude, and distance from the ground. Doolittle cast about for ways to refine these mechanisms' accuracy down to the linear foot, if possible, so that a pilot could comfortably guide his plane onto a runway and put it safely on the ground, even in a dense fog.

At Doolittle's request the Sperry Gyroscope Company, led by the renowned scientist and engineer Elmer A. Sperry Sr. and his son Elmer Jr., devised a new, highly improved directional gyroscope and artificial horizon,* which gave the pilot both a precisely accurate compass and a leveling indicator from which today's space-age electronic aviation instruments were originated.

---

* A device that tells the pilot whether the plane is flying level, banking, climbing, or diving.

Next Doolittle needed an altimeter that gave more than a rough approximation of the plane's height over the ground. Present altimeters gauged the pressure based at sea level, which was fine if you were flying along an ocean beach, but pilots needed a more accurate reading in all types of terrain. Fortunately, word had gotten out about the Guggenheim project, and inventors from far and wide began submitting various gadgets and apparatuses to the U.S. Bureau of Standards, which gave them over to Captain Jerry Land, who in turn passed them along to Doolittle if they seemed to have any merit.

A German-born American named Paul Kollsman turned up with an idea for an altimeter. He had worked for the venerable Pioneer Instrument Company until he was fired for saying the altimeter the company produced was no good. Kollsman decided the only way to prove his bosses wrong was to build a better altimeter. In this endeavor he sought the help of a Swiss watchmaker in New York, whom he induced to cut the tiny gears "more accurate than the best watch ever made."[2] Meanwhile, Kollsman, working out of his garage in Brooklyn, set about crafting a diaphragm and barometric pressure device that would allow the altimeter to adjust for precise changes in atmospheric pressure, solving one of the major problems of altitude gauging. Soon, Doolittle's instrument panel included the finest and most accurate altimeter ever constructed.[3]

None of this was as easy as it sounds. Doolittle spent many long hours in tedious flight with Elmer Sperry Jr., Paul Kollsman, and others, testing, adjusting, and refining these instruments until they were as exact as possible. Similar tweaking was done with the airspeed indicator. As well, during the better part of a year that Doolittle had spent with the Full Flight Laboratory, many other ideas and inventions had been tried and discarded.

Not only that, but Doolittle himself came extremely close to losing his life while experimenting in bad-weather flying.

On March 15, 1929, he took off at night from Buffalo for Mitchel Field, about a four-hundred-mile flight, in the O2U-1 Corsair, which was the utility plane and not equipped with any blind-flying instruments. Doolittle knew in advance that the weather would be bad the farther south he flew, but he justified the attempt by reasoning that he could always return to Buffalo if the situation got dicey. By the time he reached

Albany the weather had deteriorated; the ceiling closed in and visibility was minimal. That was also when he reached the point of no return—when he had used up too much fuel to fly back.

Doolittle dropped through the soup and managed to catch the lights of a southbound passenger train along the Hudson. He hovered above it for a while until it disappeared into a tunnel or a cut bank and he was on his own. This was the sort of weather in which pilots needed to get on the ground as quickly as possible. Doolittle thought of landing on the parade field at West Point but abandoned the idea and followed the river into New York City, which was thoroughly socked in—halfway to the tops of the skyscrapers. The fog blanket was so vast that reaching Mitchel Field was impossible. He considered landing on Governors Island but the fog was right on the ground. He turned back to the Yonker's golf course and found it similarly cloaked. He tried Battery Park but that didn't work either. And he thought about ditching in the river but the idea of water gave him chills. He tried instead to get to Newark Airport . . . to no avail; the fog was all-enveloping.

Discouraged and running out of gas, Doolittle climbed above the fog and headed west out of the populated area. A parachute landing of some kind seemed inevitable. He had flown about twenty miles into New Jersey, past Newark, when he saw through a hole in the fog what he took for an aircraft beacon and popped down to take a look. Immediately he scraped a treetop that tore his wing but he was able to maintain enough control to crash-land—deliberately, so he said—wrapping the left wing around a tree to slow the crash and break the impact. The Corsair was a total wreck, and it is nothing short of amazing that Doolittle walked away from it alive, without a bruise or a scratch.

THERE WAS ONE FINAL DEVICE needed to finish the job. Despite the remarkable refinements in the plane's instrument panel, there was nothing to tell the pilot where the airfield was, let alone the runway. Only a radio beam could do that. The team had been experimenting with beams for some time, but now they would have to perfect it so the airplane could always make contact with an accurate radio beacon that could guide the pilot in and down.

They settled on an aural beacon for long-range contact. It would direct the plane on a radio path to the airfield, where a lower-powered beacon system would take over and guide the plane in with vertical and horizontal markers, which were read in the plane itself by two vibrating reeds in loop antennae, a homing range indicator and a vibrating reed beacon-marker indicator. The beacons gave off radio signals from the reed, similar to that found in woodwind instruments. The pilot could hear it vibrate in his earphones; if it sounded *dit-dah-dit,* for example, he was too far to the left and if it sounded *dah-dit-dah-dit* he was too far to the right. It hummed when the plane was vectored in on course. As well, the plane would have two-way radio contact with the airfield.

While all these developments were taking place, an unconventional solution came Doolittle's way via a man who ran a gravel pit in Cleveland, Ohio. This man, Harry Reader, maintained a gigantic blowtorch-type of heater to dry the gravel and sand in his pit, and he had noticed, over time, that when he turned on the torch in a fog, the fog over the pit dissipated. Reader thought this information might be useful to the Full Flight Laboratory, and in due time he reported to Mitchel Field, as requested by the team, along with the giant blowtorch, which he installed along the runway where it sat for months awaiting a foggy day.

Even though it was the autumn, when thick fogs regularly roll in off Long Island Sound, the days remained sunny and dry and maddeningly clear.

Meantime, Joe Doolittle had established herself, as she did on every post, as the most charming hostess who attracted crowds of the famous and not so famous from far and wide. There was scarcely an evening when she did not entertain, and she had become by then a legendary cook, despite the fact that as a child her mother never allowed her in the kitchen. Most of her culinary skills, she admitted, were a result of the Chinese cook at the Eagle Pass airfield in Texas, who had taught her to make cheap Mexican dishes. These she spiced up and improved upon over the years until her chili con carne, meatballs, and chow mein became the talk of the town wherever she went. There was often dancing afterward, and a great deal of beer drinking, thanks to Joe's expertly prepared home brew. Those were the last days of Prohibition, but like most decent, honest Americans the Doolittles partook whenever they pleased, and Joe had learned that using first-rate hops was the secret to making good beer. Since the best hops available were grown in California, Jimmy organized a relay between army pilots flying from the West Coast to bring Joe as many hops as they could carry. Those were good times for Jimmy too. He was home enough to play with the boys, teaching them baseball, tumbling, and boxing or singing them Russian folk songs he'd learned from a pair of the czar's pilots who had fled the Soviet Union.[4]

On the morning of September 24, 1929, Harry Reader at last had the opportunity to demonstrate his giant fog-dispersing blowtorch.

The fog rolled in off the Sound sometime before six a.m., a thick gray soup that enveloped the field, the runway, and the hangar where Jack Dalton, Doolittle's chief mechanic, was working. Dalton dashed to Doolittle's quarters and woke him up, and in turn Doolittle aroused Reader, who promptly manned his torch. Doolittle also alerted other officials, including Harry Guggenheim, who had to drive from his home at Port Washington about ten miles away.

Everyone, including Captain Land, Conger Pratt, the commanding officer at Mitchel Field, Doolittle, and even Joe, gathered around Harry Reader as he got his heater going full blast. Sure enough, the fog began to disperse above the roaring torch and for some short distance around it but, as Doolittle put it, the experiment soon collapsed in dismal failure.

Although the intense heat could dissipate fog above Reader's gravel pit in Ohio, when it got into the open the slightest wind would simply push fresh fog into the hole that the torch had dispersed, filling it up just about as fast as it had dissolved the fog.

With this disagreeable setback hovering over them, and all the dignitaries hanging around while Reader resignedly packed up his torch,* Doolittle wasn't about to let such a fine fog go to waste. He told Dalton

---

* Reader's effort, later known in military jargon as FIDO, for "Fog, Intense Dispersal of," was actually used effectively both in Los Angeles and in England during World War II. Enormous heat-dispensing devices were set up on runways to heat the air directly above the runway to the dew point. Doolittle, who was commanding the Eighth Air Force then, said some twenty-five hundred bombers and fighters returning to England's pea soup fogs were saved.

to crank up the NY-2 Husky. He was going to try a blind landing in the fog now!

It was vintage Doolittle. Here was a man who six months earlier had barely escaped with his life in a fog-bound crash now anxious to jeopardize it again in a completely untried experiment. This time, however, he'd done the math on paper, and in practical experiments; he'd watched the theories being put into practice as the various instruments took shape. He saw the possibilities in his mind and the odds seemed in his favor.

Technicians rushed to man the radios and beacons as Doolittle taxied onto the runway, pulled his canvas hood shut, and took off. He climbed out of the fog at 500 feet and flew in a wide circle above the field for about ten minutes before lining up for a landing. He tuned his headset to listen to the vibrating radio beacon reeds. Every time he steered off a beeline course the humming told him to realign. When he was near the airport the local beacon took over and he began to descend. He looked at the altimeter, 200 feet, 100 feet, 50 feet—the reeds were vibrating perfectly—25 feet, 10 feet. Despite his best efforts he came down sloppy with his nose too high and bounced. But he'd just made aviation history with the first completely blind flight alone in a fog.

By then Guggenheim and others had arrived, and it was decided that Doolittle should do an "official" blind flight, meaning that everything, every move, would be thoroughly measured and recorded. The heaviest fog had begun to disperse but there was just enough left.

With the hood over the cockpit "tightly closed," Doolittle taxied out onto the grass runway and let the engine rev while he once more adjusted the directional gyroscope to the magnetic compass heading and set the altimeter at zero. Then he opened the throttle until the aircraft was straining at every bolt and rivet. When he was satisfied he had full power on, Doolittle let go the brakes and roared off westward. (At Guggenheim's insistence another pilot was put in the forward cockpit but he kept his hands off the controls the entire flight.)

Leveling out at 1,000 feet, Doolittle flew five miles, then made a series of 90-degree left turns; the last put him in the landing pattern for the west runway. The two vibrating reeds were humming left and right in the cockpit, homing him in to the Mitchel Field beacon. Whenever he veered off course, the reed in that direction would vibrate more, telling him to steer the other way. If he kept the reeds vibrating at an equal rate he knew he was flying on a direct path to the runway. Slowly descending until his new altimeter registered precisely 400 feet, he leveled out and picked up the local runway beam that guided him down, 200 feet, 100 feet, until he crossed thirty feet above the fence at the end of the runway and then glided to a touchdown, rolled, settled back on the tail skid, and came to a stop. There was uproarious cheering and applause as everyone rushed to the plane. Guggenheim joyfully pulled back the hood, revealing Doolittle with a vexed expression because he thought he'd made a sloppy landing.

"What happened to the fog?" he asked, looking around.

"It sort of rolled away while you were up there," Guggenheim told him.[5] But it didn't matter.

The entire flight from takeoff to landing was only fifteen minutes, but Doolittle had made aviation history again—twice in one day!

During the course of a grand celebration they threw that night with excellent homemade beer and a broccoli-lemon cheese dip, Joe introduced a new tradition to the Doolittle family. There was a large, white damask tablecloth on the dinner table and everyone who had worked on the project was invited to sign it, beginning with Guggenheim and Land. Later, Joe embroidered the signatures in black thread and in the years to come anyone who ate at the Doolittles' was invited to sign the tablecloth. In her lifetime Joe meticulously stitched more than five hundred signatures into the tablecloth, and when it was full she began using white table napkins. The only signature not actually made at the Doolittles' table was that of Orville Wright, who signed the tablecloth in old age when it was brought to his home.*

---

* The Doolittle tablecloth remains one of the most remarkable signature collections in history, including not only all the famous pilots of the day and their wives but politicians, movie stars, singers, writers, scientists, and more. Today the collection resides in the Smithsonian's National Air and Space Museum in Washington, D.C.

JIMMY DOOLITTLE BECAME ENSHRINED, along with Rickenbacker and Lindbergh, among the giants of American aviation. "Man's greatest enemy in the air, fog, was conquered yesterday at Mitchel Field," declared the *New York Times,* "when Lt. James H. Doolittle took off, flew over a fifteen mile course, and landed again without seeing the ground or any part of his plane but the illuminated instrument boards."

Of course there was an enormous amount of work remaining to perfect blind flight, but Doolittle and the Full Flight Laboratory had shown the way. "The occasion marked the first instance in which a pilot negotiated a complete flight while flying absolutely blind," continued the *Times* story. "The demonstration was more than an exhibition of blind flying and instrument perfection. It indicated that aviation had perhaps taken its greatest step in safety."

Guggenheim was somewhat more cautious, saying, "The last great hazard to airplane reliability is vanishing as this principle is developed, which will make the airplane more independent of weather conditions."

Doolittle was even more cautious than that. Calling the *Times* reporter "optimistic," he said for the record, "Although more work was needed, we made an initial contribution to instrument flight." Privately, he considered his work on the blind-flight project "my most significant contribution to aviation."

In the autumn of 1929, right after Jimmy's famous blind flight, the stock markets crashed, plunging the country—and the world—into a great financial depression. Nobody at the time knew how bad it would be, but an immediate shock convulsed the petroleum industry; people stopped buying cars, making cars, and driving cars. Executives at St. Louis's Shell Oil division were farsighted enough to understand they needed to open new markets, and the notion of having Doolittle compete in air races under Shell's sponsorship was suddenly very appealing. They offered him *three times* his army salary to join the company, and even gave him his own private airplane, a $25,000 Lockheed Vega.* It was an offer he would not refuse.

---

* The Lockheed Vega was a highly sought after four-passenger modern plane. It was flown by Amelia Earhart in her renowned transatlantic crossing a year earlier, and also by the well-known pilot Wiley Post in his round-the-world flight in 1931.

It was a hard decision for Doolittle; he loved the army and had given ten years of his life to it. He would miss being the army's crack test pilot and chumming around with the airplane designers, builders, and dreamers who were behind all the innovations of modern flight. He did not leave the army entirely, however. He applied for and received a commission as major in the army reserve, just to keep his hand in. With that the Doolittle family packed up and left Mitchel Field for Lindbergh's old stomping grounds St. Louis, Missouri.

St. Louis and the cities around it had become a mecca of aviation design and construction. Jimmy's responsibility at Shell, he soon found out, was much greater than he had been given to understand. He was to manage aviation affairs at all three of Shell's U.S. subsidiaries, including the one in San Francisco where his friend who had recommended him, John Macready, was posted. In particular, Jimmy was to oversee and coordinate the development and sale of all of Shell's aviation products. He was also expected to race or stunt in the big air shows.

He had been at the company less than a month when all that changed. An old friend from his army aviation class, Jack Allard, now president of Curtiss-Wright's export branch, arrived with a proposition. He wanted Jimmy—whose blind-flight fame had preceded him—to go on a whirlwind four-month, eleven-country European air show tour demonstrating the new Curtiss Hawk biplane, the standard U.S. Army fighter aircraft of the late 1920s. At first the Shell people were skeptical, but Allard won them over by explaining that Jimmy was immensely popular in Europe and that it would be to his, and Shell's, advantage for him to meet the leaders of European aviation. Besides, there was the promise that at every show it would be announced the Hawk was exclusively serviced by Shell products.

From Greece, the Doolittle entourage toured Turkey, the Balkans (Yugoslavia and Bulgaria), Poland, France, Germany, Hungary, Austria, France, Norway, and Sweden. Doolittle had two forced landings, due to faulty engines, got lost in fog and had to ask for directions from Swiss Boy Scouts, and received a diplomatic reprimand for "flying under two of the Danube bridges at Budapest, on a challenge, at night (the opening line of the ambassadorial complaint read, 'I would do little to belittle Doolittle but . . .')."[6] Meanwhile, he took note of the state of European aviation and its advances, especially in Germany, where the Germans were building "good-looking Dorniers and Junkers."

At this pre-Hitler stage of international affairs, Germany was not yet seen as a threat, but Doolittle, who was foremost a military man, was quick to notice that all of the advanced European nations were technologically much further along in aviation than the United States. In Europe, governments supported air shows and plane racing, which were essentially test laboratories for the designers, engineers, and the military. The political climate in Europe had not yet turned rancid, but Doolittle concluded that World War I had not settled matters once and for all, that many old antagonisms remained and new menaces lurked. They did not, for example, tour Italy, where the fascist dictator Benito Mussolini had recently consolidated his power.

Doolittle returned to the States in July of 1930 to learn that his mother, who had been ill for several years, had taken a turn for the worse. She passed away in September, carrying with her at least the satisfaction that her son had not grown up to be a jailbird.

That same fall, Doolittle purchased a wrecked Travel Air—a stripped-down, low-wing racing monoplane known in aviation circles as the Mystery Ship because he had it reconstructed to his own modernized specifications, streamlining it with a backward sweep, or curve, in the wings as they came off the fuselage. On June 23, 1931, he took it to a local air show for a test flight.

At first the Mystery Ship responded to Doolittle's complete satisfaction as he performed several aerobatic stunts. Then he dived down to 100 feet, right above the crowd at almost 300 miles per hour, but when he zoomed up toward 500 feet there was "an ominous sound of cracking metal." The plane went into a horrible spasm of vibration as the wings started to break and the ailerons bucked and snapped off. That, for all practical purposes, was the end of the Mystery Ship. What remained to be seen was whether it would also be the end of Doolittle.

Spectators were horrified. Doolittle had flipped the stick to point the plane away from the crowd and scrambled out of the cockpit, immediately pulling the rip cord on his parachute, but he was already so close to the ground that he actually watched his own plane crash and explode half a mile off, just as his feet touched earth. Like Lindbergh,

Doolittle was now a member of the Caterpillar Club two times over, having twice jumped with a parachute to avoid what would have been certain death. His is said to be one of the lowest unplanned jumps in parachuting history. Jimmy had put a considerable amount of his and Joe's life's savings into the Mystery Ship, the remains of which were now no more than a steaming pile of hot, twisted metal.[7]

Undaunted, and needing to recoup some of the cash he had lost, on behalf of Shell, Doolittle entered a much-publicized cross-country race sponsored by the Bendix Aviation Corporation, which held out a $7,500 prize for the winner.* Billed as the Transcontinental Free-for-All Speed Dash, the eight racers, including Doolittle, would take off after midnight from Burbank, California, and the first one to cross the finish line at Cleveland, Ohio, before seven p.m. that same day would be the winner. In a straight line it was 2,046 miles.

Doolittle arranged for refueling stops in Albuquerque and Kansas City where Shell crews were prepared to service the plane with 140 gallons of gas in under ten minutes. Doolittle figured that would shave off enough time to give him an edge.

He was flying a plane made by the aviation designer E. M. "Matty" Laird, called the Laird Super Solution. Doolittle figured it would average about 200 miles per hour to Cleveland. His opponents included a Hollywood stunt pilot, a stockbroker, an airline pilot, an army captain, and a retired barnstormer with the delightful name of Beeler Blevins.†

The contestants took off shortly after one a.m. Pacific Time, with each pilot choosing his own route, speed, fuel stops, and altitude. At Albuquerque, Doolittle barely had time to drink a glass of milk that someone handed him before the Super Solution was fueled full by the Shell "pit crew" and ready for takeoff.

He made the Kansas City airfield three hours and five minutes later, averaging 228 miles per hour, and won the Bendix Trophy with a

---

* In the depth of the Great Depression this had the purchasing power of about $100,000 in today's money.

† The army captain was Ira C. Eaker who, along with Doolittle, would become one of the highest-ranking commanders of the air force during World War II.

record flight time of nine hours and ten minutes to Cleveland. Joe and the boys were waiting for him on the airfield, but after a brief reunion Jimmy refueled and took off again for New York, where an additional $2,500 awaited him for completing that leg of the flight. He crossed the Alleghenies in a rain squall and landed at Newark before five in the evening—coast to coast in eleven hours and eleven minutes, beating the old record by a full hour. With $10,000 in cash prizes, he'd made up in full for the loss of the Mystery Ship.

BY THE BEGINNING OF THE 1930S Shell Oil was selling more than twenty million gallons of aviation fuel a year, mostly to private pilots, and there was even a feeling among the population that the airplane might actually supersede the automobile as the principal means of personal transportation. At world's fairs in Chicago and elsewhere, exhibits portrayed modern cities with personal airplanes flying all over the skies. Commercial airlines were just beginning to catch on as well. The Depression slowed but did not stop production of aircraft, nor the sale of aviation fuel.

There were many advanced engine designs, but the more powerful the engines became, the more they tended to blow or burn out their pistons. If aircraft were to fly heavier loads faster, they were going to need increasing power, but first the piston problem needed to be solved. Doolittle summed it up this way: "More powerful engines would demand better aviation fuel."

Pilots had long known that there was a difference in fuels. They called it the "knock rating," before the term "octane rating" was coined, because a low-grade fuel would cause any internal combustion engine— car, plane, motorbike—to "knock." Scientists both in the United States and abroad were studying the problem and at last came up with tetraethyl lead as a gasoline additive to reduce knock in an engine. It worked but was more expensive. Soon there were eighteen different grades of fuels, ranging from 65 octane to the standard 87 octane used by most commercial airlines. Doolittle was for standardizing these into three or four grades, but most of all he pushed Shell to manufacture 100 octane aviation fuel.

It would be the fuel of the future, he told executives, because he'd studied the new engine designs and all of them called for far more powerful engines than were in existence at the time. Military planes, fighters and bombers, Doolittle argued, would soon be built with extremely powerful engines, and the same was true for commercial aircraft, which by the early 1930s were being designed to carry up to twenty-one passengers instead of the present six or eight.

Shell was convinced enough by Doolittle's argument to put $3 million into research and development for the 100 octane fuel, the demand for which at the time was absolutely zero.* Doolittle took much criticism from various naysayers and disbelievers in the company, who behind his back branded it "Doolittle's Folly." In fact, his standing within the company was on the line, and he knew it.

The first hurdle Doolittle had with selling the 100 octane fuel was the U.S. Army, which had solved the multifuel grade problem by designing all its military engines from motorcycles to fighter planes so they would use a single-grade fuel (87 octane). It was believed that this would simplify supply problems in wartime.

Doolittle organized and closely monitored tests of various grades of fuel conducted by the Air Corps at Wright Field in Ohio, where engineers made an amazing discovery: using 100 octane fuel would increase power even in existing engines up to 30 percent, and that with high-compression engines the higher-grade fuel would get up to 15 percent in fuel savings.

Jimmy made his case to the army brass and in 1936 a committee was appointed that recommended all combat aircraft engines be designed for 100 octane fuel. The commercial airlines didn't need a committee, and by 1938 Shell Oil was selling millions of gallons of high-octane fuel monthly. By 1943, with the war on, Shell was producing fifteen million gallons of 100 octane *a day.* It had been a big gamble, and Jimmy had risked his career with Shell over it, but "Doolittle's Folly" paid off in spades.

Meantime, Jimmy announced he was retiring from air racing. He had been gravitating toward the decision for years, gently pushed by Joe, as

---

* $3 million in 1934 translates into more than $40 million today.

so many of his friends and acquaintances had died in crashes. He was the number one air-racing pilot in America, but he was also thirty-four and balding, and his happy smile was beginning to look rueful. What finally pushed him into retirement was when he learned that during his last race, a Thompson Cup, news photographers had clustered around Joe and the children, hoping to capture the looks on their faces if he crashed.

The air races, he told the press, had served their purpose. They aroused public interest and created great innovations in aircraft design such as retractable landing gear, streamlined wings, and of course more powerful engines. But now, he said, the emphasis should be on reliability and safety. When pressed on the decision, he told reporters, "I have yet to hear of anyone engaged in this work dying of old age."

Very soon afterward, the Curtiss company came calling once more, wanting Doolittle to make a trip around the world to sell its P6 Hawk, in conjunction with Shell Oil, of course. He took Joe along this time—after arranging for the boys to be cared for—and sailed from San Francisco in early 1933, arriving nearly a month later in Yokohama, Japan. Jimmy immediately became a subject of suspicion when the Japanese saw his passport, but he was allowed ashore anyway to visit Tokyo and sightsee other areas. He wrote later that if he'd had any inkling that the United States would one day soon be at war with Japan he would have taken careful notes of landmarks and military targets.

Jimmy gave demonstrations of the Hawk in several Chinese cities, including Shanghai; each time he noticed on the outskirts of the field a group of Japanese photographers with telescopic lenses taking pictures of the military plane. Twice he had strong misgivings that a saboteur had tampered with the plane and damaged critical parts. They pushed on to the Philippines without further incident, making brief stops in the Dutch East Indies, the Middle East, and Europe, before sailing back to New York from England in August 1933.

While he was in England, Jimmy had made a determined pitch to the Royal Air Force, pointing out the extra power boost its planes—especially the defensive fighters—would get by converting to 100 octane gas. He showed British engineers that a 1,000-horsepower-rated Merlin fighter engine would produce 1,700 horsepower when fueled with 100 octane gasoline. This gave the RAF an enormous edge during the Battle of

Britain, when its Hurricanes and Spitfires could develop much higher manifold pressure and outclimb and outrace their German counterparts, which used only 87 octane fuel.[8]

Because Doolittle's words did not fall on deaf ears, by the middle of 1940 all RAF fighters had begun to use 100 octane fuel, and after the war the British petroleum secretary said of the conversion: "This octane was thirteen points higher than the fuel used by German aircraft. Those extra thirteen points ended the threat of any Nazi invasion of England."[9]

IN FEBRUARY 1934, a significant and expanding scandal erupted when, in answer to charges of favoritism, President Franklin D. Roosevelt without warning canceled all airmail contracts with civilian airline companies and nationalized the airmail service by ordering the Army Air Corps to fly the mail. The president's action stemmed from his assertion that the major airlines, with the collusion of his Republican predecessor's administration, had criminally conspired to keep all mail contracts within their own hands and nobody else's.

This provoked severe and biting criticism of the president by such aviation luminaries as Eddie Rickenbacker and Charles Lindbergh. Lindbergh, still famous for his transatlantic flight and a large stockholder in TWA, one of the affected airlines, was never a man to mince words. The day following the announcement, he sent Roosevelt a personal telegram, simultaneously released to the press, charging that the president's action would "unnecessarily damage all American aviation," and condemning the president for taking arbitrary action against the airlines without a fair trial.[10]

Rickenbacker, who by then was also inextricably involved with the airline industry, was even more strident. After Lindbergh's comments were printed, reporters rushed over to Rickenbacker's New York office to get a comment. He explained that army pilots were not suited to flying the mail. They were neither trained nor equipped for blind flying or even night flying. Their planes were not adapted to airmail flying. Pointing out that no chief pilot for a commercial airline had less than four thousand flying hours, compared with a few hundred for the average army pilot, he told the newsmen, "Either they [the army pilots] are going to pile up ships all across the continent, or they are not going to be able to fly the mail on schedule."

The Roosevelt administration had already developed a highly skilled attack organ within its public relations machine. In an obvious case of "if you don't like the message, attack the messenger," Roosevelt's secretary Stephen T. Early immediately accused Lindbergh of, basically, being ungentlemanly for releasing his telegram to the press before Roosevelt had had a chance to read it himself.

Not only that, but prominent Democratic congressmen began attacking Lindbergh in the press, accusing him of being a publicity seeker, a shill for the airlines, and there were assertions hinting of bribery and corruption. It was Lindbergh's first encounter with adverse publicity, but if he was stung by it he didn't say. It would not be his last difficult encounter with the Roosevelt administration.

The army was scheduled to begin flying the mail by February 20. By then, all of the commercial airlines had practically gone out of business, since carrying airmail had been their mainstay, and there wasn't yet enough passenger traffic to keep the companies going. Staff and workers were laid off to cope with the Depression however they could. On that same morning, newspaper headlines announced that three army pilots had been killed the previous day flying in snowstorms or fog, merely *on their way* to their airmail assignments. Rickenbacker was having breakfast with several reporters when the newspapers were brought in, and he abruptly declared, "That's legalized murder!" When the reporters asked if they could quote him, America's Ace of Aces said, "You're damned right you can!"[11]

He had been scheduled to give a fifteen-minute nationwide speech on NBC several days later and had asked the *Los Angeles Times* publisher Harry Chandler for help "from his best editorial writer" to weigh in on the airmail controversy. As he was leaving for the studio, Rickenbacker said, he received a call from a friend at NBC who informed him that "orders had come from Washington [i.e., presumably from the White House] to cut me off the air if I said anything controversial."

Rickenbacker toned down his speech, but not enough to keep from being cut off entirely several days later, he said, by orders of the president, when he was scheduled to make another speech via NBC's national radio forum.*

Just as Lindbergh and Rickenbacker had predicted, in the ensuing weeks there were sixty-six crashes and ten more army pilots were killed delivering the mail, provoking a public outcry that at last caused Roosevelt to reverse himself and put the airmail service back on commercial airline contracts. But the president, in a final fit of pique, decreed that no one who worked for any of the original companies that had traditionally carried the mail would be eligible to receive a government contract. This produced a charade of musical chairs in which all the airlines simply changed their names (e.g., United Aircraft became United Airlines), a solution that Lindbergh sourly characterized as "something to be found in *Alice in Wonderland*."[12]

Instead of speaking out like Lindbergh and Rickenbacker, Doolittle kept his counsel during the controversy, though privately he shared the opinion of Lindbergh and Rickenbacker that the president had been imprudent in making army pilots fly airmail routes. Perhaps his silence was because he was trying to sell the government 100 octane gasoline.

Responding to the public's outrage, a committee was convened in Washington to investigate why the Army Air Service was in such bad condition. (In 1934, out of the three thousand aircraft that the Air Service owned, only three hundred had been suitable and serviceable for airmail duty.) Known as the Baker Board after its chairman, Newton D. Baker, who had been U.S. secretary of war during World War I, only four of the twelve members were active pilots. Lindbergh had been asked to serve but declined after his feud with Roosevelt, but Doolittle jumped at the chance to accomplish something constructive.

In the end he came away deeply disappointed. The majority report was openly antagonistic to the aviators, declaring that the notion that

---

* In his autobiography Rickenbacker implies that the hush order came from Roosevelt, but more likely it came from Rickenbacker's superiors at General Motors, including Pierre du Pont, who was heavily invested in the company. Like Rickenbacker, du Pont was horrified by Roosevelt's autocratic regime but acted out of fear for the company.

airpower could produce "decisive results" in war was "visionary"—in other words, unrealistic—and heaped scorn on those sounding alarms about the Air Service, stating, "The fear that has been cultivated in this country by various zealots that American aviation is inferior to that of the rest of the world is, as a whole, unfounded."* It went on to accuse those officers—presumably, Doolittle included—who wanted an air corps separate from the army, or even a separate budget, as "continuing agitation" and disturbing "harmonious development."[13]

Doolittle wrote an incisive, even eloquent, dissent or "minority statement," and said afterward that he was "disgusted" with the conclusion of the Baker Board. He told the newspapers, "The country will someday pay for the stupidities of those who were in the majority of this commission. They know as much about the future of aviation as they do about the sign writing of the Aztecs."

THE MID-1930S WAS A TENSE and unpleasant era for most Americans. The country remained in the grip of the Great Depression, which had dramatically lowered the living standard for all but a privileged few. By mid-decade it began to seem as if the paralytic malaise would linger forever. Money was tight; getting and keeping a job was difficult, impossible even, for some 15 to 20 percent of the working population. This of course had reduced government revenues, and President Roosevelt was putting so much money into relief and jobs programs there was relatively little left for the military, most especially the Air Service.

Meanwhile, in Germany, things had begun to brighten up, at least most Germans thought so. Adolf Hitler, an Aryan racist and odious provocateur against Jews and Slavs, had taken power as chancellor and imposed his Nazi brand of socialism on the nation.

At first it seemed to work. Germany suffered terribly following World War I and during the 1920s had undergone a period of hyperinflation that left the German mark virtually worthless. Hitler made numerous

---

* This was basically a slur aimed at Billy Mitchell and his lobbying but was also a slap at nearly every pilot in the Army Air Service.

vague promises and exuded an almost mystical confidence in himself, and in Germany's destiny, which proved irresistible to beleaguered voters. The fact that the Nazis were largely thugs did not seem to bother most Germans and, in a political contest that could almost be used as an argument against the concept of democracy, they voted Hitler into power, thereby unleashing a twelve-year-long reign of terror across Europe.

Hitler began by putting Germans back to work. A network of autobahns, or superhighways, was built throughout the country; the Germans built plants, mills, and car factories; they farmed, they exercised, they gave each other the *Heil Hitler* Nazi salute. But most of all they made weapons, because the leaders knew that the only way to pay for all that building was to conquer and rob their neighbors. Originally, Hitler's plan was to absorb Austria and a large part of Czechoslovakia, to occupy Poland and exile or exterminate the Poles, then turn on the Soviet Union, which at the time was plunged into the dark miseries of communism.

This was in order to provide Germany with what Hitler called lebensraum, or "living space," a dream of many Germans since the Middle Ages. Hitler had explained all these hostile ideas carefully in his book *Mein Kampf,* which he had written while in prison for treason, but few Germans had taken the time to read it carefully or understand its implications.

For the time being, most Germans were happy, possibly the happiest people in Europe, except perhaps for the Italians, whose trains were at last running on time thanks to Mussolini and his fascist Blackshirts. The Germans, at this point, had no idea that their great dream would become a national nightmare. All they knew was that Hitler had pulled them up from poverty and despair and eliminated the menace of communism.

Hitler took a keen military interest in airpower, because it now offered the threat of destroying entire cites from the air without the enormous casualties of a ground attack. He surrounded himself with such fops as Hermann Göring, a shrewd and often amusing World War I ace who had flown with the Richthofen bunch and was now a full field marshal in charge of the German air force. Having grown immensely fat since his flying days, Göring was fond of wearing ridiculous uniforms right out of *The Student Prince* but had in turn surrounded himself with stellar airmen such as Ernst Udet, another ace in the Great War, who had remained a staunch supporter of German aviation.

Under the terms of the Treaty of Versailles that ended World War I, Germany had been required to surrender some twenty thousand aircraft that it possessed at the end of the fighting, along with all other armaments and military equipment, the intention being that Germany would pose no further threat to the peace of Europe.

However, in the 1920s, a group of former German war pilots had secretly organized themselves into various "flying clubs" in which they not only trained young men how to operate their seemingly harmless civilian planes but also schooled them in military tactics, including simulated gunnery, pursuit, evasion, dive bombing, and other maneuvers. Thus, by the mid-1930s Hitler and Göring had a solid corps of trained aviators.

Though it was in flagrant violation of the terms of the peace treaty, the Germans began cranking out fighters and bombers at an estimated rate of three hundred per month. In 1933 Udet arrived in America to purchase two Curtiss Hawk fighter planes, which he said he intended to use to perform stunts at air shows.

Udet was a happy-go-lucky continental playboy who had been known during the war as the "wasp" for his habit of striking down at Allied planes alone and from above, but he had become known in social sets as the "flea," Doolittle said, "because of his habit of hopping gaily all over Europe." Udet was also one of the world's greatest fliers, fully in the league of Doolittle, Lindbergh, and Rickenbacker, and would soon be working hand-in-glove with Göring's Luftwaffe, designing and test flying warplanes and consulting at the highest levels, presently with the rank of full colonel.

He asked to test fly one of the planes before the purchase was closed, but Curtiss-Wright refused on grounds that the planes cost $15,000 apiece and couldn't risk a crack-up. The impasse was solved when Doolittle appeared on the scene and took one of the Hawks up for a spin. He performed some sleek aerobatics before putting the Hawk into a terrifyingly steep dive straight into the ground then zooming up at the last possible moment. That not only satisfied Udet, but the two men, who were about the same size and build, and born in the same year, quickly became fast friends.

In 1937 Doolittle went to Germany on Shell Oil business and was amazed to see troops of young boys in Nazi-like uniforms marching all over town singing Nazi songs. In Berlin he looked up Udet first thing and was given the royal treatment by the high-ranking Luftwaffe officer. Not only did Udet arrange for Doolittle to visit the large German aircraft plants, such as Junkers,* Heinkel, Dornier, Messerschmitt, and Focke-Wulf, he offered him a military aide and the use of his personal plane.

Doolittle was astounded by what he saw. The Germans were cranking out top-of-the-line fighters and bombers at an alarming rate. He was thoroughly impressed by the quality of the engines and airframes, which were decidedly better than those being manufactured in the United States. At least at that level, Hitler's socialism ensured a quality control and economy of labor that was superior to the more or less catch-as-catch-can American method of building planes. It was obvious to Doolittle that the manufacturing of so many warplanes could mean but one thing, that Germany was planning for war. But with whom and when?

Though he spent his days inspecting aircraft factories, Doolittle's evenings were spent with Udet, who remained an amusing bon vivant and daring pilot who looked on the Nazis with disdain, particularly Hitler and Göring. He was a kind of Renaissance man who spoke fluent English, recited poetry, sang well, and was an accomplished cartoonist. He was also a renowned marksman.

One night while they were drinking champagne in Udet's eclectically decorated apartment, Udet challenged Jimmy to a shooting match. When Doolittle asked where, Udet produced a steel box filled with sand that had a curved top, which deflected bullets down into the sand. He set it on the mantelpiece over the fireplace, and over it Udet hung up a paper target, handing Doolittle a powerful air pistol.

They both "had some pretty good shooting," Doolittle recalled, which apparently improved in direct relation to the amount of champagne they drank. As the night wore on, Udet decided that a greater challenge was needed. He handed Jimmy a huge .455-caliber pistol, much larger and more powerful than the U.S. standard-issue .45 automatics. Doolittle

---

* At the Junkers factory Doolittle was stunned to discover that the two Curtiss Hawks he had sold Udet had become the basis for the German Stuka dive-bomber that was presently destroying cities such as Guernica in the Spanish Civil War.

fired it with a terrific roar but, owing to its weight, shot low and into a stack of classified Luftwaffe papers that Udet had brought home to study.

Instead of being upset that the documents were blown all over the room, Udet seemed delighted, and he took the weapon from Doolittle to show him how it was done. But Udet himself misaimed, high, putting a hole in the wall that went all the way through to the next apartment, whose terrified occupants "could look right through at us," Doolittle remembered, "but they never said a word." Udet proceeded to fire another round, hitting the bull's-eye, and with that the shooting match was ended.

DOOLITTLE RETURNED TO THE STATES disturbed by what he had seen in Germany. It was obvious that Hitler should not be taken lightly, and that Germany must someday be reckoned with, but everywhere he went an odd air of complacency appeared to him to have affected political opinion. The unsatisfactory outcome of the previous war, with its horrendous casualties and destruction, had soured everyone except Hitler on the notion of further armed conflict. A League of Nations existed that was supposed to resolve international disagreements, and Britain and France, in particular, remained exhausted from the effects of World War I.

In early 1939 Jimmy again returned to Germany on Shell Oil business. By then Hitler had accomplished the opening acts of his new world order. He had absorbed Austria. He'd taken all of Czechoslovakia after persuading the British prime minister Neville Chamberlain at the Munich Conference that he had intended only to occupy a small, German-speaking portion of that nation. Chamberlain had returned to London and famously predicted "peace in our time," only to find himself now, a year later, grumbling that Hitler "was not keeping his word."

In the midst of this tense and disagreeable situation, Doolittle arrived in Frankfurt to find a marked change in the city, with "hundreds of uniformed men with swastika armbands and civilians with unsmiling faces on the streets and in the shops." There was an "ominous air of impending catastrophe," he said.

He stayed only a few days and did not go to Berlin, but he did find time to look up his good friend Ernst Udet, who by this time was a full major general in the Luftwaffe. Udet had likewise changed. "The old ebullience and grin and laugh were gone," Doolittle said. "He had difficulty remembering English words, and seemed much subdued." Udet did not offer him an escort this time, or allow him into military facilities, but he did take Doolittle to an air show in Frankfurt, Jimmy recalled, where he seemed "embarrassed to have me around." The show was confined entirely to military aircraft and tactics.

There was a grim sense of urgency everywhere Doolittle went. He managed to meet a few German pilots but their conversations, he said, were always "one-way." They asked questions about U.S. aircraft production, Doolittle remembered, with "an impudence bordering on rudeness," and "talked openly about a war in Europe."

Udet invited Jimmy to join him on a vacation he was taking in Munich, but "something told me," Doolittle said, "it was not the right thing to do." It was the last time he would see his old friend.

Doolittle stopped in London on his way home and visited the American embassy where he looked up the air attaché, Major Martin "Mike" Scanlon, whose lackadaisical attitude regarding the possibility of war was recorded by more than one observer. Scanlon was completely uninterested in hearing about the vast changes in Germany. "There's nothing I can do about it," Scanlon told him, suggesting to Jimmy that he tell his story to Hap Arnold when he got home, which is precisely what Doolittle did.

Arnold early on had been Jimmy's commanding officer at Rockwell Field and Doolittle had an extensive relationship with him. He was now the chief of the Air Corps with the rank of major general. Instead of going home to St. Louis, Jimmy went immediately to Washington when his ship landed in New York. He told Arnold he believed war in Europe was "inevitable" and offered to return to the service. Arnold knew it would mean a huge pay cut for Doolittle and the two agreed to leave the offer open.

Not long after, on September 1, 1939, Hitler attacked Poland with planes, tanks, and infantry. Two days after that Britain and France declared war on Germany. World War II had begun.

★ ★ ★ ★ ★

CHAPTER 8

I WAS SAVED FOR SOME GOOD PURPOSE

WHEN HE RETURNED TO THE UNITED STATES on February 1, 1919, Captain Eddie Rickenbacker was the highest decorated U.S. airman in World War I and, after Douglas MacArthur, the second highest decorated American soldier. In other words, he had become a household name.

He had won nine Distinguished Service Crosses, the nation's second highest award, one of which was later upgraded to the Medal of Honor. He held five French Croix de Guerre, the Distinguished Service Medal, and numerous other military honors.

After hostilities ceased on November 11, 1918, the 94th Aero Pursuit Squadron had been detailed by General Billy Mitchell as part of the Allied Army Occupation of Germany, and Eddie had been looking forward to some sightseeing in the land that had been the cause of so much grief. That opportunity was short-lived, however, for after several weeks in the German city of Koblenz he received notice from Washington that his services as a war hero were required back in the United States to kick off the fifth Liberty Loan drive that was being put on by the War Department.

With all the strain of war, and then the jubilation at the Armistice, Eddie was just beginning to wonder about what he would do for the rest of his life. There was no doubt it would have something to do with aviation. He was a master of the sky, as skilled as anyone, and could see a great future for airpower, both military and civilian. He conceived a scheme with Captain Reed Chambers, his friend and squadron mate, to persuade the army to sponsor a cross-Atlantic flight that they were convinced would open the public's mind to the value of aviation.

Meanwhile, Eddie had some free time before his orders sent him back to America. He played Santa Claus for a group of the 94th's enlisted men, who presented him with a silver cup at their Christmas Day dinner, a gay affair punctuated by the consumption of a great deal of wine, beer, and "punch." He also met and began a lifelong friendship with the Hearst newspaper corporation's star reporter Damon Runyon, who had been covering the war. And he met an unusual man named Laurence La Tourette Driggs, who would cowrite Eddie's popular autobiographical book *Fighting the Flying Circus,* published the following year. Driggs was a ubiquitous sort. The son of a wealthy Oregon lumberman, he was a lawyer, a politician, and an accomplished writer, who had once almost joined the Army Air Service as a colonel in charge of a group of rich young aviators before the idea was shot down by President Woodrow Wilson for petty political reasons. Driggs nonetheless made his way across the Atlantic under the aegis of the press baron Alfred C. W. Harmsworth, Viscount Northcliffe, who was England's minister of information. As an observer and "special correspondent," Driggs was given wide access to the Allied military units and some months earlier had befriended Rickenbacker. Early on, Eddie lent Driggs his diary, and after hostilities ceased he dictated about 140 single-spaced pages, his account of flying with the Hat in the Ring squadron.

On the day after Christmas, Eddie began preparing for his trip home. One of his unhappiest moments was parting with his German shepherd Spad. It was simply too difficult to bring the dog back to America, especially since Eddie was going first to Paris and then to England, which had strict animal-entry laws. He'd made arrangements for Spad, but the night he started packing for Paris Eddie said Spad "knew something was happening, knew I was leaving because he hung around and cried and licked my hand and whined."[1]

Eddie's first stop was Paris, where he and friends would visit old haunts such as Ciro's, and the Folies Bergère, then on to London for a few days, where he intended to retrieve his briefcase and the engineering designs that

Scotland Yard had confiscated in the spy fiasco of 1916. After the satchel and papers were returned, he went to Liverpool to board the White Star liner *Adriatic,* but not before searching around for the insufferable long-nosed Scotland Yard sergeant who had treated him so shabbily when he'd tried to come ashore to work for the Sunbeam company.

The sergeant soon appeared with his usual disdainful countenance, and Rickenbacker marched right up to him and the man got a load of the rows of ribbons on his dress uniform. Fairly wallowing in the sergeant's oily supplications of apology, Rickenbacker later said that it "made up to some extent for all the browbeating and insults heaped on my shoulders by the Scotland Yard boys."[2]

It was an uneventful crossing. When newspaper reporters aboard ship asked what he would be doing when he returned to the States, Eddie told them he wanted to educate Americans about the possibilities of airpower. "America's future depends on its air service," he told them. There was also a rumor that he would start a military flying school, similar to West Point or Annapolis.[3]

Eddie arrived just in time for the new Prohibition law that had been enacted two weeks earlier (which wouldn't go into effect until the following year). The ship actually arrived at the army docks in Hoboken the night of January 31, but Rickenbacker had been ordered not to disembark until the following morning.

As he walked down the gangplank Rickenbacker noticed that there were no throngs of reporters, and when he reached the pier a lieutenant came up and said, "Captain Rickenbacker, report to the provost marshal's office!"[4] Wondering what he might have done wrong, Eddie followed the lieutenant across the yard from the docks to a building and, when the lieutenant opened the door, he entered a room to find—his mother, Elizabeth, who rushed into his arms to the great flashing of photographers' powder pans and the happy smile of General Charles T. Menoher, the perfect photo op for the army public relations office.

Rickenbacker checked into the Plaza Hotel, soon to gain notoriety for its role in Fitzgerald's novel *The Great Gatsby,* and after a two-day reunion with his mother he attended the first of many opulent dinner banquets that would honor him as the country's hero. The affair was held in the ballroom of the Waldorf Astoria, sponsored by the American Automobile

Association, which, it was rumored, had offered Rickenbacker $200,000 to return to racing.

Among the many dignitaries at the event were the chairman of the House Ways and Means Committee, Clifford Ireland, who was toastmaster, and U.S. Secretary of War Newton Baker, the same Newton Baker who would later chair the committee that so disparaged the military aviation enthusiasts and left Jimmy Doolittle "disgusted."

Baker inappropriately used his time at the podium to deny charges that corruption and chicanery were behind the regrettable fact that not a single airplane flown by U.S. fliers during the war had come from an American factory. Rickenbacker agreed, believing instead that the cause was "lack of foresight and mis-management,"[5] but judiciously kept his counsel.

At the conclusion of a lengthy oration by Princeton University's Dr. Henry van Dyke, Eddie was presented with a set of gold flier's wings, bejeweled with diamonds and sapphires, after which he was expected to respond. "I have never known such a moment of helplessness," he wrote later. "I became frightened and embarrassed."

As he stood at the dais in a near defenseless panic, Rickenbacker spied his mother, described by a reporter as "a beaming little women in black silk whose eyes shone proudly through gold-rimmed spectacles,"[6] and his sister, Emma, sitting in the gallery. In a moment of sudden inspiration, he held up the golden wings toward them and cried, "For you, Mother!"

It brought down the house. There was an instantaneous standing ovation. Some women began to weep. Men shouted patriotic slogans. There was the roar of applause and people pounding furiously on the floor with their walking sticks. When the crowd had calmed down Eddie made some awkward, off-the-cuff remarks—namely about the possibility of transatlantic flight—and sat down, supremely self-conscious that anything he said paled in comparison to the elegant orations of Dr. van Dyke.

At one point Eddie engaged Newton Baker, whom he was seated next to, in conversation about his and Reed Chambers's notion of having the army sponsor a transatlantic flight, but the secretary of war would have none of it and brushed off the idea as a waste of time, or as Rickenbacker put it later, "indicated that he couldn't care less."

However, among the spontaneous remarks Eddie made that night was a statement that he "envisioned a future in which aircraft would link the world's peoples in peace." This notion may have left a special impression on one of the dinner guests, the rich French-born hotel owner Raymond Orteig, because only a few months afterward, in May of 1919, he would announce the offer of a $25,000 prize for the first person or persons to fly nonstop between New York and Paris.

Rickenbacker next traveled to Washington, D.C., where he was given a standing ovation in the House of Representatives. But he spent a fruitless week there, buttonholing anyone who would listen about the sorry state of American aviation, and that England, France—even Italy—were far superior in planes and pilots to the United States. Nobody was interested in Eddie's cross-Atlantic proposal except Billy Mitchell, but Mitchell did not have the authority to go forward with such an expensive proposition. The day before he left, Rickenbacker was made guest of honor at a tea party given by a rich Washington society matron, an experience he afterward described as "worse than an engagement with seven Fokkers."[7]

His hometown, Columbus, awaited Rickenbacker with an enormous celebration and automobile parade and official welcome by the governor of Ohio. Some extent of his notoriety can be gauged by the fact that while on the train, even in his private compartment, he was compelled to sign scores of one-dollar bills for souvenir-seeking passengers, excited to be on the same train with the great war hero.

Rickenbacker soon returned to New York to become featured speaker on the Liberty Loan bond tour—the government still needed to pay for the war. He was embarrassed, however, at the quality of his speech and his poor delivery and so turned to his friend Damon Runyon, who had returned from overseas to the city he had deemed "Baghdad on the Hudson" and resumed covering shady characters around Broadway for the Hearst newspaper corporation. After Runyon finished redoing the speech, Eddie was completely satisfied but still worried that his delivery left much to be desired.

Runyon tried to instruct him in the art of public speaking but soon gave up and sent Rickenbacker to an elocution instructor at the Metropolitan Opera House, one Madame Amanda by name, a stout woman who put him on the stage, while she hovered in the upper balcony—which she called the "chicken roost." He was instructed to yell his speech up to her, and she would shout instructions down to him. "Louder!" she would holler. "Raise your right arm! . . . Raise your left arm! . . . Look up!" At Madame Amanda's suggestion he purchased the book *Modern Eloquence* and later picked up a copy of Emily Post's book on etiquette.

The bond tour opened in Boston's Symphony Hall before six thousand people, hosted by the governor of Massachusetts, Calvin "Silent Cal" Coolidge, whose voice was so thin and irritating, Rickenbacker said, that when it came his own turn to talk it made him feel like he was Daniel Webster.

The tour, which lasted through May, was generally a success and it introduced Eddie to great numbers of Americans, some of whom were substantial people, such as Orville Wright, whom Eddie met when he spoke in Dayton, Ohio. In his speeches, Eddie made glowing predictions about long-distance air travel in America and abroad, where trips that now took days or even weeks would be reduced to a matter of hours. Airplanes would one day seat hundreds of people and have salons; he said they would travel thousands of miles, and would be safe, with "wireless controlled compasses."[8]

The tour's schedule was grueling—seven days a week, each day in a different town—and toward the end it began wearing him down. Eddie lost his voice, and became weak and tired, but he emerged from his final performance in Toledo as an accomplished public speaker. At the same time, he reentered the population as a civilian, the army having finished with him after promoting him to major.*

Likewise, he emerged as one of the nation's greatest socializers and lodgemen, having been tapped in towns and cities across the land as an honorary member of just about every men's organization in the country: the Loyal Orders of Lions, Moose, Elk, Owls, and Eagles, the Independent Order of Odd Fellows, the Sons of Norway, the Knights of Pythias, the Woodmen of the World, the Shriners, the Sons of the Golden West, the Little Men's Chowder and Marching Society, and so on. Furthermore, he had amassed enough keys to the city to start a respectable collection, but it was more than just the beginning of a long career of speechmaking by Eddie Rickenbacker. It was the start of a new chapter in his eventful

---

* Rickenbacker didn't like the ring of "major" and was always "Captain Eddie" throughout his long career.

life in which he began to understand that he was no longer merely good ole Eddie Rickenbacker, death-defying car driver and army aviator. He had become venerable, a man of substance, and a man to whom people deferred, whose opinion would often be sought on lofty national issues. He had been suddenly pitchforked into popular greatness.

IT CAME TO HIM IN THE DESERT, he said, the notion of manufacturing a high-end automobile. He had visited the Arizona desert in a get-back-to-nature mood and camped out for days at a stretch. The car would be called the "Rickenbacker," and feature all the newest innovations. He had a picture of it in his mind, and an idea of where he could get financing. After the bond drive he'd gone to Arizona to clear his senses and get out into the open spaces, he said, which was when the concept of the car began to jell.

Afterward, Rickenbacker attended the 1919 Indianapolis 500 and sat in the stands despite the AAA's strenuous attempts to get him back on the racing circuit. There he witnessed a bloody and disquieting afternoon in which two drivers and a mechanic drove to their deaths, alleviating any regrets he might have felt over his retirement from auto racing.

In the meanwhile, Rickenbacker was continuously besieged by promoters who offered enormous sums of money to endorse their products—"cigarettes, chewing gum, wearing apparel." Publishers pushed to have their ghostwriters tell his story. Hollywood producers loitered around with fantastic offers, the most brazen of whom, Eddie said, was Carl Laemmle of Universal Pictures. Along with his whiz-kid assistant Irving Thalberg, Laemmle shadowed Eddie throughout the bond tour, "booking compartments next to mine on trains and rooms next to mine in hotels," he said. "On one occasion he [Laemmle] produced a certified check for $100,000 made out to me!" Rickenbacker remembered.

He turned it all down, of course, unwilling to cash in on his honest fame, which was all the more honorable considering that Eddie was about out of money. Much of what he had accumulated during his racing days had been spent or was given to his mother to raise the family. He wasn't particularly worried; anybody in the country would buy a meal and a drink for Eddie Rickenbacker, and many opportunities had come his way. But he was savvy enough to know that, whatever he did, his name and reputation would be heavily associated with it.

He investigated a career in aviation manufacturing but the war had flooded the market with thousands of army surplus Jennys, the Curtiss JN-4 training plane, and other warplanes that were produced but never made it to France. There were in fact enough of these planes at cheap prices to glut the market for years. It became apparent that making a proper living in aviation at that time would be difficult. There was no commercial aspect to speak of yet, and barnstorming or taking up passengers for rides was both iffy and risky. Curtiss offered Rickenbacker a steady job selling airplanes but he didn't want it; something didn't seem quite right.

Eddie had important contacts through the racing world, and he tapped an auto man named Harry Cunningham, who persuaded three investors to put up $200,000 for development of the Rickenbacker automobile. Soon several models were on the drawing boards at the Rickenbacker Motor Company in a factory building in Detroit and a prototype was in the works.

The new company was aiming at a car in the $1,500 to $2,000 bracket, well beyond the $500 Ford Model T, but not quite so pricey as a Packard or Cadillac. According to Eddie, it would be tailored to the "white collar worker, junior executive, the fairly prosperous farmer and the woman of taste." Eddie wanted an innovative car with brakes on all four wheels, instead of the usual two, which Eddie considered safer,* a high compression motor, a low center of gravity, and a crankshaft with flywheels at both ends to reduce vibration. Somebody came up with a splendid slogan: "A Car Worthy of Its Name."

Meantime, in Detroit, Eddie oversaw production and test-drove the Rickenbacker prototypes, and in the autumn of 1921 Rickenbacker Motors made an initial public stock offering that sold $5 million worth of shares, which the company used to buy the factory building and begin production.† Eddie and his partners retained 25 percent of the business.

---

* Four-wheel braking was not incorporated in the final design because engineers agreed it was a little "too innovative."

† About $63 million today.

There were three models, initially: a coupe, a touring car, and a sedan. These were on gleaming display at the 1921 New York Automobile Show, a huge event attended by dealers nationwide. Adorning the polished chrome radiator of each Rickenbacker car was the insignia of the Hat in the Ring squadron. Orders "flooded in."[9]

As it happened, the floral arrangements for the Rickenbacker display on the third floor of the Grand Central Palace on Lexington Avenue had been done by an acquaintance of Eddie's, the beautiful and graceful Adelaide Durant, who had married, and recently divorced, a wealthy sometime race car driver who was the ne'er-do-well son of the founder of General Motors. Eddie had known the couple in California and was delighted to renew the friendship with Adelaide, who had left an indelible impression on him when they first met several years before the war.

Rickenbacker had generally steered clear of women since he got back to the States. But his handsome photograph was plastered in all the newspapers with rows of ribbons, high, polished boots, and the Sam Browne belt and he became, for better or worse, the object of constant approaches by females, ranging from the higher classes to those of indifferent virtue, many of whom sent him mash notes, called him on the phone, and even lay in wait for him outside hotels when it was announced he was in town. But Eddie understood, almost to the point of being self-conscious, that he now represented not just the army flying service, or even the U.S. Army itself, but the entire United States before the world, and had thus best put up a proper front.

He had a brief fling with a girl named Dorothy Bill, the daughter of a well-to-do Connecticut family, whom he had met on a lengthy train ride through Canada. But as a romance it slowly fizzled out. He also had a rapport with a popular actress and entertainer named Elsie Janis, whom he had met on his way home in London, where she was raising the morale of U.S. soldiers in a hit show called *Hello America*. He renewed the relationship five months later, on June 3, 1919, by escorting Elsie to the elegant Farewell Dinner of the 94th Aero Pursuit Squadron at the Commodore Hotel in New York City. Rumors soon abounded of their impending marriage, but the relationship went nowhere when she turned out to be a lesbian.[10]

Adelaide Frost was raised in comfortable circumstances in Grand Rapids, Michigan, the daughter of a wholesale grocer. She was noticed by Cliff Durant while singing in a cabaret, and they married in 1911. The couple lived on a luxurious estate near San Francisco with the finest of everything, but Durant was "a heavy drinker and womanizer . . . [and] Adelaide's life with him was marred by physical abuse and his extramarital affairs." She was said to have had a number of miscarriages and ultimately a hysterectomy to avoid the chance of having children with a man such as her husband.[11]

A divorce decree was granted in 1921, on grounds of "extreme cruelty." She moved around with a girlfriend for a while and took a lengthy tour of Europe and North Africa courtesy of $250,000 worth of gifts and trust funds lavished upon her by her former father-in-law, William C. Durant, the General Motors magnate, in gratitude, he said, "for doing her best in a lost cause."[12]

She had only recently returned and was staying in New York, where it was said that her "money, charm, and beauty, made her a much sought after figure in the social circles." Rickenbacker ran into her while she was on a shopping spree in Manhattan and invited her to dinner. After they'd renewed their acquaintance, and she agreed to do the flowers for the automobile exhibition, a courting period began. Eddie was living in Detroit and working closely with Rickenbacker Motors now, but he used every possible opportunity to travel to New York. He began sending her a dozen red roses in advance of his visits and soon started buying her jewelry. After they had spent the 1921 New Year's Eve together, he told her, "I can't keep making excuses for coming to New York on business . . . so you'd better marry me or come to Detroit," he said.[13]

Adelaide agreed to do both, but soon an "avalanche" of unseemly and mean-spirited gossip in the newspapers staggered them. Like Lindbergh, Rickenbacker was learning the downside of being famous. The couple couldn't be married until Adelaide's divorce was final, which occurred in July 1922. They were married privately on September 16 of that year, in an Episcopal church in Greenwich, Connecticut, with only a handful of witnesses. Assisting the Episcopal priest at the wedding was the Lutheran minister Jacob Pister, who had baptized and confirmed Eddie back in Columbus. Immediately after the ceremony they went aboard the White Star liner *Majestic* for an extensive European honeymoon. Rickenbacker, who was thirty-one years old and beginning to go bald, later described it as the happiest day of his life.

Aboard ship during the six-day voyage, Eddie was able to relax for the first time in his memory. He and Adelaide were, in his words, "the laziest people on board," sleeping late in the morning and lounging in deck chairs or strolling the decks, nodding and smiling at the other passengers, who gawked at them as if they were royalty or movie stars.

Paris became their home base. From there they visited the battlefields of the Argonne Forest, above which Eddie had prevailed in so many deadly encounters. The war was four years past but the haunting desolation of the battlefields was a stark reminder of the tragedy. At Verdun everything was still in ruins and the Rickenbackers saw horrifying piles of skulls and bones that were destined for the new marble and granite ossuary at Fort Douaumont. This enormous tower contains the skeletal remains of at least 130,000 soldiers whose bones were picked up on the battlefield after the war but whose identities remain unknown.

They drove to Toul to pay their respects at the little cemetery on the hill where Lufbery and a dozen other friends were buried, only to find the caskets had been removed and the place turned into a rifle range for the French army. This put Rickenbacker in a wrathful mood, and that night he raged against "statesmen" and governments, who start wars where other people suffer but who never suffer themselves. "The fallacy of war is livid," he wrote, "and I am certain though I may never live to see the day, when instead of people being the *victims* of government, statesmen and government will be their victims."

They took a night sleeper train to Berlin on October 2 after Eddie had balked at paying 500 francs for airfare, but it was cold and uncomfortable and the customs agents kept waking them up at all hours. In the morning they arose to find themselves in Germany, passing through a region of neat, autumnal farm fields and houses, which looked prosperous and undisturbed because the war had never reached that far into Germany. But the impression was illusory.

As they exchanged their American dollars for German marks they discovered that the horrendous hyperinflation they had heard about was far worse than they'd imagined. Their large suite in a luxury hotel cost 14,000 marks—about $8.50 when, before the war, a mark had been roughly on par with the dollar. At dinner, Eddie tipped the waiters what he thought was about $3 apiece but, after recalculating the ever changing exchange rate, it turned out to be only six cents. He rectified the mistake, and later wrote that the Germans themselves were in complete shock and disbelief at what was happening to them.

The Weimar government, set up at the insistence of the Allies, seemed helpless and hapless against the financial onslaught. The war had prostrated Germany, and Eddie remarked on the numbers of undernourished children in rags and without soles on their shoes. In the end, people were actually burning German banknotes in their stoves to keep warm because the money was so nearly valueless. Ultimately it was this economic tragedy that created the atmosphere into which Hitler emerged with his peculiar friends and ideas.

Eddie visited German automobile showrooms, which seemed shoddy, and the cars were "too high and heavy," old-fashioned and uninspired. Adelaide was bored because there was no place worth shopping. They had been there only a day, and were intending to leave, when Eddie had a surprising visitor.

It was Ernst Udet, the German Ace of Aces, who had learned that Rickenbacker was in town and sought him out with an invitation to dinner with a group of German fighter pilots, among whom were Hermann Göring and Erhard Milch who, along with Udet, would one day rise to the very top of the Nazi regime. "Naturally I accepted," Rickenbacker said.

Dinner was in a secret room under a small café. Eddie was introduced to about a dozen of the German airmen but only Udet, Göring, and Milch spoke English. Milch "was on the slender side; he was dignified and well educated."* Udet, according to Eddie, was "short, stocky and jovial." Göring, who had commanded the Flying Circus after the death of von Richthofen, was conspicuously in charge. "He was then a fine figure of a man, positive and dedicated to the rebirth of the fatherland," Eddie would write.

Göring became expansive as the wine and the evening wore on and they reminisced about the war. Then, surprisingly, Göring laid out a

---

* Milch walked a tightrope during the Hitler regime, since his father's parents were Jewish, but he was a favorite of Göring, who had Milch's mother produce a certificate saying that his father was not actually the sire of the child. "It is I," Göring famously said, "who decides who is a Jew."

chilling blueprint for the resurrection of a rearmed imperial Germany.

"Our whole future is in the air," Göring said, as Rickenbacker recalled, in his harsh, guttural accent. "It is by airpower that we are going to recapture the German Empire. To accomplish this, we will do three things. First, we will teach gliding as a sport to all our young men. Then we will build up a fleet of commercial planes, each easily converted to military operation. Finally we will create the skeleton of a military air force. When the time comes, we will put all three together—and the German Empire will be reborn. We must win through the air."

As astounding as this information was, the conversation ended on a cordial note, as Udet and Milch each weighed in on the need to save Germany from its current plight.

Next day Eddie and Adelaide returned to Paris for a breath of fresh air at the horse track at Longchamp with Mr. and Mrs. Harry Crosby. Crosby was an alcoholic pervert and scapegrace son of a Boston Brahmin family, but in the meantime he was also a brilliant editor, poet, and founder, along with his wife, of the notable Black Sun Press, which published among others James Joyce, Ernest Hemingway, and Ezra Pound.* Heaven knows how the Rickenbackers got mixed up with that outlandish couple—history doesn't tell us—but the Crosbys must have been on their better behavior that day because Eddie found the encounter pleasant. Next day they went out to Le Bourget, which Eddie described as the "finest airport he had ever seen."[14] It was just then under construction and Eddie was stunned by the size and concept of the project, with its capacious runways and row after row of enormous hangars, interspersed by offices, warehouses, baggage rooms, and a plush new hotel for passengers arriving on commercial airliners from Amsterdam, Brussels, and London. There was nothing remotely like it in the United States.

Toward the end of October the Rickenbackers embarked on the remainder of the Grand Tour, hitting Nice, Monaco, Rome, and Naples in a chauffeured Packard, and returning by Florence, Venice, Turin,

---

* Crosby and his wife, the former Polly Peabody, scandalized Boston from the time of their marriage in 1922 until his death seven years later in a murder-suicide pact with another man's wife in New York City.

Avignon, and Lyon. Adelaide did so much shopping it was said that their excess baggage amounted to well over a thousand pounds on the flight from Paris to London. In Naples they had a glimpse of the future when thousands of armed Blackshirts began to assemble for Mussolini's victorious "March on Rome."

In London, on November 11, 1922, the celebration of the fourth anniversary of Armistice Day included a splendid formal dinner and dance at the Savoy, where the Rickenbackers were staying. Eddie never did learn to dance very well, though he had taken lessons in New York at a dance studio for several months after his return from the war. "He knew the two-step," Adelaide said, "and then one step back. That was about it." Eddie was reminded of the time he stayed at the Savoy in 1916, and he stood at the window watching squadron after squadron of British warplanes flying over the Thames.

During their last days in Paris there were auto and air shows to attend and at last, on November 22, the Rickenbackers boarded the *Majestic* for the seven-day voyage home, with Hermann Göring's threatening concept of a rearmed Germany still ringing in Eddie's ears. During the voyage he sketched out a design he thought of as the Rickenbacker Plan for World Peace, which he took to Washington at the first opportunity and gave to various politicians he had met after the war and on his speaking tour.

Rickenbacker deplored the poverty in Germany and concluded it could lead to no good end, so the first part of his proposal was for a reduction in the amount of the German indemnity for the war forced on her at the Versailles Conference, as well as an extension of the terms that would "make it possible for her to pay the balance." The second part of the plan consisted of a bridge loan from the U.S. government that would allow Germany to meet her immediate indemnity payments, as well as "stabilize the government and get the currency on a firm basis."

He saw it as a no-lose scheme that would allow Germany to repay the European Allies, which, in turn, would allow them to repay the war loans made to them by the United States, so that "it would be merely a matter of bookkeeping," and everyone would settle up and live happily ever after. He released this manifesto to the press, which gave it widespread coverage, but that's where the matter ended. Nobody in Congress wanted to fool with it and the general public didn't care. The war was over and Europe was a long way off.

When the Rickenbackers returned to Detroit they moved into an apartment at Indian Village Manor, an exclusive new building overlooking the Detroit River and Lake St. Clair. There, with the antique furnishings and artwork she had purchased in Europe, Adelaide created a tasteful and sumptuous home for dinner parties and other obligations of an automotive company executive.

Eddie had taken the position of vice president in charge of sales for the Rickenbacker Motor Company. He took his work seriously, and soon the company had some five hundred dealers in the United States and about three hundred abroad. Profits were steady, if not huge, but the company paid dividends, increased its stock issue, and by the end of 1923 reported a profit of $511,060.[15] Then, to his eternal regret, Eddie pressured the directors to include four-wheel braking on all models for the next year.

The system had been considered too innovative for the first models, but Eddie had driven the European race cars that used it and insisted they were the wave of the future. Unfortunately, all he did was set a trap for himself.

Rickenbacker Motors announced with great fanfare and a national advertising campaign that its 1924 automobiles would include a reliable, state-of-the-art, four-wheel braking system. This caught the other auto companies by surprise, because they had large inventories of cars and it was too late for them to change for the model year.

Their response to the Rickenbacker announcement was immediate and devastating. Led by the prominent automaker Studebaker, full-page ads were taken out charging that the four-wheel braking system offered by Rickenbacker was inherently unfeasible and unsafe. In rain, these rival attack ads claimed, the brakes would cause a car to skid out of control. Further, the ads said that oftentimes the front-wheel brakes would lock up and hurl the passengers into (or through) the windshield. Also, it was widely suspected by many Rickenbacker dealers that these same competitors had backed a whispering campaign* to start rumors that a

---

* Illegal even then, whispering campaigns, complete with paid rumormongers, were often used in the early twentieth century to help put competitors out of business.

huge number of accidents, many with broken necks and other terrible injuries, were being kept out of the papers by Rickenbacker bribes.[16]

Here was the dilemma Rickenbacker Motors was caught in: even though the unfavorable publicity was affecting sales, the company couldn't go back to two-wheel brakes after making its announcement of the superiority of four-wheel brakes. All the company could do was hunker down and try to move the cars they had.

At the same time, in 1925 the American economy went into recession. Many of the Rickenbacker dealers were going broke, and Eddie put all of his own considerable savings into shoring them up. Then he borrowed more from banks or got credit from suppliers.

But the recession became worse. One of the directors of the company, a man respected for his knowledge and wisdom, was killed in a car accident. The company stock dropped. Then a new competing automobile appeared, a Chrysler, with a fashionable design, dependable engineering, and a reasonable price. There were more than one hundred U.S. automakers in the 1920s, and dozens of them foundered, including, at last, Rickenbacker Motors. The owners began quarreling among themselves and Eddie resigned his position as vice president, hoping that might inspire some miracle that would bring the company back.

In 1927 the Rickenbacker corporation filed for bankruptcy. Eddie was thirty-six years old, broke, unemployed, and $250,000 in debt. It is the ultimate measure of a man what he does under tremendously adverse circumstances such as these, and Rickenbacker was no piker. Friends advised him to file for personal bankruptcy, but he would have none of it. His own words bear repeating: "I owed the money, and I would pay it back if I had to work like a dog to do it. I was not ashamed and not afraid. Failure was something I had faced before and might well face again. I have said it over and over: 'Failure' is the greatest word in the English language. Here in America failure is not the end of the world. If you have determination, you can come back from failure and succeed."

It was certainly a test of Rickenbacker's character. He was a man of his times, and of his country. He had come up from nothing, an immigrant family's child of the streets who'd sold rags and bones at the age of six and climbed up the ladder, rung by greasy rung, a Horatio Alger story without the pervasive helping hand. Though he couldn't know it then, his severest trials lay in the future, with only the barest hank of hair or piece of bone between himself and eternity. Without a winning mind-set such as he had, Eddie Rickenbacker never would have made it.

IN THE MEANTIME a showdown was brewing in the court-martial of General Billy Mitchell. Mitchell had accused the Army Air Service hierarchy of behavior that was in his estimation criminal in its neglect of planes and pilot training. He reasserted his demands for a separate air force—or at least one that was controlled by flying officers—ideas that did not sit well with the twelve generals who sat on the court-martial jury, including General Douglas MacArthur, who thought Mitchell was insubordinate.

The highlight of the trial came when Rickenbacker, who had once been Mitchell's driver in France—and was still the most famous airman in America—took the oath to testify in Mitchell's behalf. As the final witness in the trial, he told the court that the United States ranked an embarrassing seventh in aviation power, behind France, England, Italy, Germany, Russia, and Japan. He had some sharp clashes with the court-martial officers, including Major General Hugh A. Drum, who insisted to Rickenbacker that he could defend Washington with a dozen antiaircraft guns.

Eddie responded with a tirade, pointing out that when the United States entered World War I there was no American aircraft industry, and that hundreds of pilots lost their lives needlessly flying obsolete foreign planes. He excoriated the military brass for denying pilots parachutes in the war.

"This nation owes General Mitchell a debt of gratitude," he told the court, "for daring to speak the truth. He learned his lesson from the only true teacher—experience. It is pathetic to think that military leaders can destroy the life of a man who has done us the service Mitchell has . . . It is a crime against posterity. This nation will pay the price of its selfishness. Not perhaps in this generation, but in that of the boys who are growing up today, or their sons." In the end it all came to naught. Billy Mitchell was found guilty of conduct prejudicial to the military service and suspended from active duty for five years without pay. "I might as well have been talking to a stone wall," Rickenbacker said bitterly.

EDDIE RETURNED FROM THE TRIAL to the cutthroat world of big business with a splash. The first thing he did was to buy the Indianapolis Speedway, home of the Indianapolis 500.

Of course it wasn't quite as simple as that. But Eddie's very name was leverage. He had investigated buying a small company in Indianapolis, Allison Engineering, which manufactured auto and airplane parts, but its owner, who was also looking to sell the Speedway, talked Eddie into buying it instead of the engineering plant. It hadn't taken much talking. Eddie had many fond memories of his glory days on that track, and the alternative was that the property—which was now surrounded by the fast-growing city—would have been broken up and sold off in real estate parcels.

A banker acquaintance of Eddie's in Detroit had told him after the bankruptcy of Rickenbacker Motors that if he ever had a business proposition to come to him with it for financing. Eddie had been profoundly grateful that such an offer had been made when he was broke, unemployed, and deeply in debt. Now Rickenbacker went to him with a plan to finance the Indianapolis 500. The bank floated a $700,000 bond issue—the purchase price for the property—and within a few months Rickenbacker held a 51 percent interest in the Indianapolis Speedway, with the bank holding the other 49 percent as its fee. He was back in business.

First off, Eddie resurfaced the track, putting asphalt over the old bricks of what is still known in car racing circles as the Brickyard, making it smoother and safer. Since the race was only a one-day-a-year event, he added an eighteen-hole golf course to generate more revenue. Moreover, he persuaded the National Broadcasting Company to begin airing the entire race on its nationwide radio network—a huge coup.

Still, Rickenbacker needed more income to pay off his creditors, so he took a job at General Motors for $12,000 a year as vice president for sales, promoting and publicizing the company's LaSalle and Cadillac brands. He put a man in charge of the Speedway operation in Indianapolis, and GM agreed that he could have a leave of absence during the month of May when the Indianapolis 500 was held.

The job with GM necessitated working out of New York City, where Eddie purchased a comfortable, rambling home in Bronxville, an affluent suburb in Westchester County. He needed the space because by now he was the father of two young boys, William Frost, age one, and David

Edward, three. Adelaide and Eddie had adopted them, since she could no longer have children of her own.

In May 1927 Charles Lindbergh stunned the world when he flew nonstop between New York and Paris, landing in the dark at Le Bourget airport, which had so impressed Rickenbacker when he'd visited there in 1922. Eddie was just as excited by the feat as everyone else, but he also realized he himself was no longer the most famous airman in America.

As usual, Eddie took his work at GM very seriously, as he had when he commanded the 94th Aero Squadron. Rickenbacker refused to sit behind a desk, instead traveling into the field visiting hundreds of dealerships throughout the country. Once he called on seventy-one different dealers in eighty-one days. After Eddie had made an assessment of an operation, he would call the entire workforce together and harangue them with lengthy motivational speeches offering encouragement, criticism, and advice. In the end he recommended to GM that it discontinue its LaSalle model—not that there was anything wrong with it—because it was competing against its own Cadillac brand. Next season, LaSalle was no more.

Meanwhile, using leverage again to do a deal, Rickenbacker at last purchased Allison Engineering, and soon he sold it to GM, pocketing a tidy sum, most of which went to reduce the notes to his creditors.

In June of 1929 GM bought the Fokker Aircraft Company, which was connected to Trans World Airlines, and Eddie was asked to be vice president in charge of sales. It seemed ironic that he would now be working for the same outfit that built airplanes that had tried so hard to kill him, but he accepted. It was the end of his affiliation with the auto industry and the beginning of an illustrious career in commercial aviation.

By now Fokker was building large passenger planes. It had introduced the famous Fokker trimotor F-10 in the mid-1920s and was now producing a four-engine plane, the F-32, which had "an unfortunate habit of blowing the cylinder heads off." When this happened, Rickenbacker said, the huge cylinder head, or part of it, would fly back into the rear engine, "which would throw it in any direction." A friend of Eddie's told of the time he was enjoying a flight between San Francisco and L.A. when the cylinder crashed through the window by his seat, flew past his nose and out the other window, and smashed into the opposite engine. These were the kinds of things that needed to be dealt with.

During his time at Fokker Eddie acquired the Pioneer Instrument Company, which would be so beneficial to Jimmy Doolittle's blind-flying experiment with the Guggenheim fund. When news of Doolittle's perfect blind flight broke into the headlines later that same year, Rickenbacker, perhaps more than anyone else, knew what a godsend it would be for commercial aviation. At last airlines could adhere to firm schedules, without fear of fog and storms.

In the autumn of 1929 the stock market crashed. Especially hard hit were the automotive and aviation industries. Since no one had lived through anything like it before, or ever heard tell about such a thing, no one knew what to do or how long it would last.

Amid the gloom, the War Department announced on July 14, 1930, that Eddie Rickenbacker would be awarded the Medal of Honor, "For conspicuous gallantry and intrepidity above and beyond the call of duty in action against the enemy near Billy, France, September 25, 1918." The citation referred to his first day as commanding officer of the 94th Aero Pursuit Squadron when, flying alone over enemy territory, he took on seven German planes—five Fokkers and two Halberstadt photography aircraft—shooting down two and causing the others to flee.

This honor had been initiated several years earlier by a Michigan congressman, Robert Clancy, and was supported by everyone from Rickenbacker's squadronmates from the Hat in the Ring gang to Charles Lindbergh, who had also received the award.

It had been opposed, however, by prohibitionists in the Senate, who pointed to newspaper stories revealing Eddie's penchant for flouting the Volstead Act by having cocktails, and also by high-ranking staff members in the army who remembered Eddie's spirited defense of Billy Mitchell. These objections were soon overcome when the American Legion became involved; the organization represented too many votes to ignore. On November 6, 1930, at Washington's Bolling Field, President Herbert Hoover slipped the blue ribbon of the medal over Rickenbacker's head, with Adelaide and the boys in the forefront of those looking on.

Afterward, there was a substantial air show, including a performance by the 94th Aero, then located in Michigan. Eddie was incensed, however, that Billy Mitchell was left off the invitation list. At one point, Eddie made an attempt to persuade Hoover of the importance of an independent air service but to no avail. "The president was polite and courteous," Eddie said, "but his interests were not in military aviation."

In March 1931 a TWA Fokker trimotor airliner en route to Los Angeles was involved in a horrible crash over the wheat fields of Kansas. It was the kind of accident that every aviation company dreads. A wing tore off the plane as it flew out of a low cloud formation. It simply nosed over and dove straight down, burying itself several feet into a cow pasture. A farmer had watched horrified as five passengers fell out and bounced when they hit the ground. Everyone of course was killed. Among the dead was the University of Notre Dame's legendary football coach Knute Rockne. It was accidents such as this that gave Eddie fits.[17] In 1932 GM moved the TWA Fokker operation to Baltimore, but without Eddie Rickenbacker, who did not wish to move his family away from New York.

Rickenbacker soon became involved in a series of aviation companies owned by two young Wall Street geniuses, W. Averell Harriman and Robert Lehman. During the next few years he found himself serving as vice president of American Airways, which had east-west routes serving between New York (whose only airport was in Newark, New Jersey) and the Midwest. He had tried to persuade the owners to buy a small outfit then called Eastern Air Transport, which flew passengers on a north-south route from New York to Atlanta and Florida, but he was rebuffed. A year later American was bought by E. L. Cord, manufacturer of the Cord and Auburn automobiles, who moved the home business offices to Chicago, again without Eddie Rickenbacker, who declined to uproot the family and take the boys out of school.

It was around this time that the big airmail brouhaha erupted, which put Rickenbacker in direct conflict with President Roosevelt. He'd voted for Roosevelt in the election of 1932 but was highly critical of what he called Roosevelt's "socialistic" agenda, which is how Eddie viewed the New Deal. He believed that Roosevelt's original platform "was sound and conservative and what the country needed." But it seemed to Rickenbacker that when he got into office the president "made a complete 180-degree turn, and took off in the other direction."

In December of 1934 an opportunity presented itself that would change Rickenbacker's life forever. He was approached to become the general manager of Eastern Air Transport, now known as Eastern Air Lines after the government airmail fiasco. It was owned by his old employer GM, and it was losing money to the tune of $1.5 million that very year. Eddie saw it as an opportunity to get back into aviation and accepted the position as a challenge. Florida was gaining a reputation as a vacation destination, and Eddie thought there could be a fine opportunity flying people there, with stops all along the East Coast. New York to Miami by train took two days, whereas an airliner could make it in a matter of hours.

Rickenbacker approached the problem with his usual vigor and persistence, the same way he had with the car companies, popping up everywhere from the Eastern ticket counter selling tickets to the cockpit flying planes; from the mechanics' shops changing spark plugs to the men's rooms off the lobby inspecting for cleanliness. He analyzed every aspect of the business, then gave the workers inspirational speeches. He was a stern taskmaster, but employees soon came to understand that he was fair and, more important, they saw that he was working day and night to improve the company. In those days widespread passenger travel was just beginning, as airlines started designing planes with creature comforts in mind—large enclosed cabins, comfortable seats, heating, and meals. Even so it still took at least twenty-five hours to fly from New York to Los Angeles, including several different airlines and changes of planes and more than a dozen stops. With Eddie now running Eastern, the company made $35,000 in 1935. It was a start.

Rickenbacker's celebrity took off in a different direction with the creation of a comic strip called *Ace Drummond,* which he scripted with the cartoonist Clayton Knight. Loosely based on the Rickenbacker character from World War I, the hero flies his plane all over the world foiling bad men and saving damsels in distress. The comic ran as a Sunday page from 1935 to 1940, and at its peak it was distributed by King Features Syndicate in 135 newspapers. Soon the strip spurred the formation of the Eddie Rickenbacker Junior Pilots Club, which in turn inspired a thirteen-chapter movie serial starring John King as Ace Drummond. The first chapter featured the adventures of Ace Drummond in Mongolia and included dragons, dungeons, and a death ray.

On February 19, 1936, a telegram caught up with Rickenbacker on the road saying that Billy Mitchell had died. Mitchell had been only fifty-six but a bad heart and influenza combined to kill him in a New York City hospital. Eddie went to New York immediately and helped escort the casket from the undertakers to Grand Central Station where it was to be shipped to Mitchell's childhood home in Milwaukee. It was a poignant, emotional occasion. The casket had been left at the far end of Grand Central, and Eddie and a handful of Mitchell's close friends carried it through the dark catacombs to the express car on the train. "I felt so bitter, so grief-stricken, so shocked at this ignominious, demeaning end to a brilliant career, that I found the whole episode hard to believe," Eddie wrote afterward.

Soon enough Mitchell's crusade would be shockingly vindicated when the Japanese carried out a surprise attack on Pearl Harbor, which put much of the U.S. Pacific Fleet out of commission. In all, sixteen battleships were sunk by airplanes during the Second World War, making clear that airpower was supreme against these large, powerful vessels.

Mitchell was belatedly showered with honors. The B-25 Mitchell bomber was named after him, and would be flown by the crews of Jimmy Doolittle on his famous 1942 raid on Japan. In that year, too, President Roosevelt restored Mitchell to the rank of general and added an additional star, making him a major general. He was awarded the Congressional Gold Medal, posthumously, and inducted into the Aviation Hall of Fame. Additionally, everything from mountains and high schools to airports, roads, streets, dormitories, and the eating hall at the United States Air Force Academy were named after him. In 1955 a first-rate movie was released, *The Court-Martial of Billy Mitchell,* starring Gary Cooper and directed by Otto Preminger. In 1999 his portrait was put on a U.S. postage stamp.

All this was to recognize that in fact Mitchell was right and those in power were wrong. Eddie Rickenbacker went even further, giving it as his opinion that if the military had listened to Mitchell right after World War I ended, the United States would have built up such a powerful air force that Hitler and Göring never would have dared to start World War II—a noteworthy ideal.

WITH MITCHELL BURIED, Eddie decided he needed "a change of scenery," and he took Adelaide and the boys to Europe, ostensibly to examine the state of aviation there. In London they had breakfast with Eddie's friend the Canadian newspaper baron Max Aitken, now Lord Beaverbrook, publisher of the *London Evening Standard* and the *Daily Express.* After learning Rickenbacker's itinerary, Beaverbrook asked if Eddie would have dinner at his home when he returned. It was a portentous request.

They toured England, France, and Italy by air, the better to see the commercial aviation progress that the Europeans had been making. Germany was high on Rickenbacker's list, however, because he had heard unsettling rumors since Hermann Göring, now a field marshal, had announced the existence of the Luftwaffe a few months earlier. This was done in flagrant disregard of the Treaty of Versailles, which, under Hitler, the Germans continued to ignore—just as Göring had predicted to Eddie back in 1922.

Arriving in Berlin, Eddie and Adelaide were met once again by Ernst Udet and Erhard Milch, now high-ranking officers in Hitler's Third Reich, dressed in full Nazi regalia. Milch and Udet escorted the Rickenbackers to the new Air Service building at Tempelhof Airport, which Eddie described as "one big bomb shelter . . . the size of a city block," where a grand banquet had been prepared in their honor, hosted by none other than Göring, wearing a grin and a brilliant white uniform so that he resembled a drum major in a marching band.

"Herr Eddie," Göring greeted him effusively, "do you remember when I told you about the future of our air force when you visited us in 1922?"

Eddie assured him he remembered it clearly.

"Gut!" the German beamed, rubbing his hands together in a characteristic gesture. "Now we will show you." With Udet as guide, they spent three days touring German aviation installations, beginning with Göring and Udet's old squadron the Richthofen Flying Circus, which was hidden in a pine forest and so well camouflaged that Eddie didn't realize it was there until he was "right in the middle of it." In addition to the fighter planes, there were numerous two-seat trainers. When Eddie inquired about these, Udet surprised him by revealing that every man in the squadron was trained to fly—not just the officers but sergeants, privates, mechanics, cooks, clerks, and so on. No manpower was wasted.

They visited subterranean aviation factories that were producing both commercial and military planes and underground aeronautical labs that were using wind tunnels to test stability—a new development. In the concealed design departments, Eddie saw the newest plans for aircraft and engines. He was sure that Göring's purpose in showing him these things—many of which would ordinarily have been highly classified— was to leave an impression for him to carry back to England, France, and America, of the new Germany's great air strength, of her invulnerability. Further, he deduced that, because of Eddie's reputation as a combat pilot, they couldn't resist trying "to overawe me with their Teutonic might." The Germans, Rickenbacker realized, had no respect for England or France as military powers. "Through their discipline, sacrifice and preparation . . . the Germans earnestly believed they had a right to wage war and win it."

The day before the Rickenbackers left Berlin Udet threw a cocktail party in their honor at his apartment. Udet was no fan of Hitler, and seemed to have no qualms about criticizing him—so much so that Rickenbacker took Udet aside once to caution him, saying, "If you keep on talking like that, Ernst, you're going to get your head shot off." Eddie remembered that the walls of Udet's apartment were "lined with pictures of blond Hollywood stars, all affectionately inscribed to [Udet],"* and dead center on one wall was a target, surrounded by more pictures of Hollywood stars. The German ace had an enormous collection of handguns, and after everyone "had their favorite tipple," Udet suggested they play a game—the same he had played with Doolittle. With each man choosing a pistol, they would stand so many paces from the target and see who could hit it without breaking one of the surrounding pictures.

This went on for most of the party, with Udet showing off his marksmanship. The noise was deafening. Adelaide worried, "Those poor neighbors . . . what will they think? Surely they'll think someone is being liquidated . . . and wonder whether they'll come next."

Once back in London Rickenbacker looked up Lord Beaverbrook as promised and, good as his word, Beaverbrook invited Eddie and Adelaide to dinner next night. Eddie was astounded when he arrived at Beaverbrook's London townhome to find nearly every high-ranking

---

* Udet was an international-class seducer of women, whose conquests included Martha Dodd, the daughter of the American ambassador to Germany.

cabinet member there except for Prime Minister Stanley Baldwin himself. He was cornered by the foreign undersecretary Robert G. Vansittart and asked his opinion of when Hitler would be ready for war. Eddie said three to five years, but Vansittart nervously countered, "Two years at the most!"

Rickenbacker quickly understood that the gathering had been called to elicit his appraisal of the German military buildup. In his opinion, "Germany was building a great war machine, and would not hesitate to use it if necessary to regain world dominance." But only Vansittart—an ally to Winston Churchill—was convinced that the Nazis meant war; everyone else, Rickenbacker wrote later, "disagreed so bluntly and positively" that he realized it was pointless to go on. The British leaders had spent so much time squabbling among themselves they had become oblivious to the threat posed by a rearmed Germany, Rickenbacker concluded. It was, he said, "a government of compromise and self-delusion."

Things were no better when the couple reached the United States. At a meeting in Washington Rickenbacker tried to warn high-ranking Army Air Corps officers of the danger, but they brushed him off and ridiculed him when he described how the Germans were making pilots out of clerks, cooks, and mechanics. Even Eddie's friend Hap Arnold, by then a brigadier general and assistant chief of the Air Corps, was incredulous. "Eddie, you're nuts," he said. "It can't be done. You can't make pilots out of mechanics."

Even after Rickenbacker pointed out that he had been a mechanic himself, he was unable to convince them or raise alarm.

EVERY YEAR AFTER RICKENBACKER took over Eastern Air Lines, the company was more profitable, and Eddie was having a grand time running it until late one night when he answered the phone at home and realized that John Hertz, who had made a fortune with his Yellow Cab Company and car rental business, had apparently dialed his number by mistake and thought he was speaking with someone else.

Before Rickenbacker could say a word Hertz began railing about how he was "going to get that Rickenbacker." Eddie let him go on until at long last he identified himself, and after "a very loud silence, he hung up." In short, as Eddie put it, "There was no love lost between John Hertz and me."

In January 1938 a phone call from a Hearst magazine aviation writer gave him news that landed like a blow to the stomach. "I've just heard," the writer told him, "that John Hertz has taken an option on Eastern Air Lines for $2 million."

Eddie was floored. Hertz had sold the cab business to GM in 1925 for $43 million. Then he'd bought Transcontinental and Western Airlines from Lehman Brothers and immediately wanted to raise prices for passenger air travel when Eddie wanted to lower them all around.

Furthermore, Eddie learned there was skullduggery afoot. Besides Hertz, there was a shadow buyer for Eastern Air Lines, one Ernest R. Breech, an assistant treasurer for GM, who had been asked by the company to move to Detroit but did not wish to leave New York. Breech thought that by investing in Eastern he could gain a good executive position there, and thus was backing Hertz's bid. A further rub was that Breech had been the person who had gotten Eddie his job at Eastern in the first place.

Rickenbacker wasn't going to take it lying down. After all, GM had been trying to sell Eastern in 1934 for $1 million when Eddie came aboard. Now, after only three years, it was worth three times that because of his stewardship, and "My reward," he said, "was to be kicked out on my ear."

The first thing Rickenbacker did was visit Alfred P. Sloan, chairman of General Motors. He pressed the case that it was unfair not to at least give him a shot at buying the company after he had built it up from a losing white elephant. Since taking over, Rickenbacker had replaced dozens of station managers and gotten rid of all the older aircraft. Eastern was now operating with a brand-new fleet of DC-2s, the innovative forerunner of the Douglas DC-3, which became the most popular airplane in the world. For shorter distances, Rickenbacker had acquired a fleet of five Lockheed L-10 Electras, which carried ten passengers and flew 180 miles per hour. Eastern now had fifteen flights a day between New York and Washington, the first de facto shuttle service, which took eighty minutes each way. By 1937 Eastern was flying ten of the new DC-3s, and most of Eastern's routes, including Chicago, Atlanta, and New Orleans, were sellouts and fares had far eclipsed revenues from carrying U.S. mail. Eddie pleaded to Sloan for GM to give him an option to buy the company for $3,500,000 in cash rather than Hertz's offer of $1,000,000 cash and $2,250,000 in notes.

Sloan gave Rickenbacker thirty days to get the money, roughly $50 million in today's dollars, and certainly not the sort of figure that could be raised overnight. Eddie was not sophisticated about high finance but he was learning. First he approached Smith Barney, a venerable banking firm, but he was told it didn't have that kind of money and so he was sent on to the banking giant Kuhn, Loeb and Company. With the able assistance of Laurance Rockefeller, Kuhn, Loeb was able to cobble together a complex deal involving the Securities and Exchange Commission and consisting of a public offering with cash backing. Rickenbacker went to bed worried on Friday, April 30, 1938, and woke up next morning to a phone call from Frederick Warburg of Kuhn, Loeb who asked, "Where do you want your three and a half million dollars, Eddie, and when?"

"If it's convenient, Freddy, make it in Eastern's hangar at Newark Airport at ten a.m. tomorrow," Rickenbacker said.

"I'll be there with a certified check" was the reply.

He had met the thirty-day deadline.

After that, Eddie Rickenbacker became the president and general manager of, and a major owner in, Eastern Air Lines. The Rickenbacker luck had held out again.

DURING THE LAST YEARS OF THE 1930S Eastern, known as the Great Silver Fleet, was constantly expanding, with flights from Texas to Mexico City and new routes in Alabama and Tennessee. By 1939 Eastern was showing profits of just under $1 million, and at last, though it had taken nearly fifteen years, Eddie was able to pay off the remainder of the $250,000 he had borrowed for the Rickenbacker Motor Company.

Airline travel had become increasingly popular so that by the end of the decade American-owned airline companies could boast of flying more than two million passengers a year. Planes such as the DC-3 were amazingly modern and made coast-to-coast flights in eighteen hours or under, stopping only several times to refuel. The cabins were practically soundproof, which added greatly to the attraction of flying. As Orville Wright explained, "Noise was something we always knew would have to be eliminated to get people to fly. Somehow it is associated with fear." A number of the long-distance flights were "sleepers," containing curtained-off berths with posh pillows and feather comforters. Meals were often gourmet—lamb chops, Long Island duckling—"served on Syracuse china with Reed & Barton silverware." All this came with a price—as much as $5,000 in today's dollars for a coast-to-coast flight—but it had reached a point where many airlines could sustain themselves with passenger traffic alone.[18]

At this stage in his career Rickenbacker was completely engaged in his work, putting in sixteen-hour days, traveling most of the time to inspect the ever widening facilities of the company. He had long since disregarded his vows to quit smoking and drinking. He went through several packs of cigarettes a day and engaged in what was then the fairly commonplace four-martini lunch and after-work imbibing, not at all unusual among executives nationwide. It has been suggested that he and Adelaide grew apart—she had her friends and he had his—and that she considered divorce. They didn't go through with it. She had considerable wealth in her own right and proved in the future to be a devoted wife and friend of Eddie to the last.

The boys went to boarding schools, which was not uncommon among the wealthier class of families, and turned out to have vastly different personalities. William was gifted intellectually, was a talented classical musician, and made good grades, while David had more of a mechanical mind and was not a superior student. Eddie was devoted to them but with competing schedules there was not much time spent with them. Eddie took the boys to such events as the Indianapolis 500 and taught them sports, including shooting and golf. Yet there was, as in so many cases with famous parents, that kind of lofty void that so often separates and divides. William Rickenbacker once described what it was like as a boy sitting across the breakfast table from his father. "It was like looking at the Washington Monument," he said.[19]

ON SEPTEMBER 3, 1939, England and France reluctantly declared war on Germany.

During that summer, as the crisis in Europe reached its peak, Eddie had taken the family for a leisurely vacation in Europe. With fourteen-year-old David and eleven-year-old William, Eddie and Adelaide revisited a Germany that exuded "the new, confident belligerent spirit of the Third Reich." During their two days there Eddie caught up with his old friend Udet who was now a major general in charge of all aircraft production for the Luftwaffe, but he gave no indication one way or the other as to whether Udet's personality seemed altered, as Jimmy Doolittle had found earlier that same year.

From Germany the Rickenbackers went to Norway and took a "sturdy little ketch, complete with crew," for a sail along the coast of Scandinavia. Afterward they visited Oslo and were en route to Helsinki when they were suddenly warned by a friend who ran the Norwegian division of Scandinavian Air Service (SAS) that they should leave Europe immediately.

"All hell is going to break loose," the man told them.

Rickenbacker had made reservations to fly home early for an appointment but suggested that Adelaide take the boys to Paris for a few days, then board the *Hansa* at Cherbourg for the voyage home. "I thought there was a tragic possibility," Eddie said, "that, if they did not see it then, they might not see it at all. I knew what the German bombers could do." That had been during the last days of August 1939, when Hitler had signed a nonaggression agreement with Russia and was demanding a "corridor" through Poland to connect the two Germanys separated by the Treaty of Versailles.

Just as Adelaide and the boys arrived, refugees from Poland and other East European countries began pouring into France and the authorities ordered a national mobilization of the armed forces, a move tantamount to war. In the confusion the Rickenbackers only just made it to Cherbourg, where they found that the *Hansa*, a German ship, had been called home. They were barely able to make reservations on a Polish ship, the *Batory*, which was so overrun with refugees that Adelaide had to share a room and a bath with a Polish army general on a secret mission to Washington. While they were at sea war was declared and the Germans began torpedoing Allied ships, causing Eddie great consternation until the *Batory* arrived safely in New York on September 5.[20]

As the months passed following the outbreak of war, Americans were ever more divided into "interventionist" and "noninterventionist" camps. A political movement had begun on the East Coast urging the United States to intervene on behalf of the Allies. It was spurred by confidential British entreaties to the White House and political pressure by certain groups of Anglophiles, Francophiles, and Jewish organizations whose friends and relatives had suffered terribly under Hitler since the passage of the Nuremberg Laws in 1935.* Most of the rest of the country was opposed to involvement, however.

Eddie was a noninterventionist. It was his sense that what President Wilson had called the "war to end all wars" had solved nothing and that the Europeans weren't worth squandering any more American lives or treasure for. Because of his standing as a great American war hero, Eddie fell into the role of public spokesman for the antiwar crowd.

He began to write articles for big circulation magazines such as *Collier's* and *Forbes,* recalling that, aside from costing more than fifty thousand lives, American participation in World War I had utterly disrupted the economy and started a ten-year-long depression. Entry into another such conflict, he warned, would cost "millions of our young men and billions of our wealth." In speeches and radio addresses, Eddie reminded audiences that he was not a pacifist; his military record certainly proved that. But he felt that America should be strengthened militarily to the point where no nation would dare attack her. He drew up a plan for national preparedness, calling for fifty thousand warplanes and a hundred and fifty thousand pilots, always emphasizing that America should keep out of the European war. At that time under the Lend-Lease programs, the United States was supplying Great Britain with vast quantities of war materials, in exchange for long-term leases on British military bases abroad.

The Germans quickly overran Poland—with the help of the Russians courtesy of the Non-Aggression Pact with Germany—and then, after a period of relative calm known as the Phony War, in the spring of 1940 Hitler quickly attacked and conquered, in turn, Norway, Holland, Belgium, and France. By autumn the Germans were bombing England in preparation for 'an invasion. Rickenbacker was both alarmed and disgusted that the Nazis had been able to subdue these countries so

---

* These Nazi "laws" stripped non-Germans—in particular Jews, blacks, and Gypsies, or Roma—of their civil rights and severely restricted their ability to live productive lives. It was the first step on the way to the Holocaust.

easily. His most venomous disgust was reserved for France, which he had condemned as "decadent" following his postwar visits there.

In August 1940, as the French army was collapsing, General Robert E. Wood, the chairman of the board of Sears, Roebuck and Company, sought to have Eddie join an antiwar organization that emphasized American preparedness. The principals of this committee paralleled Rickenbacker's public position: they favored a staunch buildup of U.S. military might and noninvolvement in the European war.

There is some evidence that by then Rickenbacker was beginning to rethink his views. Despite his horror at the very notion of another war, he was slowly coming to the conclusion that there was no way the United States could *not* be entangled in the war. If Germany conquered all of Europe, he reasoned, America would have to become a gigantic defensive camp—at a terrible expense that would plunge the nation deeply into debt. That is precisely what happened to Germany when Hitler embarked on his ferocious military buildup, but now that the Nazis had subjugated most of Europe Hitler could loot his neighbors at his leisure. America, being America, would have no such options.

Nevertheless, Eddie gave General Wood permission to use his name in connection with the committee and soon found out that he was listed in the margin of the new America First Committee (AFC) as a member of the so-called National Committee, alongside such diverse others as Herbert Hoover, Alice Roosevelt Longworth (TR's daughter), Henry Ford, the actress Lillian Gish, and Robert Maynard Hutchins, president of the University of Chicago.

The Franklin D. Roosevelt administration lashed out at such organizations as America First, suggesting they were pro-Nazi. The charge was absurd but it stung anyway. Members of the president's cabinet used the press to create the impression that opposition to the American assistance to England was unpatriotic. Charles Lindbergh, for example, who was stridently against American involvement, was singled out for particular abuse by Roosevelt's interior secretary Harold Ickes, who declared that Lindbergh "forfeit[ed] his right to be an American."

It became obvious to Rickenbacker that the America First Committee—as it had with Lindbergh—wished to use his status as a war hero to bolster its cause. But Eddie was having second thoughts.

Rickenbacker had always been a strong advocate of preparedness, but now he used his fame as a bully pulpit to spur the formation of an air force. In 1939 he had called for fifty thousand planes. Whether or not it had anything to do with Rickenbacker's advice, Roosevelt soon announced to the country that the United States was building fifty thousand planes. By 1941 Rickenbacker was calling for a quarter of a million military planes and half a million pilots.* The war, he said, was now too big to ignore. In January 1941 Rickenbacker sent a telegram to General Wood formally resigning from the America First Committee.

A MONTH LATER RICKENBACKER'S LUCK came uncomfortably close to running out entirely. He had canceled a speech he'd promised to make to some businessmen in Birmingham, Alabama, about improving air service to that city and to the state. But a last-minute call from Alabama's governor Frank M. Dixon changed his mind. Dixon was a fellow veteran who had won the Croix de Guerre and the French Legion of Honor flying with the Lafayette Escadrille, and he had made a special plea to Rickenbacker, implying that people might think he was "too good" to come to Alabama.

In the early evening of February 26, Eddie packed an overnight bag and got aboard Eastern Air Line's Mexico Flyer, a DC-3 sleeper plane headed for Atlanta, Birmingham, Texas, and beyond. It carried thirteen passengers and a crew of three. The weather was poor when they took off—rain, windy, cold—but Eddie settled into a small private room behind the cockpit called the Sky Lounge, where he intended to do some paperwork. The weather remained foul several hours later, and when they were passing over Spartanburg, South Carolina, the pilot came into the Sky Lounge to report that the weather in Atlanta was deteriorating. Eddie told him to do what he thought was best.

In due time the lights of Atlanta appeared below. Among the intermittent showers Eddie recognized the glow of the federal penitentiary. He had made the flight numerous times and knew the

---

* The U.S. government actually built more than 300,000 planes during the war.

routine for an instrument landing. They were to fly past the radio beacon beam, then make a 180-degree turn to pick it up again and follow it down for a landing.* He was still working on papers when he felt the pilot put the left wing down to go into the 180-degree turn following permission from the tower at Atlanta to land at 11:44 p.m. Then things went terribly wrong. The wing hit something, which turned out to be the tops of pine trees. The pilot reacted by jerking the left wing up, and then the right wing began to hit the trees. Eddie knew his best chance was in the rear of the plane but, before he could move, the right wing was suddenly torn off the fuselage and the plane veered violently to the right, flipping up on its nose. The lights went out as the pilot cut the power switch, stopping everything electrical or mechanical.† Eddie was jerked around so powerfully that he shattered his hip on the arm of a seat.

All of this happened in an instant.

Next the plane flipped over in a somersault, snapping huge pine trees as it hit the ground with its tail and sheared in half right where Eddie sat, then came to an abrupt halt. Eddie found himself pinned in the wreckage where the plane had cracked in two, crushed against the dead body of the plane's steward. It was pitch dark, freezing cold, and pouring rain, and the heavy smell of aviation gasoline was in the air. Out of the gloom there came moans, and gasps, and shrieks of pain. Amazingly, out of the sixteen people aboard, eleven survived the initial crash.

Somehow Eddie remained conscious and tried to take stock of what had happened. His head was wedged in tight between a fuel tank, a bulkhead, and the corpse of the steward; something had dented his skull in "a groove you could lay your little finger in." He later learned that his left elbow had been shattered and the nerve destroyed, and several ribs were broken off so that the jagged ends poked out through the sides of his torso. His pelvis was broken in two places and his left knee was crushed.

---

* This was the same vibrator beam, or a modified version of it, that had been developed by the Guggenheim Full Flight Laboratory in 1929, the year of Jimmy Doolittle's historic flight.

† Had he not done this, it is likely that everyone aboard would have been immolated in a fiery crash.

Everything else that wasn't broken was tightly pinned in the wreckage, except for his right hand and forearm. He was covered in blood.

Gasoline was everywhere—in the plane and flowing out onto the ground. Most of the sounds were of people moaning and Eddie, too, was in agony, but at one point he distinctly heard someone say, "Hey, let's build a bonfire and get warm."

"No!" Rickenbacker screamed. "For God's sake, don't light a match!"

Eddie, on the last edges of panic, decided to see if he could somehow loosen up the trap he was in, and he strained forward in the darkness with his neck and head. He managed to wrench himself upward a couple of inches when his head hit a jagged piece of metal that was pointed directly at his left eye with such force that it ripped his eyelid wide open and his eyeball popped out of the socket and dangled down on his cheek. In desperation he gave another heave and heard several more ribs snap that "sounded like popcorn popping." He gave up.

Close by there were two other passengers trapped and apparently in worse shape than he was. He kept reassuring them that help was on the way and apologized on behalf of the airline. His reassurances helped him, too, he recalled, by keeping his mind off of his predicament and his pain. But it did not help the two passengers, both of whom died during the night.

Meantime, a crude search had been under way since the DC-3 had failed to land. Controllers in the tower immediately began calling Eastern personnel, who began to assemble at the airport. In five cars each manned by three people, they fanned out in the rainy dark with flashlights and kerosene lanterns. All night they prowled the dirt roads around Jonesboro and vicinity, but it wasn't until daybreak, deep in the woods, that one of them saw something glint, high up in a tree, something that ought not to have been there. It was part of the wing of an airplane.

The scene the rescuers came upon in the dull grays of dawn was Dantesque. The DC-3 itself was barely recognizable as an aircraft except for the tail section, which had sheared off and was resting upside down on a pile of rubble that was the rest of the plane. The nose and cockpit had plowed into the ground, burying the pilot and copilot in it. There were bodies everywhere, living and dead; when the rescuers got to Rickenbacker he was covered with blood and of course his eyeball was resting on his cheek. By this time he must have been delirious because he asked for a cigarette, only to be told, "Captain, you can't smoke here," at which he came to his senses and apologized profusely. The press had gotten word of the crash and a photographer arrived as they attempted to cut Eddie out of the wreckage. The photographer tried to get a picture but one of the Eastern Air Lines employees shoved him aside, "and not too gently."

It took a lot of cutting and prying to get Eddie free but at last he was put on a stretcher and a doctor gave him a shot of morphine, which didn't seem to help. They were deep in the woods, in a ravine, and the path to the road was muddy and slippery, and more than once the carrying party stumbled and lurched, causing him intense pain. When they reached the road there was an ambulance, but it was filled with dead bodies and drove off. When Rickenbacker asked why, he was told that the state paid the ambulance company a fee of $20 to haul off corpses but authorized only $10 for living people.

Rickenbacker waited nearly an hour for another ambulance, all the while thoroughly conscious and in great pain. When an ambulance finally arrived an Eastern pilot who had been in the search party got in as well to ride with him to the hospital. "I must have been a horrible-looking mess," Rickenbacker said later, because the pilot suddenly became nauseated from looking at him and threw up. "Why are *you* sick?" Rickenbacker complained. "*I'm* the one who's supposed to be sick!"

In the emergency room two doctors, both of them interns, were working feverishly over the crash victims, and when one of them looked at Eddie he told attendants to push him out of the way, saying, "He's more dead than alive." A Catholic priest entered the room, looked at Eddie, and asked a nurse if she knew what religion he was. Rickenbacker piped up, "I'm a damn Protestant like ninety percent of the people."

Right about then the chief surgeon of the hospital, Dr. Floyd W. McRae, arrived. Coincidentally, McRae's father, also a doctor, had treated Eddie in France in 1918. Dr. McRae shoved Eddie's eyeball back into its socket and then sewed up his eyelid without anesthesia because, the physician said, it would have affected the muscles of the eye and so make the operation more difficult. When one of the attendants who was holding him down pushed harder, Eddie heard his ribs crackle and pop again and he flooded the room with a cascade of horrible profanity, for which he later apologized.

As more doctors arrived, they and the interns stood around arguing over what to do with Eddie. One of them, he said later, wanted to drill a hole in his head where the dent was to relieve the pressure; others discussed whether or not to operate on the crushed hip or let it alone. Rickenbacker joined the conversation by asking for an osteopath. "Get me a good osteopath," he said uncharitably, "and I'll be out of this place in three days." In the end, it was decided to leave him be for now and see what happened. He was fifty years old.

Writing later about the experience, Rickenbacker noted that he had excellent vision in his left eye ever since, even better than the right eye. What is more, he said, "The crash actually improved my nose, which had been broken six times in my life. That time, the seventh, left it perfectly straight."

Adelaide had been visiting friends in Charlotte, North Carolina, and rushed down to Atlanta after picking up the boys, who were attending boarding school in Asheville. Next day when asked if he was hungry, Rickenbacker demanded a ham and egg sandwich and a bottle of beer. Ralph McGill, legendary editor of the *Atlanta Constitution,* had arrived to inquire after Eddie's status, and McRae said he was very much improved. In fact, McRae said, he had just asked for a ham and egg sandwich and a Coca-Cola. It was only partly true, but since the Coca-Cola company was then, as now, Atlanta's biggest business, this was apparently an effort to take advantage of a public relations opportunity. News was soon broadcast throughout the world and Coca-Cola sent a large cooler to Eddie's room and kept it stocked with Coke.

So many of Eddie's bones had been broken that at last the doctors decided to place his entire body from head to toe in a cast—except for his right arm—to let the knitting process begin. His bed was rigged with trusses and other contraptions to keep his limbs elevated and immobile. The next day he took a turn for the worse, and death seemed to surround him in his hospital bed.

Reporters hanging around the hospital quickly picked up word that Rickenbacker was dying. That evening Walter Winchell, the popular gossip columnist, announced on his national radio show that Eddie would be dead within the hour. With his good right hand Rickenbacker seized a bedside water pitcher and flung it at the radio.

For the next ten days Eddie remained in the delicate state between life and death. There were times when he would sink; his pulse would either quicken or become dangerously slow. But inevitably he would rally. Dr. McRae told him he'd never seen a patient with so much determination to live. All during this time Adelaide was a tower of strength, encouragement, and bravery. She sat by his bed night and day, holding his hand, attentive to his every need.

They kept him sedated with morphine but Eddie was suffering from hallucinations and begged to be taken off it. The doctor told him he wouldn't be able to stand the pain, but at last he took Eddie off the drug for twenty-four hours. The pain was awful but Rickenbacker felt himself rally and "began to get better immediately."

After six weeks doctors removed the full body cast, introducing an entirely new period of torture. In order to repair the smashed hip socket a hole was drilled through his thigh bone so that a technician could slowly work the ball of the socket back in place. They put his arm back in a cast but the pain was so excruciating that Rickenbacker gnawed the cast off with his teeth. After that, the doctors left it uncasted.

During the four months that Rickenbacker stayed in the hospital some eighteen thousand letters, cards, telegrams, and gifts arrived for him. Get well wishes came from such diverse individuals as Fiorello La Guardia, J. Edgar Hoover, and Ernst Udet. Enough flower arrangements and potted plants arrived during his stay to decorate every ward and room in the hospital. In time Rickenbacker graduated from a wheelchair to a self-propelled pushcart and then to crutches and walking canes, and finally on June 25, 1941, he was released from the hospital. He looked god-awful—thin, ashen, disheveled—when he boarded a special plane that Eastern Air Lines had sent for him.

When the flight arrived at New York's LaGuardia Airport, Rickenbacker was greeted with cheers by several hundred Eastern employees as he stepped down the stairway with the aid of a cane. Reporters asked Eddie if he thought America should enter the war and he replied, "We are in it, and have been in it for a year. A lot of people don't realize that. The sooner everyone knows we are in, the better it will be." Another reporter asked whether it was vital to the United States that Hitler be defeated. Rickenbacker replied, "The sooner we crush Hitler, the better." He had by then come full circle.[21]

The family took a cottage on Connecticut's Candlewood Lake where they spent the summer during Eddie's slow recovery. An orderly from Atlanta's Piedmont Hospital came along as massage therapist and exercise coach. Eddie found that rowing a boat every day was beneficial; he also found that for the first time he was able to spend his days uninterrupted with the boys.

Eventually Rickenbacker began to spend several days a week in New York tending to business. He was in his office on Sunday, December 7, 1941, when news came over the radio that the Japanese had bombed Pearl Harbor—just as Billy Mitchell had predicted. The news left him not only angered but also frustrated that a big war was now on and he was so infirm. His body wasn't straight anymore, and he had a permanent limp in his left leg because of a severed nerve. In fact, he had to give up driving because he couldn't use that leg to disengage the clutch of his automobile.

There were a few things he could do, though, and first was to announce that the Indianapolis Speedway was closed for the duration. The nation could not afford to waste the fuel, metal, and tire rubber the race used up, Rickenbacker said, and the engineers, mechanics, and drivers would be needed in the military. Second, he began making arrangements for Eastern Air Lines to cooperate with the military in all ways possible.

As winter came, Eddie and Adelaide retired to a houseboat in Florida, where he continued his rowing and exercising, hoping to get back into the best possible shape. Meantime, the war had become a perfect cascade of disasters. Germany had declared war on the United States right after Pearl Harbor and launched a relentless campaign of submarine warfare that threatened to destroy the U.S. Merchant Marine. The Japanese continued their rampage across the Pacific, occupying lands from Alaska to Southeast Asia and south through Indonesia to New Guinea and the Solomon Islands. Wake Island had fallen, the Philippines was near collapse, and Australia and India were threatened.

For all of the horror and pain that it caused, the plane crash did have some positive effect on Eddie. Once more he felt that he was being tested, that he'd been allowed to live "for some good purpose . . . for some opportunity to serve." In March 1942 he was still wondering what that might be when he received a phone call from Hap Arnold, who was now the commanding general of the U.S. Army Air Forces.

Arnold asked if Rickenbacker could come to Washington for a private talk, something he could not say over the phone. The following Monday, in Arnold's office, he disclosed to Eddie that his staff was receiving reports that the morale of air force groups being trained for combat was abysmal. "They're indifferent. They haven't got the punch to do the job they're being prepared for," Arnold said. He asked Eddie if he could go on a tour, immediately, and "put some fire in them, and while you're there, look around and see what our problems are."

Rickenbacker said he'd be honored, but that he needed ten days to clear his desk, that his boys were coming home for Easter and he'd be ready afterward. Arnold told him the problem was too large to wait. Some of these troops would be on their way overseas by then and they needed a Rickenbacker talking-to *now*. "It is that serious," Arnold said.

"I'll go right away, General," Eddie told him.

To give him some gravitas, Arnold offered to make him a two-star general, but Rickenbacker turned it down. He wanted to remain "Captain Eddie," a civilian, unencumbered by military orders, and with the right to speak his mind. He left on March 10, 1942, for Tampa's MacDill Field on a mission that once more would put him deep in the shadow of death.

CHAPTER 9

AN INSPIRATION IN A GRUBBY WORLD

L INDBERGH HAD PLANNED TO CHECK into a cheap hotel or *pensione* for the night when he landed in Paris, and then spend a week or so fooling around the aerodromes and flying fields, perhaps meeting some French pilots and engineers. Instead he became the object of the greatest celebration in France since the end of World War I, and which became possibly the greatest public outburst in the history of the world.

The members of the press went berserk over the story. In anticipation of Lindbergh's arrival, it was said that United Press International had arranged for exclusive use of all the public phones at Le Bourget, which nearly resulted in a mini-riot. The phone booth occupied by the chief UPI correspondent was overturned by his competitors with its door down, trapping him inside with all the phone wires ripped out. The night editor of the international edition of the *Chicago Tribune* had not believed that Lindbergh would make it and hence had left no news hole for the story. Thus, next day, a brilliant one-on-one interview with Lindbergh rated only a two-column head, when every other newspaper in the civilized world splashed his success in banner headlines—not to mention that the "interview" itself was a fake,*

---

* This was made known only decades later by the *Tribune*'s esteemed correspondent Waverley Root.

written by the paper's Paris correspondent ahead of time to beat the crowd.[1]

Lindbergh was just as astonished as anyone else at the animating effect his successful landing had on the rest of the world. "To me," he said, "it was like a match lighting a bonfire." When the Paris telegraph flashed out the news of Lindbergh's achievement it reached New York radio stations at about five p.m., and the city spontaneously erupted into delirious celebration: all the boats in the harbor, including the ocean liners, began blowing their horns. This in turn set off the fire trucks from Harlem to the Battery, which responded with their own horns and sirens; police cars from Brooklyn to Staten Island chimed in; people in the streets yelled and shook their fists in the air, while those in the high-rise buildings began shredding papers and phone books and throwing the stuff out the window like confetti. On Broadway, performances were interrupted with the news, and theater orchestras arose in their pits and played "The Star-Spangled Banner" and "La Marseillaise." Scenes such as these were repeated in cities and towns all over America as the radio, telegraph, and telephone broadcast the news.[2]

People scrambled to name babies, streets, schools, parks, landmarks, and so forth, after the new hero. The *New York Times* headline LINDBERGH DOES IT! covered the entire top of the fold. In the South and Midwest, farmers rang their dinner gongs and churches set their steeple bells clanging. There was a similar outpouring worldwide. From Stockholm to Singapore, from Tokyo to Tegucigalpa, people were seized with the notion that an entirely new horizon had been discovered—as if all men were now bound much closer to one another in a more harmonious, immutable way. Only from the surly bonds of the Soviet Union was there no uproarious celebration or hearty applause; instead, from the Kremlin came a wary silence.

When he arose from sleep at the American embassy in Paris a little after noon, Lindbergh was treated to a warm bath drawn by a butler who left him fresh towels and a robe. Outside, no fewer than twenty-five movie cameras and fifty photographers had set up since early morning, waiting to capture the valiant young flier on film, while several hundred newspaper reporters were loitering in the embassy's public rooms downstairs. Because Lindbergh had neglected to pack even so much as a business suit, the matter of clothing became urgent. Ambassador Herrick's valet came to the rescue with a dark suit borrowed from a tall, slender acquaintance, which would have to do while a bevy of Paris tailors arrived to measure Lindbergh for everything from slacks to a top hat and tails. Herrick recognized a good thing when he saw it, for the arrival of Charles Lindbergh was the best thing that had happened to his ambassadorship and he intended to capitalize on it for all it was worth. He cabled Washington: "If we had deliberately sought a type to represent the youth, the intrepid adventure of America . . . we could not have fared as well as in this boy of divine genius and simple courage." As one writer observed somewhat snidely, Herrick was delighted that he "had on his hands not a gauche hick from the Middle West backwoods, but a young man who seemed to be normal and comfortable in every situation."[3]

Indeed he was. Lindbergh had his idiosyncrasies, as we shall see, but on the face of it he was highly intelligent, especially about aviation, had a sunny disposition, a naturally smiling countenance, and a lyrical demeanor, and being a captain in the army had taught him always to defer to his elders and betters as "sir."

In the borrowed suit he spoke from the balcony of the embassy to the assembled mob of journalists, movie and camera crews, and Parisians who were chanting *"Vive Lindbergh!"* in the courtyard below. In reply Lindbergh used the only French phrase he knew, which was *"Vive la France!,"* and waved a French flag, thus entering the great corpus of historical photography while the flash pans hissed and sparkled and the movie cameramen cranked on. At the suggestion of Ambassador Herrick, he mentioned that Benjamin Franklin, when he had been the American envoy to France, had shown great interest in French aerial balloons. Like Rickenbacker before him, Lindbergh was beginning to realize that what he had done was bigger than him, or anything he had ever conceived it might be, and wrote later that he found himself "surrounded by unforeseen opportunities, responsibilities and problems."

Back inside the embassy he spoke with his mother on a transatlantic radiophone linkup, and he was introduced to the first of the enormous amount of personal mail and tributes that would inundate the embassy in the coming days. The first thing he was shown was a congratulatory telegram from President Calvin Coolidge, and next a huge floral spray, about which Lindbergh laughingly remarked from the height of his own experience with aviation that "I am glad to be able to receive it personally," since "a lot of times flowers come the wrong way, and you aren't able to appreciate them." It was his first public joke and everyone broke out in cheers.

There was much pulling and tugging at Lindbergh's sleeves but to his credit the first thing he insisted on doing was pay a visit to Charles Nungesser's mother. In an apartment up six flights of stairs, Mrs. Nungesser was waiting for Lindbergh at the door, and a teary embrace ensued, while Lindbergh told her not to give up hope.* The afternoon was spent in press conferences, including a session with the *New York Times,* with which the St. Louis syndicate had arranged to have an exclusive interview.

Next day, after inspecting the *Spirit of St. Louis* and finding everything in reasonably good order, Lindbergh was driven to the Élysée Palace, where the president of France pinned the French Legion of Honor cross on his lapel, the first ever such distinction for an American civilian. Riding past throngs of cheering Parisians, he went to a luncheon at the Aéro-Club and was bestowed its gold medal, as well as his first glass of champagne, which he could hardly turn down after a lengthy toast was offered on his behalf and a waiter in livery served the sparkling glass conspicuously up to him on a silver platter. This showed a rare flexibility in Lindbergh's character, because he almost religiously shunned alcohol. In this case he was canny enough to realize it was diplomatically important to observe the customs of the French rather than adhere to his principles. There were times in the future, to the regret of many, when he would not prove so adaptable.

Lindbergh turned down a gift of 150,000 francs that the Aéro-Club had offered him, instead (once more) diplomatically asking that it be given to help the families of French fliers who had died "for the progress of aviation" (doubtless with the mother of the missing Charles Nungesser in mind). Then he was taken to the window, where thousands of people

---

* No trace of Nungesser's plane was ever found.

in the streets cheered the sight of him, and, to the delight of Ambassador Herrick, he gave a short speech praising the attempt by Nungesser and Coli to fly the Atlantic.

That night, Lindbergh was astonished and angered to find that the *Times* reporter he'd been talking to had used Lindbergh's information to create a first-person account of the transatlantic flight that ran all over the front page of the *New York Times*—under *Lindbergh's byline!* He considered it a violation of trust, as well as blatantly dishonest, because the reporter had put words in his mouth in an ingratiating, hayseed style. The incident had a lasting effect on Lindbergh; he concluded that the press "had an agenda all its own" and would exploit him for their own ends. They were not to be trusted—even those publications with the stature of the *New York Times*.[4]

The celebrations, ceremonies, luncheons, dinners, and interviews went on until Lindbergh was exhausted. Americans wanted him home and President Coolidge had sent the U.S. Navy battlecruiser *Memphis* to fetch him at Cherbourg. The Belgians wanted a piece of him also, as did the English. On May 29, a week after he'd landed in Paris, Lindbergh took off from Le Bourget. A million Parisians gathered in the streets to watch his departure. He did not disappoint, performing a breathtaking repertoire of stunts: loops, rolls, Immelmanns, dives, and spins from his barnstorming days, and dropping a French flag with a note attached— "Goodbye! Dear Paris! Ten Thousand Thanks for Your Kindness to Me!"—before proceeding north toward Belgian Flanders.[5]

Some of the hardest fighting of the war had taken place there, and many of the scars remained: shell-hole-pitted fields, jagged remains of trench lines, demolished towns and villages, and entire forests blown completely to splinters. When he landed near Brussels, Lindbergh and his plane were not mobbed as in Paris: King Albert had thoughtfully ordered five thousand Belgian soldiers with fixed bayonets to guard the field when the *Spirit of St. Louis* came down.

Lindbergh was feted by Albert and made a Knight of the Order of Leopold. He spent the night and next day was received by cheering tens of thousands as he was paraded through the capital city. That afternoon he flew away, but not before dropping a wreath of flowers over the American cemetery near Ghent. When he reached the Channel he headed for Croydon Field, a dozen miles south of London, with perfect flying weather in the merry month of May.

If Lindbergh had believed that the usually sedate British would, like the Belgians, give him a hearty but formal welcome, he was sorely mistaken. An estimated hundred and fifty thousand people crashed through ropes and barricades and ignored the frustrated whistles of hundreds of bobbies. They so mobbed the flying field that Lindbergh was compelled to do a touch-and-go landing when he feared he might plow into the crowd. When at last the field was cleared and he put down for good, police and other officials arrived in cars to spirit him away, but not far. He was taken to the control tower where he climbed to the top and addressed the surging masses. "I just want to tell you this is worse than I had in Paris!" he said delightedly and to great cheering.[6]

When he reached the American embassy in London Lindbergh was informed that the king wanted to see him, and on the morning of May 31 he was driven to Buckingham Palace and presented to King George V. The U.S. ambassador was away and the chargé d'affaires was a "boiled shirt who was in rather a state because I was in an ordinary business suit and not a frock coat!" Lindbergh said. As it turned out, it was just the two of them, Lindbergh and the king, who, Lindbergh said, showed a remarkable knowledge of aviation. Right off, the king leaned forward and said, "Now tell me, Captain Lindbergh, there is one thing I long to know. How did you pee?"[7]

Lindbergh addressed this startling inquiry by explaining that he carried with him "a sort of aluminum container," which he said he threw out of the plane in France before landing at Le Bourget.[8] The king seemed satisfied with this explanation and they moved on to other topics. Soon Queen Mary swept into the room and watched as the king pinned a medal on Lindbergh, the Air Force Cross, "for great flying achievement." Before he left, Lindbergh was taken into a room and introduced to the king's granddaughter the baby Princess Elizabeth, who had just turned one year old.

What followed were the now customary rounds of celebrations, ceremonies, and presentations, and the adulation reached dizzying heights. Lindbergh was taken to Parliament by Lord and Lady Astor, where the entire House of Commons recognized his exit by rising to their feet in a standing affirmation believed to be the only such demonstration ever extended to an American. Afterward, on the terrace, he met Winston Churchill, then chancellor of the exchequer, who later told the Parliament, "From the little we have seen of him, we have derived the impression that he represents all that a man should say, all that a man should do, and all that a man should be."[9]

EVERY DAY NEWSPAPERS WERE QUOTING this person or that on what Lindbergh should do with the rest of his life. Some said he ought to start a flying school, others that he ought to be appointed to some high official position in government, and others still with the predictable suggestion that he should become a movie star. Much of the to-do was similar to what Eddie Rickenbacker had endured when he came home a hero from World War I. Huge financial offers were made if Lindbergh would endorse everything from cigarettes to shaving cream to hats and gloves. During the first months it was estimated that these offers totaled at least $6 million.[10]

Will Rogers, the midwestern humorist, wrote, "There is a hundred and twenty million people in America all ready to tell Lindbergh what to do. The first thing we want to get into our heads is that this boy is not our usual type of hero that we are used to dealing with. He is our prince and our president combined, and I will personally pay benefits to him for the rest of my life to keep him from having to make exhibitions out of himself. We only get one of these in a lifetime."[11] Will Rogers notwithstanding, however, and as the *New Republic* put it, Lindbergh was "ours. He is no longer permitted to be himself. He is the U.S. personified."[12] In other words, for better or worse—and to his eternal regret—Lindbergh had become public property.

People soon began to argue as to what Lindbergh's accomplishment "meant," and two schools of thought emerged. One claimed the feat was the heroic achievement of man over nature; the other asserted it was the ultimate triumph of "the machine," or science. In either case Lindbergh was the hero, but of exactly what was not clear.

Those who hailed him as a pioneer were on firmer ground. He was compared with Daniel Boone and Davy Crockett, two loners who struggled across the Alleghenies and opened up the western lands beyond. There were also more lofty claims. Heywood Broun in his newspaper column enthused that this "tall young man raised up and let us see the potentialities of the human spirit," while a Harvard professor gave an address in which he described Lindbergh thusly: "He has come like a shining vision to revive the hope of mankind." Another speaker put it a bit more succinctly: "He stands out in a grubby world as an inspiration."

Lindbergh had, in fact, opened up a new frontier, which, in hindsight, was certainly no small feat. A *New York Times* reporter wrote that "what [Lindbergh] means by the *Spirit of St. Louis* is really the Spirit of America." That might or might not have been so. What stands out is that Lindbergh himself at that time had little or no idea of the meaning of the flight of the *Spirit* other than to land in Paris in one piece, and he was utterly unprepared for the reception and attention that followed.[13]

On the afternoon of June 10, 1927, the cruiser *Memphis* entered the Chesapeake Bay with Lindbergh standing on the bridge, escorted by four destroyers, with two army blimps and several squadrons of army aircraft overhead. Crated below was the *Spirit of St. Louis,* which had just as much well-earned rest as her pilot on the six-day voyage. At sunrise next morning, the battle cruiser entered the Potomac River and steamed toward Washington. As it neared the dock at the Navy Yard all the bells and whistles began to sound as they had in New York, and additionally a battery of field guns roared out a welcoming salute.

Lindbergh stood in the ship's bow, wearing his blue serge suit, waving to the crowed on the dock with his hat. When the boarding ramp was let down, Admiral Guy Burrage, commander of U.S. Naval Forces, Europe, escorted aboard a little brown-clad lady wearing a large straw hat. He took her arm up the ramp and the crowd, including the ship's crew, collectively gasped as they realized who she was, and when the thoroughly surprised Lindbergh ran down the ramp to embrace his mother, Evangeline, pandemonium reigned supreme. A brass band began to play, prompting some men to weep while others threw their hats into the air, women clutched their breasts, and everyone was overwhelmed with feeling.[14]

Lindbergh and Evangeline were paraded up Pennsylvania Avenue in the backseat of President Coolidge's limousine—escorted by a squadron of U.S. cavalry in full regalia—to the Washington Monument, where a quarter million cheering people awaited them. The mid-June heat bore down as Coolidge bestowed on Lindbergh the Distinguished Flying Cross as well as a full colonel's commission in the U.S. Army Reserve. The din was overwhelming as the twenty-five-year-old pilot stood on the podium with a bemused expression. When at last the multitude fell silent he made a brief speech about how the European outpouring of affection had been not just for him, but actually a demonstration of their friendship with the United States. Hundreds of photographers took pictures while Lindbergh's remarks were carried by radio to some thirty million Americans.

Afterward there was the usual round of celebrations and ceremonies, including the announcement by the U.S. Postmaster General that a new ten-cent "Lindbergh" airmail stamp would be issued depicting the *Spirit of St. Louis,* the first ever that honored a man still living.*

Two days later Lindbergh took off in *Spirit* for New York City where another mind-boggling shindig awaited him. He was placed aboard Mayor Jimmy Walker's yacht and paraded down the Hudson to the Battery while hundreds of harbor boats followed and dozens of airplanes strewed hundreds of thousands of flower petals on the procession. He was then put in the back of a touring car and, led by ten thousand marching soldiers, paraded up bunting-decorated Broadway past Wall Street, which had shut down for the occasion, through a perfect blizzard of shredded stock ticker tape tossed from thousands of windows along the route of the Canyon of Heroes.† It was printed that four million people attended the celebration, including a hundred thousand who had crammed into the plaza at City Hall to witness the occasion. The loquacious Mayor Walker, wearing a black top hat, opened the ceremony by declaring, "Colonel Lindbergh, New York City is yours—I don't

---

* While the stamp honored Lindbergh by name, long-standing custom dictated that no U.S. stamp would be issued with the likeness of a living person. Thus, while tradition was broken using Lindbergh's name, the airplane itself was the featured art.
† The New York City street cleaning department announced later that it had picked up two thousand pounds of confetti.

give it to you; you won it!"* Walker pinned on Lindbergh the gold and platinum Medal of New York City.

The parade then continued up Fifth Avenue where it stopped at St. Patrick's Cathedral so Lindbergh could receive the blessing of Cardinal Hayes, who told him, "I greet you as the first and finest American boy of the day." The parade at last ended in Central Park's Sheep Meadow where Governor Al Smith presented Lindbergh with the Medal of Valor of the State of New York—a first for a non–New York resident—and proclaimed him "an ideal example for the youth of America."

As if that weren't enough, Lindbergh was trundled out to Long Island that night for a big fancy dinner dance, before embarking on the next round of receptions the next day, and the next. Everyone wanted some of Charles Lindbergh, and so far he seemed to be accommodating most of them. Like Ambassador Herrick back in Paris, Lindbergh seemed to sense a good thing when he saw it, and rather than give in to his natural tendency toward shyness and introspection, he endured the endless palaver for the sake of the future of aviation—or so he said. He was smart enough to realize this adulation might not go on forever, and that some positive good might come of it.

This positive good revealed itself on Lindbergh's fourth day in New York. After an exhaustive twenty-two-mile parade before nearly a million residents during Lindbergh Day in Brooklyn—followed by a ceremony at Roosevelt Field, followed by an appearance at Yankee Stadium in the Bronx—the exploit finally paid off. Never mind the medals and the adulation and the promotional offers he would never accept; on Thursday evening, June 14, at the Hotel Brevoort on Fifth Avenue, Lindbergh was presented by Raymond Orteig with the Orteig Prize, consisting of an elegant scroll, a medal, and a check for $25,000. In accepting it, Lindbergh generously congratulated Orteig for issuing a challenge that initiated the construction of, and consequent improvements to, so many aircraft seeking his prize. Likewise, a short time later he received another $25,000 from the Vacuum Oil Company, the lone endorsement that he

---

* Later accused of taking bribes, Walker was forced to resign and in 1932 fled to Europe to avoid prosecution.

had agreed to before the flight.* This put him on a firm financial footing for the first time in his life.

The next day, a Saturday, Lindbergh flew to St. Louis, a nine-hour trip mostly in the rain, to show his appreciation to his backers. The entire city turned out on his behalf of course; half a million people lined the parade route that was decorated with his picture on every wall, in addition to the usual patriotic bunting. On Sunday, when the weather cleared, he delighted the crowds by flying stunts.

By now Lindbergh hoped for some well-deserved time off from the frantic schedule that had overtaken him the instant he put down in Paris. This was easier said than done, however. When he went downtown a day later in a new car, Lindbergh was relieved that people stared at the car and not at him. But no sooner had he set foot on the pavement than somebody recognized him and as if from nowhere a mob of people appeared and chased him, grabbing at his clothes and his person.[15]

BY THIS TIME LINDBERGH was engrossed in the stupendous amount of mail he had received. Thus far there were some three and a half million letters from all parts of the globe and a hundred thousand telegrams— everything from "congratulations" to "welcome home" to marriage proposals by the dozens. As with Eddie Rickenbacker, there was interest in Lindbergh by every Rotary, Kiwanis, Optimist, Sertoma, and Exchange club in the country, as well as the usual mammalian lodges. There were messages of congratulations, often accompanied by a gold medal of some description, from practically every country in Europe and Central and South America, including Bulgaria, Romania, Peru, and the Canal Zone—which presented him with a large gold Indian idol to the Eastern Sun. The gold alone in all of these medallions, at today's prices, is worth a small fortune.

The president of Honduras sent a watch hidden within a twenty-dollar U.S. gold piece. In addition to a gold medal, Nicaraguans sent

---

* The combined value of these awards was worth nearly $1 million today, enough to relieve for the foreseeable future the day-to-day living concerns of a young man who'd been barnstorming for $5 a day only a few months earlier.

a native-made hammock. Not to be outdone, the nation of Guatemala presented him with "native-woven linen scarves and girdles and a set of decorative gourds." Many U.S. states also sent gifts, mostly gold medals, although Colorado sent a picture of the newly named Lindbergh Peak, painted by "the children of the Rocky Mountain Region."

Even more elaborate presents were sent from cities worldwide, including an engraved gold dress sword from the city of Hamburg; a chest of 197 pieces of sterling flatware from Providence; 140 pieces of dinner china from Syracuse; and from Hartford a cane carved from a tree out of Mark Twain's garden. Most touchingly, Limerick, Ireland, sent a lace shawl "for Capt. Lindbergh's mother," and the children of Patchogue, New York, gave her "a golden thimble set with diamonds." From San Diego came a sterling silver model of the *Spirit of St. Louis,* while from El Paso there arrived a serape and sombrero.

From Saint Croix in the Virgin Islands "an inlaid sword from the 1830s" turned up. Perhaps the most unusual gift came from the city of Port-au-Prince, Haiti, which sent Lindbergh a mahogany paperweight set with a hunk of iron from the anchor of Christopher Columbus's flagship, the *Santa María,* as well as a resolution from the city government naming the city's main thoroughfare Lindbergh Avenue.

There were honorary academic degrees by the dozens, as well as honorary memberships in practically every flying club in the world, most accompanied by a plaque, scroll, or medal. From an association known as the Gold Mines of Honduras arrived a "gold chest of native gold nuggets." How these were obtained went unsaid. For reasons of his own, William Randolph Hearst presented Lindbergh with an exquisite pair of silver celestial and terrestrial spheres, circa 1700—the only known pair in existence. The American Society of Mechanical Engineers presented him with a silver cigarette case—somewhat oddly, for it had been well publicized that Lindbergh didn't smoke. And there were far bigger deals than that: Ryan Aircraft gave Lindbergh a five-seat, high-wing cabin monoplane, to which the Wright Company added a Whirlwind J-5C 220-horsepower engine. The Franklin Automobile Company gave him a brand-new four-door sedan, and Henry Ford matched that with a four-door sedan for Lindbergh's mother, while GM gave him a two-door Cadillac convertible. Both professional baseball leagues gave him lifetime passes, as did the Shubert theatrical organization to all of its Broadway plays. Standard Oil gave him stock. A donor who wished to remain anonymous sent Lindbergh a stickpin with the *Spirit of St. Louis* cut from a single diamond. Another donor who wished to be unknown sent Lindbergh a German shepherd police dog.

There were art pieces offered, depictions of Lindbergh in all mediums and stages of excellence, and sculptures "made of pure silver, ivory, plaster, and soap; airplane models of solid gold as well as fragile silk." In all, there were more than fifteen thousand gift items,[16] inspired by everything under the sun—from an ivory inlaid billiard cue to a copy of the Gutenberg Bible. Lindbergh declined an offer of a live monkey, a free home in Flushing Meadows, and several motion picture contracts, one worth $5 million. As he had with the cash award from the French Aéro-Club, he declined an offer of 5,000 Swedish crowns from a Stockholm newspaper, suggesting instead that it be distributed "for aviation purposes."*

LINDBERGH'S EARLIEST BIOGRAPHER, Fitzhugh Green, probably did not overstate matters by much when he described the adulation lavished on the young aviator as "the greatest torrent of mass emotion ever witnessed in human history." Lindbergh was by then unquestionably the most famous man in the world, a heroic phenomenon—the perfect combination of bravery, aviation genius, modesty, sagacity. An affable personality, good looks, and a winning smile. Some people saw in him the work of "Divine Providence," while to others he very nearly resembled the Second Coming.

---

* Beginning in 1927 Lindbergh permitted the St. Louis Historical Society to exhibit the items for an indefinite period, and in 1935 he deeded the entire collection over to the society for permanent display. The collection was seen by 1.5 million people in 1927 alone.

It is noteworthy that the Spirit of St. Louis Organization (the backers) refused any claim on or share in the gifts to Lindbergh, which remain highly valuable.

There was some discussion, reported in the newspapers, about creating a new cabinet-level position for Lindbergh as secretary of aviation, but nothing came of it. Harry Guggenheim, president of his family's aviation trust fund, had quickly recognized that Lindbergh was the best thing to happen to aviation since the Wright brothers, and he offered him $50,000 to take the *Spirit of St. Louis* on a three-month tour of America to promote air travel, a proposition that Lindbergh accepted.

Lindbergh wasn't rich at that point, but it must have dawned on him that he would never again be poor. He was scheduled to write a quick book about his flight for the George P. Putnam publishing company that was sure to be a best seller. Unfortunately, Putnam's had contracted with an embellishment-prone *New York Times* reporter to write the manuscript, and when Lindbergh saw the galley proofs, which had been produced only two weeks after his return to the United States, he nearly became unhinged.

Again, the story was written in the first-person purplish "aw shucks" prose and took great liberty with the facts. Lindbergh refused to have anything to do with it. He suggested a compromise in which he would write the book himself, but the publisher was appalled to learn that he didn't intend to start until after his U.S. tour was over in the fall. At last an agreement was reached in which Lindbergh would isolate himself for the remaining month before the tour began to see if he could repair the offending manuscript and, where necessary, write his own version of the events.

To say that Lindbergh's enforced isolation was "splendid" would be an understatement. Harry Guggenheim offered him the best bedroom suite at Falaise, his Norman-style castle at Sands Point, which opened onto a magnificent terrace overlooking Long Island Sound and a view of the Connecticut shore beyond.* There, Lindbergh had the run of the 350-acre estate, laced with riding trails and sculptured glades inhabited by flocks of peacocks, as well as the private beach on the Sound.

Guggenheim, who liked to be called "Captain Harry," after his service as a combat aviator in World War I, took it upon himself to school the young flier in the social graces and made a determined but failed attempt

---

* According to Lindbergh's biographer Leonard Mosley, from that time on this was Lindbergh's personal bedroom and was never used by anyone else.

to dress Lindbergh in stylish clothes. Good to his word, Lindbergh a month later delivered a finished and much improved manuscript to Putnam's that was published under the title *We*, which is how Lindbergh habitually referred to himself and the *Spirit of St. Louis*. As predicted, it quickly became a best seller, earning Lindbergh royalties of $250,000.*

That done, on July 20, the aviator took off from Mitchel Field and flew across the Long Island Sound to Hartford, Connecticut, where a hundred thousand people awaited him. For the next three months, Lindbergh's tour became the world's longest victory lap. At each stop as he zigzagged across the United States he was met by adoring crowds, swooning girls, autograph hunters, reporters, and photographers. He loved the flying, and performing stunts, but by then the novelty of fame had worn off, and Lindbergh began to dread his own popularity and the attendant publicity. He even stopped sending his laundry out under his own name in hotels because the laundresses would steal his underpants. Accordingly, as one of his biographers has written, he treated the crowds with "icy disdain" and the press with "anger and contempt."[17] This, eventually, led the press to retaliate, alluding to Lindbergh's "war with the press." Nevertheless, no matter how contemptibly he treated them, the reporters and broadcasters were eternally on the make for news and always came back for more.

During the tour, Lindbergh flew a total of 22,350 miles and was personally seen, it has been estimated, by more than 25 percent of the American population. He was living history. He visited eighty-two cities and flew over countless towns. At each stop there would be a parade, a luncheon, a press conference, and a dinner, usually accompanied by a band playing "Lucky Lindy," a song written in his honor.† In the morning there was takeoff again, once more attended by a fawning public, all of it set up by advance men supplied by the U.S. Department of Commerce.

During the tour he spent at least one night in each of the forty-eight states, and when he wasn't performing social duties Lindbergh made a point of inspecting airports and possible airport sites for future aviation

---

* This in a time of 5 percent maximum taxes, when a four-story town house on New York City's Upper East Side could be purchased for $100,000 or less.

† Lindbergh did not like the song because he considered it ostentatious.

expansion. In Detroit, he took Henry Ford up for his first airplane flight, as well as his mother, who had returned to the city to continue teaching her high school chemistry classes. In all these places, Lindbergh continually eschewed advances by the women who almost beyond number brazenly threw themselves at him. Occasionally, though, to the "middle-aged, and the spinsterly," he would stoop to the kindness of a smile, or even a ride in *Spirit*—doubtless the thrill of a lifetime.[18]

Throughout it all Lindbergh had become a one-man aviation chamber of commerce. When at last the tour was done, on October 23, 1927, he wrote that he had seen America, quite literally, "as no man had ever known it before."

LINDBERGH DUTIFULLY FIELDED questions from the press, but the one thing he bridled at was inquiries about his personal life. Women reporters in particular tended to ask him about love, marriage, girlfriends, and so on. His standard answer was a scornful, "What's that got to do with aviation?"[19] No one would ever have suggested he was gay, but neither could the gossip writers explain why, unlike, say, Eddie Rickenbacker who for a time always seemed to have a girl on either arm, the preposterously handsome Lindbergh was strictly a lone wolf.

Despite his reserve, however, love soon would come into Lindbergh's life in a most surprising way. From the outset he had attracted the attention of Dwight Morrow, a powerful lawyer, future U.S. senator, and senior partner at J. P. Morgan's formidable Wall Street banking firm. Morrow had chaired the eminent airpower commission known as the Morrow Board, convened in 1925 by President Coolidge in the wake of the Billy Mitchell controversy, which resulted in the creation of a separate U.S. Army Air Corps within the army. It was also Morrow who had suggested to Harry Guggenheim that the aviation foundation pay Lindbergh $50,000 to do a U.S. aviation promotion tour.* In return, Lindbergh put all of his money in the hands of Morgan's investment bankers.

---

* It did not hurt that Morrow was a college classmate at Amherst and friend of Coolidge.

Lindbergh and Morrow had met at the president's dinner the day Lindbergh arrived in Washington from Europe, and Morrow had invited the attractive young aviator to visit at his stately home in Englewood, New Jersey. At some point before going on his tour, Lindbergh accepted the invitation, and there was a fleeting introduction to Morrow's three daughters, whom he scarcely remembered but all of whom, and one in particular, would remember him, for she would become his wife.[20]

The same summer that Lindbergh embarked on his goodwill tour, President Coolidge tapped Dwight Morrow as ambassador to Mexico. Long considered a diplomatic backwater, the Mexico that Morrow was now charged with overseeing had become highly important to the United States. There were vast U.S. mining interests there (chiefly Guggenheim's) as well as enormous oil discoveries by American companies, while Mexico remained, as usual, in a state of eternal war. A year earlier its current president, Plutarco Elías Calles, a revolutionary with Marxist leanings, had begun a war of extermination against the Catholic Church, murdering Catholic priests and razing churches and cathedrals—all of that aside, of course, from the run-of-the-mill rape and pillage that accompanied any Mexican revolution. Morrow decided that to draw the spirit of the Mexican people closer to the United States, nothing could be better than an official visit by the most popular fellow in the world, Charles Lindbergh, American. Lindbergh readily agreed, and not only would he come to Mexico, he said, he would make the occasion even more memorable by setting a new record—a nonstop flight to Mexico City from Washington, D.C.! When Morrow protested that because of the mountains it was too dangerous, the newly minted colonel told him, "You get me the invitation, and I'll take care of the flying."[21]

A LITTLE AFTER NOON on December 13, 1927, the *Spirit of St. Louis* took off from Bolling Field in Washington. Everything went well throughout the night and until the next afternoon when Lindbergh entered the Valley of Mexico and found it blanketed in fog. He had prepared a map that outlined rail lines but was having trouble matching the map with the tracks on the ground. Like many a pilot, Lindbergh swooped down to get a peek at the names of the towns on the railroad stations along the tracks but became baffled when each town he passed was named "Caballeros." Only later did he discover that he had been reading the signs for men's rooms.[22]

After wandering off course for several hours, Lindbergh at last got his bearings and landed at Mexico City's airport, which was mobbed by at least 150,000 cheering Mexicans. President Calles himself handed Lindbergh the keys to the city. It had taken twenty-seven hours and fifteen minutes. On the way from the airport to the embassy the exuberant Mexicans nearly buried Lindbergh in flowers and bombarded him with invitations to every kind of Mexican entertainment from parades to bullfights to rodeos.

It was the Christmas season and the Morrows asked Lindbergh to spend the holidays with them at the embassy. They even arranged for his mother to come down on the train to San Antonio, where she would take a plane to Mexico City. Of the three Morrow girls, Lindbergh spent time bantering with the gregarious fourteen-year-old Constance, and warmed up to the beautiful twenty-three-year-old Elisabeth, but his world began to change, imperceptibly at first, with the arrival of twenty-one-year-old Anne Morrow. She had come home for Christmas from her senior year at Smith College.

Beneath her somewhat fragile-looking exterior, Anne was a tower of determination and brave as a bull. She was petite with a reserved beauty set off by a wide smile beneath a prominent nose,* keen, luminous eyes, and dark, silky hair that she kept short in the sort of rolled pageboy fashion of the 1920s. She also kept a diary in a perceptive writing style that belied her age and experience.

"I saw standing against a great stone pillar . . . a tall, slim boy in evening dress—so much slimmer, so much taller, so much more poised than I expected," she wrote. "A very refined face, not at all like those grinning 'Lindy' pictures—a firm mouth, clear, straight blue eyes, fair hair, and nice color . . . He did not smile, just bowed and shook hands."[23]

It was Anne's first time in her new home at the embassy, and she found the experience "intoxicating," with its enormous flower-filled rooms and "baronial" hall. "Why is it," she asked her diary after she found herself

---

* A newspaper later described her nose as sticking out of the cockpit of Lindbergh's plane "like a red grape."

244 ★ THE AVIATORS

included in a sitting room with Lindbergh and her sisters, "that attractive men stimulate Elisabeth to her best and always terrify me and put me at my worst!? . . . Colonel L. stood awkwardly by a desk, shifting from one foot to another. Elisabeth talked.

"He was very young and terribly shy," she continued, "looked straight ahead and talked in straight direct sentences which came out abruptly and clipped. You could not meet his sentences; they were statements of fact, presented with such honest directness . . . It was amazing—breathtaking. I could not speak. What kind of boy was this?"[24]

That night she could not sleep well as she "tried to comprehend, tried to analyze, the popularity of this man." It wasn't so much what Lindbergh had done, she wondered to her diary, "it must be either that he is the symbol of the most beautiful achievement of our age . . . or is it just personal magnetism? For everyone does feel immediately, I think, silenced and amazed at this man." Clearly then, after a day, Anne Morrow was smitten but, typically, she kept telling herself she didn't have a chance—especially against her taller and more beautiful older sister, Elisabeth.

After Christmas, Lindbergh set off on a goodwill aviation tour of South America and the Caribbean, and Anne Morrow set her jib for him. In the waning days after Christmas she made a point of paying particular attention to his mother, Evangeline, a fact that was not lost on Evangeline's son. One afternoon Lindbergh had taken the ladies of the family for a flight over Mexico City that so thrilled Anne once she was back on the ground she felt compelled to tell her diary, "I will not be happy till it happens again." And soon the diary filled with poetry—John Masefield, Edgar Lee Masters . . .

> . . . When first I met
> Your glance and knew
> That life had found me
> And Death too . . .

These were heady thoughts for a smart, sensitive, well-educated—and determined—young woman. When she returned to Smith after the holidays, Anne began buying copies of the magazine *Popular Aviation* at newsstands near the campus and scrutinized a volume about how to fly called *Airmen and Aircraft,* while trying to explain Lindbergh to herself.

"The intensity of life, burning like a bright fire in his eyes. Life focused in him—When he in turn focuses his life, power, force, on *anything,* amazing things happen . . . he wastes nothing, words, time, thought, emotion . . . His tremendous power over people—untried for, unconscious . . . His effect coming into a room, going out. His effect on men . . . never a false note, a hint of smallness . . . utter lack of recklessness, an amazing, impersonal kind of courage," she told her diary, and could have gone on—and did—"the way his smile completely changes his face; the small-boy-hands-in-pockets looking-straight-at-you attitude . . ."

Even after his lengthy South American tour the world continued to shower honors and money on Charles Lindbergh, including the presentation of the Medal of Honor, bestowed by President Coolidge on behalf of Congress. *Time* magazine named him its first "Man of the Year" for 1927, and the University of Wisconsin, whose doors he had not darkened since being expelled six years earlier, awarded him an honorary doctorate of law degree.

In the meantime, Lindbergh was becoming considerably wealthier. He had been asked to come aboard a new aviation company named Transcontinental Air Transport that purported to establish a coast-to-coast air route beginning with ten Ford trimotor single-wing or monoplanes. Lindbergh's position was chairman of the company's technical committee, but his name lent enormous prestige to the enterprise.

In exchange for his services he was given a signing bonus of $250,000 to purchase shares in the company and a yearly salary of $10,000. Transcontinental subsequently became known as "the Lindbergh Line." Several months later he accepted a similar position at a similar salary with the new Pan American Airways, owned by the legendary Juan Trippe. And within the year Harry Guggenheim had appointed him a consultant to his Aeronautical Foundation at a salary of $25,000 a year. In today's dollars Lindbergh was taking in nearly $700,000 a year plus stock offers and options, and there were additional advisory or board member positions as the months and years passed.

For Lindbergh these jobs were no sinecures; he actively advised both companies on all aspects of aviation from engines and toilets to air routes and the laying out of landing fields. He tested new equipment and inspected the personnel, constantly crisscrossing the country, looking for the better way. "Celebrity without purpose seemed pointless to Lindbergh," wrote his most recent biographer, "and commercial aviation became his crusade."[25]

BACK AT SMITH COLLEGE, Anne visited the airfield near campus after school, quizzing mechanics about planes and the art of flying. One day she even got a pilot to take her and a classmate up for a spin, an experience that left her with "tangled hair, [and] ecstatic." None of this, however, kept her from excellence in her college work; she was the recipient that year of the Montagu and Jordan prizes for literature and graduated from Smith summa cum laude in the spring of 1928.[26]

She spent the rest of the spring and most of the summer telling her diary all the reasons Lindbergh would not want her, e.g., that she was dumb and silly and far too insignificant for the magnificent Colonel Lindbergh, the most eligible bachelor on earth; that her sister Elisabeth was so much prettier and wittier and so on. Then one day he called her at home in New Jersey. He wanted to take her for a plane ride.

Lindbergh took her first to the fabulous Guggenheim mansion where he was living, because of the press—if they went to any of the regular airfields "we'd be engaged the next day." So Lindbergh left her there in the fabulous Guggenheim mansion ("Madonnas in every niche . . . It was priceless—I and all the Madonnas!" she wrote later to her younger sister) with the equally fabulous Guggenheims, Harry and Caroline, while he brought the plane around to Harry's private landing strip. Meantime, the Guggenheims "horrified" Anne, "with tales of 'Slim's' practical jokes." (Lindbergh had been known to change the keys on people's typewriters, give hotfoots, and so forth.)[27]

Suddenly, the ice had been broken. "I can't explain to you, Con, what a change had come in my attitude—just from that hour ride out," she wrote to her little sister, Constance. I discovered that I could be *perfectly* natural with him, say anything to him, that I wasn't a *bit* afraid of him, or even worshipful any more . . . He's just *terribly* kind and absolutely natural . . . He's rather a dear."[28] The courtship of Charles Lindbergh and Anne Morrow began, and by the end of the year he had asked her to marry him.

Anne had no illusions about what she was getting into. In one sense she was marrying beneath her class—that charmed mid-Atlantic life of private schools and clubs and woodsy manors, with baby carriages and christenings, weddings and formal hunt club balls—but in another sense she was marrying way above it. They spent much of their time in the confines of the Guggenheim mansion, where young Charles and young Anne socialized with the likes of Vanderbilts, Morgans, Whitneys, Rockefellers, Putnams, Roosevelts, and others too swell to mention, all of whom could be trusted to keep a secret.

To an old friend, Corliss Lamont, son of Thomas Lamont, chairman of J. P. Morgan and Co., Anne wrote of her impending marriage, "It must seem hysterically funny to you, as it did to me, when I consider my opinions on marriage. 'A safe marriage,' 'Things in common,' 'A quiet life,' etc. etc. . . . Don't wish me happiness—I don't expect to be happy; it's gotten beyond that somehow." She was headed, she knew full well, into "a life of relentless action! But after all," she wrote, "what am I going to do about it? After all, there he is, and I've got to go. Wish me courage and strength and a sense of humor—I will need them all."[29] Thus was Anne Morrow swept away by a simple boy from the Midwest on a magic carpet powered by an internal combustion engine.

THEY WERE MARRIED ON MAY 27, 1929, in a private ceremony at the Morrows' grand new Georgian manor house, Next Day Hill, in Englewood, New Jersey. Back in February, reporters had been given a cursory engagement announcement with no wedding date. The few guests, consisting of family and close friends, understood that they had been invited to a reception for Lindbergh's mother and were completely surprised to find themselves witnesses at the wedding of Charles and Anne.

She wore a white wedding dress with a lace cap and veil and carried a bouquet of spring flowers, larkspur and columbine, picked and arranged by her sister Elisabeth. The Reverend Dr. William Adams Brown, of Union Theological Seminary, conducted the ceremony.[30]

Their honeymoon immediately afterward resembled, as much as anything else, a prison break. It had been arranged that they would slip out the back of the house and spirit themselves to a yacht on Long Island

Sound, in which they would leisurely cruise to the Morrows' summer home in Maine. "We escaped in a borrowed car," Anne wrote. "I seem to remember lying down in the bottom while passing the crowd of reporters at the gate." They then swapped cars at a friend's house, donned hats and dark glasses, and motored to the spot on the Sound where they found a dinghy tied to a tree and rowed it out to the thirty-eight-foot boat, named *Mouette,* a gift to the Lindberghs, which was moored right offshore.*

By the time news got out about their wedding, Mr. and Mrs. Charles Lindbergh were motoring far down the Sound, headed to Block Island under cover of darkest night. Meanwhile, when the press people learned they had been foiled, reporters hunted them down like animals.

When they made Block Island on the second day, even though they remained disguised, the Lindberghs were spotted and revealed. "One man in an open boat circled around us in harbor for seven straight hours, his wake rocking us constantly," Anne said, "as he shouted demands that we come out on deck and pose for him . . . I felt like an escaped convict. This was not freedom."

They pressed on toward Maine with full fuel and water tanks and an icebox loaded with block ice, dining on fancy canned foods such as pâté de foie gras, exotic fruits, and cases of ginger ale, and they were having the best of honeymooners' time between the attacks of the reporters, which quickly caused them to flee a comfortable anchorage at the Woods Hole, Massachusetts, harbor and spend a storm-tossed night anchored on a fishing bank in the open ocean, "hearing the dishes crash at every big wave," all to elude the pestilent press.[31]

At last they reached the coast of Maine, only to be assailed by "that terrifying drone of a plane hunting you, and boats," Anne wrote to her mother, even as a press-hired seaplane hove into view. "I don't feel angry about it anymore—it is inevitable. But it was a terrible shock to wake up from

---

* The boat was a wood cabin cruiser made by the Elco corporation, which previously had made electric engine launches. The author went aboard *Mouette* in 1978 when she was for sale in Three Mile Harbor in East Hampton, Long Island. Among her accoutrements then was the original set of yachting china, monogrammed for the Lindberghs. Recently, she was listed for sale again, in California.

that blissfully quiet existence of being nobodies . . . without being followed, stared at, shouted at; to be waked by the harsh, smirking voice of a reporter outside our window one morning: 'Is this Colonel Lindbergh's boat?' "[32]

THE LIFE THAT THE LINDBERGHS LED was every bit as hectic and exciting as Anne had imagined. Like Eddie Rickenbacker before him, Charles was now the world's resident guru not only for aviation but seemingly for practically every other matter under the sun.

Anne was soon infected with Charles's distaste for the press, all the more so after the running pursuit of their honeymoon cruise. "Never say anything you wouldn't want shouted from the housetops," Lindbergh had warned her, "and never write anything you wouldn't mind seeing on the front page of a newspaper." She had taken these admonishments to heart during their courtship, disguising her letters home and to friends on the suspicion that her mail was being opened, and using code words for Charles (he became Boyd) and for other important events and elements in her life.

Even though there was plenty of good reason for his antipathy Lindbergh fundamentally misunderstood the press. He believed that the less said the better, on the theory that the reporters would thus have fewer chances to misquote him or misinterpret him. The same went for photographers; both he and Anne began putting on disguises when going out in public to keep from being recognized, and they continued the practice for many years afterward.

Lindbergh failed to recognize that his very secrecy was what created so much of the unwanted attention by the newspapers. He might have taken a lesson from his contemporary the great Swedish actress Greta Garbo, whose aversion to the press and publicity produced a constant and outsized flurry of activity by the paparazzi of the day.

Instead, Lindbergh seems to have taken the officious, offensive, and boorish behavior of the newspapermen as a personal affront and any attempt to pry into his personal life as a deliberate insult. He did not seem to grasp that these people—reporters, photographers, editors, etc.—were for the most part merely trying to make a living from their bosses, who were in turn driven by orders from above to keep circulation moving. Eventually, his relations with newspapers degenerated to the extent that he became convinced that America's founders had erred when they included "freedom of the press" in the First Amendment.

In any event, Lindbergh's work with Transcontinental and Pan Am kept him almost perpetually on the go in between other adventures. Anne was no stay-at-home wife but went with him as a sort of assistant and, in time, a radio operator-telegrapher and navigator. Together they crisscrossed the country—San Francisco with the famed woman flier Amelia Earhart; Cleveland for the air show and races; Santa Fe; Detroit to see Evangeline; Los Angeles for dinner with Mary Pickford and Douglas Fairbanks, the two biggest movie stars of the day; Washington; Kansas City; New York; and the newly elected president of the United States Herbert Hoover's fishing camp in the Shenandoah Valley. In fact, there was no Lindbergh home to return to. During all these months they lived in hotels or stayed with Charles's many new friends, who tended to be men of "substance"—bankers, lawyers, airline or railroad owners—and, of course, at Harry and Caroline Guggenheim's mansion Falaise. Eventually, Anne became an enthusiastic pilot herself, with the great Lindbergh himself as her instructor. As a perfectionist, he expected nothing less from his wife, and in time she became an excellent flier.

The couple complemented each other in a symbiotic way. She was educated in classics and fine arts, while his interest in literature ran to (and stopped in the neighborhood of) Robert Service. He knew nothing of music and had a tin ear, while Anne played the piano. She was a student of fine arts and sculpture and he appreciated pictures of things he could readily identify.

On the other hand, he had developed a scientific mind that grasped the positions of the stars in the heavens and the curvature of Earth; ultimately he delved deeply into history, ancient and modern, anthropology, politics, philosophy, economics, and animal husbandry, of which he was already something of an expert. Above all he was a man of science. Nevertheless, Anne came to know him as a person of great sensitivity, as she had suspected almost from the beginning, and someone she could talk with easily.

And while all of that and everything else was going on, by the last of 1929 she managed to get pregnant.

AFTER A WHIRLWIND GOODWILL and air-route survey tour of the Caribbean basin with Mr. and Mrs. Juan Trippe of Pan Am—during which Anne was frequently discomforted by morning sickness, which she mistook for airsickness until the doctor confirmed she was going to have a baby—Anne moved into her parents' house for the duration of her pregnancy. The press began gearing up for the big event by hovering around the gates of Next Day Hill like a stupendous flock of geese, and hyping the story of the forthcoming Lindbergh nativity as if it involved a royal heir. It was reported that newspapers were offering substantial bribes to telegraphers and phone operators for information regarding the event. For their part, Charles and Anne decided against giving the press even the courtesy of *an announcement* of the birth and arranged to notify Evangeline in Detroit by coded wire.

On June 22, 1930, coincidentally Anne's twenty-fourth birthday, Charles Augustus Lindbergh III came into the world, but it would be two more weeks before the Lindberghs would reveal to the press even the name of the child. Nevertheless, the occasion set off a delirious new round of worldwide rejoicing as tens of thousands of telegrams, flowers, cards, letters, and baby gifts—many of them quite elegant—flooded into Next Day Hill. Desperate for news and photographs of the Lindbergh heir, some newspapers began floating disgusting rumors of a birth gone wrong, forcing Lindbergh at last to call a press conference and give details about the baby. For its own part, the press in general was beginning to sour on what many interpreted as the constant whiff of arrogance in the great transatlantic hero, and a sort of mini-backlash occurred, with columnists suggesting that Lindbergh was, in effect, biting the hand that fed him. All in all it was an unpleasant episode in the Lindberghs' seemingly intractable "war with the press," but afterward, like fighters who have beaten each other into exhaustion, a kind of uneasy truce was declared—if not by Anne and Charles, then by the press—until the next round could begin. Around the same time, the Lindberghs were suffered to endure a shocking incident of reckless and inhumane invasion of privacy when gawkers managed to drive through the gate at Next Day Hill and run over Anne and Constance's childhood pet terrier, Daffin, mortally injuring but not immediately killing the dog, and not even stopping to try and help.[33]

IT WAS DURING THIS SAME SUMMER OF 1930 that Lindbergh went to Cleveland for the air races and met for the first time the German flying ace Ernst Udet. They got along famously. While there, Lindbergh also ordered a new plane for himself and Anne, a low-wing, dual cockpit capable of flying long distances. It was modern in every aspect, from the latest navigation aids, a generator-based electrical system that could heat flying suits at high altitudes, and sliding plastic-style cockpit canopies of the type later used in World War II fighter planes.[34] Lindbergh took delivery of the plane in Los Angeles and the two of them set out for New York, breaking the current speed record by three hours.

Now that a family had been started, Lindbergh at last turned to the task of making a home. Anne, who had hinted once that she would love to live in New England, knew that would never do because of its frequent fogs. Charles needed to be near but not *in* Manhattan, because of his association with Transcontinental and Pan Am and other business connections. They discussed Long Island because of its many flying fields, but Charles finally settled on an approximately five-hundred-acre tract of property not far from Princeton, New Jersey, where they could build a home that would at once give them privacy and access to airfields around the New York area and also remain close to Anne's parents' place at Englewood. It "had a brook, and fields and woodlands filled with beautiful oaks," and as they began designing a house with the help of an architect, they meanwhile rented a quaint old farmhouse where Anne settled into motherhood.[35]

Charlie, as they called him, soon began to resemble his famous father, with the cleft chin, blue eyes, broad smile, and wavy shock of blond hair. Like many fathers, Lindbergh at first did not seem to know what to make of the baby, but as he grew into a toddler his father was soon "flying" him around the room above his head—"ceiling flying," Lindbergh called it. There were two dogs in the family, a fierce Scottish terrier named Skean (Gaelic for "dagger") and an equally intrepid fox terrier named Wagoosh (after Charles's dog back in Little Falls). At that point the Lindberghs employed a maid, a cook, a butler, and soon hired a new baby nurse after the departure of their first one. She was twenty-four-year-old Betty Gow who had left her native Glasgow, Scotland, at the age of fourteen to earn her keep as a servant in America. Now she was about to figure in a horror that would soon darken the bright sun presently hovering over the Lindbergh household.

Charles had become increasingly restless during Anne's pregnancy, which in its latter stages had more or less grounded him, except for a trying episode involving the investigation into the cause of the dreadful plane crash in Kansas that had killed Knute Rockne and seven others. This was the crash that had so concerned Eddie Rickenbacker, then general manager of TWA. As chairman of a federal aviation commission Lindbergh explained that the crash was due to a wing failure.

Now Lindbergh was proposing another "survey" flight such as the one recently undertaken through the Caribbean to sketch out new passenger air routes for Pan Am—only this time it would be a three-month grind reaching halfway around the earth from Washington to Alaska, Japan, China, and the Soviet Union, with occasional stops along the way for food and fuel.

It is self-evident that any new mother who would consent to such a departure from her child must have uncommon devotion to her husband, and Anne filled this role to its uttermost degree. Charles had helped her become a pilot, as well as a radio-telegraph operator, and with dual controls in the Sirius she could spell him in periods of flying. It was this kind of partnership that he had envisioned when he proposed to her, though Anne had not understood it at the time.

Anne knew her life was now an adventure inextricably linked with her husband and, contrary to the opinions of some of her more recent biographers, didn't seem uncomfortable with it.* "I went on them proudly," she wrote later, "taking my place as a crew member. The beauty and mystery of flying never palled, and I was deeply involved in my job of operating the radio."[36]

LIKE HIS TRANSATLANTIC TRIUMPH, the path to the Orient that Lindbergh chose to take had never been flown before—a 7,100-mile great circle route that would have him flying over some of the most desolate,

---

* This is not to suggest that Anne Lindbergh did not at times become homesick or miss her children. Of course she did.

inhospitable, and uncharted territory on the planet. In preparation, he again measured every item to be taken in terms of its weight, including a six-pound shotgun and limited number of shells in case they were forced down and had to hunt for food. The big, sleek, black-painted Sirius had been converted to a seaplane with pontoons for wheels, and a more powerful 600-horsepower engine was installed.[*]

On July 29, 1931, the Lindberghs landed the Sirius at the North Haven, Maine, summer home of the Morrows, and next morning Anne and Charles said good-bye to her parents and to baby Charlie, whom Charles had taken to calling "Buster," and flew away to Washington, D.C., starting point for their great Arctic air exploration journey, which was expected to take four months.

From Ottawa they flew over "hundreds and hundreds of lakes, absolutely flat, and tall, thin pines," to Moose Factory, Canada, where they were met after landing on the water by a delegation of Cree Indians and Hudson Bay Company men. They ate moose and raspberries (canned) and slept in a house built about 1650 that reminded them of an Edward Hopper painting, checked in with the Canadian Mounted Police, and flew on to Churchill, finding it "a little snappy, like fall." Next morning they flew to Baker Lake, refueled at Point Barrow, then on to Aklavik where Anne got her first (and last, before Tokyo) bath in a tin tub, the only one in town.

During a long day after Nome they crossed the Bering Sea and found themselves flying off the northern coast of Siberia; fog was frequently a problem though Lindbergh usually managed to fly beneath it, except when he rose up to give antenna height for Anne's radio-telegraph messages in which she several times daily tapped out their progress for all the world to note.

Night flying was no problem since there was virtually no night in those latitudes at this time of year, when the North Star was almost directly overhead. They landed in the harbor at Petropavlovsk and were given

---

[*] Like yachtsmen, it was customary for pilots to name substantial planes such as the *Spirit of St. Louis,* but for some reason the Sirius remained unnamed until several years later on a stopover in Greenland when an Eskimo boy deemed it *Tingmissartoq,* or "one who flies like a big bird," which stuck.

dinner of pork, beans, radishes, and Russian tea by the head of the local governing committee in a room plastered with posters of Lenin and other Soviet leaders.

On August 29 they landed in Tokyo Bay, but outside Tokyo, and spent the night in the home of a man who raised foxes for a living. At Nemuro the mayor gave them a ceremonial dinner complete with geisha girls to serve and dance. At Tokyo, however, it was different, more like the old days in France, England, and New York. Millions of Japanese mobbed them, shouting *"Banzai! Banzai,"* which means "May you live ten thousand years!"

They stayed in Japan for two weeks, visiting cities, then pushed on to Nanking and "the great expanse of China." Seeing it from the air, Anne observed that "every bit of ground is cultivated in small, narrow strips, not at all like our Great Plains in the West . . . here it is almost terrifying; no trees, no wild land, nothing left but narrow back-yard strips of fields and mud huts representing thousands of people as far as one can see."

The Yangtze River was in a dangerous flood stage, inundating an area equal to the size of Lake Superior, and those people who weren't drowned were starving and in need of medicine. Lindbergh of course volunteered to help and nearly lost the plane. He and two doctors landed at the city of Hinghwa with a bag of vital medicines, which the Chinese thought was food and swam out to one doctor's sampan, swamped it, and then swam to the plane and began to clamber aboard, tipping the wings dangerously, until Lindbergh took out his revolver and fired into the air, driving them away.

By this time Anne was missing Charlie, writing to her mother, "I dream about the baby every night, almost, and am quite homesick for you. But I want to see Peking before I start home." She never got the chance.

They were headed to Shanghai when they spotted the big British aircraft carrier *Hermes* anchored in the rushing stream of the Yangtze, dropped down for a look, landed, and were greeted so cordially by Admiral Colin MacLean that they decided to stay for a few days, and Anne became the first woman ever to spend the night aboard the World War I–era warship. At night, MacLean considerately arranged for the ship's crane to lift the Sirius aboard the carrier to protect it from river currents, thieves, or vandals, which very nearly lost the Sirius and the Lindberghs as well.

When the ship's crew was attempting to drop the plane back into the water—with Charles and Anne in their cockpits—the Sirius wrenched around against the current while still in the grip of the ship's crane's cables and began to turn over. Charles cried, "Jump! Jump quickly!" and the two of them plunged into the Yangtze, quite possibly the most insanitary river on earth. Hampered by their heavy flying suits they floundered around until the ship's tender came and fished them out, and once aboard the carrier the surgeon plied them with Bovril, a nourishing English tea-like drink, and castor oil, which was about all that was available in those times to ward off the Yangtze's contaminated organisms.

The accident had caused a wing to be torn off the plane and other damage, but when at last it was dredged out of the rushing river Lindbergh believed it could be repaired in Shanghai and was in the process of arranging to take it there. Anne, somewhat agitated, wrote to her sister Elisabeth, "How long will it take to repair, and *when* will we get home?"

Sooner than she expected, but not in any way she might have wished. On October 5, a telegram came from home saying that her father, Dwight Morrow, by then a U.S. senator from New Jersey, had died of a brain hemorrhage. Anne was of course devastated and Charles immediately canceled the expedition, arranging their immediate passage to America and for the Sirius to be crated and sent to San Francisco.

Pan Am and the other airlines did not adopt Lindbergh's northern route across the Pacific. Instead they chose the middle Pacific route with the famous Pan Am Clipper service that landed at Midway, Wake Island, and Guam before reaching the Orient.

IN EARLY FEBRUARY 1932 the Lindberghs moved into their new home in Hopewell, near Princeton, New Jersey, a white rambling six-bedroom brick, stone, and slate two-story manor-style house they named Highfields. They had hoped the place, with its extensive grounds and remote location, would give them the privacy they desired. Instead it became a house of horror.

Anne battled a case of ptomaine poisoning most of the winter and stayed at Next Day Hill with her mother. She seemed to gravitate to her family home, and a routine had settled in where she, Charles, and the baby—whom she called her "fat lamb"—would spend their weekdays at Englewood and go down to the Hopewell house on weekends. Betty

Eddie Rickenbacker, known as "Captain Eddie," 1918, stands beside his plane emblazoned with the Hat in the Ring squadron emblem.

LEFT: *Rickenbacker ca. 1903, approximately the time he quit school to help support his family.*
RIGHT: *The Rickenbacker home, built by Eddie's father on the outskirts of Columbus, Ohio.*

*Eddie Rickenbacker ca. 1915. By age twenty-one he was one of the top
race car drivers in the United States.*

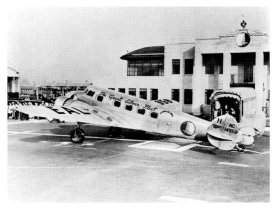

LEFT: *Eddie and his future wife, Adelaide, in 1922.*
RIGHT: *In 1938 Rickenbacker bought Eastern Air Lines, which flew the innovative DC-3 and the Lockheed Electra pictured here.*

Following a 1941 plane crash Rickenbacker was initially given up for dead.

LEFT: *Jimmy Doolittle as a young boy.*
RIGHT: *Jimmy and Joe Doolittle in 1918, shortly after their marriage.*

*Doolittle beside the Consolidated NY-2 he used for his famous
"blind flying" experiment in 1929.*

Doolittle flew the stubby Gee Bee to win the Thompson Trophy in 1932.

*Jimmy and Joe Doolittle pose with the Vultee aircraft in which
Doolittle set a transcontinental record in 1935.*

LEFT: *Charles Augustus Lindbergh with his father, a U.S. congressman.*
RIGHT: *Charles at age six with his mother, Evangeline, ca. 1908.*

LEFT: *"Slim" Lindbergh in his early flying days, ca. 1925.*
RIGHT: *Second Lieutenant Lindbergh graduated top of his class*
at the U.S. Army's flying school.

In England crowds mobbed the Spirit of St. Louis *following Lindbergh's historic 1927 New York to Paris flight.*

LEFT: *The* Spirit of St. Louis *soars past the Eiffel Tower.*
RIGHT: *Lindbergh receives a warm welcome home with a Wall Street ticker tape parade.*

Charles and Anne, whom Lindbergh married in 1929, became famous
as a flying team with around-the-world aerial explorations.

LEFT: *One-year-old Charles A. Lindbergh Jr. at Highfields, the Lindbergh estate.*
RIGHT: *Accused kidnapper Bruno Richard Hauptmann is led into court, January 1935.*

Gow, the nursemaid, had taken up residence at Next Day Hill and Anne looked after Charlie, the fat lamb, herself. Soon her doctor confirmed that Anne was pregnant again. Charles said he hoped for a girl.

On the weekend of February 27, Charlie came down with a cold. He was still sick on Monday, which dawned cold and rainy, when Anne phoned Betty Gow to tell her they would remain in Hopewell. Charles had gone into his office in New York and phoned to say he was staying over and would be home next day.

On Tuesday, March 1, Anne caught the baby's cold and asked Betty to come to Hopewell. That afternoon the weather had much improved and so had Charlie, and Anne took a walk around the grounds, then spent the rest of the afternoon with the baby in the living room. About 6:15, after feeding him, Anne and Betty tucked him into his crib and started closing the shutters, but those on the corner of the room were warped and would not close properly. Betty opened the window on the southern side about halfway, observing a custom of the day so as to let in "fresh air," despite it being the dead of winter with temperatures in the low thirties. Then she turned off the light and closed the door. It was a little after 7:30.

Anne sat at her desk writing and waiting for Charles, who was late and did not arrive until after eight, and the two had dinner about 8:30. Around nine o'clock, Charles heard a heavy noise, a kind of "thud" that sounded as if someone in the kitchen had dropped something—"such as a wooden box or orange crate."

Charles went upstairs and bathed, then about 9:30 returned to the study to read, sitting beside the fire next to a window that was directly beneath the baby's nursery windows where the shutters would not close. Charles read and Anne went up and bathed. While Anne bathed, Betty Gow went to check on the baby. It was ten p.m. She went into the bathroom and turned on the light, enough to see but not disturb him. She closed the window but suddenly realized she couldn't hear him breathing. "I thought that something had happened to him," she said later, "that perhaps the clothes were over his head. In the half light I saw he wasn't there and felt all over the bed for him." She rushed down the hall to the Lindberghs' bedroom.

"Do you have the baby, Mrs. Lindbergh?"

"No."

"Then maybe the colonel has him!" Betty said, and bolted down the stairs to the library where Lindbergh was still reading.

"He isn't in his crib?" Lindbergh asked, alarmed. He dashed upstairs to the nursery and found it empty, with Charlie's imprint still on the bedclothes. Charles bounded down the passageway to the master bedroom where Anne was standing, bewilderedly; she had been to the nursery, and finding it empty she'd returned to her bedroom. She asked her husband if he had the baby, but Charles brushed past and went to his closet where he kept a rifle and headed back to the nursery. When he arrived, with Anne and Betty at his heels, and finding the crib of course still empty, he turned and said, "Anne, they have stolen our baby."[37]

An all points bulletin went out from New Jersey state police headquarters notifying police locally and nationwide that the twenty-month-old son of Charles and Anne Lindbergh, wearing a gray sleeping suit, had been kidnapped. That of course alerted the press, which descended on the Lindbergh home like ants on a wounded beetle. It quickly became the "crime of the century" or, in the words of H. L. Mencken, "The biggest news story since the Resurrection." Within the day photographs of the child, provided by Lindbergh, appeared on the front pages of newspapers around the world. For once, in Lindbergh's estimation, here was a chance that the press might actually make itself useful.

All through the night, as state police officers arrived, the grounds were searched for clues, more of which were likely destroyed than found. The window of the nursery had been ajar and a white envelope was lying on the sill. Deciding that it might be a ransom note, Charles had not touched it in case there were fingerprints. Outside, he and the butler found footprints beneath the window. Thirty yards from the house officers found three sections of a homemade extension ladder.

An officer who dusted the envelope taken from the windowsill found no fingerprints. He opened it and gave the single sheet of paper inside to Lindbergh. Written in blue ink with odd curlicues, misspellings, and Germanic intonations, the ransom note began "Dear Sir," demanded $50,000 in various denominations, warned against going to the police, promised contact "after 2–4 days," and included a strange symbol in the lower right corner consisting of two interlocking circles.

From the note, police deduced that the crime had been committed by someone of Nordic descent who was either agonizingly unskilled at writing or trying to disguise his penmanship.

President Hoover offered the full resources of the U.S. government, including the attorney general's office, postal inspectors, the Internal Revenue Service, and the military. Congress began working on a bill, later known as the Lindbergh law, making kidnapping a capital crime and allowing the FBI to intervene if a kidnapper went across state lines. Everyone from Boy Scouts to men's and women's service clubs offered help. Labor leaders promised to put their members on the lookout. Churches regularly began conducting prayers until the child was found. Moreover there was an enormous outpouring of sympathy from the general public, confirmed by the thousands of letters each day that began to arrive at Highfields. Most of these were merely expressions of sympathy by individuals far and wide, but far too many were from cranks, crackpots, and con men. There were all sorts of clairvoyants, seers, and other oracles, people claiming to have had dreams about the baby's whereabouts, people who claimed to have seen him, many of these seeking money. And, unfortunately, as the days went by with no news, some elements of the press began publishing made-up stories of the most lurid variety, which was not only unhelpful but infuriating and hurtful to the Lindberghs.

Anne held up well, all things considered, and mostly stayed in her room, out of the way, while Charles read police reports, sat in conferences, and hovered around the command center. It is heartrending, even now, to read her account, reflected in the letters she wrote at the time. On the second day, Anne tried to be upbeat to Evangeline Lindbergh, pointing out that the kidnappers' "knowledge of the baby's room, lack of fingerprints, well-fitted ladder, all point to *professionals*, which is rather good, as it means they want only the money and will not maliciously hurt the baby."

As the days wore on, she tried in quiet desperation to keep up hope and on March 3 was prompted to write Evangeline: "C [Charles] is *marvelous*—calm, clear, alert, and observing. It is dreadful not to be able to do *anything* to help. I want *so* to help."

And March 5: "We seem to have pretty tangible word that the baby is safe, and *well cared for* . . . we are progressing toward recovery of the child . . . at any time I may be routed out of my bed so that a group of detectives can have a conference in the room."

And March 8: "It is a slow hard game but they all have faith in the ultimate success."

March 10: "There *really* is definite progress. I feel *much* happier today."[38]

Charles was telling her only in a general way what was actually happening. Police were investigating hundreds of leads daily. On March 5 a genuine ransom note arrived (there had been numerous phony ones). It warned that the Lindberghs would now "have to take the consequences" of going to the police and the press, and now upped the ransom from $50,000 to $70,000. But the note also gave assurances the baby was well cared for and that the kidnappers intended "to send him back in gut health."

With no good leads, Lindbergh saw no other course than to pay the ransom. He did so personally, and with a strange accomplice, seventy-one-year-old John F. Condon, retired doctor of pedagogy, who had been the swimming and boxing coach of Fordham University in the Bronx, New York. Condon had inserted himself in the case and made contact with the person who claimed to be the kidnapper.

At a park in the Bronx on the night of April 2, with Lindbergh waiting in the car with his army .45, Condon gave the kidnapper a box of bills that had been specially marked for identification by agents of the U.S. Treasury Department. In exchange, the alleged kidnapper told Condon the baby could be found on a small boat named the *Nelly* located on a windblown island south of Cape Cod, Massachusetts. A search of the island and surrounding area next day turned up no such boat. "We've been double-crossed," Lindbergh said.

EARLY IN THE MORNING of May 12, 1932, a truck driver pulled over on a road several miles from Highfields so that his passenger could go into the woods to urinate. There, the passenger stumbled across what he thought was a small human skull in a shallow grave. Upon further investigation he saw a bloodstained burlap sack with what appeared to be the decomposed remains of a child, with golden curls intact. Animals had apparently dismembered some of the body.

Colonel Norman Schwarzkopf, head of the New Jersey State Police,[*] got a full description of the clothing that the baby was wearing the night of the kidnapping, which was supplied by Betty Gow, down to the last undergarment. At the scene, Schwarzkopf told one of his police inspectors to carefully examine and sample the clothing on the body, and piece by piece it matched what the nursemaid had said the child had worn that night. Sorrowfully, but resolutely, they returned to the Lindbergh home where Betty verified that the sample of clothing had belonged to little Charlie.

Anne's mother, Betty Morrow, who had lost her husband only a few months earlier, was the first family member told of the discovery. When she went upstairs into Anne's bedroom the look on her face must have told the awful truth. Just recently Anne had wakened from a dream in which the baby was actually returned, and someone was saying, "Why, she hasn't even kissed him yet," wrote Anne in her diary. "They don't understand—I don't want to kiss him but just put my hand over the top of his curls."

"The baby is with Daddy," Mrs. Morrow told her daughter.[39]

CHARLES, WHO HAD JUST ARRIVED HOME exhausted after chasing down another phony lead, was distraught over the news. He went to Anne's room, where he found her nearly inconsolable. He "spoke so beautifully and calmly about death that it gave me great courage," she wrote afterward.

The remains of the body were taken to a funeral home in Trenton that doubled as a morgue, where an autopsy was performed and the cause of death revealed to be a heavy skull fracture. At first authorities thought "a maniac" had committed the crime and deliberately murdered the child, but later it was determined that the broken step in the ladder had probably caused the kidnapper to drop the burlap sack in which the baby had been placed and the child landed headfirst on a concrete windowsill.

---

[*] He was the father of the late U.S. Army general Norman Schwarzkopf Jr. of Operation Desert Storm fame.

Possibly, that was the sound that Lindbergh had heard on the night of the kidnapping as he sat in his chair reading in the library below the nursery.

Next day, Lindbergh insisted on identifying the body himself. It left some people to wonder why a father would put himself through that kind of ordeal, but thoroughness was ingrained in Lindbergh's makeup. He knew he didn't want for either of them that, somewhere down the road, there would arise any spark of doubt that it was their son's dead body that had been found.

After being shown the autopsy report, Charles concluded that the child must have died immediately from the fall. "I don't think he knew anything about it," he told Anne. The scene around Trenton was already turning into a sideshow, with people vending food to curiosity seekers. Even more nauseating, and painful, a photographer had broken a window and gotten into the morgue, where he took a photograph of the dead baby, copies of which were being sold on the street. Lindbergh decided a funeral and burial would merely attract more unwanted attention and desecration and made arrangements to have the body cremated. Schwarzkopf accompanied him as they drove to the crematorium behind the hearse that contained the small body, and the state police chief remained with Lindbergh until the process was finished and Lindbergh had accepted the ashes to scatter in the air.

The search phase of the crime had now ended, but Schwarzkopf swore to redouble his efforts to arrest the perpetrators. The scum of it was the realization that, after the child was dead, the kidnapper or kidnappers threw him into the woods like garbage and even took his sleeping suit to use as a bargaining chip. Police made a duplicate of the ladder and tried to reenact the crime to see if some clue turned up. The ladder was a clue in itself; Schwarzkopf sent a few pieces of it to the Forest Service Laboratory of the Wisconsin department of agriculture, where one of its scientists, Arthur Koehler, said that by examining its unique grain, which exists in all wood, he might be able to trace the timber in the ladder to the place where it was sold. Meantime, some of the bills of the ransom money began to appear in New York.

ANNE, NOW IN HER SIXTH MONTH OF PREGNANCY, suffered deeply from the ordeal but tried to put the best face on it for herself. "I am glad," she said, "that I spoiled him that last weekend when he was sick and I took him on my lap and rocked him and sang to him. And glad he wanted me those last days." Charles, the epitome of courage and strength, was drained to the point of exhaustion but determined to find a way to reclaim their lives. He tried desperately to overcome the temptation toward bitterness, but he was not always successful. The fact that something like this could happen, in the face of all his resolve to secure privacy at Highfields, left Lindbergh feeling guilty, and he damned his own naivete for assuming that the family was safe. But mostly, beyond the hurt, he felt violated.

The outpouring of sympathy was stunning. From all parts of the globe tens of thousands of messages arrived in telegrams and letters and bouquets of flowers. Trees were planted and other memorials made in the dead child's name. One woman even offered her own one-year-old son to the Lindberghs for adoption. The Guggenheims graciously invited Anne and Charles to Falaise for a long weekend, where they tried to gather their thoughts for the future. Anne was due in August, and she felt the most important thing was to prepare for the new baby. Highfields seemed cursed now, and Anne felt more comfortable being at home with her mother at Next Day Hill.*

It had been building for a long time, but the Lindberghs had developed almost a siege mentality when it came to their privacy—largely it consisted of the intrusions of reporters and photographers who seemed to dog them to the ends of the earth—but now a new danger had arisen: murderers and kidnappers. As one of Lindbergh's biographers put it, "They were no longer in the world, but surrounded by it, and it was menacing."[40]

---

* Ultimately, the Lindberghs donated the Highfields property to the State of New Jersey, and today it is the Albert Elias Group Center, a home for delinquent and troubled boys.

CHAPTER 10

HIS HALO TURNED INTO A NOOSE

O N AUGUST 16, 1932, a second baby boy was born to Anne and Charles Lindbergh. They named him Jon, the Scandinavian spelling for John. They acquired a German police dog named Thor to watch over the child, and Thor performed as advertised, rarely leaving the baby's side unless he was called away by Charles or Anne. To get away from the summer heat, they took the baby up to the Morrow place in Maine. Anne's sister Elisabeth was there, newly engaged to a wealthy Welshman, but she was doomed, and everyone knew it. Doctors had discovered lesions on her heart that were inoperable. On December 28, 1933, she married Aubrey Niel Morgan in an elaborate wedding at Next Day Hill. Within two years she would be dead.

Charles became very interested in his sister-in-law's case and inquired of Elisabeth's physician why an operation could not be performed on her heart to save her life. The answer was that the heart would have to be stopped to do the surgical work, and she would die on the operating table.

The mechanically minded Lindbergh went to the glassblower at Princeton University and began fashioning a crude heart pump that, when perfected, would ostensibly pump blood through a human body long enough for the heart to be stopped and operated on. Ultimately teaming with Dr. Alexis Carrel, a Nobel Prize–winning French vascular surgeon, he produced a series of these pumps, but none of them quite worked yet. He also invented a centrifuge for separating blood plasma without destroying it. It was because he was working on yet another version of the pump that he arrived home late on the night Charlie was kidnapped. After that, work ceased, but over time it was resumed.

Meanwhile, Anne devoted everything to the new baby; her letters and diaries speak of little else. "You'll wear the baby out, just looking at it," Charles told her. All through that dim winter she doted, but she also found time to write her account of the trip to China.* Then Charles, restive as ever, approached her about another aerial survey—this time to test the feasibility of seaplane routes for Pan Am, which was beginning its famous China Clipper trips to the Orient.† The itinerary this time would surpass even the Grand Tour: Greenland, Iceland, Norway, Sweden, Finland, Denmark, Estonia, Russia, England, Scotland, Ireland, France, Holland, Switzerland, Spain, and Portugal—then home through the Azores, Canary Islands, Cape Verde Islands, Brazil, Trinidad, Puerto Rico, Santo Domingo, Miami, and New York.

Anne winced at the notion of being away from Jon for so long, but in the end Charles convinced her that her partnership had become invaluable, and that such a trip as this would help to lift her spirits from what by than—despite the arrival of the new baby—had become noticeable signs of the onset of depression, a kind of late-whipsaw reaction to the kidnapping and its aftermath.

The trip took five months and covered more than thirty thousand miles and was considered a grand success; the Lindberghs were received as royalty and mobbed almost everywhere they landed.

Afterward, they received a warm congratulatory welcome home telegram from the new president of the United States, Franklin D. Roosevelt, thanking them "FOR THE PROMOTION OF AMERICAN AVIATION."

---

* Titled *North to the Orient* Anne's book would become an instant best seller when it was published in 1935.

† The China Clippers were four-engine behemoths that were featured on U.S. airmail stamps of the 1930s.

This fraternal relationship did not last long, however, for it was only a few months afterward that the Roosevelt administration issued its startling order requiring army pilots to carry the U.S. mail. Lindbergh saw this as a purely political maneuver to both blacken the reputation of the previous administration and besmirch the characters of the businessmen who ran the major airlines—men Lindbergh knew intimately.

Roosevelt's order was no laughing matter to the airlines, which were panic-stricken since air-passenger revenues were not then nearly enough to keep the businesses alive. Without the government mail contracts, they would have to shut down or drastically curtail their schedules. We have already seen how this dispute turned out, with the appalling deaths of the inexperienced and misused army pilots, as well as the insertion of Lindbergh and Rickenbacker into the argument, with Jimmy Doolittle standing on the sidelines. In a direct rebuke to the president, Congress passed the Air Mail Act of 1934, giving the airmail contracts back to commercial aviation, which not only vindicated Lindbergh, as he saw it, but made him aware that he had great stature and influence on public opinion. This merely set the stage for what was to come between himself and Roosevelt.

In the meantime, Lindbergh had returned to the Rockefeller Institute for Medical Research and Dr. Carrel to resume work on his experimental heart pump. Ever since his childhood when he had worked on his father's Ford Model T, and on the electric milking machines at the farm, Lindbergh had developed an almost uncanny understanding of machinery.

"Lindbergh understood the machine like few people of his time," wrote a professor at the University of Minnesota, who took no note of the fact that Charles must have come a very long way from his days in academia. "No piece of mechanized equipment escaped him. He looked into each as if he had X-ray vision, took it apart, and put it back together in his head."[1]

In the glassblowing lab Lindbergh fashioned his first successful "perfusion pump," or "system for cardiopulmonary bypass." *Time* magazine described it as "Looking like a twist of vitrified bowel oozing out of a clear glass bottle," while others said it looked like an inverted saxophone with a football on top. In experiments with laboratory animals the pump was found to be able to keep cells, tissue, and organs alive for long periods outside the body and led to the development of the artificial heart pump used so frequently today in bypass procedures. Lindbergh published a scholarly and well-received article in the *Journal of Experimental Medicine* titled "An Apparatus for the Culture of Whole Organs." And with Dr. Carrel, he published an equally well-received book titled *The Culture of Organs,* which afterward landed them both on the cover of *Time.* That was in the summer of 1934. The fall brought a different kind of news.

IN SEPTEMBER, ANOTHER OF THE BILLS, a gold certificate, used for the kidnap ransom money turned up at the Corn Exchange Bank in the Bronx. An alert filling station owner had written down a license plate number in the margin of the bill.

A check of the license with the New York Bureau of Motor Vehicles revealed that the plate belonged to a blue 1930 Dodge sedan owned by one Bruno Richard Hauptmann, a handsome, muscular, thirty-five-year-old German-born carpenter and former machine gunner in the German army. Hauptmann claimed he had struck it rich in the stock market, but nobody believed him since the stock market had been at all-time lows since the crash of '29.

Hidden in the wall of Hauptmann's garage was found tens of thousands in bills that matched the ransom bills. In one of his notebooks police discovered a carpenter's rough draft drawing of a three-piece extension ladder, similar to the one used to kidnap the Lindbergh baby. Paper found in the home matched that of the ransom notes and a small empty green bottle marked "ether" was uncovered as well as maps of the New Jersey area where the Lindberghs lived. Police also noted that Hauptmann's tool chest was missing a three-quarter-inch chisel, such as one that was left at the crime scene. Experts said Hauptmann's handwriting bore conclusive similarities to that in the ransom notes in the Lindbergh case. It was further discovered that he had a significant criminal record in Germany, including using ladders to break into houses.

Still the police had no confession, so they attempted to obtain one by the accepted method of the day. They shackled Hauptmann to a chair and attacked him with a hammer and other blunt tools. For some reason this did not produce the desired result, so they went back to his home to see what else they could find. It proved to be a fruitful visit.

In the attic they found that a piece of wood flooring was missing. When a rail from the ladder left at the Lindbergh residence after the kidnapping was brought in, it not only fit exactly the length of the board that was missing but the four nail holes in it lined up perfectly with four nail holes in the floorboards. Further investigation uncovered more of the ransom money, a loaded revolver, and also a hand plane that the wood expert from the Forest Service lab declared conclusively to be the tool used to hone the Lindbergh ladder. The *New York Times* declared "MYSTERY SOLVED." It had been two and a half years since the kidnapping. "Oh," Anne groaned to her diary, "now it starts all over again."

NEXT MONTH, IN NEW JERSEY, a grand jury convened by the state attorney general indicted Hauptmann for the murder of little Charlie Lindbergh under a state law that automatically made any death connected with the commission of a felony—whether accidental or on purpose—a felony murder, eligible for the death penalty. Mobs under torchlight milled around the Hunterdon County courthouse and jail in Flemington, New Jersey, when Hauptmann arrived on the night of October 19 after being extradited from New York. Lindbergh told Anne that Hauptmann was a good-looking man, but that his eyes "were like the eyes of a wild boar—mean, shifty, small and cruel." Hauptmann's trial opened January 2, 1935. As one of Anne's biographers put it, "The madness took hold again—the crowds, the reporters, the frenzied energy of the human hunt."[2]

Once more, a carnival midway overtook the Lindbergh kidnapping case. Vendors and hucksters hawked everything from food and drink to photographs of the Lindberghs with forged autographs, pictures of the dead child, and replicas of the ladder. It was reported that someone was even selling golden curls of hair—from his own head! Aside from the usual rubberneckers, morbid gawkers, and courtroom habitués, hundreds of reporters and columnists, movie cameramen, press photographers, radio announcers, and all their assistants and technicians descended on the town and spilled out of the local hotel, taverns, and saloons and into the streets freshly covered with snow where limousines deposited hopeful movie stars, comedians such as Jack Benny, café society socialites, and other would-be celebrities, all come to witness the so-called Trial of the Century, as it had come to be known. The *New York Times* hired a series of novelists, including Edna Ferber, to cover the proceedings, which she did in a piece titled "Vultures at Trial," declaring that the spectacle "made you want to resign as a member of the human race." The quaint little town of Flemington, she wrote, "looked like a picture postcard gone mad . . . We are like the sans-culottes, like the knitting women watching the heads fall at the foot of the guillotine." As Anne Lindbergh's biographer Susan Hertog noted, "Indeed, there was the smell of execution in the air."[3]

The trial lasted six weeks. Each day the newspapers regurgitated paroxysms of frenzied copy and headlines of testimony by witnesses recounting Hauptmann's numerous falsehoods, his possession of the ransom money, his "signature" interlocking circles on the ransom notes, the missing chisel, the theory of the ladder, the child's sleeping garments—a growing mountain of circumstantial evidence to prove that he and he alone had kidnapped and killed the Lindbergh child. On weekends they followed up with recaps and analyses.

At last, on January 24, Hauptmann took the stand in his own defense—a calculated mistake. He had no respectable answers for his lies to the police, the ransom money, his link to the kidnapping ladder, or any of the rest of it. Edna Ferber wrote, "We sit and stare hungrily like vultures perched on a tree, watching a living thing writhe yet a while."

By the afternoon of February 14, 1935, the summations had been made and the case was put into the hands of the jury. That evening the Lindbergh family gathered for dinner at Next Day Hill in the presence of a new personage who had been drawn into the Lindbergh drama, Harold Nicolson, later to become Sir Harold Nicolson, British politician, diplomat, journalist, biographer, and tell-all diarist. Like many of his contemporaries who were educated at Oxford and Cambridge, Nicolson was a terrific snob. Openly homosexual, he was married to the English poet and novelist Vita Sackville-West, a well-known lesbian who came from money. His appearance at Next Day Hill was at the behest of Betty Morrow and the publishers Harcourt, Brace as the writer of a biography of the lately deceased Dwight Morrow, whom he had met during the London Naval Conference of 1930.

In the drawing room where the radio was playing, Nicolson wrote, one "could hear the almost diabolic yelling of the crowd. They were all sitting around—Miss Morgan with embroidery,* Anne looking very white and still. 'You have now heard,' broke in the voice of the announcer, 'the verdict in the most famous trial in all history. Bruno Hauptmann now stands guilty of the foulest . . .' 'Turn that off, Charles, turn that off!' "

They went into the pantry and had ginger beer. "Charles sat there on the kitchen dresser looking very pink about the nose," according to Nicolson. Lindbergh said, "My one dread all these years has been that they would get hold of someone as a victim about whom I wasn't sure. I'm sure about this—quite sure. It is this way . . ."

Charles then proceeded to recite the entire case against Hauptmann to Nicolson, point by point, with the others looking on. "It seemed to relieve all of them," Nicolson later told his diary. "He did it very quietly, very simply. He pretended to address his remarks to me only. But I could see that he was trying to relieve the agonized tension that Betty and Anne had passed through. It was very well done. It made one feel there was no personal desire for vengeance or justification."

It would be tempting here to say something like, "Thus ended the tragedy of the Lindbergh kidnapping case," but it is not so. There was of course the execution of Hauptmann, but beyond that the case has provoked one of the great historical controversies in the annals of crime. Every few years a new book is introduced, either making the case for Hauptmann's innocence or revealing accomplices or fingering masterminds. Many of these are quite intriguing, and the fact remains that no one has ever satisfactorily explained how Hauptmann knew exactly where the baby's nursery was located at Highfields, and which

---

* Nicolson must have confused "Miss Morgan" with Miss Morrow, referring to Anne's sister Constance. Elisabeth Morgan, Anne's other sister, had died two months earlier. But in fact, three years later, in 1937, Constance Morrow, at the age of twenty-three, had married Aubrey Morgan, the widower of her dead sister, and they lived happily ever after until their deaths in the last part of the twentieth century.

window to go through, and at what time, and also that the baby would even be there on that particular night when the family was nearly always away—or was he just guessing?

BETWEEN THE CLOSE OF THE TRIAL and Hauptmann's scheduled execution date, January 17, 1936, the Lindberghs endured a number of alarming incidents that eventually drove them out of America entirely. Shortly after the trial a deranged mental patient got loose and found his way one night inside the grounds of Next Day Hill, where Charles caught him peeping through a window.

After Jon was born, Lindbergh issued a rare statement appealing to the press to "permit our children to lead the lives of normal Americans." The family wished to remain in the country, he said, but it would be "impossible for us to subject the life of our second son to the publicity which we feel was responsible for the death of our first." This was a heavy indictment, but it did not in the least deter the members of the press, who redoubled their efforts; Lindbergh—both Lindberghs now—still sold newspapers.

There were numerous stalkers and people who thought that Hauptmann was innocent and wrote horrible letters to Charles and Anne. Charles began carrying a .38 revolver wherever he went. People made so many death threats against their son Jon that Lindbergh had to have him escorted by a bodyguard armed with a sawed-off shotgun whenever he was out of the house. By Lindbergh's account, "Post Office authorities made fourteen arrests during a single year in connection with threatening letters we received." Their car was sometimes followed.[4]

One day Anne received a call from a teacher at the Little School in Englewood, which Jon attended, saying that "a suspicious-looking truck" was parked just outside the grounds. The children were called inside, and shortly afterward state troopers apprehended the vehicle, which turned out to be "full of newspaper photographers, who had snapped pictures of Jon Lindbergh through slits in the canvas." Not long afterward, Jon's nurse was driving him home when a car full of men "forced them into the curb." The nurse thought they were gangsters and, terrified, clutched Jon, who began to cry. A man jumped out, stuck a camera to the window, and began taking pictures of the wailing child, then returned to the car and drove away. Because of the power of the press and the First Amendment, there were no laws to protect Lindbergh from this unwanted media attention, and "no effective action I could take," he lamented.

Then the kidnapping case began to erupt again. Even though the New Jersey Court of Errors and Appeals quickly upheld the Hauptmann guilty verdict, for some reason New Jersey's governor, Harold G. Hoffman, stuck his nose into the case. In a personal meeting with Hauptmann that was supposed to be secret (it wasn't) Hoffman somehow concluded there was enough evidence to at least investigate further, prompting the press to report, "LINDBERGH CASE REOPENED." Abundant theories found their way into the newspapers, one being that while attempting a practical joke Lindbergh had killed his own child accidentally and covered it up with the kidnapping story. Another wild theory held that Anne's sister Elisabeth had hired people to kidnap and murder the baby out of jealousy because Charles had picked Anne instead of her. In the midst of all this, Hauptmann's wife Anna's new leading lawyer, C. Lloyd Fisher, asserted that he had found a child on Long Island that he said was "the Lindbergh baby."

LIFE, IN LINDBERGH'S WORDS, had become "intolerable," and he at last decided to take his family abroad until by some happy circumstance conditions would change enough in the United States to allow him and his family a measure of personal privacy.

Cloaked in deep secrecy, Lindbergh made arrangements for the family to be smuggled out of the country aboard the *American Importer,* one of the better-appointed cargo vessels owned by United States Lines, which would carry them to England and which, Lindbergh declared, "had greater regard for law and order" than other nations.

Under cover of darkness on the night of December 21, 1935, Anne, Charles, and Jon Lindbergh bade farewell to Betty Morrow and the staff at Next Day Hill and drove to Manhattan's West Side docks where, shortly before midnight, they quietly boarded *American Importer* as its only passengers.* After nearly ten days at sea, mostly cabinbound because of North Atlantic winter gales, they arrived on New Year's Eve morning in Liverpool where they were aghast to find a swarm of photographers and reporters awaiting them, chomping at the gangplank to have their story and photographs.

Before he left, Lindbergh had contacted a reporter at the *New York Times,* the only newspaper he had any small measure of respect for—even after the phony first-person account of his flight to Paris—and offered to explain why he was leaving in exchange for the paper holding the story until he and the family were at sea. The reporter agreed and Lindbergh proceeded to spell out his reasons, basically, the safety of his family, including "demands for money, threats of kidnapping and murder." He omitted, however, the fact that his angst over the unwanted intrusions of the press had an awful lot to do with it. He assured the reporter that he and his family would remain American citizens. The scoop would win the reporter and the *New York Times* a Pulitzer Prize.[5]

When the newspaper hit the streets the morning after the ship sailed a new national uproar commenced. Everyone was shocked and horrified that a man of Lindbergh's stature had been driven from his own country, by his own people. A pall had been cast across the nation. The Hearst newspapers hypocritically lamented that Lindbergh's departure was "distressing," in light of the fact that America was filled with so many "cranks, criminals and Communists" and that it drove away "a splendid citizen like Colonel Lindbergh." The Hearst papers had been among the worst offenders, especially its photographers.

From Liverpool, the Lindberghs went immediately to Wales where Charles and Anne's brother-in-law Aubrey Morgan had a grand manor near Cardiff. There they stayed for several months, relaxing, acclimating to the country, and weighing their options. In late January the Lindberghs traveled to London where Charles was both astonished and delighted when he did not get mobbed in the streets. They stayed at the Ritz;

---

* The Lindberghs' German police dog Thor and Skean, the terrier, were on the other hand shipped to England aboard the *Queen Mary,* an honor, Lindbergh said, "I'm afraid they have not appreciated."

Betty Morrow was now there also, consulting with Harold Nicolson on his biography of her late husband. On January 20, King George V, with whom Lindbergh had a memorable audience in 1927, had died, and Charles and Anne watched his long and elegant funeral procession from their hotel window, Big Ben chiming, the minute guns firing, a cold, gray day, and the British nation draped in mourning; he was much beloved, the king who had led England through World War I. It was a stirring sight as the casket went by, on a gun caisson drawn by horses with only a wreath and the fabulous royal crown resting on top, surrounded by the regiment of guards in their red tunics, preceded by cavalry with white ostrich plumes on their golden helmets, followed by the heads of state of many nations, afoot in mourning clothes.

That night the Lindberghs dined with Mrs. Morrow and the Nicolsons and a discussion arose about their plans. Lindbergh had been vague since their arrival; there were so many choices—Sweden, France, England. Nicolson's mother-in-law had recently died, leaving his wife, Vita Sackville-West, a small fortune and eliminating the need for the couple to sell Long Barn, a "tumbled-down cottage" they owned in the tiny Weald of Kent, a quiet garden district about twenty-five miles southeast of London. Nicolson offered to lease it to the Lindberghs.

Long Barn was quite larger than the ordinary American definition of a cottage, and "tumbled-down" or not it was a comfortable, warm home, dating back to the 1420s. It reportedly came with its own ghost, according to Sackville-West, but it also provided a welcome safe haven. Harold Nicolson had phoned the local postmistress asking her to put out word that the Lindberghs should not be disturbed. There was, however, one ugly incident after Charles refused to bring the family out for news photographs, and photographers then "threw rocks at our dog," apparently to bring the Lindberghs out to see what was the matter. But the dog "caught some of the stones in his bleeding mouth," Lindbergh said, and "several of his teeth were broken."[6]

In the meantime, after several stays of execution, Governor Hoffman of New Jersey at last stopped meddling in the Hauptmann case, and on the evening of April 3, 1936, the German carpenter was strapped into the electric chair at the state prison in Trenton and electrocuted. Not only did he never confess to the kidnapping but after his death a statement prepared by him was released, proclaiming his innocence, which has provided fodder for crime sleuths from that day to this. The press naturally sent inquires to Lindbergh seeking comment, but from Long Barn came only silence.

It was not as if Charles and Anne spent all their nights at Long Barn reading by the fireside. To the contrary, they had an active social life in England; they were frequent guests at the American ambassador's dinners and became friends with Lady Astor and her set at Cliveden. They even stood for an audience—and later a dinner—with the new king, Edward VIII, and his lady friend Mrs. Wallis Simpson of Baltimore, Maryland.

In May, Lindbergh received a letter from Major Truman Smith, a U.S. Army military attaché at the American embassy in Berlin. Like all military attachés, the tall, handsome Smith was basically a spy, expected to report regularly to his superiors on the conduct of Germany's army, including its airpower. Smith was an infantryman by training who knew his limitations in estimating something so complicated as aircraft, but he was intelligent enough to know that the Germans—against the Treaties of Versailles and Locarno—were going all out to build the most modern and destructive kinds of planes.* When Smith heard tell that Lindbergh had moved to England, he asked if Charles would be willing to come to Germany if he, Smith, could put together a tour of Nazi aircraft facilities.

That summer Charles and Anne flew to Berlin. The Germans arranged for the Lindberghs to attend the opening ceremonies of the 1936 Olympic Games the last week in July—as the special guest of Hermann Göring, Germany's air minister. Charles A. Lindbergh in Berlin! It was too grand a propaganda opportunity to waste. Meanwhile, it took only a few days for Lindbergh to make his preliminary assessment of German air strength, which, as it had Doolittle and Rickenbacker before him, must have sent a shiver up his spine.[7]

"I realized," he said, "that Nazi Germany intended to become the greatest air power in the world. . . . Obviously, Germany was preparing for war on a major scale with the most modern equipment . . . I got

---

* The 1925 Treaty of Locarno was an effort by the Allies to adjust with Germany some of the points of the Treaty of Versailles that had ended World War I.

the impression the Germans were looking Eastward [toward the Soviet Union]," Lindbergh said, "but it was obvious that bombing planes would not find the Maginot Line a formidable obstacle."*8

At the Berlin Air Club Lindbergh made a speech that was reprinted around the world—even in Germany, purportedly on the orders of Hitler—in which he called for martial restraint, particularly in the air. "Aviation, I believe," Lindbergh told the guests, "created the most fundamental change ever made in war. It has turned defense into attack. We can no longer protect our families with an army. Our libraries, our museums, every institution we value is laid bare to bombardment." The fact that the speech was made in Germany, and sounded somewhat like an appeal to the Germans to stop building an invincible air force, suited the Nazis fine, because even as early as 1936 it made them sound fearsome and dangerous. Nevertheless, it was a respectable speech and praised around the world except by some Jewish publications, which even then were pulling for intervention over the Nazis' mistreatment of their fellow Jews.

Lindbergh made a point of writing his friend Harry Guggenheim, saying, "There is no need for me to tell you that I am not in accord with the Jewish situation in Germany."9 He apparently wanted to reassure Guggenheim, who of course was Jewish, that while he did not directly condemn the Nazis in his speech he disapproved of their methods. It was, in fact, an apology to Guggenheim for not condemning them, which would have been extremely awkward for Lindbergh to have done as a guest of the Berlin Air Club in 1936.

Göring, in his usual ebullient, glad-handing way, resplendent in a white gold-braided and bemedaled uniform, had the Lindberghs to lunch at his sumptuous Berlin home with its richly decorated table "in a room lined with mirrors and many carved madonnas 'borrowed,' " Lindbergh emphasized, "from German museums."

Following lunch, the party went into some sort of large drawing room when Göring's pet lion wandered in and jumped up on the couch,

---

* The so-called impregnable Maginot Line had been built by France after World War I to protect against any future attack by Germany. Unfortunately, it was finished before the danger from airpower was fully understood.

sprawling beside him. A servant followed the young beast carrying a litter box, but this proved unnecessary because the lion proceeded to urinate on the field marshal's splendid uniform. From Anne's diary: "Someone laughs . . . Göring leaps up and throws [the lion] away. All laugh. [Göring] mock-scolds the lion." After he had retired for a change of clothing, Göring proudly began to tick off Germany's aviation accomplishments in an attempt to show that the Nazis were invincible, as he had done with Rickenbacker. He displayed for Lindbergh photographs of the scores of new German airfields under construction; Lindbergh already knew from his recent inspections that "warplanes were being built for those fields."

Lindbergh knew perfectly well what modern bombs could do to cities but, seeing Nazi Germany for the first time, the idea of a new and very dangerous war became real to him. The streets of Berlin were draped in the red-and-black banners of the Nazi swastika; uniforms were everywhere, on adults and children alike. The German officers that Lindbergh met were not "preparing for a game. Their discussions gave me a sense of blood and bullets, and I realized how destructive my profession of aviation had become."

But beyond that Lindbergh found himself impressed by the robustness and organization of Germany—the ceaseless activity of its citizens and the explosive creation of new manufactories and scientific laboratories— all products of a dictatorial fascist government. In stark contrast was the lethargy of England, which had been so worn down by the last war that it merely shambled on without direction or purpose. "Germany," Lindbergh said, "had the ambitious drive of America, but that drive was headed for war." He was even more discouraged about France, warning, "There is [in France] an air of discouragement and neglect on every hand . . . such fear of military invasion, such depression, such instability."[10]

Flying back to England, Lindbergh's thoughts turned to the helplessness of cities and their citizens to planes carrying high-explosive bombs. As the coast of Great Britain appeared ahead, he contrasted the image of Napoleon standing with his great army of conquest on the shores of Normandy, wondering how he could possibly get across the English Channel, to the present fifteen minutes it would take a modern bomber to cross over.

Back in England, Lindbergh told people what he had seen and what he deduced from it, but he was usually met with stony silence; the British were war weary. A generation of their boys—more than a million of them—had been wiped out on the fields of France and Flanders. Only Churchill warned of Hitler, and no one paid him much attention. Lindbergh helped Major Truman Smith prepare his report on the German military, with special emphasis on the mighty air force the Nazis were building. Back in Washington, it was received and noted by the U.S. Army Air Corps authorities, but because of the Depression little was done in the way of rearmament.

Harold Nicolson, an ardent Nazi hater, summed up Lindbergh's position in his diary entry for September 8, 1936; he wrote, "He has obviously been much impressed by Nazi Germany. He admires their energy, virility, spirit, organization, architecture, planning and physique. He considers that they possess the most powerful air-force in the world, with which they could do terrible damage to any other country . . . He admits that they are a great menace but denies that they are a menace to us . . . he contends the future will see a great separation between Fascism and Communism. He believes that if Britain supports the decadent French and the red Russians against Germany there will be an end to European civilization."

Apparently Lindbergh had gone on to say that Great Britain had to take a stand—make a choice—whether to be on the side of fascism or of communism, since there was no middle way between the two. In this, Nicolson conceded. "I very much fear that he is correct in this diagnosis, and that our passions for compromise will lead us to a position of isolation, internal disunity, and eventual collapse . . . Never have we been faced with so appalling a problem."

It was the unhappiest of notes to end the year on, but Lindbergh had big plans. He had a fast new low-wing monoplane built for him, a Miles Mohawk, and he intended to break it in by flying to India.

ANNE FOUND OUT SHE WAS PREGNANT AGAIN, but she never let a thing like that stop her from flying. In the winter of 1937 the couple took off for Calcutta via Rome where, like Rickenbacker, they watched Mussolini's

Blackshirts in action, then flew over the old world of Carthage, Tripoli, Alexandria, Cairo, and Jerusalem and landed in a sandstorm at an oasis in the desert near the Dead Sea. They made various stops in India where Lindbergh tried to divine the secrets of the swamis and yogis and other holy men who were said to have mystical powers.[11]

Engine problems in Nagpur forced them to take a train to Calcutta. When they arrived at their private compartment they found that British friends had arranged for a "huge block of ice to be placed in the center of the floor. 'Without ice, the heat on these Indian trains becomes unbearable,' the friends said. 'This ice will keep you a little cooler. Be sure that the window stays closed.' "

The Lindberghs were appalled by Calcutta. "Human life here had sunk to levels we had never seen before," Charles wrote. "Ragged hungry people milled about on filthy streets. At night we stepped around stretched-out sleeping bodies on the sidewalks close to our luxurious European-style hotel. 'You never know the difference,' we were told, 'but sometimes one of them is dead.' I could hardly believe this country had once produced a civilization of art and architecture and religion—or that conditions were even worse before the British took over," Charles said.

They were back at Long Barn by April, and on May 12 Anne presented Charles with another baby boy—the same day as the coronation of George VI, after the abdication of Edward VIII over the scandal regarding his lady friend Mrs. Simpson. They named the boy Land, after Evangeline's family. "A coronation baby!" Anne exclaimed in her diary.

Life in England, however, had grown tedious for Charles. Even though it had created "the greatest empire ever to exist on earth," Lindbergh felt "a sense of heaviness of life in England that pressed like a London Fog. . . . England did not look to the future, but to the past," Lindbergh said, and refused to acknowledge scientific advances such as the fact that warplanes could now fly over long distances and wreak unimaginable destruction. Too much of the conversation ran to grouse shooting, the "hunt," the royal family, and their collections of everything under the sun and not to military preparedness and the specter of a rearmed and aggressive Germany.

In the fall of 1937 the Lindberghs were invited once more to Germany, a trip again quietly arranged by Truman Smith, the military attaché.

This time, it was ostensibly to participate in the Lilienthal Aeronautical Society conference in Munich.

They arrived on October 11 in the Mohawk, and Charles spent five days visiting airfields, factories, and installations. His guide was none other than the ubiquitous Ernst Udet, erstwhile Luftwaffe air ace and self-styled *pistolero,* who was by then a major general in charge of German aircraft production. Udet let Lindbergh fly the new Messerschmitt 109 pursuit, or interceptor—perhaps the most modern plane of the day— and escorted him to top secret bases where he was allowed to examine German bombers, fighters, and reconnaissance planes.*

At the end of the tour, based on Lindbergh's information, Charles and Truman Smith wrote a report for Washington titled "General Estimate" of Germany's airpower, in which Lindbergh concluded that Germany was "once more a world power in the air," that her air industry—though approximately three years from full maturity—was technically ahead of both France and Great Britain. Based on what Udet and others had told him, Lindbergh estimated that Germany had ten thousand aircraft (she had fewer than half that many) and that German factories were turning out twice the number of planes they in fact were.

Much has been made of this report. It has even been suggested that Lindbergh's estimate was the direct cause of the appeasement of Hitler by Great Britain and France at the notorious Munich Conference of 1938.† This author has found no such direct connection, although Lindbergh had in fact repeatedly made clear to many high-ranking British officials that in his judgment Germany was far ahead of England, France, and Russia in airpower.‡ After Lindbergh joined the

---

* Germany would produce nearly 34,000 of the Messerschmitts before the end of the war.

† In which England and France allowed Hitler to invade Czechoslovakia unopposed.

‡ One of Lindbergh's severest biographers, Leonard Mosley, states that at the request of the U.S. ambassador to the U.K. Joseph Kennedy, Lindbergh summarized his report and that Kennedy, an appeaser, gave it to Neville Chamberlain on the eve of the Munich Conference. Lindbergh himself says he summarized the report for Kennedy, but I can find no supporting evidence that Kennedy gave it to Chamberlain, let alone that it prompted Chamberlain to yield to Hitler.

anti-interventionist America First movement, some even suggested Lindbergh's overestimation of German air strength was a deliberate attempt to sabotage diplomacy; others called him a willing dupe of the Nazis. None of that is accurate. He was trusting of the Nazis who hosted him, that much is true. As late as 1937, the National Socialists had yet to prove themselves as duplicitous as they certainly were. There is reason to think, however, that Göring and other high-ranking Nazis lied to Lindbergh (and to Rickenbacker and to Doolittle) about the progress of their aircraft production, and that Lindbergh believed them. Any trained intelligence officer, however, would have known to discount those parts of Lindbergh's report that he indicated came from foreign (Nazi) officials. They teach you that during the first week of intelligence school.

When, in March of 1938, Hitler invaded Austria there was concern but not alarm in England. What worried Lindbergh most was that the British seemed to disregard the danger of German aviation—acting as if the Germans were still flying the boxy little fabric-covered crates of the previous war. What all of it added up to was that Lindbergh got out. He gave up his lease on Long Barn and bought an island off the coast of France, of all places, a nation he had come to despise.

Illiec was one of hundreds of small, rocky islets scattered off the northern coast of the Brittany peninsula. Barely four acres, it lay less than a mile from a much larger island owned by Dr. Alexis Carrel and his wife. Twice daily the receding tide swept all of the water away, leaving only tidal pools and a sandy bottom filled with clams, oysters, abalone, and seaweed to walk across to the other islands or the mainland. Illiec was a starkly beautiful isolated slip of sun-burnished, storm-tossed rocks, with craggy formations spiraling forty feet above the sea and trees gnarled by the wind. It came with a three-story, slate-roofed stone manor house, "like a scaled-down castle," Lindbergh said, with a large turret and a chapel—but no plumbing, electricity, or running water—built in the 1860s by the author of the *opéra comique Mignon*.

Lindbergh snapped it up for $16,000, even though he was fully aware of the deteriorating conditions in Europe. "Even one summer at Illiec would almost justify buying it," he said with the air of a man who knew how to spend money.

During the spring and summer of 1938, still in England at Long Barn while the Illiec house was being made livable, the Lindberghs embarked on a whirlwind social spree, lunching with the playwright George Bernard Shaw and former prime minister David Lloyd George; dining with the Astors and such luminaries as the duke and duchess of Kent and U.S. ambassadors William C. Bullitt and Joseph Kennedy; attending formal balls with the king and queen of England—the latter, when asked for a dance with Lindbergh, was told, "I've never danced a day in my life," and so the two of them (Lindbergh in white tails and satin knee breeches) sat and talked of many things: of worlds gone mad, and privacy, and what next year might bring.

It might have been a poignant time for Anne, leaving this glittering existence for life on an isolated rock in the English Channel, but actually she was unaffected. She'd discovered that for all its intense socializing English society was essentially closed. Before she left Next Day Hill a friend of the family told her, "You will find your own group wherever you are, anywhere." "But I haven't," she confided to her diary, right before they left. "I haven't found anyone in England—not one single soul. I have been here almost two and a half years and I have not made a single friend."

It was during this time that Harold Nicolson penned in his diary an erroneous, if not treacherous, entry that would cause Lindbergh much trouble later on when the diaries were published. On May 2, at a luncheon party at Sissinghurst, the Nicolsons' estate, Lindbergh had recited his appraisal that England would lose if she challenged Germany in the air. Nicolson, second only to Churchill in Nazi hating, had apparently tired of hearing Lindbergh's gloomy talk about German power and his open admiration for some aspects of Nazism (which included the organization and growth of modern Germany out of the chaos that had followed World War I). Lindbergh did not find anything admirable about the Nazis' brutal treatment of the Jews, or Nazism's regimentation, thuggery, or its draconian dealings with nonconformers, and had said so on many occasions. Nicolson nevertheless wrote in his diary that Lindbergh "believes in the Nazi theology, all tied up with his hatred of degeneracy and his hatred of democracy as represented by the free Press and the American public."

It was a damning statement when it was released, in 1966, because it reopened all the old sores about Lindbergh's loyalties, a matter we shall come to presently. But by then Nicolson was in his eighties and dying, and Lindbergh was unable to engage him enough to retract the assertion. It was a gross and overblown exaggeration of Lindbergh's actual sentiments, but Charles knew nothing about the diary entry at the time and continued to consider Nicolson a friend.

In Washington, meanwhile, the Smith-Lindbergh report on German airpower had caught the attention of Hap Arnold, commander of the Air Corps, who began to circulate it widely, though with top secret clearance, to high officials, including embassies around the world. This prompted interest by some air attachés, including the one in Moscow, in having Lindbergh visit their host countries and provide his opinion of their air capabilities. Unfortunately, the Smith-Lindbergh report apparently had little or no effect on the U.S. Congress, which actually *lowered* the Air Corps appropriation for the following year.

The notion of visiting the Soviet Union appealed to Lindbergh even after there were reports of the Stalin regime's wholesale slaughter of its population. He accepted the invitation, but obtaining a visa took six weeks. Nevertheless, in mid-August 1938, he and Anne flew the Mohawk to Russia, where they were shown "two museums, a new subway, a ballet, an operetta, a shoe factory, an ice cream factory, a trip on a canal, a collective farm, and a Young Pioneers' camp." What they were not shown was any appreciable portion of the Soviet air force and its manufacturing arm—whether out of secrecy or embarrassment. Lindbergh stated afterward, "We were shown so little of the Soviet aviation industry that I could make no estimate of its production capacity."[12]

What he did see, however, convinced him that Soviet air capabilities were second-rate, if that. The workers were "neither highly trained nor skillful. The bombers under construction were inferior in design" to those built by the democracies. Factories were not well laid out or organized, tools were out of date, production was sloppy, and the Russians were dependent on foreign sources for machine tools—"a serious limitation."

Likewise, at the flying school Lindbergh visited, he found the buildings "run down," and in one barracks he was startled to see "embroidered pillows on sixty lined-up cadet bunks." The Russians, it seemed, were training women to fly, and in fact when Lindbergh met some of the female cadets he found that they were on the whole neater and snappier than their male counterparts.

Though he could make no proper estimate of Soviet airpower, Lindbergh ventured that the government possessed several thousand planes that "were no match for the Luftwaffe in either quantity or quality."

His impression of the Soviet Union itself was not promising—a scarcity of goods in the stores, people who seemed browbeaten, and the ice cream factory they visited was full of flies. "The system they lived under," he concluded, "was destructive of life and incompatible with ideas of personal freedom so basic to the American mind."

For the next several months Lindbergh became a major figure at the highest levels among the European powers attempting to avert war. On September 22, the American ambassador to Great Britain Kennedy asked him to draw up the aforementioned letter outlining German air strength, in which Lindbergh concluded: "It seems to me essential to avoid a general European war in the near future at almost any cost. I believe that a war now might easily result in the end of European civilization. I am by no means convinced that England and France could win a war against Germany at the present time, but, whether they win or lose, all of the participating countries would probably be prostrated by their efforts."

Around the same time, William Bullitt, America's ambassador to France, tried to embroil Lindbergh in a scheme to circumvent the U.S. Neutrality Act of 1935 by procuring U.S.-made warplanes for the French air force through Canada. Lindbergh countered with the apparently ridiculous proposition that the French might consider buying warplanes from the Germans, since they had so many of them. Bullitt thought he was joking, but Lindbergh was deadly serious. If he could convince the Germans to sell, and the French to buy airplanes, a line of prosperous trade would be opened that Germany would be loath to close. Perhaps a balance of power could be struck. For Lindbergh, these were desperate times that called for desperate measures, and he would grasp at any straw.

At the end of September 1938, Prime Minister Neville Chamberlain returned from the Munich Conference waving a note signed by Hitler that promised "peace in our time," which temporarily halted the digging of air raid trenches and handing out of gas masks in Hyde Park. A few days later, the Lindberghs made their third trip to Germany, officially to attend an aeronautical conference, but again there were higher stakes in play.

At a dinner in Berlin, Lindbergh sat next to Erhard Milch, then inspector general of the Luftwaffe, and used the occasion to drum up visits to all the big German aircraft production plants—Heinkel, Junkers, Messerschmitt, Dornier—and, with Göring's blessings, flew many of these types of planes, including some secret prototypes with amazing capabilities. It convinced him more than ever that the democracies would be overwhelmed in a war with Germany, and that "Germany now has the means of destroying London, Paris, and Prague if she wishes to do so."

Before leaving Germany, Lindbergh attended a stag dinner at the U.S. embassy for Hermann Göring that was thrown by the new American ambassador, Hugh R. Wilson. The hope was to soften Göring up so he would loosen the restrictions on Jewish emigration from Nazi Germany. The room was sprinkled with Nazi demigods such as Milch, Udet, Dr. Willy Messerschmitt, and Dr. Ernst Heinkel, as well as the Italian ambassador and various U.S. officers and embassy officials. As usual, Göring arrived last and marched up to Lindbergh, beaming like a harvest moon. He was dressed in a hideous sky-blue uniform of his own design and carrying a small velveteen red box, which he handed to Lindbergh with a short disquisition in German. Lindbergh did not understand German, but when he opened the box he found that it contained the Order of the German Eagle, one of the most prestigious decorations of the German government—"by order of der Führer," Göring said proudly. The accompanying document stated that the award was for Lindbergh's advancement of the field of aviation and for the 1927 New York to Paris flight.

Everyone, including Ambassador Wilson, was caught off guard by this occasion. Lindbergh politely thanked the portly field marshal, "shoved the medal in his pocket," and thought no more about it as the men went in to dinner. It would soon come back to haunt him as the centerpiece of his worst personal setback since the kidnapping of the baby. When he showed the medal to Anne that night after returning from the dinner, she took one look at it and remarked, "The Albatross."[13]

Göring continued to snow Lindbergh with stories of 500-mile-per-hour German bombers and other fantastic progress being made by the Nazi air force. "I felt that he wanted to impress me with that power," Lindbergh wrote, "and through me, the United States."

Because of his continued good relationships with Göring, Milch, and Udet, Lindbergh considered that he and the family might take up residence in Berlin for a few months, since living on Illiec in the winter was out of the question, and it would give him ample opportunity to collect further intelligence on the Nazi air force. Anne had even found a satisfactory house for let. They returned to France to get the children and pack up when, on the night of November 9, 1938, hundreds of Nazis, and Nazi-style thug groups, convulsed Germany and inflamed the world with a violent pogrom-like assault on Jews and their property across the country.

Known as Kristallnacht, or "night of broken glass," the attackers burned and looted several hundred synagogues and many thousands of Jewish-owned businesses and homes, killed nearly a hundred Jews, and inspired the Nazi authorities to send tens of thousands more to concentration camps. It was the regime's most brutish treatment by far of Germany's Jews, leaving no doubt about Hitler's future intentions, and blackening Nazi Germany in the eyes of the world. The Roosevelt administration withdrew Ambassador Wilson in protest, a severe diplomatic rebuke. The Nazi government tried to pass off the attacks as a "spontaneous" reaction stemming from the shooting death of a German attaché in Paris by an insane Polish Jew, but nobody was buying it.

The Lindberghs, on lonely Illiec island, did not get the newspapers until several days afterward and were as horrified as anyone when a copy of the *Times* arrived by boat. Anne wrote in her diary, "You just get to feeling you can understand and work with these people when they do something as stupid and brutal and undisciplined like that. I am shocked and very upset." Charles was equally aghast and wrote in a new journal he had started, "My admiration for the Germans is constantly being dashed against some rock such as this. What is the object in this persecution of the Jews?"

It was now out of the question that Charles would move his family to Germany for the winter, so they took an apartment in Paris, where he began to initiate prospects for the French to buy aircraft from the Germans. As the process moved forward, Lindbergh made another trip to Germany on December 16.

Lindbergh had been there a few days when he had dinner with Udet who, unsurprisingly, challenged him to a shooting contest in his apartment. Lindbergh first insisted that they discuss the possibility of Germany selling planes to France. Udet was keen on the idea as it would promote better relations but said it would have to be decided "at least as far as Göring."

With this matter out of the way, the shooting competition began.

Like Rickenbacker and Doolittle before him, Lindbergh was somewhat taken aback by the setup. In his journal he leads us through Udet's apartment with the various aviation trophies and stuffed animals (rhinoceros, panther, etc.). "Over his bed hung an oil painting of a reclining nude," Lindbergh wrote, "and in an adjoining room photos of pretty girls [the movie stars]." This was where Lindbergh encountered the "small metal target box" on the mantelpiece in front of the photographs of the girls. "If a shot missed the box," he said, "it could not miss the photos behind it."

Lindbergh, a crack shot since his days on the shooting team at the University of Wisconsin, won the first three rounds straight. They decided to settle the contest with a kind of sudden-death shoot-out. Lindbergh lost, though he said his total score was higher. "We will shoot again sometime," he wrote in the journal, but they never did.*

LINDBERGH DID NOT RECEIVE AMERICAN newspapers and he had no idea how politicized the issue of Nazi Germany was becoming in the

---

* Ernst Udet died mysteriously in November 1941. The German press put out the story that he was killed "in an accident with some kind of gun." Other sources said it was a plane crash. Most people think he committed suicide. Whether at the behest of the Nazis or not, no one knows. Milch suggested that Udet had deliberately impeded Nazi aircraft production.

United States. Passions were highly inflamed, mostly on the East Coast, through influential publications such as the *New York Times, The New Yorker, Time,* and *Newsweek,* among others. In New York and other East Coast cities there lived large and vocal Jewish populations horrified at what was happening to their brethren in Germany. They had formed a powerful lobby with the Roosevelt administration. Hollywood was beginning to bring anti-Nazi films to the screen. As well, the political Left (for the moment, at least) was diametrically opposed to Hitler because of the threat that fascism posed to communism, and it made those sentiments known through various media outlets. In light of these and other anti-Nazi forces, Lindbergh's acceptance of Germany's Eagle medal created a perfect storm of condemnation that caught Lindbergh unprepared.

His friend Dr. Carrel warned him from New York, "There is a good deal of ill-feeling about you." The *New York Times* ran a front-page story headlined, "Hitler Grants Lindbergh a Medal," reporting that Göring had personally pinned the medal on Lindbergh, who "wore it proudly" for the rest of the evening. One magazine even claimed that Lindbergh had made the trip to Germany specifically to accept the award.

The day after Kristallnacht, after the Lindberghs had already decided against taking a place in Germany for the winter, a front-page story in the *Times* reported that the Lindbergh family "plan to move to Berlin." *The New Yorker* published a snide article saying, "With confused emotions we say goodbye to Colonel Charles A. Lindbergh, who wants to go and live in Berlin, presumably occupying a house once owned by Jews." Editorial cartoonists had a field day drawing Lindbergh's German decoration as a Nazi swastika and other unhappy depictions.

Harold Ickes, secretary of the interior and one of the Roosevelt administration's most vituperative attack dogs, went so far as to say that anyone accepting such a medal from Germany "forfeits his right to be an American."[14] With stunning suddenness, Lindbergh had gone, in Rickenbacker's words, "from hero to zero," at least in certain parts of the country.

Lindbergh, of course, had his defenders, including a majority of the population west of the Mississippi (except for Hollywood). Most of the big city papers in the Midwest were anti-interventionist, notably the *Chicago Tribune.* In addition, it should be noted that the opinion of the American

South, in those days, was not generally considered important enough by the news makers to be included in issues of national debate. Even the *New York Times*'s influential Washington correspondent Arthur Krock pointed out that if it weren't for Lindbergh the U.S. Army Air Corps itself would not be as far along as it was and scolded such criticism of Lindbergh as being "as ignorant as it is unfair."[15]

When on Lindbergh's behalf it was pointed out that the Germans had recently bestowed the same medal on Henry Ford and the French ambassador, the critics retorted that it was only because they were anti-Semitic. When Hugh Wilson, the American ambassador, wrote a letter saying that Lindbergh had done the only proper diplomatic thing in accepting the medal, and that refusing it "would have been an act offensive to a guest of the ambassador of your country," Lindbergh's enemies turned a deaf ear. And he definitely had enemies now, not just cranks and crackpots. Among them were members of the media who had long tired of his attitude of disdain toward them. Now they had a way to hit back: a Nazi medal, a concrete symbol. They demanded that he publicly return the medal, but Lindbergh didn't have it anymore. He had already turned it over to the St. Louis Historical Society, which owned the entire Lindbergh collection. That only created more controversy and more acrimony. Anne had been all too right when, on seeing the medal that first night, she had muttered the word "albatross."

The controversy probably would have blown over if Lindbergh had gone back to work and let it alone. But he did not do that. He was convinced that another European war "would destroy Western civilization," that even if the democracies won they would be ruined financially and physically, and so become easy prey for the communist behemoth. Instead, he believed that Hitler should be able to expand toward the East, through Czechoslovakia and Poland. Sooner or later he would run into the Soviets, and in the bloody war that followed each would destroy the other. Even if Hitler survived, Lindbergh postulated, he couldn't live forever, and the evils of his Nazi regime would die with him and better men would take charge.

There were many "what if"s in Lindbergh's vision, but he saw it with such crystal clarity that he became a man with a mission. When Lindbergh got his mind around a problem and decided that he had a solution, wild horses could not drag him away from pursuing it. Whether it was flying the Atlantic Ocean, developing an artificial heart, or, in the present case, preventing a war, Lindbergh approached his goal with a single-mindedness that could also be labeled stubbornness.

ON APRIL 8, A SATURDAY, with Italy invading Albania and Europe still perched on the edge of war, Lindbergh went to Cherbourg and boarded the *Aquitania* for New York. Anne and the children would come later in the month, after closing up the house on Illiec for what would prove to be the last time. "Are we on the verge of the world's greatest and most catastrophic war?" Lindbergh asked himself. "Possibly the end of European civilization. It could be all of those things. Human life will, of course, go on, but with what changes?"

He went into the ship's dining room early to get his seating arrangements and found they had placed him at a table for five. "The trouble is," he said, "if I talk to my table companions they will be interviewed by the reporters at New York . . . they get all mixed up; then I am quoted in the papers as saying silly things I never said." The steward promised to get him a single table next day.

At sea he received radiograms from Hap Arnold, asking that he call as soon as he landed, and an invitation to attend a meeting of the National Advisory Committee for Aeronautics. The captain had made arrangements for Lindbergh to debark on the crew gangway but he decided instead to go down the passenger gangway "and see what happens." This was a mistake.

When the ship began to dock Lindbergh went to his cabin and locked the door. Soon reporters and photographers were banging on it. As he was talking to a steward, a photographer broke in through the door to the adjoining cabin, snapped Lindbergh's picture, and ran off. A dozen New York policemen arrived and formed a wedge to shove more than a hundred clamoring newsmen out of the way. In this fashion, with Lindbergh in the middle of the wedge, he exited down the gangway, crunching on broken glass from photographers' flashbulbs. He forced his way across the dock to a waiting limousine sent by Betty Morrow to take him to Next Day Hill. "It was a barbaric entry to a civilized country," he remarked.

The next morning he drove alone out of New York City and up the Hudson to West Point, where he had lunch with Hap Arnold and his wife, who were visiting their son, a cadet at the military academy. Arnold asked Lindbergh to come on active duty and make an assessment of what the Air Corps needed to meet the newest threats. He agreed, and next morning Lindbergh went to a tailor and ordered a new colonel's uniform.*

In the following weeks Lindbergh became deeply involved in military aviation intelligence and development technology at the highest levels, including meetings with Secretary of War Harry Hines Woodring, Dr. Vannevar Bush, director of the office of scientific research, and, lastly, President Franklin Delano Roosevelt.

The meeting with Roosevelt did not begin well. As Lindbergh entered the White House, at noon on April 20, he encountered "a crowd of press photographers at the door and inane women screeching at me as I passed through. There would be more dignity and self-respect among African savages," he wrote in his journal that night.

Roosevelt immediately broke the ice by asking about Anne, whom his daughter had known when they were students at Miss Chapin's School in New York City. Recounting the meeting in his journal, Lindbergh found the president "an interesting conversationalist. I like him and feel that I could get along with him," Lindbergh said, but added, "There was something about him I did not trust, something a little too suave, too pleasant, too easy." He thought the president looked "tired, and overworked." As he sized him up, Lindbergh seemed to have misgivings about Roosevelt, and ended up thinking it was just as well to work with him as long as he could, but he had a feeling it might not be long. In that he was correct.

THE NEXT FEW MONTHS WERE filled with cataclysmic events, for the Lindberghs and for the world. In August of 1939 Germany shocked everyone by signing a nonaggression pact with the Soviet Union.

---

* The army had changed uniforms since Lindbergh had last worn his.

Overnight, communists, socialists, and their fellow travelers reversed their antipathy toward the Nazis and began agitating for Germany and against England and France. The next week Hitler invaded Poland, and in response Great Britain and France declared war on Germany. World War II was on.

That same summer Anne began some sort of brief affair with the dashing French writer and aviator Antoine de Saint-Exupéry, who swept her off her feet by writing an introduction to her new book *Listen! The Wind.* Anne's publisher had sent him the manuscript in hopes of getting back perhaps a few lines of praise, but Saint-Exupéry, author of the estimable *Wind, Sand and Stars* and his most famous work, *The Little Prince,* wrote at length a penetrating analysis of Anne's book that left her giddy. When she heard he was in New York she invited him to the historic farmhouse that she and Charles had leased near Cold Spring Harbor on Long Island. She even drove into the city and picked him up. Saint-Exupéry was already burdened with a wife, family, and mistress back in France, but somehow he managed to seduce Anne Lindbergh in a single afternoon with his talk (he spoke only French so she was forced to as well) of poetry, art, novels, and so forth—or was it the other way around? What precisely happened will never be known, but from Anne's diaries we learn that something did, and if she did not fall in love it was fairly close to it; Saint-Exupéry spoke to her in the language of literature in a way Charles was never able to. Later, in 1942, Anne recounts to her diary in a fashion that can only be described as obtuse, how she asked Charles for "forgiveness" (presumably for being unfaithful) to which he replied, "If you *want* to be forgiven, then you *are* forgiven," but it's unclear if he actually knew what the hell she was talking about.[16]

At the end of August, while heavy war clouds hovered over Europe, the news commentator Fulton Lewis Jr. and some Republican Party officials approached Lindbergh about giving a speech on national radio against American intervention in the European situation. Lindbergh asked Hap Arnold about the matter and was told that he'd best go off active duty in the Air Corps before doing so. On September 15, Lindbergh received an "urgent message" from Truman Smith, now a colonel, who was serving in military intelligence in Washington. Smith wanted him to know that the Roosevelt administration was "very worried" about his proposed speech, and in exchange for him *not* giving it the president would create a special cabinet position for him as secretary for air. Lindbergh merely laughed at this smarmy bribe.

That evening, before a bank of microphones representing every broadcast network in the country, Lindbergh gave his anti-interventionist speech, which was generally well received (except by the diehard interventionists and the administration). In the speech he traced the history of fratricidal conflicts, from the Peloponnesian War between Athens and Sparta that had destroyed ancient Greece to World War I that had nearly destroyed Europe. It was the first of many such speeches he would give in the coming days. In response he received tens of thousands of letters—about 90 percent of them supportive, though the others contained the usual insults and threats to murder him and his wife and children. Lindbergh also endured the public slings and arrows of a growing number of interventionists in the media, such as the columnist and radio commentator Dorothy Thompson, who called him a "cretin" and "pro-Nazi."* Secretary of the Interior Ickes chimed in with his usual bile, branding Lindbergh a "Nazi," and the New York newspaper *PM* identified Lindbergh as "the spokesman for the fascist fifth column in America." The FBI, which had opened a file on Lindbergh during the kidnapping, now began to investigate him for his "nationalistic sympathies."[17]

It was not as though Charles had no support; in fact, polls routinely showed a majority of Americans to that point were against involvement in the European conflict. Dozens of U.S. senators, mainly from the West and Midwest, and such luminaries as Frank Lloyd Wright, Avery Brundage, John Foster Dulles, Walt Disney, and Chester Bowles, plus up-and-comers such as Gerald Ford, Potter Stewart, and Sargent Shriver, were among his staunchest allies.

Anne herself became embroiled in the controversy when she wrote an unfortunate book called *The Wave of the Future*, which postulated that

---

* Thompson, who was said to be the second most powerful woman in America (behind Eleanor Roosevelt), had been expelled from Germany for her anti-Nazi reporting and hated Hitler and his regime rabidly.

the isms—fascism, socialism, communism—seemed to have swept up the European masses so completely that it was merely a matter of time before they began to erode the democracies. The message in the book was vague, but it leaned toward the conclusion that if democracy was conquered, fascism was the better choice of the three—minus, of course, the Hitlerite touches of persecuting citizens and disturbing the peace. The book rose to the number one spot on the best seller lists and just as quickly Anne found herself on the receiving end of a firestorm of criticism—most of it ugly, and much of it obscene—accusing her of treason, along with her husband. Since she had never found herself an object of national controversy it was upsetting to Anne, the more so because she was pregnant again.

Like Charles, Anne thought universally. Both Lindberghs had a detached, deeply philosophical worldview that perceived the Europeans' problems from a height next only to God—or at least so abstractly that the fact that Hitler was murdering Jews, or that Great Britain might be having trouble keeping its empire together, had little to do with the science of their far-flung political and sociological equations. The Lindberghs thought in terms of centuries, of continents, of entire races of people and what would be for the better good. What they misunderstood was that this could not be squared with the sentiments that were building in America over the European war, which had become so passionately inflamed that detached logic no longer applied. For an increasing number of Americans, you were either "for the war and intervention" or a "callous coward and/or anti-Semite Nazi traitor." There was little or no middle ground.

Through the autumn and winter of 1939 Hitler consolidated his gains and regrouped in what became known as the so-called Phony War, during which there was little action. When the spring of 1940 arrived and the weather cleared, Hitler struck a sledgehammer blow through Belgium and into France, which capitulated after a humiliatingly halfhearted resistance of less than three weeks. Now it was England alone against the Nazi war machine, and as Hitler's bombers opened the Battle of Britain it began to look as if Lindbergh's predictions of German air superiority were correct. There was every indication that Göring's Luftwaffe was in the process of bombing England back to the Stone Age.

IN THE SPRING OF 1940 STUDENTS at Yale began to agitate for an organization that would keep America out of the war. In response to Roosevelt's signing of the Neutrality Acts—which allowed the United States to sell arms to England and the Free French, "including all aid short of war"—they began a group to preserve the nation's strength by keeping U.S. armaments in the United States. This effort morphed over time into the America First Committee.

America First was an inclusive organization, counting among its members Democrats, Republicans, Independents, Socialists, and a surprising number of influential Jews, who also supported the group with their bankbooks. Also backing the organization were the powerful American Legion and the Veterans of Foreign Wars, studded with World War I heroes including the likes of Eddie Rickenbacker.

After his reelection in 1940, and despite having campaigned on a platform of nonintervention, Roosevelt used the occasion of his inaugural address on January 6, 1941, to ask Congress to pass a lend-lease bill, which would effectively allow Great Britain to "borrow" U.S. warships and other armaments on credit while allowing the United States to lease British bases abroad. It was a giant step toward entering the war.

Lindbergh was asked to testify on the bill in Congress before the House Foreign Affairs Committee. He arrived to face a battery of microphones and newsreel cameras and an audience of a thousand spectators shoehorned into a space designed for half that many. Lindbergh clearly stood out as the star that day, "serious, smooth-cheeked, a little gray over the ears," according to *Life* magazine, though technically the junior witness among a gallery of powerful administration men such as Secretary of State Cordell Hull, Secretary of War Henry Stimson, and Secretary of the Navy Frank Knox. The congressmen, according to the magazine, "interrogated [Lindbergh] gingerly, as though they were doctors trying not to alarm an exceptionally sensitive patient."

With spectators alternately hissing or cheering, interventionists on the committee unsuccessfully tried to shake Lindbergh out of his posture of resolute neutrality, but he would not bend. When Representative Wirt Courtney of Tennessee asked him "Who do you want to win the war?" Lindbergh responded, in essence, "Nobody." Because he had shown not even the tiniest interest in seeing England win the war, *Life* characterized him as representing "the far spectrum of isolationism," and a new wave of anti-Lindbergh publicity hit the streets and airwaves. But that was a mischaracterization of Lindbergh's position. He wasn't *against* England and *for* Germany but—looking down from way up in the clouds—he saw Germany as a bulwark between western Europe and the evil intentions of the Soviet Union, which was what he'd been saying all along.

Two weeks later, in a similar hearing before the Senate, Lindbergh testified against the lend-lease bill on grounds that sending vast quantities of U.S. armaments abroad dramatically weakened America's ability to defend herself against an enemy attack from any quarter— including the Pacific. But his refusal to take sides in the present conflict, with most of Europe occupied and England under heavy attack, made him sound unpatriotic. The only moment of levity in the proceedings came when Florida's senator Claude Pepper, who considered Lindbergh a "fifth columnist" and was a little dotty even then, began his questioning by asking stupidly, "Colonel, when did you first go to Europe?"

When Lindbergh replied, "Nineteen twenty-seven, sir," the gallery erupted in hilarious jubilation.[18]

THIS PERIOD, JUST BEFORE America's entry into the war, marked the beginning of Lindbergh's fall from grace. He had become so hostile to the press that he'd developed a kind of "tin ear" when it came to anything that was written about him.

The more public criticism that Lindbergh received, the more intransigent he became, until it appeared that he was almost as callous as his accusers charged. Time after time critics pointed out that Lindbergh had never taken a moment to publicly denounce Hitler's atrocities against the Jews, nor the violence toward the Poles, Gypsies, recalcitrants in France, Belgium, Holland, Greece, Norway, and the other occupied countries, nor the indiscriminate aerial bombing of London, which ultimately cost the lives of more than forty thousand British civilians and destroyed or damaged a million London homes.

As Nazi aggression proceeded and German cruelties unfolded, the tide in what had come to be known as the Great Debate was beginning to turn. Even late in 1941, while polls still showed more than 60 percent of the U.S. public was against intervention, American sympathies clearly lay with the British and other oppressed nations. The public increasingly saw Lindbergh's "staunch neutrality" as heartless.

Lindbergh nevertheless kept up his agitating against American involvement, drawing crowds of up to eighty thousand in such venues as Madison Square Garden, Chicago's Soldier Field, the Hollywood Bowl, and points in between. At the Madison Square Garden speech, the left-wing New York newspaper *PM* described the crowd as "a liberal sprinkling of Nazis, Fascists, anti-Semites, crackpots and just people." By then, organizations had sprung up to counter the America First Committee and other isolationist groups. One of these sent ten thousand of its members to heckle the AFC attendees at the Garden rally. A group called the Friends of Democracy distributed a twenty-eight-page pamphlet titled *Is Lindbergh a Nazi?*, which included practically every accusation, true or false, linking Lindbergh to Göring, Hitler, and the British fascist Oswald Mosley.

Even Roosevelt got into the act. During a press conference on Friday, April 25, 1941, he compared Lindbergh to a "copperhead," a Civil War term for anti-Union northerners who sympathized with the South.

Lindbergh was once again incensed at Roosevelt for implying that he was a traitor. A "point of honor" was involved, Lindbergh wrote in his journal that night. His Commander in Chief had used the fact that he was a colonel in the army to fashion his insult.

It was the bitterest of pills for Lindbergh, who wrote in his journal, "My commission has always meant a great deal to me." What he opposed, he said, was "a war I *don't* believe in, when I would so much rather be fighting for my country in a war I *do* believe in . . . There is no philosophy I disagree with more than that of the pacifist, and nothing I'd rather be doing than flying in the air corps."

He weighed the decision over the weekend, and he talked it over with friends such as Truman Smith, who advised against it. But on Sunday evening, with a heavy heart, he wrote to the president that he felt "no honorable alternative" but to resign his commission as a colonel in the U.S. Army Air Corps. He could not serve under a president who would call him a traitor.

As Japan was making bellicose threats in the Pacific, Lindbergh made a speech in Des Moines, Iowa, entitled "Who Are the War Agitators?" in which he enumerated for the first time the forces that he believed were behind the clamor to go to war with Germany. When Anne found out what he was going to say it threw her into "black gloom."[19]

The three groups "pressing the country toward war," Lindbergh said, were "the Roosevelt administration, the British, and the Jews." The last reference caused Anne to blanch. "I hate to have him touch the Jews at all," she wrote, "even though what he had said was true," but "I dread the reaction on him. The price will be terrible. Headlines will flame 'Lindbergh Attacks Jews.' He will be branded anti-Semitic, Nazi. I can hardly bear it, *for he is a moderate.*"

She tried to talk him out of it but of course that did no good. The point, he told her, was not what effect it would have on him, "but whether it is *true* and whether it will keep us out of the war."

In his speech, Lindbergh said, "It is not difficult to see why Jewish people desire the overthrow of Nazi Germany . . . No person with the dignity of mankind can condone the persecution of the Jewish race in Germany. But no person of honesty and vision can look on their pro-war policy here today without seeing the dangers involved in such a policy both for them and us."

As the crowd of some eight thousand gave a standing ovation, Lindbergh went on to say that, "Instead of agitating for war, the Jewish groups in this country should be opposing it in every possible way, for they will be the first to feel its consequences."

As Anne had feared, Charles had set into motion a dreadfully acrimonious argument that would bring him to the low point of his career. Lindbergh's speech seemed to insinuate that Jews were not Americans. At least that's the way it was taken by the critics next day, and they were out for blood. Lindbergh had long insisted that America's entry into the war would only exacerbate the persecution of the Jews, whom Hitler would blame, and it was those Jews—the German Jews—that he meant when he referred to "them and us." The harshest critics accused Lindbergh of inciting anti-Semitism by blaming the Jews for pushing the United States into war—when blame had clearly not been his intention, and he said so in the speech.

The public reaction was swift and furious; the news media became nearly unhinged. Lindbergh was called everything from a Hitlerite to a fool. The terms "anti-Semitic" and "Nazi" were freely applied. The *Des Moines Register* called the speech "intemperate ... unfair ... dangerous in its implications." The *San Francisco Chronicle* wrote, "The voice was Lindbergh's but the words are the words of Hitler." Roosevelt's press secretary compared the talk with "outpourings from Berlin." Wendell Willkie, the Republican standard-bearer, called it "the most un-American talk made in my time by a person of national reputation."

There was worse. The general consensus was that Lindbergh had gone too far, to say the least. In towns and cities across the country, Lindbergh's name was removed from streets and schools. TWA even expunged the phrase "The Lindbergh Line" from its official stationery. It became clear within a few days that Lindbergh's effectiveness for America First was demolished. There were even calls for America First to be disbanded, and calls as well for Lindbergh to be deported to Germany. In the thick of it he offered to resign from America First but his resignation was not accepted.

Was Lindbergh anti-Semitic? The answer is yes, to the same extent that many if not most Americans of his era were anti-Semitic, including many black Americans who often resented Jewish ownership of property in what came to be called black "ghettos." Most Americans in the 1940s had been raised that way; it was as simple as that.

Seventy-five years ago, for most of the U.S. population, it was one thing to look on Jews as different, to exclude them from clubs, apartment buildings, hotels—as was regularly done and chronicled in many books and such movies as the 1947 *Gentleman's Agreement*—and to impose Jewish quotas, as Harvard and other Ivy League schools did, but to the vast majority of Americans it was another thing entirely to hate a race of people to the point of persecution and elimination as the Nazis were doing in Germany. Lindbergh's longtime friend Harry Guggenheim said both publicly and privately, "Slim has never had the slightest anti-Semitic feeling," but for years afterward his Des Moines speech "was enough for history to record Lindbergh as a strident Jew-hater."[20] The fact remains that what he had said was true, that as a group Jews were lobbying for the United States to go to war with Germany. But as Lindbergh's friend former president Herbert Hoover instructed, "When you had been in politics long enough, you learned not to say things just because they are true."[21]

Lindbergh, though, was a self-described "stubborn Swede." He stubbornly refused to retract his statements. Even Lindbergh's family was mortified by the incident. Betty Morrow was an interventionist (as she was certain her late husband would have been), but she also thought that the less said about it around Charles, the better. Charles's cousin Admiral Emory Land was furious with him, and his sister-in-law Constance—who by then had married the Welshman Aubrey Morgan, widower of her dead sister Elisabeth—lamented that Lindbergh had "gone from Jesus to Judas."

Stubborn though he might have been, Lindbergh was also shaken by the fallout from the incident and by watching his immense prestige evaporate.

LESS THAN TWO MONTHS after the Des Moines speech, on December 7, 1941, planes from Japanese aircraft carriers attacked the huge U.S. naval base at Pearl Harbor on the island of Oahu in the Hawaiian Islands, essentially destroying the U.S. Pacific Fleet of battleships that were moored there. The attack was a complete surprise, and the United States declared war on Japan the next day. Three days afterward, the Germans and Italians declared war on the United States, rendering the arguments of the America First Committee moot.

For Lindbergh, it was moot the moment he learned of the Japanese attack, but he now found himself in the most awkward position. Here was the war that he *believed in* fighting, but he had resigned his colonel's commission. One can scarcely imagine a more frustrating situation for a man of Lindbergh's temperament. A couple of years before, he had been Colonel Lindbergh, America's hero. Now he was ex-colonel Nobody, despised by a large portion of the population; the cause for which he had fought so hard was forever lost. And now that there was a war he wanted to fight, he couldn't get into it. Walter Winchell, a popular commentator of the day, summed it up uncharitably: "His halo has turned into a noose."

Yet America wasn't through with Slim Lindbergh, not by a long shot. The years ahead would bring a dazzling conclusion to the young man who made history by flying alone across the Atlantic Ocean. Before long he would take to the air once more—the Lone Eagle again in deadly earnest.

CHAPTER II

★ ★ ★ ★ ★

THE RAID

One of the most courageous deeds in military history.

—ADMIRAL WILLIAM "BULL" HALSEY

IN THE WEEKS FOLLOWING the Pearl Harbor attack, everyone with authority from the president on down was wracking his brain for a way to retaliate against the Japanese. Roosevelt was particularly desirous of striking a blow. As a World War I–era assistant secretary of the navy, he felt a special indignation at the near destruction of the Pacific Fleet and heavy loss of life. Plan after plan was rejected, most often, and most glaringly, because the United States, in the early months of 1942, simply did not have the strength to go forward with them.

All along the East Coast and the Gulf of Mexico, German submarines began ravaging American shipping, especially petroleum tankers on their way from the oil fields of Texas and Oklahoma to the Northeast, exploding and sinking many of them before the eyes of horrified beachgoers from Miami to Maine. On the West Coast, Japanese subs attacked merchant shipping, and on the evening of February 23 one of them surfaced and for twenty minutes bombarded an oil refinery near Santa Barbara, slaying some cattle on a nearby ranch. Meanwhile, with help from the U.S. Secret Service, Archibald MacLeish, the Librarian of

Congress, crated up copies of the Declaration of Independence, the U.S. Constitution, the Magna Carta, and other precious documents and put them on a special train for Fort Knox, Kentucky, where they remained in the gold vault for the duration.

On the Bataan Peninsula in the Philippines, General Douglas MacArthur's army was losing a life-and-death struggle with the Japanese. Elsewhere the Japanese imperial army and navy continued to swarm across the Pacific and Far East like a plague of locusts, extending their defensive perimeter outward thousands of miles from the main island chain.

The U.S. Navy had been launching and recovering planes from ships since 1922 when the USS *Langley* was converted from a coal barge into an aircraft carrier. But even by 1942 the standard carrier aircraft simply did not have the range to attack large targets in Japan without putting the carriers themselves in jeopardy of attack from land-based enemy planes, nor with the carrier planes' small frames could they carry sufficient ordnance. One optimistic idea had been to bring big four-engine B-17 long-distance bombers to the area near Vladivostok, in the Soviet Union, just six hundred miles from Tokyo, and strike from there. But Roosevelt was rebuffed by the Soviet dictator "Uncle Joe" Stalin. Hitler's treachery had once again caused all the worldwide communists, socialists, and fellow travelers to switch their allegiance back to Britain and the United States. Having been double-crossed by Hitler the previous summer, Stalin was unwilling to risk provoking Japan into attacking him as well.

Thus the stalemate continued, as the Japanese octopus crawled over Indo-China, Sumatra, Borneo, Java, New Guinea, and nearly all the Pacific Island groups, including the U.S. possessions of Guam and Wake.

Then one day in early January a bright idea popped into the head of U.S. Navy Captain Francis "Frog" Low, a World War I submariner then on the staff of Vice Admiral Ernest J. King, the chief of the U.S. Fleet. Low had gone to Norfolk to inspect the progress on the new aircraft carrier *Hornet,* and upon his return he looked out the window of the DC-3 transport plane that was carrying him back to Washington. Low noticed that the outline of the deck of an aircraft carrier had been painted on the surface of an adjacent runway, which he logically assumed was a practice area for carrier pilots-in-training so the navy could avoid the prospect of trainees crashing into the real thing. At the end of the runway, however, sat two big army bombers, of what nomenclature Frog Low did not know. With the kind of dashing cognizance that military brains sometimes exhibit, Low put two and two together—namely, the army and the navy—and when he reached Washington he made straight for Admiral King, who was aboard his flagship, the 333-foot former German yacht *Vixen,* which was moored in the Potomac River off the docks of the Navy Yard.*

Admiral King was the sort of commander people liked to describe as "more feared than loved," a hard-boiled, hard-drinking, no-nonsense sailor, of whom it was said, "Not only did he not suffer fools gladly, he didn't suffer *anybody* gladly."† When Low arrived the officers were preparing to go into the ship's dining room, so he kept his counsel until after the meal, when he followed King into his study and bared his mind.

Low told of looking at the carrier imprint and the bombers and thinking, "If the army has some plane that can take off in that short distance—one that can carry a bomb load—why couldn't we put a few of them on a carrier and bomb the mainland of Japan?"[1]

Instead of biting his head off, King looked up from his chair and said thoughtfully, "Low, that might be a good idea," adding that he should investigate the scheme further and get back to him.[2]

The carrier people Low contacted were skeptical. It might be possible for some sort of bomber to fly off a carrier, but the pilot would not be able to return because the landing speeds were too fast. Navy Captain Donald B. "Wu" Duncan, King's air officer, told Low that none of the army's big four-engine bombers would fit on a carrier because of their wingspans and they also required too much takeoff footage. He asked Low what sort of plane he had in mind.

---

* *Vixen* had been the private yacht of Julius Forstmann, a wealthy German-American wool dealer and father of the late colorful venture capitalist Theodore "Teddy" Forstmann.

† King's own daughter said of him, "He is the most even-tempered officer in the United States Navy. He is always in a rage." Upon his promotion to admiral, King is said to have remarked of himself, "When they get in trouble, they send for the sons-of-bitches."

"How in hell would I know?" came the reply. "I'm a submarine man."³

There were difficulties with most of the twin-engine medium bombers as well, Duncan said, except perhaps for the B-25, which, with a wingspan of only 67 feet, was enough to clear the carrier's "island"—the tall superstructure that looms over the starboard side of the deck. (The wingspan of a B-17 Flying Fortress, by contrast, was 103 feet.)

North American Aviation built the B-25, named the Mitchell, after the late General Billy Mitchell. It was powered by two 1,700-horsepower Wright engines to a maximum speed of 300 miles per hour at level flight carrying a payload of 2,400 pounds of bombs with a range of 1,500 miles. Best of all, it would fit on an aircraft carrier and might actually be capable of successfully taking off from one. The beauty of it was that these planes could be launched while the ship was out of range of Japanese land-based interceptors.

The hitch, Duncan said, was retrieving the planes after the raid. He suggested a sort of Rube Goldberg scheme in which the B-25s would take off about five hundred miles from Japan, make their bomb runs, then return to the carrier, which would already be retreating toward Hawaii, and ditch in the ocean to be picked up by rescue crews. But nobody was very comfortable with that last part of it.

Low suggested to Duncan that, as the air officer, he draw up an operations plan and give it to King, which Duncan did on January 15, 1942, thirty-nine days after the Japanese attack on Pearl Harbor, while some of the fires in the damaged ships still smoldered. Duncan's plan totaled fifty pages—written out in longhand, because he didn't type and didn't want to trust anything like this to office workers. Duncan immediately realized that the main element in the scheme would be surprise, which became a paramount issue; if Japanese intelligence got any whiff of the plan its forces could ambush the task force and destroy it.

Duncan proposed to use the newly completed aircraft carrier *Hornet* to launch a raid. The B-25s involved would need to be modified and lightened and navy carrier pilots would instruct the army pilots in the fine art of taking off from a pitching deck at sea. King read over the proposal with intense satisfaction, and next day, for security, he carried it personally to Hap Arnold. The two men could scarcely have been less alike, Arnold with his sunny, gregarious disposition* and dour old Ernie King. While their personalities clashed, they cooperated famously with a shared devotion to winning the war.†

Hap Arnold liked the plan and King suggested that he order some army B-25s to Norfolk to see if they could take off from the *Hornet,* instructing Duncan and Low: "Don't mention this to another soul." At this point King and Arnold also decided to bring Roosevelt into the scheme, and the president not only delightedly gave his blessings but made clear his desire that the highest priority should be put behind the mission. While the B-25 "tests" were being conducted, Arnold sent for the most trusted troubleshooter on his staff, James H. Doolittle. He figured that the army's role in this adventure would need a spearhead, someone who could pull the whole thing off seamlessly—if anybody could.

JIMMY DOOLITTLE HAD COME back into uniform at Arnold's request on July 1, 1940, as a troubleshooter for aircraft factories and related industrial endeavors as the United States ramped up its military output following the fall of France. He had spent the intervening year and a half helping companies such as Ford and General Motors convert from automobiles to airplanes.

"Do you think, Jim," Arnold asked, "that we have a plane that can take off in five hundred feet, carry a payload of two thousand pounds, and fly two thousand miles?" Doolittle immediately sensed what Arnold was getting at and asked for a day or two to study the question. When he reported back to Arnold next day that the army's B-25 might do the job, Arnold told him to work with Duncan and Low on the modifications to the planes and training of air crews. Doolittle had known "Wu" Duncan from the old flying days, and he read his plan with mounting excitement. The two met next morning, right before Duncan left for Pearl Harbor

---

* West Point class of '07, Arnold had been one of the army's first two pilots—taught to fly in 1911 by Wilbur and Orville Wright themselves.
† Despite the drawbacks of King's personality, it has been suggested by historians more than once that he was among the most brilliant naval officers of the era.

to explain the plan to U.S. Pacific Fleet Commander Chester W. Nimitz and his carrier commander William F. "Bull" Halsey.* For his part, Doolittle also left that afternoon, for Wright Field in Ohio, where he began to attack the problem of how to modify the B-25s for this strange, important, highly secret mission.

Doolittle's superb skills as an aeronautical engineer now put him in an ideal position to supervise the conversion of the Mitchells; he was already familiar with the mechanics of the plane and first set about to add enough extra fuel tanks to give the plane the range it required. Next would be to find other ways to lighten the aircraft.

Meantime Duncan, who had returned to Norfolk from Hawaii, arranged for two B-25s to be hoisted aboard *Hornet* to see if they could make a takeoff. In fact, to Duncan's delight they got off the deck so quickly that one pilot feared, as the plane reared up, that his wing would hit the projection from the ship's "island" that stuck out four stories over the flight deck. Granted, the planes carried no extra fuel, full crew, or heavy bomb load. Nevertheless the experiment was considered a success.

What allows an aircraft to take off from the ground (or, in this case, the deck) is a factor called lift, which is a direct function of the speed of the airflow over the wings. Every plane has a takeoff speed—the speed at which it can become airborne—depending on atmospheric conditions. On a carrier, there is the added factor of the speed of the vessel, plus the speed of the wind, as the carrier will always turn into the wind to launch. In the experiment Duncan conducted with the B-25s, the speed of the ship was 20 miles per hour, and the speed of the wind was 25 miles per hour—a total of 45 miles per hour of airflow over the wings. Since the minimum takeoff speed of the B-25 was a low 68 miles an hour, the pilot had only to accelerate to about 23 miles per hour to get airborne. In fact, a takeoff by a 25,000-pound plane in less than 500 feet would have been impossible except from an aircraft carrier. Wind at sea, then, would be an important factor in the raid.

---

* Halsey's friends called him Bill, not "Bull," but owing to some mix-up in communication a journalist's cable had once misidentified Halsey as "Bull" and the nickname stuck in the press.

Another problem was usable deck space aboard the *Hornet*. The navy had calculated the ship could carry sixteen B-25s on deck. The planes were too large to get down the elevator to the ship's hangar, so they would have to be lashed down and exposed to whatever weather came their way. But they took up so much room that the first planes to take off would have considerably less usable deck space in which to reach takeoff speed. Doolittle set to work on that problem along with the others.

Selecting the flight crews was singularly important, but the question ultimately solved itself. Three squadrons of the Seventeenth Bombardment Group stationed at Pendleton, Oregon, were about the only ones who fit the bill. The Seventeenth was the only intact B-25 unit in the Army Air Corps, its pilots were used to flying and navigating over water, and it had had actual experience patrolling for Japanese submarines off the Pacific coast. On Christmas Eve of 1941, less than three weeks after Pearl Harbor, it had sunk a Japanese sub off the mouth of the Columbia River.

Now, if only they would volunteer. By now, Doolittle—the great risk calculator himself—had calculated the odds of surviving the mission at under fifty-fifty. In the U.S. military "acceptable losses" would have been in the neighborhood of 5 to 15 percent depending on the mission. He was not about to *order* any airman to accept a challenge such as this.

On February 3, 1942, Doolittle brought twenty-four planes and a hundred and forty officers and men of the group to an airbase at Columbia, South Carolina, where the Seventeenth's officers informed them the army was looking for volunteers for an important but highly dangerous mission that would take them out of the country for two to three months. That was all they knew; one of the men thought to himself that "dangerous is a pretty bad word when you're talking about airplanes." However, to a man they signed on, even the married ones.[4]

From there they flew to Eglin Field, a remote bombing and gunnery range in a sparsely populated part of the Florida panhandle, arriving between February 27 and March 3. A flying instructor from the Pensacola Naval Station, Lieutenant Henry L. "Hank" Miller, was waiting for them. Miller surprised the senior captains by telling them he was there to teach them how to take off from a carrier in a B-25. They were further surprised to learn that he had never even seen a B-25, let alone flown one. And they became disturbed when they realized that he had not mentioned carrier landings in his introduction.

PRESENTLY DOOLITTLE ARRIVED at Eglin Field. When the men were assembled he entered the room to audible gasps; he was already a legend in the Air Corps. He reiterated what they had been told by their commanders, that they had volunteered for a very dangerous mission. Anybody could still drop out for any reason, and "nothing would ever be said about it," he told them. Some wanted to know more details but Doolittle was not forthcoming. He was extremely concerned about secrecy and the less anyone knew the better. Even he kept no written records. He told them the mission was top secret and not only were they not to discuss it with their wives, they were not to discuss it with each other, even if they managed to hazard a guess about where they were going. All rumors would be investigated by the FBI, he said. He again gave them a chance to back out. No one did.

They had less than three weeks to get ready. Coached by the navy lieutenant Hank Miller, they began to practice minimum speed takeoffs, which proved quite frightening to pilots used to mile-long runways. "They had always been taught to have plenty of airspeed before attempting to lift a plane off the ground," Doolittle explained. "Yanking a plane off the ground at near stalling speed took some courage and was very much against their natural instincts."

Doolittle himself underwent training by Miller because, unbeknownst to Hap Arnold and the brass in Washington, he intended to lead the mission, and he wanted to make sure that at the age of forty-five he could still cut it like the twenty-five-year-olds.

While this practice was undertaken, the planes were being modified on a rotating basis. The crews found many problems, such as that the electric machine-gun turrets did not work properly, and neither did the machine guns. By some oversight the rear turrets lacked machine guns entirely, and so machinists stuck two broomsticks in the tail and painted them black so to a Japanese fighter pilot they would at least look like twin .50s.

The planners also had to deal with the problem of collecting the planes after the mission. The original notion of flying back to the carrier and ditching turned out to be a nonsolution owing to uncertainty over weather, which made the highly dangerous practice of ditching a large airplane impossible.

The planning team finally decided that the pilots, after completing their bomb runs over Japan, would fly west across the Japanese mainland and the East China Sea to the region of Chuchow, which lay inland from the Chinese coast in territory that was disputed between the Chinese Nationalists and the Japanese imperial army. There they would land on designated airfields held by Chiang Kai-shek's army, turn the B-25s over to the Chinese Nationalist army, and then be flown to India and put aboard a ship back to the United States. It was a bold, complicated plan, fraught with danger, but getting the Chinese involved—or even the American military advisers—was the only available option.

The weight of the airplanes was an ongoing concern of Doolittle's, and everything not needed for the mission was stripped out, leaving room for guns, ammunition, fuel, bombs, the five-man crew, and little else. When they were finished they had stripped enough weight and added enough tankage for fuel to extend the range of the B-25 from one thousand to twenty-five hundred miles. In so doing they would carry more than a thousand gallons of high-octane gas—three tons of it in all. Since the bombing would be low level, they could remove the top secret Norden bombsight. One of the squadron commanders, Captain C. Ross Greening, designed a replacement consisting of two strips of aluminum that could be made in the field's metal shop for twenty cents. The heavy radios were eliminated as well.

There were constant problems to be overcome. The machine guns had to be removed and the metal smoothed by hand filing. Most of the Seventeenth's gunners had never fired twin .50-caliber machine guns, let alone from a turret at a moving target going 300 miles per hour. Then the crews found that the bomb racks would not release the bombs. The new rubber bladder gas tanks leaked. And every day the pilots and crews continued to practice taking off in five hundred feet or even less, with the plane being loaded heavier and heavier.

There was also bombing and gunnery practice and low-altitude flying, known as "hedge hopping," which a B-25 was never designed to do—

and, in fact, hedge hopping was illegal under air corps regulations—but Doolittle made them do it anyway because he figured that if during the attack they came barreling in right on the deck, twisting and turning around hills and towers and buildings, it would confuse the Japanese radar, if they had radar, and throw off their antiaircraft batteries.

Meantime, the *Hornet* weighed anchor in Norfolk and headed for the Panama Canal and the Pacific Ocean. For Doolittle, the clock was ticking. He went to Washington to make a progress report and sprung it on Hap Arnold that he wanted to lead the mission. Arnold said no, but Doolittle "launched into a rapid-fire sales pitch," which he'd long planned out, opening with the assertion that he was "the one guy on the project who knows more than anybody else," and closing with "They're the finest bunch of boys I've ever worked with."

Arnold seemed to relent and said, "All right, Jim. It's all right with me if it's all right with Miff [Brigadier General Millard F. Harmon, Arnold's chief of staff]."

"I smelled a rat," Doolittle said, "so I saluted, about-faced, and ran down the hall to Miff's office."

"Miff," he said breathlessly, "I've just been to see Hap about the project I'm working on and said I wanted to lead the mission. Hap said it's okay with him if it's okay with you."

Harmon was nonplussed—or, in Doolittle's phrase, "caught flat-footed"—and replied, "Well, whatever is all right with Hap is certainly all right with me."

Doolittle thanked him and made a fast exit, walking out the door just in time to hear Arnold's voice on Harmon's intercom, and Harmon replying plaintively, "But Hap, I just told him he could go."[5]

BY NOW A LAUNCH DATE had been selected: April 18, 1942, a Saturday. Data from U.S. submarines especially equipped for weather observations had indicated this would be the ideal date, as clear skies were expected over Tokyo. Because only sixteen bombers would fit on the deck of the *Hornet* the group was cut back to twenty-two planes—six of them in reserve—and the one hundred and ten men who would man them. The planes would be loaded aboard in San Francisco, and they would sneak across the Pacific along roughly the same northern route the Japanese had taken to attack Pearl Harbor five months earlier. In mid-ocean *Hornet* would rendezvous with the carrier *Enterprise,* which would escort them the rest of the way, providing reconnaissance flights and fighter cover in case the Japanese discovered them. Bull Halsey himself would command the task force.

On March 22, "Wu" Duncan, monitoring the mission from Pearl Harbor, sent a top secret message to Admiral King in Washington:

TELL JIMMY TO GET ON HIS HORSE.

That was the go signal to fly the B-25s cross-country to the air service depot in Sacramento where they would undergo last-minute checks and added equipment before proceeding to San Francisco. Next morning, Doolittle assembled the pilots and crews and told them they were moving out. He gave them another chance to back out, no questions asked, as well as a stern warning against even speculating or hinting to *anyone* about what they had been doing or where they were going.

Bull Halsey flew from Pearl Harbor to San Francisco and Doolittle met him there to discuss the operation. When Doolittle checked in a message was waiting: "Meet me at seven o'clock" along with the name of a popular restaurant—of all places to discuss a secret operation! He found Halsey seated at a booth at the appointed time. He had somehow arranged for the booths on either side to be vacant while they had dinner and, when the restaurant had cleared out, they got down to business. "Let's start out by having a drink," Halsey said.

Doolittle told Halsey that he understood the navy was in complete charge of the operation until the B-25s left the carrier, adding that, "My boys and I will be happy to serve under your orders."

Halsey explained about the size of the task force. In addition to *Hornet,* it would include two heavy cruisers, two light cruisers, eight destroyers and tankers. A similar task force built around the carrier *Enterprise* would steam from Pearl Harbor and rendezvous somewhere in the northern Pacific to serve as escort.

"We hope to get you within four hundred miles of the coast. But if we are intercepted or attacked [*Hornet*] will be like a sitting duck until we can clear the decks of your bombers."

Doolittle replied that in that case he would push the bombers over the side so *Hornet* could bring her fighters up to the flight deck.

"Not necessarily," Halsey told him. "You will probably have enough time to fly your planes off the deck and head for Midway." But, he added, "If the advance is sudden, without any radar warning, you will have to shove them overboard." That would be up to Marc A. "Pete" Mitscher, the *Hornet's* captain.

Halsey continued, "Suppose we are 1,500 miles off the coast of Japan and are attacked. You can either shove your planes overboard, or take off with your bombs, try to reach your targets, and hope for the best."

Doolittle thought it over. "I'd rather take the chances of finding the targets. We have rubber rafts on the planes. Maybe one of our submarines could pick us up.

On that happy note, at Halsey's suggestion, they had "one for the road."

TO THE DELIGHT OF THE PILOTS, Doolittle ordered them to perfect their hedge-hopping techniques all the way from Florida to California. As bomber pilots they were trained to understand that their job was simply to load up and deliver bombs over certain targets from altitudes of 15,000 to 25,000 feet and, like truck drivers, return and load up more of the same. It was the fighter pilots—the top-gun hotshots—who had all the fun, swooping, zooming, diving, looping, pulling G's. But now Doolittle's boys would have a chance at that, too, all the way across America. The crews, on the other hand, tucked away as they were in other parts of the plane, would just have to hold on and take it.

Meantime, in just these short weeks, the Japanese had conquered most of the Pacific, and news from the war fronts was grim. While Doolittle was still training his men, the Bataan Peninsula in the Philippines was overrun, and in the so-called Bataan Death March as many as ten thousand Allied prisoners had been killed by the Japanese. What remained of the American and Filipino forces on the island of Corregidor had been reduced to a forlorn hope. Roosevelt had ordered General MacArthur to evacuate to Australia and take command of all Allied forces in the southwestern Pacific. The trouble was, there weren't any Allied forces to speak of in the southwestern Pacific, and the Japanese were on the verge of shutting down the only remaining Allied pipeline, which was the route from the U.S. West Coast to Australia. If this was accomplished, there would be no place for the Allied forces to assemble to attack the Japanese-held islands. The Japanese were also in the process of finishing up their campaign for New Guinea, after which they intended to invade Australia and New Zealand, which would complete their conquest of the western Pacific. To that end, on February 27, 1942, they attacked and sank the small but important U.S. Asiatic Fleet in the Battle of the Java Sea.

It wasn't any better in the European and North African theaters. England was still the target of German bombers, while in the Egyptian desert British forces were, at best, stalemated with Field Marshal Erwin Rommel's panzer (mechanized tank) army. American convoys carrying war goods to England and Russia were suffering terribly from submarine attacks, while German armies were at the gates of Leningrad and Stalingrad as Russian resistance seemed to be crumbling. The year 1942 so far did not bode well for the Allies; in fact it was the only year the war actually could have been lost. But Doolittle's raid on Japan was about to change much of that, in ways no one could imagine.

ON MARCH 23 THE CROSS-COUNTRY hedge hopping began as the B-25s left the Florida panhandle and buzzed at treetop level, terrifying men, women, children, livestock, and wild animals and kicking up a two-thousand-mile dust trail from Eglin Field to Sacramento. There the planes received new propellers, additional sixty-gallon gas tanks in place of the lower gun turrets, and new back-strap-type parachutes for the crews. Supervising the work, Doolittle became furious at the slovenly attitude with which the civilian workers approached their jobs. He was rendered almost ballistic after finding out that the maintenance crews had readjusted the B-25s' carburetors in direct violation of his orders not to touch them. It prompted him, Doolittle said, to "use some expletives I hadn't used before and probably haven't since." Unable to explain the urgency of the mission, Doolittle phoned Hap Arnold, which turned things around fast.

The planes were flown to the naval air station at Alameda on San Francisco Bay, and even though all the aircraft could not fit on the deck, Doolittle told all the pilots to go aboard, as some might be needed as substitutes. Each in his army uniform marched smartly up the gangplank, saluted the flag and the officer of the deck, and "reported for duty." Meanwhile the B-25s were hoisted aboard the *Hornet* by giant cranes, and the astonished and uniformed sailors began lashing them down. It was April Fools' Day, 1942. Doolittle gave the air crews a talking-to about secrecy, then let them have a final night on the town, while he himself spent the night with Joe, who had flown out to see her sister and be with him. He told her he was going on a mission in the morning. She didn't ask what it was.

At first, aboard ship, there was some resentment between the army and navy personnel. Seeing the bombers on deck, the navy people assumed they were merely part of some sort of ferrying operation that would take the B-25s to Hawaii or another Pacific island. Since the army men wouldn't tell them any different, they felt put upon.

Then, on April 2, at noon, the carrier slipped her moorings and steamed westward beneath the Golden Gate Bridge. By late afternoon when they had rendezvoused with the cruisers and destroyers and were out of sight of land, Captain Mitscher sent a signal to all ships: "This force is bound for Tokyo." Within moments a chorus of cheers from five thousand throats rose up toward the darkening Pacific skies.

THE VOYAGE ACROSS THE NORTHERN PACIFIC was anything but boring for the army fliers. Their training would continue with daily classes in navigation, gunnery, and carrier flight operations, as well as a special course taught by one of *Hornet*'s intelligence officers, Commander Stephen Jurika, on Eastern "cultural matters." Jurika had spent the previous two years as assistant naval attaché in the American embassy at Tokyo and was well versed in the language, the city, the targets, the defenses, and the culture of the Japanese. He instructed the fliers on how to tell the difference between the Japanese and the Chinese if they reached China and were not sure if the area was occupied. The big toe of the Japanese, Jurika told them, is splayed out from the other toes from years of wearing thongs; Chinese toes are close together because the Chinese wear clogs. There was an important phrase in Chinese that they needed to learn, *Lushu hoo metwa fugi,* meaning, "I am an American." The

Chinese knew Americans as friends and would probably help them. If the Americans were shot down over Japan, however, the news was not so good. Capture by the Japanese, Jurika informed them, meant "they would be, first of all, paraded through the streets, then tried by some kangaroo court and probably publicly beheaded."

The pilots and crews made regular trips to the wooden flight deck to inspect their bombers—and to pace off the takeoff distance. They checked the lashings and looked for corrosion from the salt air, charged batteries, cleaned guns, checked tires, calculated, and prayed. One pilot was nearly blown overboard doing this at night during a storm and had to be rescued by *Hornet* crewmen. Others involved themselves in spectacular card and craps games with the sailors, and were soon relieved of their money, apparently not having been exposed to the adage "never gamble with a sailor aboard his own ship." There were rumors that, against regulations, some of the airmen had brought liquor aboard ship, which increased their popularity among the sailors.[6] Otherwise, Doolittle's boys enjoyed themselves at the ship's movie theater and ice cream station or took tours of the engine rooms and other interesting places. On April 5 a number of the airmen attended Easter service in the main mess hall.

Doolittle also conducted classes of his own, selecting targets in Japan and going over maps of the landing fields in China. Two things he ruled out, much to the dissatisfaction of the men, were using incendiary bombs to start fires in Tokyo's residential areas, where houses were made of paper and wood, and bombing the emperor's palace. He had been in England the previous year, at the height of the Blitz, and knew that killing civilians or bombing sacred places only made the enemy's population more intransigent. Also, he knew that the grounds of the palace were heavily defended with antiaircraft guns.

Meanwhile, Hap Arnold's effort to secure landing bases in mainland China was running into snags. The commander of the American forces in China and adviser to Chiang Kai-shek, Lieutenant General Joseph "Vinegar Joe" Stilwell, found that Chiang was reluctant to adopt the plan because he feared massive Japanese retaliation against the Chinese civilian population. However, by the time the task force was at sea Stilwell was able to report to Washington that the fields would be ready, with special equipment to broadcast a homing signal for the incoming B-25s—the number 57. If the planes were forced to land at night, Stilwell said, they would be guided in by torches and bonfires, weather permitting. And if weather was not permitting, well, presumably it was every plane for itself.

The task force had been at sea little more than a week when Japanese intelligence picked up radio signals indicating that American carriers were headed Japan's way. The assumption was made, however, that the carriers would launch their normal complement of carrier fighter-bombers, which would entail bringing the ships within about two hundred miles of the Japanese coast, where the task force could be swiftly and thoroughly dealt with by land-based bombers. Therefore, the Japanese awaited arrival of the American warships with a certain amount of anticipation.

As the task force plowed into Japanese waters, *Enterprise* sent up fighter interceptors as scouts, fanning out several hundred miles in advance of the carriers. On April 17, as they closed inside enemy territory, the B-25s were fueled, the machine guns loaded, and bombs brought aboard. Each plane's bomb rack included three five-hundred-pound explosive (demolition) and one five-hundred-pound incendiary, enough to do considerable damage to steel mills, factories, refineries, naval yards, machine shops, and other selected targets. That morning, the tankers refueled the carriers for the final time and returned toward Pearl Harbor.

In the afternoon, an unusual ceremony took place. A number of old sailors who had visited Japan in 1908 with Theodore Roosevelt's Great White Fleet had been given medals by the Japanese. Following the attack on Pearl Harbor they sent the medals back to the U.S. State Department, which turned them over to the secretary of the navy who, at someone's suggestion, sent them to Mitscher's task force to be attached to the bombs meant for Tokyo and other Japanese cities. This was done on the flight deck to the accompaniment of much hilarity and the inscribing of things, most of them better left unsaid, on the bombs themselves. By nightfall the B-25s were ready, and Mitscher told Doolittle, "Jimmy, we're in the enemy's backyard now. Anything can happen."[7]

OVERNIGHT, THE WEATHER BEGAN to deteriorate. It was a tense evening aboard the *Hornet* as the fliers checked their B-4 bags that contained their personal items plus two pints each of navy-issued "medicinal" whiskey. Those who could, slept—but not for long. The "general quarters" alarm sounded at three a.m. when *Enterprise*'s radar picked up two surface craft. Half an hour later the craft slid off the radar screen and the "all clear" was sounded. The weather had not improved, though, and by daylight a gale was blowing and the seas grew tall as a three-story building. Right before six a scout plane reported an enemy ship forty-two miles ahead, and Mitscher swung north, hoping to avoid it. He and Doolittle stood on the bridge peering into the gloom as the minutes ticked by and *Hornet* rolled heavily onward in the great seas. Then, at 7:38, *Hornet*'s radar picked up a Japanese ship at 20,000 yards, and almost immediately the radio operator reported that the enemy vessel had sent out a signal. In all likelihood they had been spotted.

U.S. naval intelligence was aware that the Japanese had established a defensive picket line of ships about three hundred miles off its eastern coast; it was not aware, though, that they had established a *second* early-warning line of fishing boats about seven hundred miles out. This was what the task force had encountered. Halsey, in the *Enterprise,* sent the cruiser *Nashville* to deal with the offending picket (later identified as the seventy-ton *Nitto Maru*), and soon *Nashville*'s big guns roared to life. People on the other ships ran to the sides to see what was going on. Less than two miles away in the mist lay the Japanese vessel. By then, on the carriers, there was no doubt—if they could see *it,* surely it could see *them.* Radio scanners on all ships were picking up messages in Japanese code.

It turned out not to be a glorious day for American gunnery. In the thirty-foot swells the enemy boat was bobbing so much it took an amazing 934 six-inch shells before one finally hit and blew the bows off the enemy boat, sinking her.

A Japanese survivor who was fished out of the water told of how he had spotted the American task force and ran to his captain's quarters to report "two beautiful Japanese carriers" passing by. The captain went topside and after taking a look said to the seaman, "Yes, they are beautiful, but they are not ours." Then, according to the sailor, after ordering the radio man to signal the warning, the captain "returned to his cabin and shot himself in the head."

Doolittle and the navy task force were in a nasty predicament. Halsey had wanted to get Doolittle and his bombers inside four hundred miles off the Japanese coast, but they were still eight or nine steaming hours away from that point. Japanese bombers were certainly being scrambled at this moment. Doolittle's bombers' fuel had been calculated down to nearly the last drop to get them to Japan and then to China. Worse, almost, instead of arriving over Japanese cities at night when they were fairly safe from Japanese fighters and antiaircraft, they would arrive in broad daylight; worse still, they would arrive over *China* at night. Doolittle did not hesitate. Within moments the Klaxon sounded and *Hornet's* loudspeakers blared, "Army pilots, man your planes!"

At the Hashirajima naval base near Hiroshima, the chief of staff to Admiral Isoroku Yamamoto, Japan's supreme naval commander, received word of the presence of the American ships and ordered his entire fleet to converge on the coordinates where the unfortunate Japanese fishing boat reported its location. This included an enormous five-carrier fleet under Admiral Chuichi Nagumo, who had been in command during the Pearl Harbor attack. Halsey's intelligence section thought this force to be in the Indian Ocean, but it had returned and was at that very moment passing through the Straits of Formosa. Suddenly the air crackled with urgent radio signals between Japanese headquarters and myriad warships—nine submarines, the aircraft carriers, battleships, cruisers, air forces—creating a virtual field day for American code breakers, who snatched these signals out of the air at stations ranging from Hawaii and Alaska to San Francisco and Sydney. These were the most Japanese radio signals the American cryptologists had ever heard and would prove immensely useful in the near future.

After Captain Mitscher's announcement, *Hornet* immediately became a hive of activity. The army pilots, some of whom had been eating breakfast, others dressing or shaving—and some of whom were actually still asleep through all the gunfire—dropped everything, got their gear together, and rushed to the flight deck. From below, sailors were lugging up hundreds of five-gallon jerricans of aviation fuel—twenty-five gallons per plane—to try to make up the difference in distance because of the early takeoff. Doolittle had warned his pilots to make sure holes were punctured in each can before tossing them out so they wouldn't leave a trail in the ocean leading back to the carriers. Navy men yanked the engine covers off the planes and unfastened the restraining straps. At eight in the morning a message was flashed from *Enterprise* to *Hornet*:

LAUNCH PLANES X TO COL. DOOLITTLE AND GALLANT COMMAND
GOOD LUCK AND GOD BLESS YOU—HALSEY.

THE DECK OF *Hornet* was pitching wildly in the mountainous waves and the gale force winds whipped a salty spray all across the bows, soaking anyone on deck, as the huge carrier turned slowly into the wind to launch planes. Inside their cockpits the pilots could only hold their breath and pray as their engines sputtered to life and props slowly began to turn. Everyone understood what would happen if the takeoff was unsuccessful and their plane stalled; they would plunge into the sea and the *Hornet* would immediately run over them, sealing their fate. The airmen looked down the flight deck in breathless consternation as the carrier's bow rose three stories or more on a swell, then came crashing down, only to rise up and plunge again, and yet again. If there was anything good about this weather it was the thirty-knot gale winds, which, coupled with the twenty-knot speed the carrier was making, would bring nearly fifty knots of wind speed across the wings of the planes even before the takeoff, giving them that much more lift.

At about nine o'clock Doolittle's plane was towed to the starting point, where a white line track had been painted straight down the deck. The pilots had to use this guide because there was less than a six-foot clearance between the bombers' wings and the carrier's island. There could be no wobbling. The flight officer on deck began furiously waving his flags in ever faster circles, signaling for Doolittle to rev up his engines to full power. "It was like riding a seesaw," Doolittle said, "that plunged deep into the water each time the bow dipped downward."

Doolittle gave his engines more and more throttle until Lieutenant Ted Lawson, of Los Angeles, piloting *Ruptured Duck* seven planes behind him, "thought he would burn them up." Then, Lawson said, "I saw that the [flight officer] was waiting, timing the dipping of the ship so that Doolittle's plane would get the benefit of a rising deck for his takeoff. . . . We watched him like hawks," Lawson remembered, "wondering what the wind would do to him, and whether he could get off in that little run toward the bow. If *he* couldn't, *we* couldn't." Then, Lawson said, "just as the *Hornet* lifted itself up and cut through the top of a wave, he took off. He had yards to spare. He hung his ship almost straight up on its props, until we could see the whole top of the B-25. Then he leveled out." Above the roar of the revving engines, Lawson remembered, "I could hear the hoarse cheers of every navy man on the ship. They made the *Hornet* fairly shudder with their yells. I haven't heard anything like it, before or since." At that point they were 824 statute miles from the center of Tokyo.

Several planes behind Lawson, Edgar McElroy, of Ennis, Texas, gripped the stick so tightly he thought he'd break it, as his copilot Richard Knobloch, of Fort Sheridan, Illinois, kept shouting, "Yes, yes, yes!" as Doolittle leveled off and came around in a circle over the ship.[8]

The next plane, however, piloted by Lieutenant Travis Hoover of Arlington, California, seemed to stall out when it left the deck, with its nose nearly straight up, and to everyone's dismay it began sinking tailfirst into the waves. Recounted Edgar McElroy, "We groaned and called out 'Up! Up! Pull it up!' Finally, he pulled out of it, staggering back up into the air."

One by one the B-25s roared off into the gloomy mist. One of the pilots, Lieutenant Bob Emmens of Medford, Oregon, recalled the takeoff this way: "Suddenly the island of the carrier was lost from sight as it had passed a mere eight feet from our right wingtip, and then, like a big living thing, our plane seemed to leap into the air as the deck of the ship disappeared under us."

When it came his turn, and the noise and vibration inside the cockpit became horrendous, McElroy said a kind of desperate prayer, "God please help us," as the flight officer dropped the flags the moment the deck reached its low point. "Here we go!" McElroy cried, and they began rolling down the deck straight into the angry, churning water. "As we slowly gained speed," McElroy said, "the deck began to pitch back up. I pulled up and we strained away from the ship. There was a big cheer and whoops from the crew, but I just muttered to myself, 'Boy, that was short!' "

The rest of Doolittle's squadron took off without serious incident except for the last plane, *Bat Out of Hell.* She was revved and her props were spinning in a high-pitched blur when one of the sailors assigned to remove the restraining ropes slipped on the soaking deck and was sucked into the *Bat*'s propeller. It chopped off his arm, but the horrified airman in the *Bat* took off anyway.

The moment the last plane was airborne Halsey ordered the fleet to come about and steer for Hawaii at full speed. He fully understood the danger they were in and knew that Japanese bombers—and probably the entire Japanese navy—would be headed their way. Watching from *Enterprise* as the planes took off, Halsey called it "one of the most courageous deeds in military history."

Each plane circled the carrier task force then broke into loose formations, depending on the location of their targets—Tokyo, Yokohama, Osaka, Kobe—and set courses toward the empire of Japan. Somewhere in the hazy squalls behind them they left the rising sun, with Lieutenant Jurika's pungent phrase *Lushu hoo metwa fugi*—"I am an American"—ringing in their ears.

THE B-25S SKIMMED in on the deck all the way, about twenty to fifty feet above the raging sea, flying slower than usual, about 170 miles per hour to save fuel (normal cruising speed of the bomber was 233 miles per hour and maximum dive 348 miles per hour). As they burned off gasoline the crews emptied the five-gallon cans into the tanks, stabbed puncture holes in them, and tossed them out of the plane. Lawson, in *Ruptured Duck,* remembered that "suddenly a dazzling, twisting object rushed past our left wing. It was startling until I realized it was a five-gallon can discarded by one of the planes in front of me. [It] would have downed us if it had hit a prop." The fact remained, however, that the early takeoff had put an extra four hundred miles on their flight plan, and they would need every drop of gas they had.

It took about five hours of flying to reach the coast of Japan, which the first planes encountered shortly before noon, Tokyo time. Ted Lawson felt somewhat disappointed. "I had an ingrained, picture-postcard concept of Japan," he said. "I expected to spot some snow-topped mountain or volcano first." Instead, the first land they saw "lay very low in the water in a slight haze that made it blend lacily into the horizon."

The crews had been warned to prepare for heavy antiaircraft fire and fighter attacks from the time they reached the coast, but instead they encountered numerous fishing vessels and later pretty little farms, "fitted in with mathematical precision." The fishermen and farmers looking up at them waved and smiled. The weather had cleared and they flew on in the sunshine.

The Tokyo-bound bombers—which included most of them—headed south. Before long Lawson encountered a flight of six Japanese fighters coming straight at them at about 1,500 feet. The brownish color of the B-25 must have been enough to camouflage them, as they kept on the deck and passed over a large forest. The enemy planes soon vanished from sight and were not heard from again. But the encounter caused a kind of shiver to pass through Lawson, he remembered later, like that of a man expecting at any moment to be shot in the back.

It was supposed to be about twenty minutes to Tokyo from the spot where the planes hit the coast, but it took longer. Soon, however, the crews began to spot the snowcapped peak of Mount Fuji, just as Commodore Matthew Perry had done on his famous visit to Japan not quite a hundred years earlier. On the outskirts of the city, Doolittle also came upon a swarm of Japanese fighters—nine of them, by one count, in flights of threes, but the raiders went past apparently unseen.

Doolittle reached Tokyo first. The city was immense—eight million people—and spread out more like Los Angeles than compact San Francisco. Once inside the boundaries his ship began to encounter antiaircraft fire. There were reportedly five hundred batteries within Tokyo's environs. Nevertheless, the Japanese people had been told they were immune from attack—forever shielded by the "divine wind," the *kamikaze,* which had protected them from invasion for a thousand years. By coming in at rooftop level the B-25s had the jump on the antiaircraft guns, for the most part, but Doolittle admitted the black puffs of flak "shook us up a little and might have put a few holes in the fuselage."

Doolittle spotted the large munitions factory that was his target and pulled up to 1,200 feet, which was the bombing altitude they all had practiced. His bomb bay doors opened. He was carrying the four five-hundred-pound incendiaries that were supposed to have marked the targets during the planned night attack. The bombardier dropped them and set the munitions factory afire.

Afterward, as he sped to the coast, Doolittle saw five enemy fighters converging on him from above. There were two small hills ahead, however, and he swung around them in an S turn, "pouring on the coal." The Japanese gave chase but Doolittle lost them. "They didn't see the second half of my S," he guessed. "The last time I saw them they were going off in the opposite direction."

Somewhere behind Doolittle, McElroy had climbed to 2,000 feet, "to see where we were," when he began to take flak. He put the nose down and headed for Tokyo Bay. Ahead, he could see smoke rising around the city from the bombers that got there before him. McElroy's destination was the big Yokosuka Naval Base across the bay in Yokohama, and as he approached it he could see the black bursts of flak exploding ahead. He soon was amid the layer of flak and the plane was jerked violently about by the aerial concussions, but McElroy headed straight for the torpedo factory and dry docks, where a big ship lay on the ways.* He called for the bomb bay doors to be opened.

"Those flak bursts were really getting close and bouncing us around," McElroy said, "when I heard Bourgeois shouting, 'Bombs Away!' I couldn't see it but Williams had a bird's eye view from the back and he shouted jubilantly, 'We got an aircraft carrier! The whole dock is burning!'" As McElroy turned south he looked back to see a giant crane begin to topple over. From the back of the plane there was "wild yelling and clapping each other on the back. We were all just ecstatic and still alive, but there wasn't much time to celebrate."

Ted Lawson dropped his bombs without incident, though he had some scary encounters with antiaircraft flak. He looked behind him to see a steel smelter that had been his target "puff out its walls and then subside and dissolve in a black-and-red cloud" after a direct hit from a five-hundred-pound bomb. Then Lawson took *Ruptured Duck* back down on the deck and gunned her full speed, "expecting a cloud of Zeros from moment to moment."

In the city itself, the airmen saw bicyclers and children looking up and waving as they roared over the rooftops; citizens assumed that the B-25 was some new type of Japanese aircraft. The military had conducted an air-raid drill that morning and many thought this had something to do with it. Just as had Americans at Pearl Harbor, the Japanese were expecting nothing more than a lovely spring day with their cherry trees in blossom. Then the bombs began to fall.

---

* This proved to be the new, nearly finished Japanese aircraft carrier *Ryuho*.

At the U.S. embassy, the ambassador to Japan Joseph Grew and his staff and their families were being interned by the Japanese until they could be exchanged for Japanese diplomats in the United States. They heard the explosions but were uncertain if it was an actual attack. Some of them went out on the roof and discovered it was in fact a U.S. raid, prompting Grew to report that "we were all very happy and proud in the embassy and the British told us that they drank toasts all day to the American fliers." When the wife of the American military attaché saw one of the planes she said, "Those planes are American bombers and I bet you that Lieutenant Jurika is in one of them." She was wrong by just a hair. Jurika, who until recently had been assistant naval attaché in the Tokyo embassy, was, of course, now Lieutenant Commander Jurika who had briefed the American fliers aboard the *Hornet*.[9]

The raid over Tokyo was over in a little more than an hour and achieved nearly complete surprise. In the other Japanese target cities it was the same. It had been four months and eleven days since the attack on Pearl Harbor. At one point during the action, the Japanese prime minister General Hideki Tojo was riding in a small official plane that was trying to land at the Mito aviation school on the far western side of Tokyo, where Tojo intended to conduct an inspection. As his plane descended to the runway, one of Doolittle's B-25s "roared up on its right side and flashed by without firing a shot." Tojo's secretary, an army colonel, reported that the plane was "queer looking."[10]

A good deal of damage was done but it was minimal with respect to the size of Japan's immense military power. Nevertheless, the psychological damage would prove to be devastating to the Japanese. By early afternoon the raiders were in open waters headed for China—and, in the case of one plane, Russia. None of the B-25s had been shot down although some had been hit and one in particular sustained considerable antiaircraft damage. The gunners of *Whirling Dervish* shot down an enemy fighter, and *Hari Kari-er* claimed two. Thus far the raid was a success, but there remained a long, nightmarish passage into the setting sun, where the weather ahead was worsening and the gas gauges falling ominously.

Aboard *Hornet,* which was racing back toward Pearl Harbor, all ears were tuned to the Japanese radio stations. Commander Jurika had been stationed by Captain Mitscher at the ship's radio to translate any news, but nothing abnormal was coming in, even though the bombers should have made their attack by then. Instead, the infamous Tokyo Rose, an American woman of Japanese descent who regularly made propaganda broadcasts for the Japanese, was at that moment reassuring Japanese listeners that they had nothing to fear from enemy bombers. At last at 1:45 a station interrupted its programing with a special bulletin.

"A large fleet of enemy bombers appeared over Tokyo this afternoon and much danger to nonmilitary objectives and some damage to factories," it said. "The death toll is between three thousand and four thousand so far. No planes were reported shot down over Tokyo." Another radio station referred to numerous fires set by the bombing and requested the people to pray for rain. The cheering broke out immediately aboard *Hornet* as Jurika translated the broadcast, and on *Enterprise* and the other ships soon thereafter. They had done it! After months of helpless frustration America had hit back.[11]

As the hours wore on, and the censors took hold of the information, the reports from the Japanese radio stations became less hysterical. The raid was described as "cowardly," and was said to have deliberately targeted hospitals and schools. In the days to come the damage was greatly played down and civilian casualties increasingly played up. Words such as "fiendish," "inhuman," and "indiscriminate" were applied to the raiders. But many Japanese were shaken after being told for so long that the islands were invulnerable to enemy attack, and they naturally expected and feared a repeat performance at any time. The raid induced an unsettling attitude among the Japanese population, which had been given to believe that the U.S. fleet had been destroyed at Pearl Harbor and there was no danger from the Americans. Now this!

The raid had immediate and serious repercussions for the military as well, particularly the Japanese navy, which was responsible for safeguarding the home islands. The Japanese quickly concluded that the planes must have come from aircraft carriers and after sending out every plane and warship in its fleet the navy returned empty-handed. Halsey was long gone—a highly embarrassing, if not humiliating, development. The reaction of the imperial navy was to recall as many modern warplanes as possible—mostly the famed Zeros—from areas in the South Pacific and Indochina. This of course interfered with other operations, most

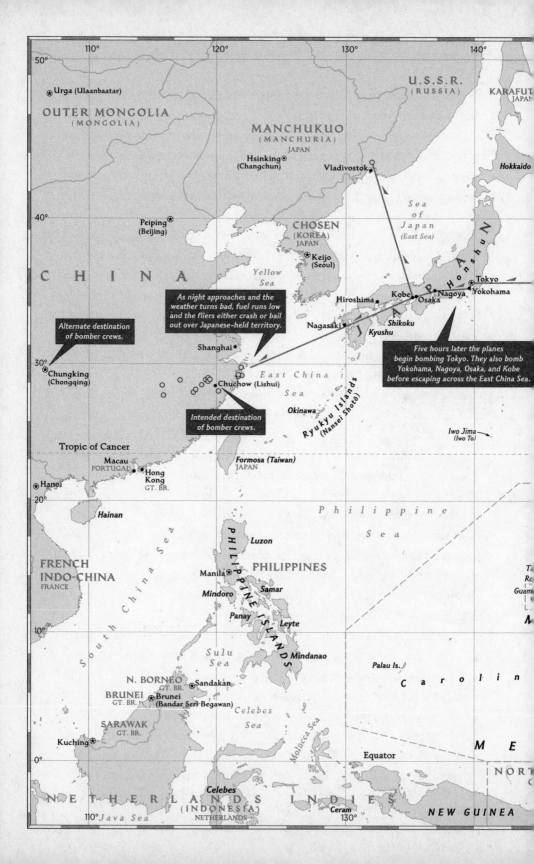

As night approaches and the weather turns bad, fuel runs low and the fliers either crash or bail out over Japanese-held territory.

Alternate destination of bomber crews.

Intended destination of bomber crews.

Five hours later the planes begin bombing Tokyo. They also bomb Yokohama, Nagoya, Osaka, and Kobe before escaping across the East China Sea.

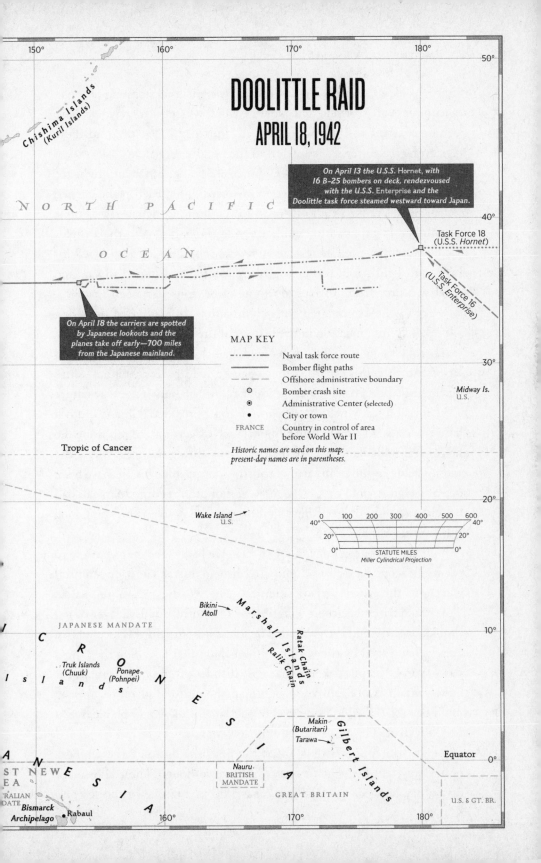

DOOLITTLE RAID
APRIL 18, 1942

On April 13 the U.S.S. Hornet, with 16 B-25 bombers on deck, rendezvoused with the U.S.S. Enterprise and the Doolittle task force steamed westward toward Japan.

NORTH PACIFIC

OCEAN

Task Force 18 (U.S.S. Hornet)

Task Force 16 (U.S.S. Enterprise)

On April 18 the carriers are spotted by Japanese lookouts and the planes take off early—700 miles from the Japanese mainland.

Chishima Islands (Kuril Islands)

MAP KEY

–·–·–·–	Naval task force route
————	Bomber flight paths
– – – –	Offshore administrative boundary
○	Bomber crash site
◉	Administrative Center (selected)
•	City or town
FRANCE	Country in control of area before World War II

Historic names are used on this map; present-day names are in parentheses.

Midway Is.
U.S.

Tropic of Cancer

Wake Island →
U.S.

| 0 | 100 | 200 | 300 | 400 | 500 | 600 |

STATUTE MILES
Miller Cylindrical Projection

40° / 20° / 0°

Bikini Atoll →

Marshall Islands

Ratak Chain

Ralik Chain

JAPANESE MANDATE

M I C R O N E S I A

Truk Islands (Chuuk)

Ponape (Pohnpei)

Islands

Makin (Butaritari)

Tarawa →

Gilbert Islands

Nauru
BRITISH MANDATE

GREAT BRITAIN

U.S. & GT. BR.

Equator

M E L A N E S I A

ST NEW
EA

RALIAN
DATE

Bismarck Archipelago

• Rabaul

notably in New Guinea, control of which was the final stepping-stone to the conquest of Australia and New Zealand, which in turn would have been devastating to the American war effort in the Pacific. And there were even greater repercussions from the raid further along.

Meantime, Jimmy Doolittle's raiders were flying into a very tight fix. With fuel running low and huge storms closing in, each plane carried a small hand-cranked radio to pick up the homing signal—the simple ID number 57—that would guide them in the darkness to the airfields of Chuchow that the Chinese army was supposed to have arranged for them with lighting and refueling trucks. But they listened in vain; no signal was broadcast. In fact, no homing beacons had been installed, nor were the fields prepared with illumination. It was one of the worst failures of communication in the history of the war.

General Chiang Kai-shek, it seemed, had thwarted the landing plans out of fear of reprisal within the Japanese-held parts of China. Since Washington didn't trust Chiang enough to inform him of the true nature of the mission for which the fields were to be prepared, Chiang did not share the sense of urgency and importance of getting the job done. So the general stalled and said he first wanted to bring the areas where the landing fields lay under his army's control. The problem might have been solved if Hap Arnold or U.S. Army Chief of Staff George Marshall had thought to send a man of high rank to coordinate plans on the China end, but this was not done.

Doolittle, of course, knew none of this. He had expected to be able to follow a beacon to a secure, illuminated airfield. Instead he found himself flying into the worst sort of situation. The weather was abominable. Pilots could barely see their wingtips for the storm clouds; a layer of fog completely shrouded the ground. The Chuchow airfield was located in a steep valley ringed by the vast mountain chain that lay along the China coast. Worse, the pilots knew that the altitudes given on their maps for the mountains were faulty: on one map the altitude given for a peak would be 5,000 feet and on another the same peak would be measured at 10,000 feet. They all were running low on fuel.

By eight-thirty Doolittle spotted the first islands along the Chinese coast. They had been in the air a full twelve hours. Their choice for survival lay between going down on the deck, ditching in the sea and hoping their life rafts would carry them to shore, or flying high on instruments and chancing to find some landing spot beyond the jagged peaks before their gas ran out.

Some took the first option, including Ted Lawson, but most, including Doolittle, took the second. Bob Emmens had somehow burned so much gas he was forced to land in Vladivostok, in the Soviet Union, despite what Stalin had said.

Lawson was about to take the high route when a hole in the fog revealed a long sandy beach on an island below. Lawson thought he'd take the chance it was not occupied by the Japanese and spiraled down on the deck to come in just feet above the water. As he skimmed along, however, suddenly both engines quit and the landing gear hit the water. It was like hitting a brick wall. Lawson, his copilot, and the navigator were catapulted through the Plexiglas windshield into the water. The bombardier was likewise thrown through the Plexiglas bubble in the nose. The gunner remained in the plane, which was upside down. Miraculously, because the tide was coming in, all five made it to the beach about a hundred yards away, though all were terribly injured. One man had both shoulders broken; another's head was deeply gashed. It was pouring rain.

Lawson was mangled the worst. His leg had been nearly cut in two and his biceps was slashed off. He put his hand to his mouth and realized his lip had been cut clear through to his chin. His upper teeth were bent in and, when he put his thumbs into his mouth to push them out, "they broke off in my hands," as did his bottom teeth. His navigator, Dean Davenport, came staggering down the beach, took a look, and said, "God damn! You're really bashed open! You're whole face is pushed in." And for Lawson that wasn't the worst of it.[12]

Doolittle had tried to fly as close to the landing field at Chuchow as possible using instruments and dead reckoning. When the gas gauges showed empty Doolittle put the plane on automatic pilot, gave the order in which the men would jump, and prayed they would land in Chinese territory. Nobody but Doolittle had jumped from an airplane before. When the fourth man had gone out the hatch, Doolittle shut off the gas valves and bailed out himself, earning his third star in the Caterpillar Club. On the way down he suddenly became concerned about breaking his ankles again, as he had done in Chile in 1926, but needn't have worried. In the pitch dark he plunged waist-deep into a soggy paddy field that had been fertilized in the typical Chinese fashion with "night soil," or human excrement. Doolittle waded out and presented himself at the door of a farmhouse shouting *Lushu hoo metwa fugi!* as he had been taught aboard the *Hornet*. But it failed to produce the results indicated by Commander Jurika. There was some rustling inside the house, Doolittle said, and then "the sound of a bolt sliding into place. The light went out and there was dead silence." He was on his own.

McElroy, flying behind Doolittle, experienced the same angst as his fuel gauge began blinking red. He told the crew to crawl forward. "I put her on auto-pilot and we all gathered in the navigator's compartment around the hatch in the floor. We checked each other's parachute harness. Everyone was scared. None of us had ever done this before." McElroy gave the order to bail out and said, "Go fast, two seconds apart! Then count three seconds off and pull your rip cord."

McElroy "kicked open the hatch and [we] gathered around the hole, looking down into the blackness. It did not look very inviting. Then I looked up at Williams and gave the order." When they had gone McElroy himself plunged into the hole. "I was jerked back up with a terrific shock," he said. "At first I thought I was caught on the plane, but then I realized I was free and drifting down . . . The silence was so eerie after thirteen hours inside the plane. Then I heard a loud crash and explosion. My plane!"

Like Doolittle, McElroy had landed in a rice paddy; he was lucky enough that his crew members were also nearby. At daybreak they assembled to find a way through the disputed territory to friendly lines.[13]

After being rebuffed at the Chinese farmhouse, Doolittle hiked on down the road in his stinking uniform and the pouring rain. A bitterly chill wind began to blow. He came to a warehouse of some kind. Inside, a large wooden box rested on two sawhorses. He removed the top to crawl inside, only to discover that "a very dead Chinese gentleman" already occupied it. He was in a morgue. He trudged on through the storm until he found a water mill, which got him out of the rain but the chill was so overwhelming that he spent the night doing calisthenics to stay warm.

At daylight he followed a path to a village where he met a Chinese man in the street. After *Lushu hoo metwa fugi* again elicited no reaction, he drew a picture of a train, whereupon the man "smiled, nodded, and trotted off." Doolittle followed him to a military headquarters where a Chinese officer attempted to take his .45 pistol. Doolittle refused to hand it over. The officer spoke a little English but seemed not to believe Doolittle's story, so Doolittle offered to show him his parachute in the paddy field of night soil.

With a dozen armed soldiers as "escort," Doolittle led them to the field, but the parachute had vanished. He told the officer that the people in the house must have heard the plane and maybe had the parachute. The occupants of the house, however, denied everything. "They say you lie," the officer informed Doolittle, and then told the soldiers to disarm him. Doolittle was backing away in what was suddenly "not a comfortable situation" when two soldiers emerged from the house carrying the white silk parachute. At this, the officer smiled, shook hands with Doolittle, and everything was hunky-dory.

Doolittle was taken back to headquarters and given a hot meal and a bath. He washed and dried his uniform but to his chagrin he could not get the odor of the night soil out of it. To his immense relief, the Chinese officer's men soon rounded up the rest of Doolittle's crew, who were in good shape except for a sprained ankle.

That afternoon Doolittle was taken to the site of his crashed plane, which was spread out on a mountaintop in pieces of debris covering about three acres. Scavengers had already picked the wreckage clean. It was a sorry sight. A photograph exists of Doolittle sitting forlornly on a piece of wing surveying the rubble and ruminating over the consequences. He had lost all of his planes and at that point heaven only knew what had become of all of his men; he felt the mission a total failure. Since he'd planned the raid, he told his crew chief Sergeant Paul J. Leonard, of Denver, Colorado, who had come along, "I guess they'll court-martial me and send me to prison at Fort Leavenworth." In fact, Doolittle believed his army career was over, but Leonard replied, "No sir, Colonel. I will tell you what will happen. They're going to make you a general." Doolittle gave a weak smile and Leonard continued. "And," he said, "they're going to give you the Congressional Medal of Honor." But this did not assuage Doolittle, who had "never felt lower" in his life.

MEN FROM THE FIFTEEN OTHER planes were having their own hard experiences. One man landed in a tree and was caught. Before freeing himself and climbing down he lit a cigarette, and when he tossed the butt he watched its orange glow descend into an unfathomable chasm. Luckily he decided to stay put in his tree, because dawn revealed he had landed on the edge of an enormous rock cliff. If he had cut himself free that night he would have plunged to his death. Here may be history's only example of a cigarette saving someone's life.[14]

Ted Lawson and his crew had a harrowing, weeks-long escape from Japanese-held territory into American hands.* Gangrene set in on Lawson's leg and it had to be amputated under the most trying conditions.

Farmers and peasants all over the province had been startled to hear the violent crashes of the Doolittle planes against their mountains and into their rice fields. Most of the five-man crews were united with one another next day, but *Lushu hoo metwa fugi* seemed to make absolutely no impression on any of the Chinese. Many of the men were injured and, miraculously, only three were killed—two drowned after ditching in the sea and one died in the parachute jump.† A few were robbed by Chinese bandits.

Japanese troops captured eight of the crew members and three of these were executed on the basis of a document invented by the Japanese army after the raid, entitled "Japanese Regulations for Punishment of Enemy Air Crews." Five of the prisoners were sentenced to death but for no particular reason their sentences were commuted to life in prison. The unlucky three, Lieutenant William G. Farrow and Sergeant Harold A. Spatz of *Bat Out of Hell* and Lieutenant Dean E. Hallmark of *Green Hornet,* were ceremoniously marched to a Japanese cemetery, made to kneel while they were tied to three white wooden crosses, and shot in the back of the head. The others were horribly tortured and phony "confessions" were beaten out of them by the Kempeitai, the Japanese version of the

---

* When he returned to the United States Lawson wrote the best-selling book *Thirty Seconds Over Tokyo*, published in 1943 and made into a hit movie the following year.
† The two men who perished at sea were lost, but Doolittle went to great lengths to see that the raider killed in the jump, Corporal Leland D. Faktor, of Plymouth, Iowa, received a proper burial.

Gestapo, in which the Americans attested to deliberately machine-gunning children and so forth. Then they were thrown into inhumane prisoner of war compounds where one of them, Robert J. Meder, died of starvation and neglect.

Upon receiving the announcement of the executions from Tokyo, Roosevelt began that evening's "fireside chat" with the words, "It is with the deepest horror . . ." The unremorseful Japanese responded by threatening in their own radio broadcast: "Don't forget, America, you can be sure that every flier that comes here has a special pass to hell. Rest assured that it's strictly a one-way ticket."[15]

The crew that landed their B-25 in Russia endured a bizarre odyssey. At first they were greeted with open arms by the Soviet military, and even conducted tours of their plane for Russian aviators. But this attitude changed quickly as they were shifted to higher and higher levels of authority in that strange and brutal country. At first they were given vodka and borscht and shown American movies—apparently "to keep them at all times as drunk as possible"—but soon the Americans were locked in a car on the Trans-Siberian Railway for a twenty-one-day journey to a remote guarded compound where they nearly froze to death. Attempts to contact the American consulate were futile, and the diet was so poor that their gums bled and several became ill. Out of desperation their commander, Captain Edward J. "Ski" York, of San Antonio, Texas, wrote a letter directly to Stalin himself, asking that they be sent to a warmer climate. To everyone's surprise it worked, and eventually they escaped to British-held Iran through the strange distant provinces of the Soviet Union.[16]

When he reached Chuchow on April 28, Doolittle learned that he had been promoted to brigadier general by Hap Arnold, just as Sergeant Leonard had predicted. Clayton Bissell, air operations officer to General Claire Chennault, pinned a pair of stars on him and gave him a swig of his high-priced scotch to celebrate, then castigated him for taking too big a swallow. By some act of providence the rest of Doolittle's people—sixty-seven pilots and crewmen—managed to find their way into the hands of friendly Chinese and were carried by practically every means of locomotion—junks, steamboats, sedan chairs, oxcarts, trains, rickshaws, donkeys, and buses—across the mountains, often through Japanese-held territory, to Chungking, a thousand miles distant in the interior of China.

There, arrangements were made for getting the raiders out of China, and Doolittle received orders to proceed to Washington quickly and by any means possible. Not, however, before he and the others were taken to the palace of Chiang Kai-shek and his wife, Madame Chiang, where they were presented medals.* Madame Chiang spoke English and Doolittle broke protocol by beseeching her to have the Chinese do everything possible to return his airmen from Japanese captivity before they were harmed. Madame Chiang replied that she would see what she could do.

In the United States reaction to the raid was at first muted. On Saturday, April 18 (April 19 in Tokyo), the *New York Times* carried a story based on what was intercepted from Japanese radio broadcasts. It said U.S. warplanes had bombed Tokyo, Yokohama, and other cities, inflicting damage on schools, orphanages, hospitals, etc., and that nine of the bombers were shot down. Military authorities in Washington refused to confirm or deny the story. They were waiting for better information.

Hap Arnold learned that most of his air crews were safe before Doolittle reached Chuchow. On April 19 the following telegraph cable was routed through various wire services:

MISSION TO BOMB TOKYO HAS BEEN ACCOMPLISHED. ON ENTERING CHINA WE RAN INTO BAD WEATHER AND IT IS FEARED THAT ALL PLANES CRASHED. UP TO PRESENT ALREADY FIVE FLIERS ARE SAFE. DOOLITTLE.

This was, of course, distressing news—all sixteen planes lost and possibly most of their crews as well? That wasn't something either Arnold or Marshall wanted to tell Roosevelt, let alone the public. Arnold soft-pedaled it to the president for the moment, saying more solid information was needed.

---

* Doolittle, who had been trying to send messages, arrived a few minutes late to find that there was no medal for him. Through some mix-up it had already been presented to his second in command. Upon learning this, Chiang snatched a handsome medal off the uniform of one of his generals and pinned it on Doolittle's chest.

Meanwhile, Dwight D. Eisenhower, at the time deputy chief of staff for the Pacific and Far East, reported that his experts believed it would be imperative for Japan to retaliate against the United States in a major way and suggested the possibility of an attack on the Panama Canal, even on Washington, D.C.[17] At this, the army seemed to panic. California radio stations were ordered off the air so Japanese planes couldn't use their broadcast signals to home in on as they had at Pearl Harbor. In San Francisco the bridges, including the Golden Gate, were temporarily closed down. Hundreds of thousands of gas masks were shipped to the West Coast.

During the next few days, as more of Doolittle's crews were found, the picture became brighter, but the military and the White House continued to drape a cloak of secrecy over the incident. One reason was fear of reprisals in China, as well as an odd notion that American authorities could somehow disguise the method in which the attack was carried out.

When reporters continued to demand answers about how the planes came to reach the Japanese mainland, Roosevelt told them mysteriously, while flipping his famous cigarette holder Groucho Marx–style, "They came from Shangri-la."*

As more information about the attack was revealed in the press, Americans became delighted. General George Marshall wrote Doolittle a felicitous message: "The president sends his thanks and congratulations to you and your command for the highly courageous manner," and so forth. Hap Arnold cabled that he was awarding the Distinguished Flying Cross to all the raiders. Halsey sent Doolittle a glowing letter, which began "The takeoff was splendid!" and went on in that vein employing the adjective "gallant" several times, before closing with a typical Halsey flourish, "Keep on knocking over those yellow bastards."

In time, as more details emerged, the press people began to celebrate the Doolittle raid nearly on a par with Lindbergh's landing in Paris and so were clamoring for his return to the United States. The story was fodder for newsreels and radio and rated banner headlines in all the newspapers. Doolittle was soon featured on the covers of popular magazines such

---

* The legendary Himalayan kingdom in James Hilton's novel *Lost Horizon,* and also the name of the presidential retreat in Maryland, now known as Camp David.

as *Life* and *Look*. As a high-ranking army officer Doolittle, who shared Lindbergh's mistrust of the press, was spared the sort of mobbing and stalking that Slim and Anne had endured.

The raid at last produced the morale boost for the American people that Roosevelt and Hap Arnold had envisioned, and it proved, unfortunately for the Japanese, a promise of things to come.

In China, meanwhile, the enraged Japanese took out their wrath on the civilian population. Emperor Hirohito himself approved orders for a punitive bloodbath against all Chinese—men, women, and children—in the areas where the Doolittle raiders had come down and were helped to safety. In a three-month carnival of boiling vengeance that is almost beyond comprehension, a hundred thousand Japanese soldiers marched into the region and slaughtered an estimated quarter of a million Chinese. They ordered Chinese laborers to ditch up all the landing fields, then gunned them down while they rested on their shovels. They burned entire towns because they didn't like the "attitude of the population." Their barbarism seemed to know no bounds. An old man, for instance, a schoolteacher, who had given some of the Americans food, told two Catholic priests how the Japanese had "killed my three sons; they killed my wife, Ansing; they set fire to my school; they burned my books; they killed my grandchildren and threw them in the well." The schoolteacher himself escaped death only by hiding in the well with his slain grandchildren. Another man was immolated by being wrapped in a kerosene-drenched blanket that laughing Japanese soldiers then ordered his wife at gunpoint to set afire.[18]

DOOLITTLE BEGAN HIS LONG VOYAGE HOME on a China National Aviation DC-3 piloted by one Moon Chin, a native of Baltimore, en route to Myitkyina, Burma, which at the time, unbeknownst to the pilot or to Doolittle, was under attack by Japanese fighter planes. Waved off until the attack ended, they arrived during a near riot, with the airport mobbed by people seeking to fly to safety. To Doolittle's extreme consternation, Chin allowed more than seventy refugees on the plane, which was rated to carry not more than twenty-one passengers. He explained to Doolittle, "We are fighting a war over here. You do lots of things here you wouldn't do at home."

Somehow the plane got off the ground and after an excruciating four-hour flight they landed in Calcutta, where Doolittle tried in vain to find a proper general's uniform to replace his soiled khaki flying suit. At length he was reduced to using a native tailor who, after taking measurements, produced a khaki bush jacket with short pants, knee socks, and a pith helmet. Since Doolittle was due to take off on the next leg of his return trip, he was compelled to accept this ridiculous costume before boarding a British Overseas Airways flying boat to Cairo.

From Cairo he flew to Khartoum in the Sudan, Dakar in Senegal, across the Atlantic to Brazil, and thence to Puerto Rico. In each of these places his attire more or less fit in with local custom. But from Puerto Rico he arrived on May 18 at Bolling Field in Washington, D.C., where he was met by a staff car sent by Hap Arnold.

Arnold pretended to ignore Doolittle's "weird getup" when he appeared in his office doorway and saluted, carrying the pith helmet under his arm, and shushed him when Doolittle began to apologize for losing the planes. Arnold assured him no blame would ever attach to him for that. The two of them then went to General Marshall's office where Doolittle was greeted by a "big smile," which he remembered years afterward because it was so rare. After a brief discussion of the raid, Arnold suggested that Doolittle go to the uniform store and acquire some clothing that more properly befitted a new brigadier general, then ordered him to retire to his Georgetown apartment and stay there, "incommunicado," until further notice.

Doolittle did exactly as he was told. He wanted badly to call Joe, who was on the West Coast staying with her mother, but didn't dare after what Hap Arnold had told him. Next morning Arnold phoned and said a car would pick him up in an hour. When the car arrived, Doolittle was astonished that it contained not only Hap but George Marshall as well.

With the three of them sitting in the backseat they rode off in silence until Doolittle inquired where they were headed.

"We are going to the White House," Arnold said.

"What are we going to do there?" Doolittle asked.

"The president is going to give you the Medal of Honor," said Marshall.

Doolittle was astounded. He began to protest that the medal "should be reserved for those who risk their lives trying to save somebody else."

He continued by praising all of his men; he even suggested that the threshold for receiving the honor had been lowered in recent years. As he spoke, however, Doolittle noticed that Arnold was beginning to look pained and that Marshall was actually scowling.

I cannot get into trouble by keeping my mouth shut, Doolittle thought, but this proved beyond him. "I don't think I'm entitled to the Medal of Honor," he said.

"I happen to think you are," Marshall said icily.

They rode on in stony silence while Doolittle blanched at the gaffe he had just made. "The highest ranking man in army uniform had made his decision. It was neither the time nor the place for me to argue."

When they reached the White House and were shown into a parlor next to Roosevelt's office, Doolittle was stunned to find Joe waiting there. Marshall had arranged for her to be flown in from Los Angeles, although after a seventeen-hour trip with several changes of planes and no lavatories she remarked that she "looked like a carpetbagger."

Bantering with White House reporters, Doolittle truthfully told them that none of his planes had been shot down over Japan and that all but one had reached their destinations, which were "somewhere in China."* He glossed over the rest of it "for security reasons."

Roosevelt was ebullient when Doolittle and the big air bosses came into his office. He had been told nothing of the raid until after the bombers had left *Hornet.* It was just the kind of thing he felt the country needed, for ever since the United States got into the war there had been bad news everywhere, and the American strike on Tokyo was an *enormously* uplifting symbol—a direct attack on the heart of the enemy homeland within weeks of the initial Japanese affront.

Marshall read the citation aloud while photographers took pictures, then handed the scroll to Joe. Doolittle had to lean over so the seated president could pin the medal on him, but because he was only five-foot-

---

* Shortly after the B-25 landed in Russia the Kremlin contacted the United States reporting that the plane and its crew were "interned," and that it was a matter of great secrecy. A few days later the Kremlin announced to the world that the plane was in Russia.

four he didn't have very far to lean (much later, Doolittle admitted that he always said he was five-six because it made him feel taller).

In the excitement Joe absently began to twist the citation scroll in her hands so hard that Marshall was tempted to take it away from her. Her single regret was that in all the pomp and circumstance she forgot to ask Roosevelt for his autograph so she could embroider it on her getting-to-be-fabulous tablecloth.

WHEN THE DAMAGE CAUSED by the raid was initially assessed by the Japanese Demolition Ministry, it was found that about ninety buildings in the Japanese target cities were completely destroyed. Nearly all were military targets such as Factory Number 1 of the Japanese Steel Corporation, the Japanese Diesel Manufacturing Company, the Mitsubishi Heavy Industries Corporation, the Nagoya Aircraft Factory, a military arsenal, the Yokohama Naval Docks, the Yokohama Manufacturing Company, and so forth. The report also said that about fifty people were killed and two hundred and fifty injured, mostly civilians. An army hospital in Nagoya was bombed, according to Japanese newspapers, as were schools and neighborhood homes in the vicinity of the attacks.[19]

Compared with the later U.S. air raids on Japan this was minuscule. Each of the sixteen raiders' planes carried one ton of bombs; by the end of the war American warplanes were dropping seventeen hundred tons of bombs a day on Japanese cities. During one raid alone in 1945, using conventional bombs, it was estimated that eighty-eight thousand Japanese were killed and six square miles of Tokyo were completely destroyed.

But the Doolittle raid, as it has come to be called, would have consequences far beyond its modest intentions. Not only did the Japanese military recall many of their forces from other war zones in the Pacific and Asia to protect the homeland from further U.S. attacks, but there was also immense political pressure on Admiral Yamamoto to push Japan's eastern defensive perimeter out another thousand miles. The centerpiece of this maneuver would be an attempt to capture Midway Island, a scant 1,250 miles from Pearl Harbor. Midway was the Allies' lone and farthest outpost in the central Pacific, from where U.S. scout planes constantly patrolled to warn of Japanese naval movements.

Yamamoto planned to lure the remainder of the American fleet to its doom. First he would stage an attack on Dutch Harbor in the Aleutian Islands, then attack Midway to bring U.S. carriers out of Pearl Harbor. He would be lying in wait in his trap when they arrived.

It was a complex scheme and, like the Doolittle raid, required complete secrecy. What Yamamoto didn't know, even on the eve of the battle, was that his plan wasn't secret anymore—and the reason, in large measure, was because of Doolittle's raid.[20]

American intelligence, and in particular one naval officer, the eccentric forty-three-year-old Lieutenant Commander J. J. Rochefort, had been working for years to break the complex Japanese naval code. His team had unraveled bits and pieces but were stymied by the nearly continuous radio silence imposed by Yamamoto on the Japanese fleet. Doolittle's shocking attack changed all of that. For several hours during and after the raid, a terrific amount of Japanese naval radio traffic went out, and all of it was just as quickly plucked from the airways by Allied listening stations and sent to Rochefort's headquarters at Pearl Harbor, where teams of code breakers and intelligence analysts worked around the clock putting the pieces together. Before Doolittle's raid, Rochefort's team had managed to decipher some 10 percent of the code; a week after the raid they were reading half of it. By the end of May, about the time that Doolittle was getting his Medal of Honor, Rochefort's people were reading nearly all of it.

Rochefort scored his coup de grâce on the Japanese when he tricked them into commenting on a fake water supply problem on Midway Island just two weeks before Yamamoto set sail. Rochefort wanted to be positive that Midway was the target and he believed the Japanese code signal for the island was "AF." So he had his radio operator on Midway send a message saying something was wrong with the island's fresh water system and sure enough, in a day or so, Rochefort's radio operators intercepted a Japanese signal saying the Americans were having water problems at "AF."

Rochefort now knew that the Japanese planned to move on Midway and the Aleutians, but he had not yet discovered *when* the attack would occur. Up until May 27, almost the last day the U.S. Pacific Fleet could act, the code breakers had not succeeded in cracking the ultrasecret cipher that contained this information. Then Lieutenant Commander Wesley A. Wright, one of the senior cryptologists, took a crack at it.

It was a feat of staggering complexity. Late into the night Wright worked it out. The date-and-time cipher used by the Japanese "comprised a polyalphabetic with independent mixed-cipher alphabets and with the exterior plain and key alphabets in two different systems of Japanese syllabic writing—one the older, formal kata kana, the other the cursive hira gana. Each has 47 syllables, making the polyalphabetic tableau a gigantic one of 2,209 cells, more than three times as extensive as the ordinary Vigenère tableau of 676 cells. Nevertheless, by about 5:30 the next morning he had a solution."[21]

Commander Wright's decipher informed Admiral Nimitz that the Japanese planned to open their attack on the Aleutians at dawn, June 2, and attack Midway at daybreak, June 3. This priceless information was obtained only by an eyelash: Japanese intelligence, already fearing that radio traffic during the Doolittle raid may have compromised its military's secret encryptions, had planned to change the code on May 1, but owing to bureaucratic delays the change was postponed until June 1.

The rest is history. On May 30 the U.S. carrier task force of *Hornet, Enterprise,* and *Yorktown* steamed from Pearl Harbor toward Midway.* On June 4, 1942, a Thursday, the Americans ambushed and annihilated the Japanese fleet. Four enemy carriers were sunk, a blow from which the Japanese never recovered and never again regained the initiative in the Pacific. Nearly five thousand Japanese sailors died, including many of Japan's best pilots. Midway is generally considered the turning point in the war against Japan,† and much of it was due, in no small measure, to the fact that the Doolittle raid had prompted the attack on Midway in the first place—and, as a direct result of the raid, the Japanese hadn't the foggiest notion that U.S. intelligence was reading their mail.

---

* But without the indomitable Halsey, who was in the hospital with a painful rash. In his stead, Nimitz selected fifty-six-year-old Admiral Raymond Spruance (Annapolis, Class of 1907), who was not an aviator, and had never commanded a carrier let alone a carrier fleet, but he had good sense and good deputies.

† *Yorktown,* however, was lost in the action. Damaged by enemy bombs, she was floating without power when a Japanese submarine torpedo sent her to the bottom.

CHAPTER 12

★ ★ ★ ★ ★

WE WERE SLOWLY ROTTING AWAY

IN MARCH OF 1942, while Jimmy Doolittle prepared for his famous raid, Captain Eddie Rickenbacker was firing up U.S. air crews on a whirlwind tour for Hap Arnold. From Tampa to Topeka he told them—after comparing the fabric-covered crates of his day that would quite literally come apart in a steep dive, with the metal 2,400-horsepower multi-machine-gunned modern warplanes such as the P-38 and the P-40—"You've got something to fight with!"

Depending on shifts he would often make three or four hour-long talks a day. It was exhausting but gratifying—especially when he visited his old 94th Hat in the Ring squadron that had been reactivated at Long Beach, California. He stood in an amphitheater and informed them: "This is my outfit. There are new names, new faces, but the same old tradition. I know you will do the job." Then the cheering began.

Back in Washington Arnold arranged for Eddie to speak to a roomful of aviation executives and Air Corps generals, many of them younger than he, but he remained undaunted and did not mince words—he was Eddie Rickenbacker, a household name, and he could talk the way he pleased because he was no longer in the army: "The first thing I've got to say is that all of you guys get rid of your chisels that you've got in your pockets. I know. You brought a pocketful of them down here so you could chisel your way out of doing things that you're going to have to do whether you like it or not."[1]

Arnold was so pleased that on April 2, the same day that the *Hornet* carrying Doolittle's raiders made its mid-Pacific rendezvous with Halsey's *Enterprise,* he wrote Rickenbacker a letter of commendation, stating, "Your magnificent record during the last war has been splendidly carried on in this fine piece of work that you have just finished, and we all salute you." But the army was far from finished with Eddie Rickenbacker.

In the end he produced an evaluation report on his findings for Hap Arnold that so impressed Henry Stimson, the U.S. secretary of war, that he summoned Rickenbacker to perform a similar duty for the newly arrived American Eighth Air Force in England, where the pitiless, nine-month, round-the-clock German bombing of English cities had only recently subsided. Eddie arrived in London in mid-September to meet with his old friend from World War I flying days John Gilbert Winant, whom Roosevelt had recently appointed ambassador to the Court of St. James's. Like many American executives serving the government, Eddie's salary was $1 per year, and he paid his own expenses—a "dollar a year man." His mission, as he understood it, was twofold: first, to analyze and report on the general conduct of the air war against Germany, and, second, to evaluate U.S. air equipment and personnel.

He noted upon arrival that the preferred bombers during the German bombing campaign on London had been the Heinkel "Spade" He 111, the Junkers Ju 88, and the dated Dornier Do 17, nicknamed "The Flying Pencil" because of its thin fuselage. Rickenbacker was appalled at the amount of damage caused by the Germans—the entire East End was a near ruin and much of the West End was destroyed. The Blitz, as they called it, lasted nine months and demolished or damaged a million homes. He reflected that it could have been much worse, if Göring and Hitler had been willing to lose two hundred planes a day.

At the same time Eddie recalled how his now deceased friend Ernst Udet had told him in 1939 that he had recommended a different type of plane—a long-range heavy bomber carrying greater loads and protected by fighter escorts—but that Göring himself had canceled that plan.

Rickenbacker had a lengthy luncheon conference with Winston Churchill and a number of highly placed government officials, during which he divined that the prime minister was not averse to having the U.S. B-17 Flying Fortress conduct precision high-altitude daytime bombing raids, while the British would continue their nighttime terror raids on Germany with incendiaries and "bunker buster"–type ordnance. The Brits themselves had tried daytime bombing, but unsuccessfully, and Washington feared that British officials would be unreceptive to such an approach by the Americans. This was important information for Henry Stimson, who would be advising Roosevelt about the upcoming Allied conference at Casablanca. Rickenbacker also was determined to convey to Stimson his opinion, heartily shared by the commander of the Eighth Air Force, Major General Carl "Tooey" Spaatz, and his assistant Brigadier General Ira C. Eaker, that the Eighth not be stripped of B-17s for the upcoming invasion of North Africa, on grounds that the bombing of Germany should receive the highest priority.

As Eddie toured Great Britain he took note of the widespread use of American earthmoving equipment carving extralong runways into the tranquil English countryside to accommodate the B-17 bombers. American factories were sending B-17s to England as fast as they could turn them out, but this proved not fast enough. It was also difficult to ferry the planes across the Atlantic—fully a third of the first shipment of thirty had been lost in the icy Arctic wastes, and Hap Arnold considered it too dangerous to transport them by ship because of the submarine menace.

Nevertheless, when U.S. manufacturers began churning out the B-17s at maximum rate there would be thousands of them in Great Britain, and a sunny viewpoint prevalent among many high-ranking RAF leaders was that Germany could be defeated by airpower alone. Because this reflected the general principles of his friend and mentor Billy Mitchell, Rickenbacker was loath to report to Stimson that the theory was unsound—though in the end he did not hesitate. An American army, he told the secretary of war, would one day have to cross the English Channel, go into Germany, and shut it down. This too was useful information for the president when he met with Churchill and other Allied leaders in Morocco, for it was there that Roosevelt would announce—to the surprise and chagrin of Winston Churchill—that the

Allies would accept nothing short of "unconditional surrender" from the Axis powers.

Rickenbacker's report also contained numerous specific and highly useful recommendations vis-à-vis various U.S. aircraft, in particular the B-17. The plane had been modified so many times, he pointed out, that its center of gravity was off, which made it slower. The oxygen supply was insufficient and the rubber oxygen masks often froze onto the cheeks of the aviators at high altitudes. Remembering back to 1918 when he had put an iron stovetop under the seat in the cockpit of his Spad, Rickenbacker recommended that the B-17 pilot's and copilot's seats be armored, that they might fly through German flak with some small measure of confidence they wouldn't get their asses shot off.

The machine guns in the plane were not flexible enough. Their range of motion was limited, Rickenbacker found, and the waist guns were too close together, so that if both gunners were firing they would often bump into each other as they swung. Furthermore, the spent shell casings that were ejected from the guns sometimes damaged other planes in the formation, and he recommended a box to catch them in.

One of his suggestions turned out to be a dud—the creation of a "flying battleship." This craft would employ the body and machinery of a B-17 but instead of bombs it would carry a huge arsenal of machine guns to escort the other planes on the mission. However, when it was tried out, the thing proved too slow and heavy to keep up with the planes it was supposed to protect.

Rickenbacker was immensely impressed with the P-51 Mustang, a prototype of which was unveiled to him by the British, and said so in his report to Stimson. With its sleek body powerpacked with machine guns, long-range capability, and 1,600-horsepower engine, it proved to be the most popular American fighter in the European theater, and before war's end it accounted for nearly five thousand enemy planes shot down. He was only slightly less impressed with the new and somewhat odd-looking P-38 fighter, which had gotten so much criticism even before being put into action that Hap Arnold was thinking of discontinuing it. With its twin engines and twin tail booms, the P-38 Lightning would become the most popular army fighter in the Pacific, and it was the plane that would be famed for killing the

Japanese admiral Yamamoto over Bougainville in the Solomon Islands the following year. The only problem Eddie found was that the twin booms and engines hampered the pilot's vision somewhat, a condition always problematic in aerial combat. In fact, he was puzzled that nearly all of the American pursuit planes were made with Plexiglas cockpit covers that hampered rear vision. In Eddie's day, pilots didn't have cockpit covers and so enjoyed an unobstructed 360-degree view of the sky. In his report to Stimson he recommended that all fighter cockpits be reevaluated with the pilot's view in consideration, especially to the rear, where somebody might be sneaking up on you.

Before returning to the United States Eddie met with the new commander of U.S. forces in the European theater, General Dwight D. Eisenhower, whose staff was furiously planning a surprise Allied landing in North Africa to throw the Germans off balance and possibly take some pressure off of the Soviets, who were having a hard time staving off Hitler's armies. Eisenhower told him that three sets of plans had been made for Operation Torch, as it was styled, and asked Rickenbacker to take one of them back to Stimson and U.S. Army Chief of Staff George C. Marshall. This Eddie cheerfully agreed to do, carrying the top secret scheme for what was then regarded as "the greatest invasion in history" in his briefcase through icy stops in Ireland, Iceland, Greenland, and Canada and handing it over to the secretary of war on October 13.

Many of Rickenbacker's recommendations were put into practice and Stimson was so pleased that he asked Eddie to continue his evaluation of American airpower in the Pacific theater. Even though he was exhausted by nearly two months of constant travel and work, walked with a cane, and his health was not yet fully restored from the plane crash, Rickenbacker agreed. In his soul he was a warrior and, even if he realized he was too old to actually fight, he felt duty-bound to give his full measure when it was called for. The war would not pause for him to rest up and such a delay could mean pilots killed or battles lost. The work he was being asked to do was important, and he intended to approach it in a timely and deliberate way. Little did he realize when he embarked for Hawaii on the first leg of his journey that he was entering the most dangerous period of his life, surpassing even the appalling Atlanta aviation accident and the trials of aerial combat over France.

ON OCTOBER 19, 1942, Rickenbacker was at Pearl Harbor, again traveling with Colonel Hans Christian Adamson, who had accompanied him as aide on the mission to England. Born in Denmark, in the same year as Rickenbacker, the delightfully named Adamson had immigrated to America at an early age and became in time a journalist, explorer, author,* and later director of publicity for the Museum of Natural History, where he organized the renowned dinosaur exhibits. He was a fine raconteur and Eddie enjoyed his company.[2]

Stimson had given Rickenbacker a remarkable note of introduction, which instructed commanders that Eddie was to be given all consideration, accommodation, and access to whatever he wanted by order of the secretary of war. Eddie was therefore somewhat disappointed when he reached Pearl Harbor and saw that the plane assigned to carry him to the South Pacific was an older model B-17 rather than the larger, roomier, and more modern B-24, but he decided not to make an issue of it. This was a very special mission, and he needed to be on his way.

In addition to a tour of inspection and evaluation, Rickenbacker had been tasked with an assignment so delicate and sensitive that Stimson had told him it could not be written down but must be communicated personally: a message to General Douglas MacArthur, who was presently fighting the Japanese in New Guinea. There has been some dispute among historians about the contents of this secret message, and ultimately Eddie took that information with him to the grave. One version of the story has it that the message was actually a reprimand from Stimson, ordering MacArthur to stop publicly criticizing the Roosevelt administration, and George Marshall in particular, for the decision to direct America's main war effort toward defeating Germany first, in regard to remarks MacArthur had been making to the press about lack of support from Washington. There was a further directive, in this account, for Rickenbacker to tell MacArthur to "ease up on personal publicity," apparently a reference to Roosevelt's almost paranoid fear

---

* Among Adamson's books was a biography of Norway's infamous traitor and Nazi collaborator Vidkun Quisling, as well as the book that became the popular 1957 movie *Hellcats of the Navy*, starring Ronald Reagan and his soon-to-be-bride, Nancy Davis.

that MacArthur would run against him in the presidential election of 1944. (Roosevelt had once described MacArthur as one of the two most dangerous men in America—the other being Louisiana's senator Huey Long.)[3]

Other evidence suggests that Rickenbacker's message was to inform MacArthur of the date and scope of the North African invasion, top secret information the army would not want to commit to the airwaves. Events of the next several weeks lend substance to this opinion.[4] Either of these scenarios is possible—in fact, both may be true—but whatever the case Rickenbacker was the ideal candidate to deliver the message because he was both trustworthy and retained his high stature as America's most famous fighter pilot and Medal of Honor recipient. MacArthur could intimidate a lot of people, but not Rickenbacker.

Rather than lay over at Pearl for a day, Rickenbacker asked for a flight to the South Pacific at once, and a little before ten-thirty that night he and Adamson stepped aboard the B-17, where the pilot, twenty-seven-year-old Captain William T. Cherry, and copilot, forty-two-year-old Lieutenant James C. Whittaker, were in the cockpit going through their preflight checklist. At 10:28 p.m. Whittaker felt a hand on his shoulder and a voice said, "My name is Rickenbacker."

The crew naturally knew who he was; everybody still knew who he was. But they had been cleared for takeoff and there was no time for formalities. Eddie and Adamson strapped themselves into the jump seats behind the pilots, and Cherry began to taxi the plane to the runway. Whittaker ran up the engines and they began to roll as Cherry released the brakes. They had reached about 75 miles per hour when a brake expander tube burst and locked one of the wheels. The plane lurched to the left, ran off the runway, and was headed for the hangars when Cherry, "by clever manipulation of the engines," in Rickenbacker's estimate, managed to get the B-17 back on the runway. But there was not enough speed for takeoff and they were headed for the bay at the end of the strip. Seeing that the speed had dropped to about 60 miles per hour, Cherry threw the plane into a violent ground loop to stop it, which very nearly tore off a wing and knocked the engines slightly out of their mountings. It came to a stop with such force someone said it could have broken everybody's neck.[5]

After a moment of silence to capture their breaths, Whittaker quipped, "Well, you know the old saying, any landing you can walk away from is a good one." By then fire trucks and ambulances, their sirens blaring, had arrived on the scene, as had a car carrying Brigadier General William Lynd, who was yelling, "Anybody hurt? Anybody hurt?" Rickenbacker shocked him by asking how soon a replacement plane could be made available. In only a few hours they were again taxiing for takeoff in a more modern B-17. Their first destination was tiny Canton Island, an atoll in the Phoenix archipelago eighteen hundred miles to the southwest, where Pan Am had once refueled its Clippers, the big four-engine flying boats.

The flying weather was clear and fine, with a few fleecy clouds and a three-quarter moon. Cherry expressed dissatisfaction to other crew members that he'd been given no time to evaluate the airworthiness of the new B-17. When Cherry complained to General Lynd back at Pearl that he needed time to check out the plane, he was told that Rickenbacker wanted to get away at once and "if he didn't want to fly the plane [Lynd] would get somebody else to do it for him," which would have effectively ended Cherry's career as an army pilot.[6]

For another, while that was going on, Johnny De Angelis, the twenty-three-year-old navigator, was carefully studying his bubble sextant, a complex navigational instrument used for celestial navigation. It contained a bubble to create an artificial horizon from which a skilled aviator could measure lunar, solar, or celestial angles and distances to find the relative earthly latitude and longitude of an airplane, ship, or other vehicle. Versions of octants have been in use for hundreds of years but the modern ones were fashioned with mirrors, ocular lenses, prisms, the horizon bubble, gears, and calibrators, all of which were extremely delicate. They were so sensitive that the Air Corps did not include them among a plane's standard equipment but left each individual navigator to care for his own sextant, which he carried in its specially designed hard leather case.

De Angelis—whom other crew members said had the "instincts of a homing pigeon"—was concerned that the octant might have become damaged because during the ground loop it had flown off the navigator's table and bounced on the deck. The most infinitesimal misalignment or miscalculation could lead to a serious error, which would simply keep compounding itself when trying to find a tiny speck of an island

in an ocean as large as the Pacific. There had been no time to recalibrate
or even check the adjustments before the second takeoff, and when
Whittaker asked De Angelis if there was anything wrong with the octant,
De Angelis replied that there didn't seem to be, though he noted it had
taken "quite a wallop."

If that wasn't bad enough, before takeoff Sergeant James W. Reynolds,
the radio operator, hadn't been able to check in for a directional fix with
any of the local radio stations, because all were signed off at that time of
night. If he had, he would have found that the new plane's radio direction
finder, or loop, on the outside of the plane, could not be adjusted because
its gears were stuck. Unaware of all of this, the crew and passengers
droned on into the night, in the belief that morning would bring them
to a sandy coral atoll in the ocean six miles long and three miles wide and
seventeen hundred miles away.

RICKENBACKER AND ADAMSON tried to get some sleep on cots
that had been arranged for them in the empty bomb bay by Sergeant
Alexander Kaczmarczyk, who was on his way back to his unit in the
South Pacific after having had an appendectomy in Hawaii. Because
his name was almost unpronounceable, he asked them to just call him
Alex. It was freezing cold at 10,000 feet, even at the equator, and the
plane wasn't heated, making sleep problematic. At dawn, De Angelis
came up from the bombardier's compartment to report that he'd taken
some "exceptional" position shots right before the stars went out and
that the plane was directly on course. Rickenbacker and Adamson had
some coffee and went forward to the cockpit, where Whittaker asked
Rickenbacker if he wanted to take the controls. Eddie demurred, saying
he knew nothing of instrument flying, but some prodding soon had him
behind the yoke.

Whittaker, a handsome, rugged, muscular man who had flown small
planes for twenty years, went to the tail and returned with more
coffee and pressed ham sandwiches. At about nine-thirty Cherry,
a former copilot for American Airlines, began "turning up the radio
and tinkering with the DF [directional finder] to get a fix on the radio
compass." It was then they discovered the thing didn't work. Cherry

took the controls and began to descend to 2,000 feet while Whittaker continued to fiddle with the DF. They broke through clouds with no island in sight.

Shortly afterward, De Angelis came up "looking worried." They were past their ETA, or estimated time of arrival. Whittaker was certain they could not have overshot it, because they had kept a careful check on their airspeed along with an estimated ten-knot tailwind. Rickenbacker, however, had a gut reaction that told him the tailwind was stronger than that, perhaps as much as three times. He admitted that he "had no way of telling," but "inside me the feeling grew that we had overshot the mark and were moving away from it, into the open Pacific."

"We're lost," Cherry said.

Sergeant Reynolds had been in radio contact with the wireless operator on Canton; there was no voice communication between them, only telegraph keys. Cherry told Reynolds to set up a "lost plane" procedure with the wireless operator on Canton.

In this process, the plane sends out two radio signals fifteen minutes apart and the ground station takes bearings on those, which gives a cross bearing or "fix" on the plane's course. Then the controller at the station or tower draws two lines on his plotting board with compass bearings that intersect on the station and project beyond it, which lets the station plot the plane's position. It was a time-tested method with only one hitch: the wireless station on Canton wasn't yet set up with the necessary equipment to accomplish it.

"That's cute," Cherry remarked when informed of this.

Reynolds told Cherry he'd just picked up another station on Palmyra Island that was in fact equipped for the lost plane procedure.

Rickenbacker asked Cherry how much fuel was left.

"About four hours" was the solemn reply. A quick calculation showed that Palmyra was about a thousand miles distant and the B-17 had only six hundred miles' worth of gas left in its tanks. Unfortunately, the lost plane procedure works only with the station you are communicating with.

"What do you expect to do now?" Eddie asked.

"Try the box procedure," Cherry said. Known also as "boxing the compass," this involved flying a square, one hour to a leg, at 5,000 feet, which allows the crew to scan a huge area both inside and outside the square. It wasn't much, considering the vast size of the ocean, but at least it was something. Rickenbacker suggested contacting the station on Canton and requesting someone fire off an antiaircraft gun, timing the bursts at 8,000 feet. It was an old First World War trick that Rickenbacker had used in France when planes were lost. They climbed back to 10,000 feet to be above the blasts.

The minutes, then the hours droned on, all eyes looking for islands, looking for puffs of flak, but there was nothing to see but clouds and endless ocean. At one point Eddie asked Sergeant Reynolds to send a message: PLANE LOST. ONE HOUR'S FUEL—RICKENBACKER. It was the B-17's last message.

During that last hour Cherry cut the two outboard engines to save gas, and to lighten the plane the others opened the tail hatch and threw out everything that wasn't bolted down—the sleeping cots, bedding, toolbox, empty thermoses, all the baggage including Eddie's new Burberry coat he'd just bought in London and fifteen postal bags of high-priority mail that had been put aboard for the South Pacific theater.

It was clear they were going to have to put the ship down in the sea. Below they could see the big rollers, headed east. As far as anyone knew, no four-engine plane had ever been put down on a high-wave ocean with survivors. Hitting water in a plane is roughly the same as hitting a brick wall. If a plane lands into the wind and hits a wave crest too hard it will break in two and sink. If it noses through a crest and hits the next crest the nose will dive beneath the water or be caved in. Whittaker suggested to Cherry that they go in sideways and land in a trough between two waves. Cherry agreed and added that he intended to go in with gas in the tanks and the engines running on the theory that a power landing is always better than an uncontrolled one.[7]

Everyone put on life vests, also known as "Mae Wests." Sergeant Reynolds pounded furiously at the telegraph key with the SOS call but there was no response. Adamson, using a kind of code because of the presence of the crew, reminded Rickenbacker that if it was Japanese territory they put down in, because of what they knew about the upcoming North Africa invasion, they can't afford to be taken prisoners. Adamson whispered that during his intelligence training he'd learned the Japanese had acquired some kind of "truth serum" drug from the

Germans. Rickenbacker acknowledged that "if the Japs find us on the rafts you and I have only one way to go, and that's *down*."[8]

There were three life rafts in compartments on either side of the plane; two were "five-man" rafts and one was a "two-man" raft in the radio compartment. These could be released and inflated by pulling a lever in the cabin. The B-17 was more than twice as heavy as the B-25s that Doolittle's raiders flew; if the landing was successful, they could count on the plane surviving on the surface for no more than one minute. The emergency equipment also contained water and some rations, and these were stored near the escape hatch. Eddie wrapped about sixty feet of rope he'd found around his waist.

Word came back that Cherry was starting down. Everyone braced themselves best he could, some strapping in, others with mattresses or parachutes to protect them. Rickenbacker could see out of a window, and he began calling out "one hundred feet, fifty feet, twenty feet, ten feet, five feet." One of the engines sputtered and died and Eddie shouted, "Hold on!"

Rickenbacker had heard the "violent jumble of sounds and motions" once before—at Atlanta. "Pieces of radio equipment bolted to the bulkhead flew about like shrapnel," he said. The tail struck the water first to slow the plane down, a furious jerk, then a stupendous lurch forward as the belly hit and the plane went from 90 miles per hour—stall speed—to a dead stop in less than fifty feet, by Eddie's estimate. "It was a wonderful landing, timed to the second . . . If [Cherry] had miscalculated by two seconds and hit the crest . . . the Fortress would have gone straight to the bottom of the sea."[9]

Green seawater poured in through a broken window port. Everyone was terribly shaken up. Adamson "staggered to his feet," Eddie said, "moaning about his back." De Angelis and Alex appeared to be all right, but Reynolds had a great gash on his nose from which blood was pouring through his fingers as he held his hand to his face. Eddie and Adamson went first through the escape hatch and out onto the wing where they had trouble keeping their footing as the plane heaved and surged in twelve-foot swells. The life rafts were already inflated and expelled and were bobbing in the waves. John Bartek, the mechanic, had cut his fingers terribly on some sharp edge trying to unfoul a line to the raft. Eddie helped Adamson, who was in "great pain" from his injured back, into one of the five-man rafts, which looked very small against the angry sea. Then Bartek got in, and then Eddie, who remarked, "There wasn't enough room left for a midget."

Captain Cherry, Lieutenant Whittaker, and Sergeant Reynolds were already in their raft on the other side of the plane and had drifted clear of it. De Angelis and Alex were in the water trying to right the small two-man raft, which had overturned. The situation was dangerous; a big crested wave slammed Eddie's raft against the plane's tail and nearly overturned them before filling it with water. Black shark fins began to appear around the plane, and the men saw many long, dark shapes cruising ominously under the water.

Both rafts had drifted about fifty yards from the B-17, which was submerging but still afloat, when somebody in Cherry's raft shouted, "Who has the water?" No one had it, Rickenbacker said. And in the shock of the crash and the scramble to get out of the plane, no one had the rations either. They argued for and against going back inside the B-17, which was rapidly filling with water, and decided it was too dangerous. Eddie was bailing water with his hat when somebody shouted, "There she goes!" The tail of the plane rose upright, hesitated for a moment, and then the B-17 slid beneath the waves. By Eddie's watch it was 2:26 p.m., Honolulu time, October 21, 1942. They were on their own.

ON THE HIGH SEAS the three rafts drifted apart and Rickenbacker found a use for the rope he'd wrapped around his waist. They paddled against the wind with small aluminum oars until they drew together, then fastened the boats in a line about ten feet apart—Cherry's raft first, "because he was the captain," then Rickenbacker, with De Angelis and Alex bringing up the rear. Eddie believed that if they drifted away from one another "few if any" would survive.

When they tallied up their belongings, they seemed meager indeed. The only food they had was four oranges that Cherry had stashed in his pockets right before they went down. A couple of men had candy bars but they disintegrated in the water. Some of the crew had taken off their clothing in anticipation of having to swim. There was a first aid kit, a flare gun and eighteen flares, two hand pumps for both bailing and refilling the rafts with air, two sheath knives, pliers, a small compass, two bailing buckets, two rubber patching kits, three pencils, and a map of the Pacific that Rickenbacker had stuck in his jacket before the crash. There were two fishing lines with hooks that Sergeant Reynolds had found in a parachute kit; they had no bait. They also had two revolvers, belonging to Cherry and Adamson.

As the afternoon wore on the men tried to adjust to their circumstances. Several became violently seasick from being tossed about in the twelve-foot swells, which would lift the rafts up on a crest, then dash them down into the trough. This was made all the worse by being lashed together because, as the rafts rose and fell unevenly, the occupants were jerked around as if in a carnival ride, making rest impossible.[10]

There was scarcely room enough in the yellow-colored five-man rafts for three men—the inside was about the size of an average bathtub—and the two-man raft, occupied by Lieutenant De Angelis and Sergeant Alex, was hardly larger than a truck inner tube. The only way to get comfortable, or even stay in it, was for the two men to put their legs on each other's shoulders. They called it the "doughnut." Alex, already weakened because of his operation, couldn't seem to stop vomiting. As sundown came and went, and the rafts continued to lurch fiercely in the darkness, the euphoria of surviving the crash gave way to a sober appraisal of their situation; the small talk faded as each man in his own way tried to comprehend the fix they were in.

Like good soldiers they established a watch, which everyone would stand for two hours a day. To lighten the tension, Eddie offered $100 to the first man who saw land, a ship, or a plane. Nobody slept that night, as waves incessantly slopped into the rafts, soaking the men and making them miserable; it felt like "being doused with buckets of ice water." As if there wasn't enough to worry about, the sharks had followed them from the plane wreckage and circled ominously in the pale moonlight. There seemed to be dozens of them.

The faint rosy glow of false dawn gave way to grays and pinks, and then the red rim of the sun appeared on the eastern horizon. As it climbed throughout the morning this sun seemed to beam like a giant pulsing ray aimed directly at their little spot of ocean, as it would every morning, as the days went by. De Angelis had calculated they were about twelve degrees south of the equator. They took out Rickenbacker's map of the Pacific and the pocket compass, and Eddie estimated they were drifting south-southwest about four hundred miles from the Fiji Island group, where they were sure to run into land—or, with any luck, Tahiti! Rickenbacker calculated they'd be there in twenty-five days at raft speed, though of course a plane could come to rescue them before this day was out. What Rickenbacker did *not* tell them was that they could just as well be drifting in a westerly direction, in which case they would run into the Gilbert or Marshall Islands, which were now part of the empire of Japan.

Rickenbacker had somehow retained the battered old gray fedora that he always wore—and Adelaide swore she was going to throw it out—but the others had nothing to cover their heads and in many cases their arms and legs.

As president of Eastern Air Lines, Rickenbacker had been in on all sorts of survival conversations with pilots and crews and fancied himself an authority, which he probably was. Bill Cherry, however, captain of the airship, remained in charge, and Eddie became a self-appointed morale officer.

The sharks began rising up and hitting the bottoms of the rubber boats with their bodies—a "vicious jolt," Rickenbacker said, that would lift the rafts several inches out of the water. Whether it was because they scented food or to rub leeches or barnacles off of their backs the men did not know. Whittaker identified them as tiger sharks, which he understood would not attack humans. It was probably just as well that Whittaker remained unaware that tiger sharks are among the most ferocious man-eaters in the ocean.

Next day the high seas subsided and the ocean became flat calm and no wind blew, not the faintest breeze, and they entered a period of doldrums, which frequently occur near the equator. Everyone listened for the drone of a plane, but the air was silent, except for the occasional gurgle created by a shark fin or tail. The sun beat down.

Eddie became the overseer of the oranges and, using one of the sheath knives, carefully divided one of them for that day's meal by cutting it into eight slices. Each man would receive a slice every other day. Instead of eating the rind, Eddie and Cherry used theirs for bait, but no fish were interested, and the orange was itself unsatisfying. "Except for the pleasant taste we might as well had not had anything," Whittaker recalled.

The rafts drifted lazily on the glassy water, the lines between them slack. Within a day every inch of exposed skin was burned. Soon they had blisters, which burst and burned again; the skin cracked and peeled and turned raw. It became excruciating when the saltwater got to it, as it frequently did because the sharks had formed the disagreeable habit of coming near the surface and slapping the sides of the raft with their tails, spraying water on the occupants. The cut on Reynolds's nose wouldn't heal and remained an open, oozing gash that Rickenbacker called "a horrible sight." These effects of sun and saltwater also caused intense pain for Bartek, with his fingers cut to the bone. In the boats, the men sprawled all over each other, with little to say, especially from ten in the morning until four o'clock every afternoon, when the sun raged down in its most pitiless intensity and sapped what remained of their fading energy.

Whittaker and De Angelis over time developed a tan, while "the rest of us cooked day after day," Rickenbacker said. Their hands and feet swelled and became covered with running sores, as did their mouths, from some kind of ulcers.

Having recently undergone his ordeal in Atlanta, Rickenbacker was uniquely equipped to provide a relative evaluation of their distress, and to him there was barely a comparison. While pinned in the plane's wreckage, his pain had been blunted by delirium, he said, but ultimately he knew that help was near because he heard people moving and talking. Here in the raft on the empty ocean, Rickenbacker said, "I was something being turned on a spit."

AT THE HEIGHT OF THE DAY, Rickenbacker filled his hat with seawater and jammed it on his head to create a brief, cooling relief. He distributed several silk handkerchiefs, on which Adelaide had embroidered his initials, to the others, who would wet them and put them over their heads or "fold them bandit-fashion, over their nose." Captain Cherry scanned the skies in vain for a seabird that might come close enough for him to kill with his revolver. Occasionally he would break the pistol down and rub the metal with oil from his nose, but the saltwater corrosion was getting ahead of him.

After dark they tried to shoot off the flares. They had planned to fire three each night, but most of the flares were duds. Once a flare went off but the parachute failed to open, and the hissing potassium nitrate threatened to fall back and ignite one of the rafts. Instead, it fell into the water where it provided a ghostly tableau as it flickered beneath the surface, sinking slowly toward abysmal depths, illuminating and disturbing the sharks, which twitched and shied away from it.

The rafts were so small that when one man needed to turn over, everyone had to turn over, which was always accompanied by groaning and profanity as raw skin was disturbed. "Many things said in the night had best be forgotten," declared Rickenbacker, who consoled himself with the notion that "someday I shall meet the man who decided these rafts could hold five men each."

Almost all the men fantasized about food and drink. Ice cream, pies, cakes were high on the list; so were sodas, strawberry soda in particular, for some reason, and "a big ole pitcher full of ice water, with ice cubes floating on top." Sometimes they talked about food with each other in animated conversations, but inevitably after a while somebody would growl "knock it off." Adamson suffered intensely from back pain and also there was the unknown fact that he had diabetes, which doctors had failed to diagnose in his yearly physicals.

For the better part of a week, during the worst parts of the day, most everyone went into a stupor that somehow dulled their thirst. The oranges helped, but not much. Afterward, as the sun sank, the men assumed a kind of mild daze, enjoying the relief from the heat until the sun disappeared, and then the chilling night was upon them again. Even though the temperature was in the seventies, being always wet and exposed felt like "Chicago in December." Nightmares vexed most of the men. During the daytime they often saw mirages, but now the moon was full and the clouds also played tricks of the eye on them. Eddie slept fitfully, if only because he "kept one eye half open and one ear cocked" for the drone of a rescue plane.

As airmen, they had been trained to know the celestial sky, but being on the equator all the customary stars were out of their familiar places. At one point in his career Adamson had been in charge of the Hayden Planetarium at the Museum of Natural History in New York City, and he now provided feeble lectures on the constellations and movements of heavenly bodies. This kept the men entertained and alert and Eddie encouraged more of it, because of "the good it did for all of us." Night and day, the sharks continued to circle.

AFTER EIGHT DAYS THE LAST OF THE ORANGES were gone. The final two had shrunken and begun to rot, but now there was not even that to anticipate. It became obvious that unless they soon had food or water, "some of us were bound to die." Rickenbacker was especially worried about Alex who, being the youngest, nevertheless seemed to weaken more than the others and "cried continually" for water. Rickenbacker at one point pulled up to his raft and "asked him why the hell he couldn't take it?" admitting later that "it was a brutal thing to do." This, however, was only the beginning of Eddie's reign of terror on any crew member who showed signs of giving up. Some of the men came to hate Rickenbacker so much they refused to die just to spite him, and in fact wanted to live to see him die. He didn't care, he said, so long as it saved lives.

On Thursday, October 30, Adamson wrote in his journal, "We are still hanging on."

In the case of Alex, however, Rickenbacker laid off after he found out he was just three weeks out of the hospital and was suffering from some sort of infection in his mouth. But steadily the boy grew weaker and moaned and said the Hail Mary in the night; he seemed to have given up. At other times he took a picture of the girl he was engaged to marry from his wallet and talked to it. De Angelis tried to shield him from the sun but when it was high there wasn't much he could do. Except for wanting water, Alex never really complained. Adamson also began growing listless, and Reynolds "was fading to skin and bones."

Rickenbacker was concerned that if the men lost faith in being rescued they would cease to cooperate, which would lead to dire consequences for all. He had noticed that every day Bartek read from a miniature copy of the New Testament and he called for evening prayers. Eddie was the first to admit that while he was "conscious of God," he was not a religious person, but he believed in the Golden Rule and had some vague notion of God. He knew the Lord's Prayer from his upbringing in Sunday school and decided that was a start. It might pull the men closer and give them spirit. If nothing else, it would help pass the time.

As the days went by the prayer period became more intimate and complex, with one of them reading a passage from Bartek's New Testament. Then they recited familiar prayers, such as the Twenty-third Psalm. These were followed by informal confessions, in which the men would talk about themselves in a completely uninhibited fashion—"their hopes, fears, ambitions, and mistakes." The talk was "entirely frank and honest," according to Eddie, who also participated, and it went without saying these conversations would never be revealed. Some initially scoffed at the practice, including Whittaker, who said he had lost whatever religion he'd been exposed to in childhood and hadn't "the least notion that this open-air hallelujah meeting was going to do any good." But in time he came to change his mind and turned out to be one of the group's most avid participants—there was no place left to go but God.

ONE MORNING, ABOUT TEN DAYS IN, as they drifted aimlessly, some of the men engaged in an appalling conversation about self-mutilation in the interest of baiting a hook. Their inability to catch fish was most frustrating. They could see the fish, but they just didn't have any bait. They tried to catch small sharks with their hands but they were too slippery. Bartek advocated slicing off the lobe of an ear, which he said people didn't need. Whittaker offered to cut off the ball of his little finger, arguing that it would be less painful and less likely to become infected. Reynolds suggested that part of a toe would probably not be missed. They went to Rickenbacker for advice, and he concurred that it might become necessary, but demurred as to "the form the butchery might take."

At just that moment the most amazing thing happened. From an empty sky, and preceded by a loud fluttering of wings, a seagull alighted on Rickenbacker's battered fedora.

Everyone froze. Rickenbacker slowly and deliberately began to twist his right hand behind his head. He knew the bird was still there "from the hungry, famished, almost insane eyes in the other rafts." After what must have seemed an eternity of adrenaline-fueled contortion, Rickenbacker seized the thing in his fingers and wrung its neck, to the wild cheers and applause of his starving companions.

The bird was plucked and carved up with as much ceremony as a Thanksgiving turkey, with everyone receiving equal parts, including bones that were thoroughly sucked and chewed. The critical thing was that Rickenbacker thought to save the intestines for bait. After they had feasted all morning on raw gull, Eddie baited a hook on one of the fishing lines and handed it over to Whittaker, who weighted it with his class ring. The line had hardly been dropped into the water when a small mackerel struck it and it was hauled into the boat. Likewise, Cherry landed one about the same size. They were handed over for filleting, with the entrails again saved as bait.

As if that provender wasn't enough, when the sun was almost down the sky became dark and cloudy. There was the faintest hint of rain in the air, but they'd been so disappointed before that the men gave it little chance. They began their evening prayers with Cherry reading his favorite passage from the Book of Matthew:

Therefore take ye no thought, saying: What shall we eat? What shall we drink? Or where withal shall we be clothed? For these are things the heathen seeketh. For your Heavenly Father knoweth that you have need of all these things. But seek you first the Kingdom of God . . . for the morrow shall take thought for the things.

Then Cherry lapsed into his own idiom and began praying in a more normal voice, as though he were having a pleasant conversation with God: "Old Master, we know this isn't a guarantee that we'll eat in the morning. But we're in an awful fix, as you know. We sure are counting on a little something by day after tomorrow, at least. See what you can do for us, Old Master." It was the way they all came to say prayers, out loud, no *thees, thys,* or *thous,* just eight men in an awful fix talking turkey with God. As Whittaker put it, "Men don't kid when the chips are down."

NEXT DAY, WHILE THE SUN TORMENTED them like some infernal blast furnace, Adamson suddenly raised up and slipped over the side of the raft. Rickenbacker immediately grabbed him and with help got him back aboard, then administered a tongue-lashing so severe it cannot be repeated here but Whittaker summed it up later by saying, "That man Rickenbacker has got a rough tongue in his head." Adamson had actually done a brave thing, thinking he was a burden on the others and that there would be more food if he was gone. But Rickenbacker spared him not, and "woe betide the man about to turn quitter."

They began lingering anxiously at the part of the Lord's Prayer that said, "And give us this day our daily bread." Captain Cherry added in his quaint Texan drawl, "Old Master, we called on You for food, and You delivered. We ask You now for water. We've done the best we could. If You don't make up Your mind to help us pretty soon, well, I guess that's all there'll be to it."

A small breeze blew up and Cherry hoisted his undershirt on two oars, which he had been doing whenever possible for a sail. Whittaker looked off and saw a cloud "that had been fleecy and white a while ago now was darkening by the second." Within minutes the sky had become a storm of rain moving toward the rafts; the men could see big drops striking the waves. They began frantically paddling toward it.

Cherry shouted, "Thanks, Old Master!" as the curtain of rain swept over them, soaking them to the skin, washing off the salt and sweat and bloody grime from their cuts and sores. They drank it greedily with cupped hands, then began to collect the rain. They'd discussed this before. Any rain that fell into the rafts would be tainted by the saltwater that always sloshed around in the bottoms, but they had two bailing buckets and the canvas covers for the flare cartridges. To collect the rain, they would take off their clothing, and when it became soaking wet, they'd wring it out into the vessels.

While they were doing this, the storm intensified with wind, lightning, and rough waves and at its height came a cry for help. The two-man raft with Alex and De Angelis had broken free and was drifting into the darkness. Eddie and the others paddled furiously after them and at length overtook the "doughnut," but no sooner had they made it fast when a sudden jerk on the bowline revealed that Cherry's raft had been overturned by a rogue wave and its three men were floundering in the sea. When at last the men in Rickenbacker's boat righted Cherry's raft they found the flare gun and the flares were lost, as was his bailing bucket and the water therein. They'd managed to save the oars.

Within half an hour the storm had moved on. The men attributed the rain to Cherry's prayers. When the seas abated they all pulled in close and held a meeting. Eddie judged that they had collected two and a half quarts of water. Because no one knew when there'd be another squall, they decided to limit their water ration to one half jigger per man per day. The next day, the sea began to roughen again but there was no rain.

After a few days Rickenbacker became concerned that the water in the bailing buckets was evaporating too quickly and was always in danger of being spilled. So he convened a conference that resulted in a novel, if distasteful, transfer of the water into the tiny air hole in one of their Mae West life jackets. The hole was so small that the only way to move the water safely was for Eddie to take a mouthful and then slowly spit it into the hole. This time-consuming transfer was closely watched by the others in order to make sure he actually spit and did not swallow, but in the end they had conserved several quarts of the precious water safely inside the Mae West.

For drinking vessels they had only the empty brass shell casings of the flares, which were about six inches long and an inch or so wide. To indicate the depth of their degradation, since it was nearly impossible to stand up in the rafts, they had to use these same shell tubes to urinate in— what there was of it—which they then dumped over the side. Afterward the tubes were washed in the saltwater.

Meantime, Eddie became increasingly worried about young Alex. He asked Bartek to change places with him, and once aboard Eddie's raft Alex was able to stretch out a bit more. Eddie put his arm around him, "as one cuddles a child," hoping to transfer his own body heat to the boy. Sure enough, an hour later Alex's shivering stopped, and he seemed to sleep, though he murmured all night in Polish. Next day he asked to be put back into the little raft with De Angelis, and Rickenbacker gave the okay. He sensed that Alex was dying and decided to let him die as he wished.

Sometime around three that morning Eddie woke up with a premonition and the vague recollection of the sound of a loud sigh. He called over to De Angelis, "Has he died?"

There was a pause, and then "I think so" came the reply.

Eddie's and Cherry's rafts pulled close and they each checked Alex's pulse. There wasn't any. Eddie asked Bartek if he could stick it out till morning.

When daybreak came they checked Alex once more to make sure he had expired, then took his wallet and dog tags to return to his family if they themselves ever got back. De Angelis said his recollection of the Catholic burial service, then they rolled Sergeant Alex over the side and he floated off facedown—a burial at sea—such as it was. They had been marooned in the Pacific for thirteen days. The sharks circled. The sun beat down.

EACH MORNING WHEN IT BECAME LIGHT Rickenbacker would count heads in the rafts; there had always been seven excluding his own. It gave him a jar now to count only six, but he got used to it. After the men had drunk up all the water from the storm, they went for forty-eight hours without another drop, and some almost went mad with thirst and began to rave. They had quit fantasizing about food, or at least if they did they kept it to themselves. It became a waiting game until the next rain shower or chance encounter with a fish. One day Cherry caught a small shark, about two feet long, which came into the boat snapping its jaws at everyone. Cherry managed to stab it to death with a knife but not before stabbing a hole in the bottom of the raft. They divided up the shark but the flesh was so disagreeable it made them gag; no one could stomach it, which must have been saying a lot. They tried using it for bait, but no fish would touch it, and finally they threw it overboard.

They tried using the patch kit to repair the rubberized canvas where Cherry had missed stabbing the shark. To do this they had to get out of the boat and into the water with the big sharks and turn it over to work from the bottom. In the end the patch failed and they had to live with the result—a leak that kept a constant inch or two of water in the bottom of the raft. Especially at night, it was enough to make them miserable.

One day an atrocious red rash broke out among the men, all over their thighs and rears and legs. The rash turned into horrid pus-filled abscesses that looked like boils and soon burst into running sores that never healed. The saltwater made them sting and burn until they seemed to pulsate. "Our bodies, our minds, the few things that we had with us were slowly rotting away," Rickenbacker said. It was too true. Their clothes were rags, saltwater corrosion had frozen the compass needle, watches had rusted and stopped, and Eddie's crucifix, which had been given to him in 1917 by a ten-year-old girl before he went to war, was starting to disintegrate. He had carried it all these years, through the air battles of the war, through the crash in Atlanta, and now the crash of the B-17. To Rickenbacker, it was more than just a lucky charm, and he despaired of its ruination.

They drifted on for days in a semiconscious stupor. The strain had begun to wear on everyone, and after the sun went down there were cross words and profanity, sometimes pointed accusations. Somebody called Rickenbacker a mean son of a bitch. He didn't deny it. "It does us no dishonor," he said, "to say that we were all becoming a little unhinged." As for himself, he had a single recurring dream of coming to an island where an old friend had a wonderful home and where there was "an abundance of fruit juices," and then after breakfast he could telephone Mr. Stimson, the secretary of war, "and [tell] him where we were." Awaking from the dream and seeing only ocean became his low point.

Rickenbacker and Cherry both estimated that they were to the northwest of the regular air and sea-lane traffic, and occasionally they would try to paddle to the southwest, and sometimes Cherry used his sail. But in the end they found they were too frail for it and gave up, saving their strength to paddle toward rain squalls when they arose. Cherry was for splitting up the party with the idea they'd have a better chance of being spotted. Rickenbacker was against it on grounds that they all had a better chance of survival if they stuck together, and that it was a lot easier to spot three rafts out on the ocean than one. But Cherry remained determined and Rickenbacker relented. So Cherry cast off and paddled away one midafternoon; Rickenbacker watched them in the distance until it became dark. Next morning he was startled to see Cherry's raft bobbing close by on the flat sea, with the men inside sleeping. Cherry said it was impossible to paddle against the current so they roped up again.

After this, the mood of the men returned to dismal. They began to hallucinate and, as Whittaker put it, "At noon the daily round of delirious shouts began. By this time nearly all of us were holding conversations with people who weren't there." Whittaker found himself talking to Davy Jones, the mythical guardian of sailors' souls, who lived at the bottom of the ocean. Jones persisted with every argument to lure Whittaker out of the raft and down to his famous "locker," but to no avail.

On about the sixteenth or seventeenth day, after a sleepless night of ferocious squalls, Rickenbacker was idly gazing at the eternal sea when his eye caught a sudden movement in the direction of Cherry's raft. He turned his head and saw the captain frozen in a forward-leaning position with his hand cupped to his ear. "Plane!," Cherry exclaimed. "I hear a plane. Listen!"

They all heard it, a "deep-toned roar"—at least those still fully conscious heard it; Adamson, Bartek, and Reynolds were barely skin and bones and had sunk into near comas. Then off to their left they saw it, coming out of a squall, flying low about five miles away, a single-engine floatplane. Those who could stood up and waved and yelled themselves hoarse but to no avail. It had been too far away for them to see its marking but someone said the U.S. Navy had a plane like that, the Kingfisher. So, however, did the Japanese. Someone shouted, "Get the flares!" but there were no flares, and soon no plane.

It was a terrible blow, perhaps the worst yet. All they could do was groan. Rickenbacker, however, blued the air with a flood of horrible profanity that became "the masterpiece of his career," according to one of the castaways. In between the profanity, Eddie told them if the plane had come once, it would come again. If there was one plane there would be many planes; they were obviously near its base. At last good things were coming. And, he added, "A MAN would have the courage, the patience, the faith, to wait for them."

"It didn't improve his personal popularity," Whittaker remarked, "but the psychological effect was just what he'd been hoping for." As if to punctuate this, a brisk breeze sprang up, cooling everything down, and Cherry ran up his undershirt sail on the two oars—Rickenbacker had so fouled the air with his cursing that apparently it stirred up a wind.[11]

EXCEPT FOR THE SICK MEN everyone talked excitedly all night, discussing the possibilities of what they had seen. At daybreak, just as Rickenbacker had predicted, the plane reappeared—a pair of them, actually—flying at about 1,200 feet, but again they were too far off and went on without seeing the castaways. Two more pairs of planes came back that afternoon, with the same result. They deduced from this pattern that the planes were probably on a routine patrol. Next day it was more of the same, and maddening. Two more pairs of planes were sighted but they were miles away. A fear began to take hold that the rafts had drifted through a chain of islands and were again out in the open Pacific.

The next morning, Cherry climbed into the small "doughnut" raft and said he was going to cut loose by himself, adding that if everyone cut loose there'd be a three-to-one better chance of being sighted. Somehow, Adamson perked up, pulled rank, and ordered them not to do it, but he was half out of his mind and no one paid him any attention.* Rickenbacker too tried to talk Cherry out of going, but again he relented and wished him luck. Whittaker, now in the boat with De Angelis and Reynolds, also cast off his lines and said good-bye. By sundown they all lost sight of one another. That night in Whittaker's raft no one got much sleep. It was as though something important was missing. In fact they were lonesome for the men in the other rafts. Whittaker, however, was overcome with a feeling of anticipation, a feeling "that something big was ahead."

Eddie was worried that they might have drifted through a string of islands. If that were so, their chances of holding out much longer were "damn poor." Next morning Bartek came out of his coma long enough to mumble, "Have the planes come back?" Rickenbacker had to tell him no. When he tried to give Bartek his water ration it merely dribbled down his chin. "They won't come back," Bartek said. "I know they won't come back."

Whittaker finally drifted to sleep about an hour before dawn, and right after daybreak he felt a strong grip on his shoulder. It was De Angelis, saying, "Jim, I think you better take a look. It may be a mirage, but I think I see something." Whittaker rose up and beheld on the eastern horizon "a line of palm trees 10 miles long." Hearts pounding, the two men gaped for a few moments, then Whittaker, who at forty-two was by

---

* By army regulations Cherry, as commander of the B-17, was also commander of the refugee party. Adamson and Rickenbacker, no matter how high ranked or exalted, were merely passengers.

far the strongest and fittest of any of them, grabbed the oars. The land appeared to be about ten to twelve miles distant. He was rowing as hard as his strength allowed. Asprawl on the bottom of the raft poor Sergeant Reynolds was "near the finish," Whittaker said. "His resemblance to a death's head was startling."

Meantime, the men all had a helping hand ten thousand miles away in the form of Rickenbacker's wife, Adelaide, who had refused to give up searching for her husband, declaring, "He's too old a hand to get lost in any airplane." After the search for Eddie and the other airmen had proceeded for two weeks with no results, and the newspapers had given Rickenbacker up for dead, Hap Arnold wrote Adelaide what amounted to a letter of condolence. She took off on a train to Washington, where she barged into Arnold's office and "practically tore the decorations off his jacket," until he agreed to extend the search. Arnold consented to prolong it for another week, and orders from Washington went out, down to and including the tiny naval base on Funafuti atoll.[12] The base on Funafuti consisted of five Kingfisher single-engine floatplanes, four PT (motor torpedo patrol) boats, and a PT boat tender named the *Hilo*. These vessels and the aircraft conducted daily patrols, scouting for any signs of Japanese, but were also alerted that there were possibly downed fliers in their search area.

Sure enough, at about four-thirty in the afternoon on the day after Captain Cherry had paddled away from the others, the radio operator of one of the Kingfishers spotted "an irregular object bobbing on the waves," about sixty miles west of Funafuti. This proved to be Cherry's yellow "doughnut"; the seas were too rough for landing but the pilot directed one of the PT boats to pick him up.[13]

About that same time, after a grueling seven-hour ordeal, the three souls in Whittaker's raft had approached to within two hundred and fifty yards of the "line of palm trees," only to be swept back out to sea by a terrific current that spun them around and shot them nearly a mile offshore and down island, so that it appeared they might be carried past the island entirely. With his last reserves of strength—which he attributed to God—Whittaker managed to overcome the current and make way for the island once more. He was almost there in enormous swells when he felt something jerk an oar. Below in the green water he saw a "dirty gray form 12 feet long"—a shark. In fact there were several, "not the droll dullards that had plagued us earlier. These were man-eaters." They kept snapping at the aluminum oars as if they were spinners on a casting line. As if that were not enough to worry about, up ahead, with breakers crashing over it, loomed a coral reef that ringed the island, sharp enough to puncture and sink the raft.

Whittaker made straight for the reef, up and over, and found himself in calmer, shallow water. Within minutes they grounded on a second coral reef only yards from a smooth white sandy beach. De Angelis stood up, stepped out, and fell flat. They got Reynolds up and out but he too fell flat. Whittaker tried it and did the same. The weeks afloat in the raft had completely disordered their sense of balance. They kept getting up and falling back down. Whittaker stumbled to the ground eight times—until he floundered back to the raft and got an oar to lean on.

At length they hauled the raft up onto the beach and hid it under dead palm leaves. There was no way of knowing whether this island was friendly or Japanese held. All of them remained discombobulated as to balance, as well as other things associated with their hunger. They opened some coconuts with a sheath knife and killed and ate—raw—some ratlike creatures, then slept in a deserted hut about two miles down the beach. The food was restorative but Reynolds remained at death's door.

Next morning Whittaker looked out to the sea and thought he saw a line of destroyers, which soon morphed into a flotilla of native dugout canoes with outriggers, rushing straight toward them. The canoes rolled easily over the reefs and drew up in front of Whittaker, who had gone out to meet them. The other boats lingered slightly offshore while one boat beached. Whittaker's appearance must have startled the man in the lead canoe, who looked him up and down as he stood there, wild-haired, burned black, barefoot, dressed in rags, and wearing a scraggly beard— a modern-day Robinson Crusoe.

"You Japanese?" Whittaker inquired.

The man frowned and shook his head and murmured disapprovingly. It was a tense moment; Whittaker and the others had all read stories about cannibals in the South Pacific.

The natives put the airmen into the lead canoe, tied the raft behind it, and took off paddling at such a rapid rate Whittaker marveled that it caused a wake. At the native village (they had landed on the speck island of Nukufetau, approximately fifty miles west of Funafuti) they were greeted by women "wearing only lava-lava's and smiles" and the smell of cooking.* The women began to cry when they saw the condition of the airmen. The man from the canoe told Whittaker the island belonged to the British,† who operated a radio station there.

The airmen were placed on scented mats under swaying coconut palm trees and given fresh fruit juices and a hearty broth made from several village fowl that had been pecking around too close to the cooking pot. If this wasn't heaven it was close enough. Presently two British officers arrived and said a U.S. Navy boat was on the way. Meantime, one of the Kingfishers alighted just offshore and a navy doctor stepped out to administer injections of glucose that ultimately saved Reynolds's life.

Rickenbacker's group was unaccounted for. Back home the country had been shocked and horrified and ultimately saddened at the news that Eddie Rickenbacker's plane had gone down. People understood that the situation was dire from the outset. Daily updates about the search were published or sent out over the wires and airways, but hope faded with each passing day. After two weeks, the normal length for a search, obituaries of sorts began to appear in the papers and radio broadcasts. The New York *Daily News* carried an editorial cartoon by the famous C. D. Batchelor depicting Rickenbacker fading away on an ocean horizon, with the caption, "So long, Eddie."

It was all premature. Cherry alerted the authorities at Funafuti about the other rafts, and word had already arrived about the deliverance of Whittaker's group. The search plan was divided on charts and PT boats were sent to each area that night. In the morning, all five Kingfishers resumed the air search. The day passed without success but about four o'clock a pair of planes radioed that they had sighted a raft with three men in it. The Kingfishers dived down and flew straight at the raft right

---

* A lava-lava is basically a skirt.

† The Ellice Islands were a colony of Great Britain until 1974. In 1978, they became the independent nation of Tuvalu. The neighboring Gilbert Islands had also been a British colony until they were invaded and occupied by Japan.

on the deck, which for a horrifying moment suggested to Rickenbacker a strafing run. But just as quickly the big U.S. Navy insignia on the wing became plainly visible, and Eddie—who was jumping and waving his hat with the others—could even see the broad smile of one of the pilots as they zoomed past.

Strangely, however, these planes continued on until they were out of sight, and the quiet of the Pacific closed in once more upon the raft. The castaways had no way of knowing it, but the Kingfishers had been searching for them all day and were now low on fuel and had to return to Funafuti, about forty miles distant. However, they sent a radio message that turned the island base into a hive of feverish activity, resulting in the crew of one Kingfisher volunteering to fly out to the position where Eddie's raft had been reported and stand by until a PT boat could rescue them. Even though the Kingfisher could land on the surface, it did not have the power to take off again carrying the added weight even of these three emaciated survivors. It became a race against nightfall. No one wanted to take the chance that some unknown current would carry Eddie Rickenbacker and his companions off in the dark and they would never be found.

The Kingfisher's volunteer crew consisted of pilot Lieutenant (J.G.) William Eadie and radioman Lester Boutte. They spotted the raft just after sundown by illuminating the search area with flares. Eadie landed on the water, taxied up to the raft, killed his engine, and shouted: "Well, Captain Rickenbacker, here we are!"[14]

"And thank God for that," Eddie answered. At some point they had drifted across the international date line; it was now Friday, the thirteenth, their lucky day.

It was quickly becoming dark, and the pilot came up with a plan to get the airmen to Funafuti as soon as possible. Adamson, being the worst off, could lie in the radioman's cockpit, while Eddie and Bartek would be strapped to the leading edges of the wings. Then, even if they could not take off, they could taxi the plane across the rolling surface of forty miles of dark ocean to the safety of the marine base. It wasn't the best accommodation but it would do in a pinch, and Rickenbacker's bunch had been in a pinch for a long time. They taxied along in the swells in the pitch dark for half an hour, with Eddie strapped down on one wing and Bartek on the other, until they encountered one of the PT boats and

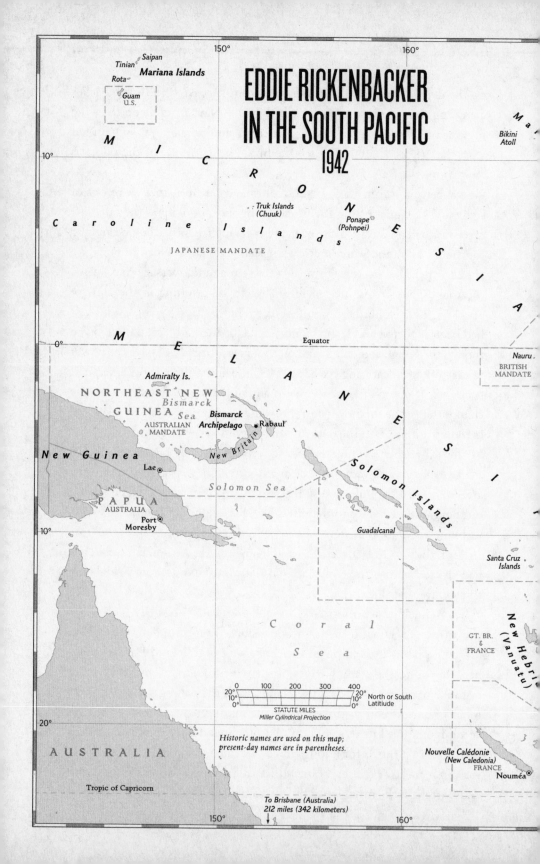

EDDIE RICKENBACKER
IN THE SOUTH PACIFIC
1942

Saipan
Tinian
Rota
Mariana Islands
Guam
U.S.

M I C R O N E S I A

Bikini
Atoll

Truk Islands
(Chuuk)

Ponape
(Pohnpei)

C a r o l i n e   I s l a n d s

JAPANESE MANDATE

10°

Equator

0°

Nauru
BRITISH
MANDATE

M E L A N E S I A

Admiralty Is.

NORTHEAST NEW
GUINEA
AUSTRALIAN
MANDATE

*Bismarck
Sea*

**Bismarck
Archipelago** •Rabaul

New Britain

New Guinea

Lae ⊙

Solomon Sea

Solomon Islands

PAPUA
AUSTRALIA

Port⊙
Moresby

Guadalcanal

10°

Santa Cruz
Islands

C o r a l

S e a

GT. BR.
&
FRANCE

New Hebrides
(Vanuatu)

0   100   200   300   400

20°
10°
0°

20°
10°
0°

North or South
Latitiude

STATUTE MILES
Miller Cylindrical Projection

20°

*Historic names are used on this map;
present-day names are in parentheses.*

A U S T R A L I A

Nouvelle Calédonie
(New Caledonia)
FRANCE
Nouméa⊙

Tropic of Capricorn

To Brisbane (Australia)
212 miles (342 kilometers)
↓

150°

160°

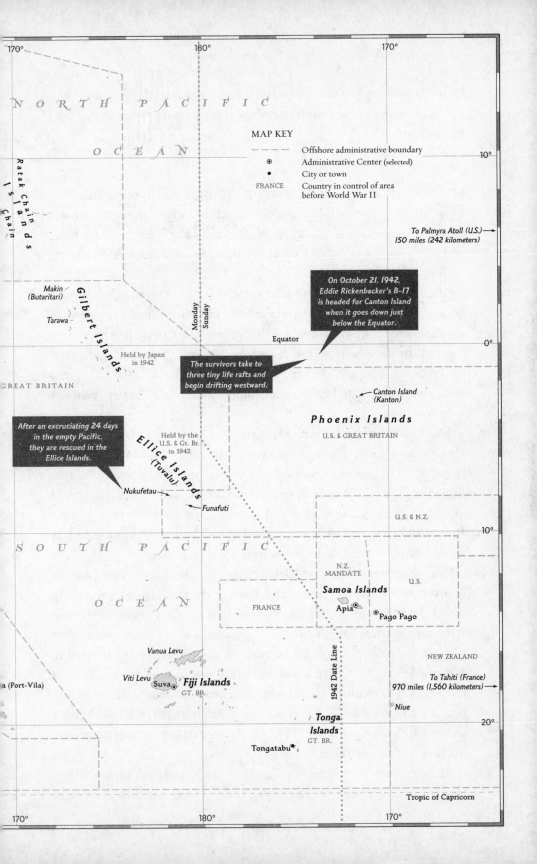

170°   180°   170°

N O R T H   P A C I F I C

O C E A N   10°

MAP KEY

– – – –   Offshore administrative boundary
⊙   Administrative Center (selected)
•   City or town
FRANCE   Country in control of area
before World War II

To Palmyra Atoll (U.S.) →
150 miles (242 kilometers)

Ratak Chain Islands Chain

On October 21, 1942,
Eddie Rickenbacker's B-17
is headed for Canton Island
when it goes down just
below the Equator.

Makin
(Butaritari)

Gilbert Islands

Tarawa

Monday | Sunday

Equator   0°

The survivors take to
three tiny life rafts and
begin drifting westward.

Held by Japan
in 1942

← Canton Island
(Kanton)

GREAT BRITAIN

Phoenix Islands
U.S. & GREAT BRITAIN

After an excruciating 24 days
in the empty Pacific,
they are rescued in the
Ellice Islands.

*Ellice Islands
(Tuvalu)*

Held by the
U.S. & Gt. Br.
in 1942

Nukufetau →

← Funafuti

U.S. & N.Z.

10°

S O U T H   P A C I F I C

N.Z.
MANDATE

U.S.

O C E A N

FRANCE

Samoa Islands

Apia ⊙
⊙ Pago Pago

Vanua Levu

NEW ZEALAND

Viti Levu   *Fiji Islands*
Suva ⊙   GT. BR.

a (Port-Vila)

1942 Date Line

To Tahiti (France) →
970 miles (1,560 kilometers)

⊙ Niue

*Tonga
Islands*
GT. BR.   20°

Tongatabu ⊙

Tropic of Capricorn

170°   180°   170°

were transferred aboard. At last the ordeal was ended. They had been in the lifeboats for twenty-four days. Eddie's parting words were, "God bless the navy!"

NAVY AUTHORITIES HAD HASTILY BUILT a small hospital at the Funafuti base just for Eddie and the castaways. There they recuperated for a few days and took stock. Rickenbacker was still covered with sores and burns and had lost forty pounds. Adamson and Cherry had lost fifty pounds each.

After several days a flying boat arrived from Samoa with two navy doctors who examined the group and decided they should return with them, where there was better care. Reynolds and Bartek, however, were too sick to be moved and were left in the care of medical personnel on Funafuti. They nearly left Adamson there also, because of his frail condition, but decided to bring him along, which Eddie always believed saved his life.

The flight took all day but they arrived in Samoa that evening, where Eddie sent a military communication to Secretary Stimson saying that he expected to be able to continue his mission in ten days or so, which to some people at the Pentagon seemed insane. Nevertheless, Hap Arnold next day sent word that he would order a special transport as soon as Rickenbacker was up to it. Arnold had already called Adelaide. At a loss for words, all she had said was a tearful "God bless you."[15]

During the next two weeks Rickenbacker and the others swilled gallons of fruit juices and ice cream and feasted gluttonously on everything under the sun until the doctors worried they would do harm to the size and shape of their stomachs. Eddie regained twenty of the pounds he had lost and gathered strength every day. Adamson eventually recovered, and word came that Bartek and Reynolds were out of danger. Toward the end of November, dressed in new army clothing, Rickenbacker boarded a new Consolidated B-24 bomber that had been converted as a transport—a luxury of a sort. This was the type of airplane he had wished for back in Pearl Harbor instead of the B-17.

Rickenbacker hopped from air bases in the Fiji islands, Nouméa, and Viti Levu and arrived at Brisbane, Australia, on December 4. A message waited from MacArthur saying that due to the almost daily Japanese air attacks he could not permit Rickenbacker to come to New Guinea in an unarmed B-24. Instead he had warmed up for him a fully armed B-17 with all machine guns working for the seven-hour trip across the Coral Sea. MacArthur was waiting on the tarmac when the plane put down at Port Moresby, and as Eddie limped toward him MacArthur wrapped him in his arms and, in that wonderfully theatrical voice of his, said, "God, Eddie, I'm glad to see you."

ASIDE FROM THE AIRPORT and a few filthy native huts, the city of Port Moresby had essentially been reduced to ruins by Japanese bombing. The heat was awful and the mosquitoes worse, Rickenbacker said. The Australian army had just repelled a Japanese advance across the towering Owen Stanley Range that got within thirty miles of the city. The fighting was horrid. MacArthur had arrived two weeks earlier with his twenty-thousand-man American army and was now engaged in the fierce Battle of Buna and Gona across the same mountains, where the Japanese had dug into heavily fortified and reinforced strongpoints, stubbornly resisting all attempts to dislodge them.*

MacArthur lived in "a framed shack [with] an outhouse containing a cold-water shower that always ran hot." Still he had courteously invited Eddie to stay with him. For a five-star† general, he said, "MacArthur lives anything but pretentiously." Eddie found MacArthur a "delightful host" and was taken into his confidence as well as that of the brilliant General George Kenney, who commanded MacArthur's air force. Kenney was an old friend of Eddie's who had also trained at the Issoudun school in France and won a Distinguished Service Cross as a flier in the last war. Kenney described for Eddie his new "skip-bombing" technique, in which an A-20 light bomber would fly low at Japanese transport ships and release its bomb load to skip across the water, similar to "dapping,"

---

* So stubborn were they that of the 6,800 Japanese engaged, only 200 were captured—the rest died.

† MacArthur had four stars at this point.

or bouncing a smooth pebble on a pond. It was one of Kenney's many innovations in a war theater of almost breathtaking dimensions, and Rickenbacker was happy to include the gist of all this in his report to Stimson.* For his part, MacArthur graciously told Rickenbacker, "You know, Eddie, I probably did the American Air Forces more harm than any living man when I was chief of staff by refusing to believe in the airplane as a war weapon, and I am doing everything I can to make amends for that great mistake."

After delivering Stimson's top secret message to MacArthur, Rickenbacker flew back to Brisbane where his luxury B-24 awaited. He did not look back fondly. "New Guinea is a hellhole of heat, dust, and vermin, [and] Port Moresby is the dust bowl of all creation." Rickenbacker found himself wishing that all the top war production people in the United States could be brought there "for just one day" so they could better understand the conditions under which Americans were fighting.

EDDIE RICKENBACKER RETURNED to the United States a hero once again. When his flight landed in California, Rickenbacker had a joyful reunion with his seventy-four-year-old mother, Lizzie, who was living in Los Angeles with her son Dewey. Eddie had supported them generously over the years. Like Adelaide, Lizzie had never given up hope that he would be rescued.

On December 19, 1942, his plane landed at Bolling Field in Washington, D.C., which was "swarming with dignitaries and top brass," including Stimson and Hap Arnold, but Eddie "had eyes for only three people: Adelaide, David and William."[16] After a joyous celebration they went to Stimson's office in the newly constructed Pentagon, where Eddie gave an account of his ordeal to reporters. That same day he and the family flew to Manhattan and a large reception thrown by Mayor La Guardia.

---

* Kenney famously put MacArthur's abrasive chief of staff Richard Sutherland in his place when he told him to get a blank white sheet of paper and put a dot in the middle with his pencil. That done, Kenney informed him, "That dot represents all you know about airpower. The rest of the paper is what I know about airpower."

In the coming days Rickenbacker recounted the story for *Life* magazine and began working on a best-selling book about the episode. At a luncheon given for him by Joseph M. Patterson, publisher of the New York *Daily News,* he had barely sat down when Mrs. Patterson leaned over and told him she'd been asked by a group of influential people to urge him to run for president. He laughed and replied, "I am too controversial, and you know it." Toward the end of the lunch the *Daily News* cartoonist Batchelor arrived at the table with the original "So long, Eddie" cartoon drawing and he presented it to Rickenbacker with the word SORRY in large letters over the front.

In the following weeks, Rickenbacker delivered a blistering speech at the Pentagon regarding lifesaving and survival gear aboard aircraft, dwelling in particular on the size of the rafts and their emergency equipment, water and rations, radios, clothing, and more. Nearly all of his recommendations were rapidly put into practice.

His return coincided with the celebration of what Winston Churchill had recently described as the "end of the beginning," after the British defeated Field Marshal Rommel's German army at the Battle of El Alamein in Egypt. All in all, the last part of 1942 had been a good half year for the Allies, who had previously suffered nothing but grievous defeats and setbacks. Now it seemed the tide of battle was turning, beginning with Doolittle's raid on Japan, followed by the enormous U.S. naval victory at the Battle of Midway, the turning back of the Japanese army in New Guinea, the dearly won successes by U.S. marines at Guadalcanal, the German defeat at Stalingrad, and the triumphal American invasion of North Africa. All of these events were encouraging, and for Americans Eddie Rickenbacker's return from the dead was a symbol of American indestructibility. Many a Sunday sermon dealt with the parable of Eddie's seagull as an act of deliverance by God himself. As the biographer W. David Lewis observed, "He was no longer a hero but a prophet."

★ ★ ★ ★ ★

CHAPTER 13

THE LONE EAGLE GOES TO WAR

THREE DAYS AFTER THE PEARL HARBOR attack Charles Lindbergh released a statement through the America First Committee, which was in the process of disbanding: "We have been stepping closer to war for many months. Now it has come and we must meet it as united Americans regardless of our attitudes in the past toward the policy our government has followed. Whether or not that policy has been wise, we have been attacked by force of arms, and by force of arms we must retaliate."

If being reviled by the press and a considerable part of the American population ever bothered Charles Lindbergh, there is no record of it. Whether he thought this statement would get him back into the good graces of the government is also unrecorded, but it's doubtful. His frustration and desperation is palpable from what he wrote in his journal several days after Pearl Harbor when Germany and Italy declared war on the United States.

"Now that we are at war I want to contribute as best I can to my country's war effort. My first inclination was to write to the President . . . [but] if I wrote him at this time, he would probably make what use he could of my offer from a standpoint of politics and publicity and assign me to some position where I would be completely ineffective and out of the way. I sometimes wish, for a moment, that I had not resigned my commission; but whenever I turn the circumstances over in my mind, I feel I took the right action. There was, I think, no honorable alternative . . . I simply cannot remain idle while my country is at war. I *must* take some part in it, whatever that may be." Days later he was still wondering, "What part am I to take in the war in view of the obvious antagonism of the Administration?" It did not take him long to find out.

During Christmas week Lindbergh wrote to Hap Arnold offering his military services, taking note of the "complications" that might ensue as a result of his open opposition to the Roosevelt administration. A few days later the offer somehow leaked to the press, which prompted Lindbergh's old antagonist Interior Secretary Harold Ickes to contact Roosevelt, warning of "a tragic disservice to democracy to give one of its bitterest and most ruthless enemies a chance to gain a military record." Ickes represented Lindbergh to the president as "a fascist, motivated by hatred for you personally," and urged Roosevelt to consign him "to merciful oblivion."[1]

Thus it was that when Lindbergh heard nothing back from Hap Arnold, he went to see Secretary of War Stimson, who told him, quite frankly, that in view of Lindbergh's opposition to intervention he was "extremely hesitant" to put him in a position of command.

Next day Lindbergh went to see Arnold and Assistant Secretary of War for Air Robert Lovett. Lovett asked whether Lindbergh could serve Roosevelt loyally. Lindbergh replied that while he disagreed with the president, he would follow his orders "as President of the United States [and] Commander in Chief of the Army." Arnold wondered whether Lindbergh's fellow officers would have confidence in him, given Lindbergh's outspoken anti-intervention views. The meeting lasted less than half an hour, but by the end of it Lindbergh conceded there were too many obstacles for him to try to have his colonelcy reinstated. He said the country might be better served if he returned to the aviation industry. Lovett said he thought the War Department would be agreeable to that.

Lindbergh, however, soon came to see the breadth of Roosevelt's vindictiveness. Wherever he went in the aircraft industry he was rebuffed. His old friend Juan Trippe at Pan Am, after first welcoming Lindbergh aboard, soon called back to say there were "obstacles." It was the same at Curtiss-Wright and United Air. Lindbergh was "dynamite," they said, and it had been made plain that any association with him could jeopardize their lucrative contracts with the War Department and other government agencies. Lindbergh later learned that when his name had come up during a White House meeting with several Democratic senators Roosevelt had said, "I'll clip that young man's wings."[2]

On January 15 Charles ran into Eddie Rickenbacker in the lobby of the Carlton Hotel, two blocks from the White House, and the two agreed to meet for lunch in Rickenbacker's apartment there. Still recuperating from his atrocious plane crash in Atlanta, Eddie told Charles (whom he always called "Slim") that the Roosevelt administration was making things as tough as possible for him, too, because of his past opposition to the president's war politics. (This was several weeks before Rickenbacker's tour of U.S. air bases and the mission to England.) Lindbergh thought Rickenbacker looked "much better than I expected," considering his ordeal.[3]

For her part, Anne Lindbergh felt exasperated over the situation. Six months pregnant, and living in their rented home on Martha's Vineyard, she told her diary on March 12, "C is away—again looking for work. I am hurt for him when he gets another telephone call from a company which wants him, but cannot afford to take him, because of Administration disapproval. And I feel that his exclusion from the world of aviation is much more than mine from the world of books.* He is not bitter or discouraged, and it does not seem to affect his daily life or what he gives to others, for he radiates a kind of health and gaiety and steadiness. It is a constant marvel—and lesson—to me."

Wartime Washington made it all the more difficult not to have a position in the military. There were machine guns at the White House and on the roofs of buildings. The entire city was blacked out at night in fear of air raids. Lindbergh dwelled in his frustrating limbo until the end of March 1942, when deliverance at last came from the man who then owned the largest aircraft manufacturing company in the world, Henry Ford.

Ford was in the process of completing the stupendous government-backed warplane plant at Willow Run, Michigan, outside Detroit. Two

---

* Anne's preface to Saint-Exupéry's latest book had been expunged by its publisher because of the controversy surrounding Charles and, by extension, her.

years earlier it had been a farm owned by Ford and used to employ Depression-era youths. It was only now beginning to produce the B-24 Liberator, a four-engine, high-wing heavy bomber.* The Consolidated Aircraft Corporation in San Diego was presently assembling the plane by hand, but the army thought production could be vastly improved using assembly-line methods that had been developed by Henry Ford for manufacturing automobiles.

Like Lindbergh, Ford had his own sharp distaste for the Roosevelt administration and had been a backer of America First. He also maintained a subsidiary of the Ford Motor Company that continued to operate in Germany until the United States entered the war. His relationship with Charles had begun in 1927, the year of Lindbergh's historic flight, when Lindbergh had given Ford his first—and last— airplane ride in the *Spirit of St. Louis.*

Deeply anti-Semitic, the seventy-eight-year-old Ford was also known for his eccentricities, but Lindbergh felt that his sheer scientific and business genius overrode the other shortcomings and had come to see him almost as a father figure.

Ford needed Lindbergh as a troubleshooter, which in the argot of the manufacturing world translated to "technical consultant," but in fact meant "test pilot." Charles told him he'd better check with the War Department and White House first, but Henry Ford, being Henry Ford, did not appreciate the notion of having to "check" with *anyone*—up to and including the White House—when he wanted to hire somebody.

Lindbergh insisted that he wanted no part of bringing difficulties upon the Ford Motor Company, but as it turned out even Roosevelt didn't want to tangle with Ford. By virtue of silence from the White House Lindbergh was allowed to take up his manifest duties as "technical consultant" for Ford's aircraft production operations.

---

* Willow Run became the largest "room" in the world, at a mile long and a quarter mile wide. At its peak, in 1943, Willow Run employed 35,000 people and was producing one B-24 Liberator an hour, twenty-four hours a day. By the end of the war 9,000 had been made there.

WORKING IN DETROIT contained an added bonus for Lindbergh—he could be close to his mother, Evangeline, who, at the age of sixty-six, was showing the first signs of Parkinson's disease but continued to teach chemistry at a local high school. He argued that she should retire; he had plenty of money to support her. But Evangeline was adamant that she wished to go on teaching and riding the crosstown bus to school each morning.

Because of the tremendous wartime migration to the Detroit area, finding a house became difficult, but Charles located a two-story mock Tudor in the tony section of Bloomfield Hills. With the baby due in several months' time Anne dreaded the idea of having to leave their idyllic place on the Vineyard—especially for Detroit—but accepted that her place was with her husband. Her arrival was marred when, just as they were moving in, their small terrier Kelpie was run over and killed. Anne hoped it was not an omen.[4]

Lindbergh had just arrived at Willow Run when—only eleven days after he had returned to the United States from his celebrated raid on Tokyo—Jimmy Doolittle landed at the airfield in a Martin B-26 twin-engine bomber he was flying to compare with the B-25s his men had flown on the raid. He and Lindbergh had lunch, along with some army officers and Ford officials. Charles gave few details of their meeting other than to say that Doolittle "looked somewhat tired."

During his early days at Willow Run Lindbergh immersed himself in the aerodynamic characteristics of the B-24 by flying it for days on end, and soon he set to solving the many problems associated with the plane. After meeting with Hap Arnold in Washington he reported that among the combat air crews the B-17 was by far the preferred heavy bomber since, as Arnold confided, "when we send the B-17s out on a mission most of them return. When we send the B-24s out, a good many of them don't." Even if this somewhat overstated the case, it was a serious indictment, and Lindbergh pledged to find solutions.

By interviewing pilots who had flown in combat, he quickly assessed a number of areas that could be improved upon: the B-24 radios didn't work properly; the armament was in the wrong place or more was needed; there were mechanical problems with the cylinders, the bottom turret, and the nose gun turret; controls were stiff; takeoff run was too long; and so forth. One overarching difficulty was that the workmen on the B-24 had previously worked on automobiles, and the difference between a car and a huge, complicated four-engine bomber with miles of electrical wire, precision parts, weaponry, unfamiliar widgets, and gadgets was overwhelming. The sheer grandiosity of the thing was simply baffling to men who had been accustomed to bolting cylinder heads on 90-horsepower Ford Coupe engine blocks with socket wrenches or slapping a car chassis on a Ford frame.

But beyond all that was the most unsettling trouble of all: Lindbergh detected widespread laziness among the workers. "They appeared to be doing something when I approached," he said, but when he looked back they seemed to be loafing. He did not mention labor unions in this particular appraisal but later expressed his dissatisfaction with organized labor and its seeming lack of interest in creating an atmosphere of the careful and meticulous work ethic necessary to construct aircraft.

On August 12, 1942, Anne gave birth to Scott Lindbergh, although, in typical Lindbergh fashion, it would be four more months before the parents filled out a birth certificate.

IN SEPTEMBER 1942, Lindbergh volunteered to be a human guinea pig in a dangerous series of tests on the effects of high-altitude flying. Oxygen deprivation, or hypoxia, begins at about 8,000 to 10,000 feet. By around 20,000 feet humans cannot live but a brief time without bottled oxygen. Above 20,000 feet is considered "extreme altitude," which was where many military fighter planes were now operating. (Mount Everest, for instance, is 29,000 feet.) At the time, many believed that being deprived of oxygen above 40,000 feet would cause the blood to boil, as the water in the blood changed to vapor, resulting in permanent, or fatal, damage to the brain and other organs.

Lindbergh had heard of some experiments in high-altitude flight being conducted at the notable Mayo Clinic in Rochester, Minnesota, where an operation known as the Aeromedical Research Unit was located. Chaired by Dr. Walter Boothby, the unit operated a simulated altitude chamber, a scary-looking apparatus similar in appearance to a gas chamber, which could replicate atmospheres of 40,000 feet and above. Lindbergh got in the thing and, ascending with a rate of climb faster than an airplane, began testing different oxygen masks to determine which was best for pilots.

Here his two great interests, aviation and medicine, intersected, and the scientist in him began to overtake his reflective persona. Next morning he was back in the chamber to an altitude of 44,200 feet for nearly half an hour. He took a ride in a "G" machine that the unit operated, a kind of human centrifuge that simulates the acceleration a pilot experiences coming out of a dive, pulling 5.8 G's, which is near the outside of what a person can tolerate without special pressurized gear.

In the coming months he returned to the altitude chamber time and again, testing the army's emergency oxygen equipment, often pushing himself so far that he lapsed into unconsciousness. This produced severe headaches later. Dr. Boothby and others worried that Charles was overdoing his trials, but—like Jimmy Doolittle and his outside loop—Lindbergh persevered with the well-known Lindbergh disdain for caution.

He also performed simulated parachute jumps in the chamber to determine if the oxygen bottle attached to the chute was adequate to get the pilot down to safety. In the end he concluded that army pilots flying at altitude were equipped with insufficient protection.

After two weeks at the Mayo Clinic he was home again in Bloomfield Hills, having dinner with Anne in the parlor where she read him her latest poem ("Christopher"). The boys were growing up now; Land was entering first grade, and Charles one day discovered ten-year-old Jon at his mother's Detroit home "in the basement, bending glass tubing over one of Grandfather's old Bunsen burners."

At the end of October Lindbergh extended his experiments to actual flight and began high-altitude experiments at Willow Run with the P-47 Thunderbolt, the largest, most powerful, and most expensive single-engine fighter plane thus far in history. A modern low-wing aircraft, the Thunderbolt boasted a 2,000-horsepower Ford-built Pratt & Whitney radial engine that could climb above 40,000 feet and fly at a speed of about 430 miles per hour—a far cry from the 90-horsepower Curtiss Jenny he'd learned to fly in twenty years earlier.* There had been a rumor that ten P-47s had crashed in Florida

---

* The ability of fighter planes to dive at altitude (from above) gave them an advantage over an enemy who would have to operate at lower altitudes, making them easy prey.

A B-25 bomber takes off from the deck of the USS Hornet, April 18, 1942.

News of the Doolittle raid made front-page headlines around the world.

Doolittle and some of his raiders and their Chinese friends.
All sixteen planes either crash-landed or were abandoned by bail out.

A forlorn Doolittle beside the wreckage of his B-25.
He was convinced he would be court-martialed for losing all the planes.

President Franklin D. Roosevelt decorates Doolittle with the Medal of Honor, with Joe, U.S. Army Air Corps chief Hap Arnold, and Chief of Staff George C. Marshall looking on.

LEFT: *Now at the Smithsonian, Joe Doolittle's tablecloth features the names of hundreds of celebrities.*
RIGHT: *President Ronald Reagan and Senator Barry Goldwater pin the fourth star of a full general on Doolittle in 1985.*

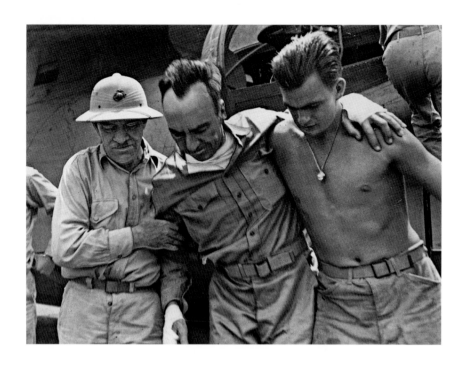

Rickenbacker shortly after his rescue following
twenty-four days lost in the South Pacific in 1942.

LEFT: *Rickenbacker and the crew were confined to small life rafts,*
virtually lying atop one another.
RIGHT: *In 1943 Rickenbacker wrote a best-selling book about the experience.*
This pamphlet, based on a speech Rickenbacker gave, also described the ordeal.

After two weeks' recuperation, Rickenbacker completed his secret mission in the South Pacific and continued to support the war effort.

After the war, Rickenbacker resumed his duties with Eastern Air Lines.

LEFT: *Lindbergh is escorted through a South Sea base on an inspection tour for an American plane manufacturer in 1944.*
RIGHT: *Lindbergh used himself as a guinea pig to test the effects of altitude on pilots.*

In 1944 Lindbergh, pictured here with fighter pilots in Emirau Island, talked his way into battle in the South Pacific as an "aviation technician."

Lindbergh and the Apollo 8 astronauts sign their autographs to a commemorative document that will hang in the White House Treaty Room as President and Mrs. Lyndon B. Johnson and Vice President Hubert Humphrey look on, 1968.

After the war, Lindbergh roamed the world in the service of environmental projects.

Veterans of Doolittle's raid inspect a B-25. The raiders' final public reunion was held in April 2013, seventy-one years after their history-making flight.

on takeoff, killing their pilots, but Lindbergh tracked it down and proved it false.

He was able to fine-tune the fuel mixture to coax even more altitude from the plane, and in months of testing he made such a number of changes in emergency equipment—especially in the event of a high-altitude failure—that he is credited with saving countless pilots' lives. On several of these experiments he nearly lost his own life.

Once at 36,000 feet Lindbergh's cockpit suddenly began to fill with smoke, but he managed to land on the Willow Run runway with barely enough fuel to fly. Another time the strip holding the emergency-hatch exit blew off. And on another occasion still, at 36,000 feet his oxygen suddenly cut off, though the gauge showed it was flowing correctly. In moments he was overcome by "that vagueness of mind and emptiness of breath which warn a pilot of serious lack of oxygen." He wondered if his mask was leaking and shoved it against his face. At this altitude a pilot without oxygen has no more than fifteen seconds before losing consciousness. Reflexively, Lindbergh shoved the stick forward into a dive; the altimeter began spinning; he began to lose consciousness; he was going so fast the plane started to shriek; the noise woke him up. At 15,000 feet, consciousness returned and he pulled up on the stick and zoomed. His mental clarity was restored.

"Returning from the border of death always makes one more aware of life," Charles wrote later. The mechanic told him the oxygen gauge read fifty pounds too high. "That had caused all my troubles," he said, "a quarter-inch error of a needle."[5]

Lindbergh's testing often took him away from Willow Run. At one point he found himself in the Florida panhandle at Eglin Field, where Jimmy Doolittle had trained his raiders and where Charles flew a British Mosquito, a two-seat bomber with twin Rolls-Royce engines—made out of wood. Many of these planes he flew were experimental or obsolete and the work was hazardous. All the planes were unfamiliar and many had mechanical or aeronautical deficiencies.

On one occasion he visited the Hartford, Connecticut, plant of United Aircraft Corporation, which manufactured the Vought F4U Corsair, the workhorse fighter plane of the U.S. Navy and Marine Corps in the Pacific.* Eugene Wilson, the company's president, who had told Lindbergh back in the summer of '42 when he inquired about a job that he was "dynamite," now informed him that "considerable water has gone under the bridge since we last talked with you" and asked if Charles was in a position to help United as a technical consultant to the Corsair.[6]

Lindbergh was thrilled. His work with the P-47 Thunderbolts was nearly finished, as they were now going into production at Willow Run, and likewise his contribution to the B-24 was almost complete. He jumped at a chance to work with the Corsair, a low-curved, folding-wing, 2,000-horsepower, eighteen-cylinder single-seat fighter that reached diving speeds in excess of 500 miles per hour. Lindbergh began spending a lot of time in Hartford, at first teaching navy and marine pilots the fine points of flying the Corsair, and later engaged in simulated combat maneuvers. Deak Lyman, the reporter to whom Lindbergh had given the exclusive story that he was taking his family to England, had left the *New York Times* and was now an executive with United Aircraft. He distinctly remembered the time Charles took on two of the top-rated marine pilots in a high-altitude gunnery contest, in which the forty-one-year-old Lindbergh "outguessed, outflew and outshot" both of the twenty-something-year-old would-be aces.[7]

Charles had also grown somewhat disenchanted working for Ford, in particular because of the shoddy work on the B-24s that he could not seem to get resolved. Once he complained to a high company official about the poor quality of workmanship. "He says again that I am a perfectionist!" Lindbergh wrote in exasperation, as if an aircraft in trouble could simply be pulled off the road like a car.

As 1943 CAME TO A CLOSE, Lindbergh felt that he had done all he could at both Ford and United Aircraft in the United States. But what he had not been able to do was observe how the aircraft they were manufacturing

---

* United Aircraft was the forerunner of the Boeing Company, United Airlines, and United Technologies, which manufacture everything from Otis elevators to guided missiles and the Black Hawk helicopter.

fared in actual combat. Twenty years earlier the army had trained Lindbergh to be a fighter pilot and, ever since, he had been itching to go into combat. Now, at the age of forty-one, he saw his chance. What he had in mind was a trip to the South Pacific theater to compare—under extreme flying conditions—the army's twin-boom P-38 with the navy's Corsair and see what could be done to improve their performance.

By that stage of the war, following the island-hopping scheme, MacArthur's army was still having a rough time of it on New Guinea in the southwestern Pacific, while the marines were moving on to the central Pacific where they continued to fight big island battles—Tarawa, Kwajalein, Eniwetok. Meanwhile, the Americans had left behind relatively undisturbed a string of large Japanese bases, coiled on other islands like wounded, angry beasts, which—though they were not believed to pose a major threat to the American rear—were still highly dangerous and prone to lash out with their airpower. For their part, the Americans left behind did not intend to let these pockets of Japanese resistance remain undisturbed and unmolested, and so a nasty little air war was being conducted on a daily basis, high above the placid tropical islands. It was there that Lindbergh hoped to conduct his tests of American combat aircraft.

He broached the subject quietly, through back channels, using old friends as contacts, among them his first cousin (now) Admiral Jerry Land (who had at last forgiven him for his strident isolationism). On January 5, 1944, in Washington, Lindbergh approached U.S. Marine General Louis E. Woods about going to the South Pacific to survey Corsair bases. Woods was receptive and said he would raise the matter with higher naval officers. That day in his journal Lindbergh wondered, doubtless with bated breath, "But will they feel they have to bring the matter to Roosevelt's attention?"

Apparently not, for the reply came next day in the affirmative. The adventure was postponed for several months due to "major military movements expected in the South Pacific," but by the end of February 1944 Lindbergh was cleared to go, and he returned to Detroit to say good-bye to Anne and the children.

Charles had a couple of weeks before heading to the Pacific and he made the most of it with Anne and the younger kids, playing with them on the floor a game he invented called "Vild-Cats" using a blanket for a cave and malted milk tablets for bait. For several hours each day Charles immersed himself in writing chapters that became his best-selling book *The Spirit of St. Louis.*

Both of the Lindberghs remained pariahs in certain parts of the country, most notably the Northeast. The Book of the Month Club had just rejected Anne's new book after receiving "a number of fanatical letters saying that if the club took my book they'd resign. I cannot believe, like [Charles]," she said, "that it all will change, that integrity will come out on top in the end."

The animosity was particularly acute among Jews, who remained convinced that Lindbergh had betrayed them. An embarrassing scene illustrating just how far the Lindberghs' esteem had fallen developed one morning at the Bucks County, Pennsylvania, country home of the playwright George S. Kaufman and his wife, Beatrice, who were entertaining the novelist John P. Marquand and his wife, Adelaide, a friend of Anne's since childhood and from Miss Chapin's School. When everyone had gathered downstairs for brunch about eleven-thirty, "Beatrice Kaufman spoke up in her clearest and coolest voice. 'Adelaide,' she said, 'while you were asleep this morning Mrs. Lindbergh telephoned you here.' 'Oh,' said Adelaide, 'I'll ring her back.' 'You may call her back if you wish,' Beatrice Kaufman said, 'but you may not do so from this house.'"

At this, Mrs. Marquand burst into tears and rushed from the room, and when she returned she asked her husband to drive her to the train station. Later that afternoon Marquand and Kaufman were standing glumly on the porch of the house where the two men—old friends— had been collaborating on a Broadway adaptation of Marquand's novel *The Late George Apley.* Kaufman at last said to Marquand, "John, why do you associate yourself with people like the Lindberghs?" to which Marquand replied, "George, you've got to remember that all heroes are horses' asses."[8]

While Lindbergh got his affairs in order, Anne worked on a sculpture for a class she was taking at the Detroit Institute of Arts, read Arthur Koestler, and worried about Charles going to the war. As the day drew near she consoled herself that this was the worst time, that it would be better once he had gone. Anne sat on the bed while Charles packed, sewing buttons on his raincoat, taking one from hers. That, at least, pleased her. "I seemed so lost, unable to do anything else," she told her diary, "not gloomy, just suspended."

ON MARCH 30 LINDBERGH DEPARTED Detroit for the South Pacific. His first stop, though, was Brooks Brothers in New York City, where he was outfitted for his military uniform and other gear. As a so-called technical consultant in combat areas Lindbergh was required to wear the uniform of a U.S. Navy officer, minus insignia of rank. At Abercrombie & Fitch he purchased a waterproof flashlight, and from Brentano's he acquired a small copy of the New Testament, remarking in his journal that, "Since I can carry only one book, it is my choice. It would not have been a decade ago, but the more I learn and the more I read, the less competition it has."

He withdrew $1,750 in cash and traveler's checks* and, after learning that the Associated Press was trying to contact him, left word at the United Aircraft offices that "I could not be reached."

On April 9 Lindbergh took off in a Corsair and flew cross-country to the West Coast, stopping at marine and navy bases for mock gunnery exercises at altitude and even a little live-fire skeet shooting on officers' club ranges. He had no urgent timetable and his flight to the South Pacific scheduled by the navy was two weeks distant. At the El Toro Marine Corps Air Station in Orange County near Los Angeles, he participated in a series of live-ammo combat gunnery exercises with a tow target and was pleased to report to his journal, "I had the highest percentage of hits of anyone in the flight, and have not fired machine guns from a plane since I was a cadet nineteen years ago," adding that, "Planes and tactics have changed tremendously since then."

On days off, he lay on the nearby beach and swam in the Pacific surf, marveling that there were "no cameras, no reporters, no publicity here." It was so wonderful, he said, it was about the only good thing to come out of the war.

On the evening of April 24 he took turns flying an unheated navy DC-3 to Oahu, which nearly froze him because he did not have a thick fur-lined

---

* About $22,000 today.

pilot's suit. At Pearl Harbor, Charles received an invitation to lunch from the military governor and commander of the Hawaiian Department, Major General Robert C. Richardson, an old friend whom he had known at Brooks and Kelly Fields in 1925. Several other generals attended the lunch. In fact, during the next several days Lindbergh was feted by a vast array of generals, admirals, and Marine Corps flying officers—veterans of the early air battles. Despite any remaining hard feelings toward him by some on the mainland, Charles Lindbergh was the most famous and sought-after civilian in the Pacific since Betty Grable.

On April 29 he flew to Midway Island in a marine Commando, the largest two-engine plane in the war. There was a squadron of navy Corsairs stationed at Midway, which was still a little gun-shy after the narrow escape from the Japanese back in '42. Lindbergh was immediately invited to fly on a dawn patrol with the marine aviators, looking for any signs of the enemy.

None was found and on Monday he boarded a four-engine Martin flying boat bound for Marine Corps Air Station Ewa on Oahu island. The pilot, Commander L. S. Drill, proudly informed Charles that he had been chairman of the Miami chapter of the America First Committee. Again taking turns flying the huge craft, Lindbergh couldn't help but marvel how far aviation had advanced since he first went up in his rattletrap Jenny. "Three regular pilots, a navigator, crew, cabin aft full of passengers, baggage, even a cook and ship's galley with stove, icebox, and tables for four. . . . I cannot quite get used to it," he said.

At Ewa, Lindbergh practiced masthead—low, level—bombing and dive-bombing in the morning, and in the afternoon he went spear fishing with the commanding general. This was the first time Lindbergh had put on a glass face mask and he was amazed at the difference it made underwater. "It was like suddenly entering a new world, one which turned from enemy to friend the instant you entered it."

On May 5, Lindbergh departed for the South Pacific war zone. The general came to see him off and gave him his face mask to take along. They made the usual refueling stops at Palmyra and Funafuti, where Charles and some of the others visited the native village. There they were treated to a dance, "a sort of tom-tom affair, with good rhythm and at times very graceful gestures," and in the evening they attended an outdoor theater where an old gangster film was featured, which Lindbergh regarded as vulgar.

Next morning they took off for Espiritu Santo, in the New Hebrides, deeper into the combat zone, where the sides of the runways were littered with parts of wrecked planes from Japanese air raids. Charles stayed for several days testing Corsairs and not liking what he found: problems with wing tanks, manifold pressures badly off, propellers out of sync, rough-running engines, rust and corrosion everywhere, something wrong with blowers and water injection, oxygen mask leaks, lack of proper instruction books, and so forth. The squadron, in gratitude for Charles's help and advice, presented him with a waterproof wristwatch on an engraved steel bracelet that they had made in their machine shop.

Next day he was invited to a pigeon shoot on one of the cocoa plantations, but Charles found the plants and wildlife so interesting that he "slipped off into the jungle alone and did no shooting."

On May 19 Lindbergh caught an airplane ride to Guadalcanal with a brigadier general. Known to marines and Japanese alike as the Island of Death, Guadalcanal was the site, late in 1942, of the first major combat between American and Japanese troops. It was a savage battle from which the Americans had come out victorious, but not before 7,100 marines and soldiers had been killed and 650 U.S. aircraft were lost. In turn, the marines and soldiers killed 31,000 Japanese and shot down 800 of their planes.

Now the fighting had moved three hundred miles up the Solomon chain of islands to Bougainville and the squadrons of marine Corsairs had moved with them. After meeting with the major commanders, Lindbergh bid them adieu on May 20 and flew to Bougainville. The first thing he asked was to be taken to the front. The Japanese had occupied Bougainville in 1942 with a sixty-thousand-man army and built numerous airfields there in order to interdict Allied shipping. Marines had invaded the island the previous November but the fighting remained bitter and protracted.

U.S. Army General William H. Arnold, the island commander himself, offered to escort Lindbergh to the battle area. They drove out in the general's jeep as he explained how the Japanese had been attacking the narrow beachhead that the Allies had established a few months earlier. There had been a full-scale assault two months before, in which seventeen hundred Japanese were killed. They walked among the trenches as the general pointed out key positions and heavy fighting spots. The ground was littered with Japanese skulls and bones and clothing, rotting on the humid earth.

The Japanese had come on two hours before daybreak, in a fierce suicide charge up the hill where they were now standing. They had captured the hill and the American emplacements, but a countercharge by U.S. troops drove them back into the jungle, leaving the hillside and the ground below carpeted with dead bodies. An unsavory smell hung over the battlefield; the Japanese had tried to bury many of the corpses in the shallow trenches and foxholes they had dug before the battle, but as the corpses bloated in the tropic heat they rose out of their graves and emitted a kind of death cloud for several miles around.

Arnold and Lindbergh walked further through the depressing detritus of battle: Japanese clothing, packs, shoes, entrenching tools, canteens—a stockinged foot protruded from the ground along the path. Many of the bodies were charred black from immolation by flamethrowers. The general said the soldiers did not dare enter the wire entanglements to bury the bodies because they were persistently mined and booby-trapped.

They drove to another spot where Arnold told Lindbergh the Japanese had penetrated the American lines for a considerable distance before being driven back by a tank attack. Lindbergh wondered if there might be Japanese snipers still at large, but the general seemed unworried. They pressed on to a forward artillery position that was in the process of firing into the jungle. Presently the general told the driver to turn back. He explained to Lindbergh that although he did not think a sniper would give away his position by firing at an ordinary vehicle, the sight of a general's star on the jeep might be too tempting. "The same idea had been occupying my own mind for some time," Lindbergh remarked afterward.

That evening, back in the tent that served as an officers' mess, Lindbergh spoke with a number of pilots from the fighting Corsair squadrons. At length, he wondered aloud if he might accompany them on a patrol, and he was immediately invited to take part next morning in a joint raid on Rabaul, the main Japanese military and naval base in the South Pacific, on the neighboring island of New Britain.

LINDBERGH ROSE AT DAYBREAK and performed his morning ablutions from a rough board table at the side of his tent, using the steel helmet he was given for a washbasin and cold water to shave in. After breakfast he went to the pilots' ready room, received the preflight briefing, and drew his equipment: a .45 automatic, leg knife, parachute, life raft, and jungle kit. There would be four Corsairs in his flight; Lindbergh's radio call sign was Jones.

At 8:40 they were airborne. Rabaul lay approximately two hundred miles to the northeast, which took them less than a half hour to reach. Once over water they cleared their guns—fired off a few shots—each plane carrying sixteen hundred rounds.

Allied forces had been bombarding Rabaul regularly ever since they'd gotten within fighter-bomber range, in order to isolate the Japanese troops, air forces, naval ships, and supply and repair installations there. A year earlier, using information developed from an intercepted Japanese radio message, a squadron of American P-38s had ambushed the Japanese imperial navy commander Admiral Yamamoto as he departed the base at Rabaul for Bougainville, shooting his plane down and killing him.

From a distance, Rabaul looked peaceful and serene, Lindbergh noted, lying at the edge of a huge volcanic crater, or caldera,* but its tranquillity was shortly to come to an end. Several different formations of aircraft had already converged on the city from as far away as MacArthur's base on New Guinea—army P-38 Lightnings, navy torpedo bombers, P-39 Airacobras, P-40 Warhawks, even a Dumbo, or flying boat, to rescue downed pilots. Lindbergh's Corsair's mission was to fly cover for the bombers in case the Japanese sent up Zeros.† If there was no opposition, then the Corsairs were to go on a strafing mission against predesignated targets.

---

* In 1994 the volcano came alive in a huge eruption that destroyed Rabaul and left it under ten feet of ash. The capital was moved elsewhere.

† The Japanese had perhaps a dozen types of fighters, fighter-bombers, torpedo fighter-bombers, etc. Each had a specific name in U.S. military jargon—Nell, Oscar, Kate, Claude, Tony, and so forth. But generally they were all considered to be "Zeros," after the big red circle surrounded by a thin white border that marked all Japanese fighter-type planes. The true Zero itself, a Mitsubishi-made carrier fighter, was known to American fliers as a "Zeke."

As the torpedo bombers began their dives, black puffs of antiaircraft fire began exploding around them. The Japanese gunners on Rabaul were considered the best in the South Pacific, Lindbergh said, for the simple reason that "they have had the most practice."

The Corsairs were circling at 10,000 feet when someone reported a "bogey," or enemy plane below. Lindbergh armed his guns and dived down to meet it, only to find it was a friendly plane. The radio reported a life raft on the water. Fighters were circling, protecting it, and the Dumbo was directed to the scene.

In Rabaul, fires were visible and smoke rose into the air; planes were diving and zooming in all directions amid the black bursts of the antiaircraft flak and against the backdrop of tropical greenery, coconut palms, and the red, orange, and white explosions from the bombs. Somewhere among all this were tens of thousands of people, Japanese soldiers and sailors and civilians, yet nary a one could be seen.

Above it all Lindbergh's Corsairs continued to circle. Another bogey was reported, which also turned out to be friendly. A plane came out of the melee burning badly, Lindbergh said, leaving behind it a long trail of white smoke, "like sky writing." The radio continued to direct the rescue of the downed pilot in the raft. As suddenly as it began, the strike was over and the planes began re-forming over the water, out of range, before going their various ways. Now it was Lindbergh's turn.

His objective was a low oblong building near the beach from which gunfire had been reported on an earlier raid. He set the controls to dive and followed the flight leader in at about 2,000 feet, lining the building in his sights. But the flight leader's plane was in the way, too close to shoot. Lindbergh waited, still diving as the ground rushed up at him, then it was clear and he pressed the trigger as the streams of tracers tore up the roof and wall.

He leveled out twenty feet above the treetops, hoping the building did not contain women and children. At 400 miles per hour he was going too fast to shoot at much this close to the ground. He turned out over the water and rendezvoused with the other planes above nearby Duke of York Island, where there was an enemy-held airstrip and huts said to be occupied by Japanese. Orders were to "strafe everything in sight."

Lindbergh was blasting away at these huts when a much larger building came into his sights. He was about to press the trigger when a tall structure atop the building revealed itself to be a steeple. It was a church. He zoomed past. He'd been told to shoot at churches anyway because the enemy used them for their troops. "However, I will leave churches for someone else to shoot at," Lindbergh said.

He joined up with the other planes and they returned to their airstrip at Green Island, keeping a sharp lookout for a yellow life raft from a plane reported missing in the St. George's Channel. Lindbergh saw no antiaircraft fire himself, but one of the other pilots reported that Japanese flak had burst behind his plane.

On the path back to his hut he ran into the commanding officer of the marine air group who was upset that Lindbergh had gone on the patrol. "You are on civilian status," the C.O. told him. "If you'd had to land and the Japs caught you, they would have shot you."

Lindbergh replied that, according to reports he'd read, they shot you anyway, no matter what your status.

The C.O. wanted to know if Lindbergh had fired his guns. When the answer was affirmative, he became even more upset, saying, "You have a right to observe combat as a technician, but not to fire guns."

One of the other pilots allowed that it would certainly be all right for Lindbergh to "engage in target practice" to see if the guns worked properly.

Others chimed in as well, agreeing that target practice was very much allowable. "There's nothing wrong with that."

"The tenseness began to ease up," Lindbergh said. "Let's wait a day or so and see if anybody kicks up a fuss," someone suggested. That was how they left it. "The more I see of the Marines the more I like them," said former army colonel Charles Lindbergh.

THE FOLLOWING MORNING LINDBERGH visited a native village. The condition of the natives was sad, he found. Traditionally, the inhabitants of these islands had been cannibals but they had not practiced for many years, since the arrival of Christian missionaries. "Their wild, barbaric freedom has been taken away from them and replaced with a form of civilized slavery which leaves neither them nor us better off," Lindbergh observed. "The white man has brought them a religion they do not understand, diseases they are unable to combat, standards of life which leave them poverty stricken, a war which has devastated their homes and taken their families away."

Later that day he went on a strafing and reconnaissance run. It was a two-plane afternoon harassing flight over the coast of Japanese-held New Ireland to locate antiaircraft guns and attack targets of opportunity. Everything and everyone on the island was "enemy" and subject to being shot at, they were told.

At one point Lindbergh, flying low along the beach, got a man in his gun sights. He was standing in the water, and for a moment Lindbergh considered pulling the trigger, but he resisted the impulse and was glad he did. The man ("probably an enemy") apparently saw him coming but did not run. Instead he merely strode out of the water and across the beach. "I should never quite have forgiven myself if I had shot him," Lindbergh told his journal. "Naked, courageous, defenseless, and yet so unmistakably man." Charles returned before sundown and spent the evening ruminating in his journal on war and life and death.

Next day, May 25, after a conference with commanders about operating problems with the Corsairs, Lindbergh moved on up the island chain to Emirau, a tiny speck on the ocean north of New Ireland and about five hundred miles north of Bougainville. The Corsair squadron leader there was Major Joe Foss, the Marine Corps' leading ace with twenty-six enemy "kills," who had recently been awarded the Medal of Honor for his actions during the Battle of Guadalcanal.

When he arrived at headquarters, Lindbergh found that Foss was elsewhere on the island attending the funeral of one of his pilots, who had been killed the day before. However, he was just in time for the arrival of Admiral Halsey, who was making a farewell tour of his South Pacific outposts before moving his command northward to the central Pacific. In moving north from Guadalcanal at the beginning of 1943, Halsey had cleared all critical areas of the enemy and established American bases with air and sea superiority while isolating hundreds of thousands of Japanese soldiers in places such as Rabaul, Kavieng, and other strongholds.

The following day Lindbergh took part in a Corsair raid on Kavieng, which lay on the northernmost tip of New Ireland. Two months earlier the Japanese admiral in charge ordered the execution of all European prisoners on the island, resulting in the deaths of twenty-three men, women, and children in what came to be known as the Kavieng Wharf Massacre. Save for the war, these places had been the very embodiment of tropical paradise, with crystal clear water, endless white sand beaches, swaying palms, friendly natives, lavish European-style plantations. Then the Japanese came.

The town of Kavieng had been badly damaged by Allied raids and there were no signs of life from the air; the patrol stayed offshore for much of the time, however, to avoid known antiaircraft positions. They did sight and destroy a Japanese supply barge, with Lindbergh firing hundreds of rounds in three passes, at close range, through "spurts of water and flying splinters." May 27 was Charles and Anne's fifteenth wedding anniversary. He spent it in the air checking out reports of a submarine (nothing found) in the channel between Kavieng and New Hanover.

It was decided to rig the Corsairs in Lindbergh's patrol with five-hundred-pound high-explosive bombs to drop on Kavieng. Lindbergh's bomb overshot its mark but landed near buildings where enemy fire had been reported. "I do not like this bombing and machine gunning of unknown targets," he reported.

That afternoon Lindbergh took a Corsair up for an aileron test instead of joining the Kavieng patrol mission, and it may have been a good thing. Three dive-bombers were shot down over the city and at least two men were killed and a third was missing. Three were saved. It was a difficult dinner that night at the pilots' mess.

For the next week Lindbergh continued his daily bombing run on Kavieng, with negligible results. Too often he overshot his target, but by the end he felt he was getting the hang of it. On June 6, however, his final day on Emirau, he managed to place a five-hundred-pound bomb squarely in the middle of the main Japanese runway, blowing a sizable crater in the coral and rendering the strip inoperable. That afternoon he flew to Green Island and resumed making trouble for the Japanese on Rabaul, and when he returned from that mission the radio was full of news about the Allied invasion of France—D-day!

Next morning the Rabaul patrol found a column of Japanese trucks and enjoyed a turkey shoot, reducing several to flames. Later they learned that a pilot had been killed in the patrol that relieved theirs when he went after a similar column of Japanese trucks. It was a trap and the trucks were decoys: damaged equipment surrounded by concealed machine guns meant to lure American pilots to their doom. Somehow word of this ruse had not reached Lindbergh's patrol. "Death lies hidden all around us," he remarked, "so subtly that we cannot realize it is there."

On his last day in the Solomons Lindbergh was witness to a spectacular air assault on Rabaul: twin-engine Lockheed PV Harpoon bombers came in first dropping thousand-pound bombs, followed by the dive bombers and torpedo bombers, then the P-38s and P-39s, and finally a flight of B-25s bombing from altitude. It was a devastating show of pyrotechnics that raised a great deal of dust but started no fires or secondary explosions, a fact that indicated there might have been nothing left in Rabaul to bomb.

Lindbergh had learned a great deal about the navy's Corsairs and how they behaved in combat, all of which he would put into a report, once he had flown the twin-engine P-38, the army's predominant fighter.

ON JUNE 14 HE CAUGHT a four-motor transport to New Guinea where the army's Lockheed P-38 Lightning twin-engine, twin-boom fighter planes were flying in General MacArthur's air force. With help from his old friend Major General Ennis Whitehead, who had been merely Major Ennis Whitehead at the beginning of the war, Lindbergh checked himself out in the P-38s for several days, nearly cracking up on his first flight from a locked wheel brake, but eventually logging enough flying time to feel comfortable in the craft.

New Guinea was a dangerous and haunting place during World War II. It is the world's second largest island (after Greenland), shaped like a peacock, and containing some of the remotest jungle terrain on Earth. It is mostly hot, steamy rain forest, punctuated by a spine of mountains, known as the Owen Stanley Range, which rise to heights of 16,000 feet or more; some are actually capped in snow much of the year. Beginning in the nineteenth century Europeans, largely Dutch, established coconut plantations along the coast, but the interior remained a dark, inhospitable place where civilization had made few appreciable inroads, and whose inhabitants were thought still to be headhunters and cannibals.

Two years earlier, in the spring of 1942, the Japanese had sent an army by sea from Rabaul to capture Port Moresby—New Guinea's capital and largest city, only a couple of hundred miles from the northern tip of Australia—but that force was turned back by American carriers at the Battle of the Coral Sea. The Japanese then proceeded to land their army on the northern coast of New Guinea, on the peacock's "back" (Port Moresby would be at the bottom, or southern, side, its "tail"), and began a march across the precipitous Owen Stanley Range until they were in view of Port Moresby. They were defeated by a ferocious Australian defense and neared starvation. However, they continued to occupy the northwestern part of New Guinea where, from scores of jungle landing strips, their air force harassed Allied shipping.

Both sides continued to throw more men into the fight throughout 1943 and early 1944, but by the spring of that year General MacArthur had accumulated the strength to attack with some eighty thousand fresh men in a two-pronged pincers movement from one end of the peacock's back to the other. That operation began two months before Lindbergh arrived, and the fighting remained intense and deadly on the ground.

Two months earlier, General Kenney, MacArthur's air chief and Eddie Rickenbacker's old friend from World War I flying days, had learned through Magic (the U.S. code-breaking project in the Pacific) radio intercepts that the Japanese had approximately three hundred and fifty warplanes at the far northern end of the peacock's back and sent two dozen B-24 heavy bombers to destroy them. He was largely successful, having caught the Japanese off guard, but there remained determined pockets of Japanese air resistance, as well as formidable antiaircraft defenses. It was against this backdrop that Lindbergh now inserted himself to learn the combat qualities of the P-38.

The story goes (as told by Colonel Charles H. MacDonald, third leading ace in World War II with twenty-seven enemy planes to his credit)[9] that Lindbergh entered the operations "shack" of the renowned 475th Fighter Group (Satan's Angels) of the Fifth Air Force, where Colonel MacDonald, who was the group commander, was absorbed in a game of checkers and did not immediately catch the name of the tall civilian standing behind him. Lindbergh stated his business, which was to test out P-38s, but MacDonald's interest continued to linger on

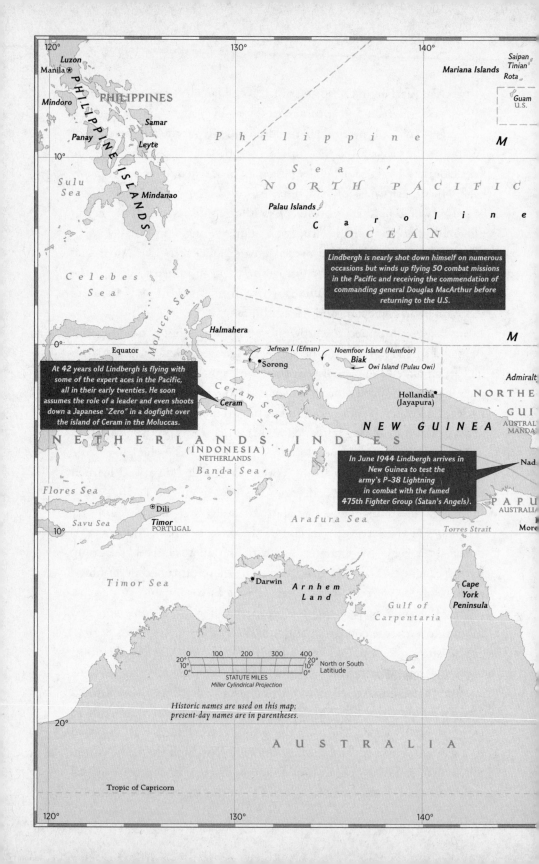

120°   130°   140°

Luzon
Manila ⊕
Mindoro

PHILIPPINES

PHILIPPINE ISLANDS

Panay
Samar
Leyte

Mindanao

*Sulu
Sea*

*Celebes
Sea*

Molucca Sea

Equator   0°

Halmahera

Jefman I. (Efman)
Sorong

Ceram

Ceram Sea

NETHERLANDS INDIES
(INDONESIA)
NETHERLANDS

Banda Sea

Flores Sea

Dili
Timor
PORTUGAL

Savu Sea

10°

Philippine

Sea

NORTH PACIFIC

OCEAN

Caroline

Palau Islands

C

Saipan
Tinian
Rota

Mariana Islands

Guam
U.S.

M

M

Noemfoor Island (Numfoor)
Biak
Owi Island (Pulau Owi)

Hollandia
(Jayapura)

NEW GUINEA

Admiralt

NORTHE
GUI
AUSTRAL
MANDA

Nad

PAPU
AUSTRALI

More

Arafura Sea

Torres Strait

Lindbergh is nearly shot down himself on numerous
occasions but winds up flying 50 combat missions
in the Pacific and receiving the commendation of
commanding general Douglas MacArthur before
returning to the U.S.

At 42 years old Lindbergh is flying with
some of the expert aces in the Pacific,
all in their early twenties. He soon
assumes the role of a leader and even shoots
down a Japanese "Zero" in a dogfight over
the island of Ceram in the Moluccas.

In June 1944 Lindbergh arrives in
New Guinea to test the
army's P-38 Lightning
in combat with the famed
475th Fighter Group (Satan's Angels).

Timor Sea

Darwin

**Arnhem
Land**

*Gulf of
Carpentaria*

**Cape
York
Peninsula**

0   100   200   300   400
20°
10°
0°
STATUTE MILES
Miller Cylindrical Projection

20°
10°
0°
North or South
Latitiude

Historic names are used on this map;
present-day names are in parentheses.

20°

AUSTRALIA

Tropic of Capricorn

120°   130°   140°

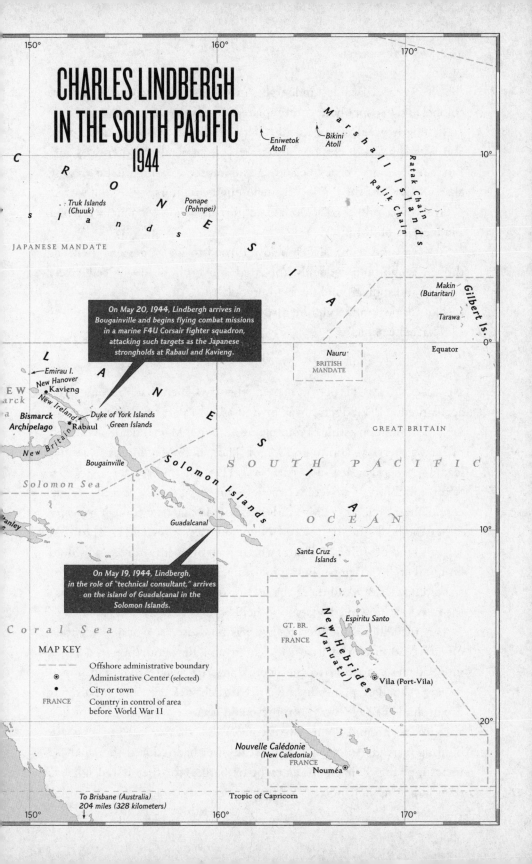

CHARLES LINDBERGH IN THE SOUTH PACIFIC
1944

Eniwetok Atoll

Bikini Atoll

Marshall Islands

Ratak Chain

Ralik Chain

C
R
O
N
E
S
I
a
n
d
s

Truk Islands (Chuuk)

Ponape (Pohnpei)

JAPANESE MANDATE

M I C R O N E S I A

Makin (Butaritari)

Tarawa

Gilbert Is.

Equator

Nauru
BRITISH MANDATE

On May 20, 1944, Lindbergh arrives in Bougainville and begins flying combat missions in a marine F4U Corsair fighter squadron, attacking such targets as the Japanese strongholds at Rabaul and Kavieng.

L A N E S I A

Emirau I.
New Hanover
Kavieng
New Ireland

EW
arck
a

Bismarck Archipelago

Duke of York Islands
Green Islands

Rabaul

New Britain

GREAT BRITAIN

Bougainville

Solomon Islands

S O U T H   P A C I F I C

Solomon Sea

anley

Guadalcanal

O C E A N

10°

On May 19, 1944, Lindbergh, in the role of "technical consultant," arrives on the island of Guadalcanal in the Solomon Islands.

Santa Cruz Islands

Coral Sea

MAP KEY

Espiritu Santo

GT. BR. & FRANCE

New Hebrides (Vanuatu)

Vila (Port-Vila)

⊙ — — — Offshore administrative boundary
⊙ Administrative Center (selected)
• City or town
FRANCE Country in control of area before World War II

20°

Nouvelle Calédonie (New Caledonia)
FRANCE

Nouméa ⊙

To Brisbane (Australia)
204 miles (328 kilometers)

Tropic of Capricorn

150°   160°   170°

the checkerboard while Lindbergh shuffled around awkwardly and the colonel and his opponent contemplated their moves.

At length MacDonald asked, "What did you say your name was, and what phases of the operation are you particularly interested in?" Lindbergh restated his name and said he wanted to compare the fighting characteristics of the P-38 with single-engine fighters.

"Are you a pilot?" MacDonald inquired, having seen no wings on Lindbergh's uniform.

"Yes" was the reply. MacDonald returned to his game, and then—as though a lightbulb suddenly appeared above his head—he reflexively cringed and spun around for a closer look.

"Not *Charles* Lindbergh!" he gasped.

"That's my name."

BY CHOW TIME THAT EVENING the two men had become well acquainted and Lindbergh was invited to be a part of a combat patrol next morning, consisting of four planes: Colonel MacDonald's and those of Major Meryl M. Smith and Major Thomas B. McGuire (the second leading American ace of World War II, with thirty-eight victories). After Lindbergh had left to retrieve his baggage the deputy group commander exclaimed, "My God! He shouldn't go on a combat mission! When did he fly the Atlantic? . . . Nineteen twenty-seven? [He's] too old for this kind of stuff." McGuire, who was all of twenty-three and would be Lindbergh's wingman in the morning, spoke up: "I'd like to see how the old boy does." And there the matter rested until the patrol took off the next morning for the Japanese-held bases of Jefman and Samate.

As it turned out, Lindbergh's age was no cause for worry. They took off at 10:28 after the weather cleared and flew four hundred miles into Japanese territory to the enemy airstrips where they had hoped to catch Japanese planes in the air. No such luck, and the antiaircraft fire around the fields was so intense and accurate (black bursts of flak appeared all around them at 9,000 feet) that they decided to go barge hunting instead. American air and sea power had reduced the Japanese to resupplying their troops at night by barges, for they dared not use their large ships anymore.

Flying up the coast Lindbergh's patrol sighted a barge almost immediately, anchored about two hundred yards offshore and camouflaged with branches and leaves. The enemy had cleverly placed its barges in coves close to towering cliffs so that Allied pilots would have to either fire while banking or do a chandelle—a climbing 180-degree turn—and "any error in judgment would leave you crashed on a mountain," Lindbergh observed.

It was risky and dangerous business, but they destroyed the barge and moved to the next cove, where there were two more barges, one of them much larger than the others. Lindbergh made an accurate hit with both his .50-caliber guns and his 20 millimeter cannon, and the thing burst into flame as its fuel tanks exploded. They continued on, destroying more enemy barges and occasionally being shot at by antiaircraft guns in what Colonel MacDonald had described as an "anti-boredom mission," until their fuel ran low and they returned to base six hours and twenty minutes after they had departed. That night in the operations shack, "Lindbergh was no longer a visitor," Colonel MacDonald said. "He was a fighter pilot and he talked like one." Lindbergh further surprised the 475th veterans by revealing that he had flown fifteen combat missions with the marines during the Solomon Islands campaign. "He wasn't the novice we had thought him to be," MacDonald wrote later."[10]

Next morning, June 28, there was no mission, so Lindbergh decided to take a walk in the woods. No one wanted to go with him, and he was strongly advised, "You'd better take a .45," as there were still Japanese stragglers roaming the jungle. Sometimes, they even came sneaking into the American encampments intending to steal food. On the upside, word was that the jungle had long since rusted their guns, so they were not as dangerous.

Lindbergh took his pistol, canteen, compass, and a chocolate bar and marched off down one of the trails that led into the camp. Soon he was swallowed up by the triple-canopy equatorial undergrowth—lush, steaming, dim, green, and alive with a riot of magnificently colored birds squawking in the treetops. After about half a mile he came upon the ruins of an ancient Dutch mill beside a bubbling jungle stream that pooled into clear water shallows. He followed the trail for nearly two more miles and finally found a large rock to sit on where he munched his candy bar and ruminated over troublesome sights and conversations he had encountered ever since he'd arrived in the South Pacific.

He lamented the way American troops treated the bodies of dead Japanese, such as sticking their severed heads on posts, as he had witnessed in the Solomons, and the cavalier attitude by the average foot soldier toward mistreating or killing Japanese prisoners of war. A marine general, no less, had approvingly told the story of two old jungle hands slitting the throat of a prisoner after offering him a cigarette, merely to impress a noncombat sergeant. Such savagery repelled Lindbergh, who felt there was something racial about it. On the other hand, he was continuously told by experienced troops that "they do the same thing to us." He was appalled when American pilots discussed machine-gunning Japanese pilots dangling in parachutes after bailing out of their planes, but the same rationale applied: "They do it to us."

It was not Lindbergh's idea of war. Perhaps he was naive, or perhaps a lot of the stories he'd heard were merely soldiers' billingsgate. Whatever it was, he had not heard, or seen, the last of it. "They have no respect for death," he wrote of the troops, "the courage of the enemy soldier, or many of the ordinary decencies of life. They think nothing of robbing the body of a dead Jap and call him a 'son-of-a-bitch' while they do so. I do not see how we can claim we represent a civilized state if we killed them with torture."

Before he left the jungle, Lindbergh found time to stop and strip naked and swim for half an hour in one of the clear pools; it made him feel cleaner.

The 475th's next mission was to bomb the airstrip on a Japanese-held island, but they turned out to be poor marksmen. A flight of twin-engine Douglas A-20 medium bombers were dropping their loads and causing havoc on the enemy runways when the 475th arrived on the scene. When it became Lindbergh's turn—he was the only one among them with any recent dive-bombing experience—he "rolled off the edge of a squall," came in steady and level, then dove, releasing the bomb at 2,500 feet, and then he pulled out with a big blast on the runway behind him. But most of the others' bombs landed in the jungle or the ocean and they returned to Hollandia amid much grumbling and dissatisfaction, mostly arguing along the lines that the P-38 was designed as a fighter, not a bomber.

However, the P-38s would be "hauling freight," as the men derisively called bombing, for much of the rest of the war.[11]

Next day a report came in that thirteen bogies had flown out of the Japanese base at Jefman Island and the 475th went up to intercept, with Lindbergh now leading one of the sections. They flew at treetop level in case the Japanese had radar (by 1944 the Japanese had developed a rough version of the Allied radar) but saw no Japanese planes in the air or on the ground, and no barges to shoot up. All they had to show for their effort were several holes shot in the plane of Lindbergh's wingman and a plane from another squadron was missing. The only bright aspect was revealed when Lindbergh returned from the nearly seven-hour adventure with 210 gallons of fuel remaining in his tanks, while everyone else was near empty.

All the while he had been flying missions in the P-38s, Lindbergh had been fiddling with ways to get improved fuel consumption. By a combination of adjusting the throttle, the fuel mixture, and the manifold pressure and lowering the revolutions per minute, Lindbergh had managed to increase the plane's range by an average of nearly three hundred miles—a tremendous improvement.

Some of the crew chiefs took notice of this and soon, at the behest of Colonel MacDonald, Lindbergh was giving lectures to the assembled squadrons of the 475th on how to manage fuel. By raising manifold pressure and lowering rpms, the pilot could save up to one-third of his usual fuel consumption, which broadened the effective range of the P-38 up to eight hundred miles, Lindbergh told them.

Many of the younger pilots were skeptical, complaining that holding manifold pressure that high would foul their spark plugs and scorch their cylinders. But Lindbergh stood his ground: "These are military engines, built to take punishments, so punish them." He added that "you must make your own decisions. You are the captains of your ships." In the coming days, pilots and mechanics came over to Lindbergh's P-38 after he had finished a mission to inspect what they were sure would be damage and fouling, but to their amazement his engine was perfectly normal. Lindbergh's advice eventually worked its way in to all three squadrons of the Satan's Angels group, and men who previously were limited to six-hour missions were now soaring over enemy territory for eight to ten hours, far in advance of anything the Japanese expected.[12]

Charles Lindbergh had all but become a full-fledged member of the 475th Fighter Group. "Lindbergh was indefatigable," said Colonel MacDonald. "He flew more missions than was normally expected of a combat pilot. He dive-bombed positions, sank barges, and patrolled our landing forces on Noemfoor Island. He was shot at by almost every antiaircraft gun the Nips had in western New Guinea."[13]

The camaraderie among the men of fighter-plane or pursuit squadrons had been famous ever since their appearance in the First World War. It was most especially so in the 475th, stuck as it was between the edge of a hostile jungle and the endless sea. There was no Paris, nor the diversions of Paris, to turn to for leave. Lindbergh was a natural leader, and far from being merely the "old boy" that McGuire had initially taken him for, Lindbergh was soon looked up to by the youthful pilots for guidance and, occasionally, consolation. Because of their age they might have been a bit faster on the stick or the trigger, but Lindbergh had many thousands of flying hours to their hundreds, and even the aces soon came to regard his aeronautical engineering wizardry with a respect bordering on awe. They were flying with Charles A. Lindbergh, the Lone Eagle, they told each other. That he had come to their squadron was a gift from Providence. Then it all seemed to unravel.

The trouble began when Colonel Robert L. Morrissey, Lindbergh's contact at U.S. Army Air Forces headquarters, South West Pacific, told him that a rumor had come in from the Australian army that Lindbergh was flying combat in New Guinea, and if that was true "there should be no more of it." Pressed for more information, Morrissey had none. To Lindbergh, it "look[ed] like politics." Had Roosevelt or someone in his cabinet found out?

Next morning he took off in a P-38 for headquarters at Nadzab to see the commanding general. Once there, the situation began to brighten. It seemed that Lindbergh's orders had been misplaced and it was merely a technical snag. While he was waiting for clarification, Lindbergh used the opportunity to visit with his longtime friend Lieutenant Colonel Archie Roosevelt, one of TR's sons, who was recuperating from a shrapnel wound suffered during the invasion of Biak Island two months earlier. The two old America Firsters got a laugh, he said, as they compared the combat records of "those of us who opposed getting into it," Lindbergh said, "[which] are far better than those who demanded intervention."

After dinner and an early turn-in, Lindbergh prepared to rejoin his comrades in the 475th in the morning. Instead, he was awakened at midnight by an army colonel with a message that had just arrived from Brisbane requesting him to come immediately to Allied headquarters. It was signed, simply, "MacArthur."

LINDBERGH TOOK OFF FOR BRISBANE at the crack of dawn next day. First he visited General Kenney, who was friendly but firm. Apparently the problem arose when rumors had filtered back to headquarters that Lindbergh "had somehow managed to get into the forward areas in New Guinea without their knowing about it" (a serious offense in itself) but, worse, that Lindbergh "was flying combat missions with the army squadrons," which violated every regulation in the book.

If the Japanese caught him, Kenney fulminated, then Lindbergh, as a civilian in combat, "would have [his] head chopped off immediately." Kenney then began to carp about the navy giving Lindbergh orders to come into the theater without going through MacArthur's headquarters. Lindbergh responded that he had turned his orders over to the proper authorities when he arrived, and "had been under the impression that all formalities had been satisfactorily met." Further, he told General Kenney that the last thing he wanted to do was cause trouble.

Kenney was "very decent" about it, Lindbergh said, and told him he would cut orders so that he could remain in New Guinea but asked him to refrain from any more combat flying. Lindbergh replied that he didn't want to go back to the front and just sit around, that the best way for him to properly evaluate the problems associated with the P-38 would be to test the plane under combat conditions, and that his recommendations might save lives. Wasn't there some way around the regulations?

Suddenly Kenney "became thoughtful and his eyes twinkled," Lindbergh said, and "the ice was broken." Kenney told Lindbergh he would put him on observer status, which allowed flying but no shooting, adding with a wink that "no one back in the States will know whether you use your guns or not."

Kenney picked up the phone and raised General Sutherland, MacArthur's chief of staff. He explained the situation and recommended letting Lindbergh continue his assessment of the army's fighter aircraft at the front. Sutherland's response was to ask to see Lindbergh personally.

The chief of staff received Charles very warmly, inquiring about their mutual friend Colonel (now General) Truman Smith. At one point Lindbergh mentioned what he was doing vis-à-vis fuel conservation and the fighter planes, and the crusty chief of staff not only perked up but immediately suggested they go in to see General MacArthur, whom Lindbergh had once met when he was the army's chief of staff in the 1930s.

The general, who "looked younger" than Lindbergh had expected, was riveted to learn about the notion of lengthening the fighter's range. Lindbergh explained that with adjustments in fuel mixture and manifold pressure the P-38 consumed only fifty gallons of gasoline per hour at cruising speed instead of its usual eighty. This would give the fighter more air time, which would stretch its effective radius three hundred additional miles. It was a stunning revelation.

When Lindbergh told MacArthur that, without any modifications whatever, his fighter planes were capable of an 800-mile radius, the commanding general was astounded. Such a thing would be "a gift from heaven," MacArthur exclaimed, and highly important to his battle plans. As Colonel MacDonald explained it later, "It meant the bombers could hit targets three hundred miles farther out [than was previously possible] and still have their 'little friends' along. This was the greatest advantage. Lindbergh had, in effect, redesigned an airplane."

When the general asked if Lindbergh would return and instruct all the fighting groups in his fuel-saving techniques, Lindbergh replied, "There was nothing [I] would rather do," suggesting that he would go back and begin at once.

At last it was settled; Lindbergh was a welcome addition to the South Pacific theater of war. "He [MacArthur] said I could have any kind of plane I wanted, and do any kind of flying I wanted to," Lindbergh wrote in his journal. Then, to Lindbergh's astonishment, MacArthur took him into his confidence and revealed in detail his entire present and future battle plans, on the maps, against the empire of Japan. In retrospect it seems like a dangerous thing to have done, since Lindbergh, technically a civilian, could have been captured and, if not immediately shot or beheaded, somehow forced to reveal the information. But MacArthur was a world unto himself.

After his meeting with MacArthur, Lindbergh went out shopping in Brisbane, marveling that "no one recognizes me here." He bought a spool of thread, a shaving stick, and shoe polish and visited a zoological park where he saw kangaroos, wallabies, and koalas. Next morning he was airborne for the fighting front in his own personal P-38, courtesy of General Douglas MacArthur.

THE SOUTH PACIFIC IS LITTERED with small islands and the Japanese had crawled all over them like an army of ants, building small airstrips, turning them into stationary, unsinkable aircraft carriers from which to interdict Allied shipping. Many of these would have to be cleared out before MacArthur could make the big move north to fulfill his famous promise to the Philippines—"I shall return." Thus, fighter command had moved on northward to the small speck of Owi Island, next to the much larger Biak Island, eighty miles off the northern coast of New Guinea, where heavy fighting was still in progress.

From Owi, Lindbergh began his lessons instructing the various fighter squadrons of the South West Pacific in fuel conservation techniques. He continued to fly on combat missions with Colonel MacDonald and the 475th. In the evenings, he would sometimes walk to the top of a coral cliff that was a stone's throw from the tent serving as officers' quarters and watch the fighting on nearby Biak. After two months of steady slaughter, the Japanese abandoned the tactic of the banzai charge, which they discovered used up all the men too quickly, and were engaged in a shot-for-shot slugging match with American soldiers.

It turned out to be one of the worst battles of the war. The Japanese had an army of more than eleven thousand on Biak when the United States invaded on May 27, 1944, with approximately thirteen thousand men from the Forty-first Infantry Division. By the end of July the Japanese had been pressed back from their airfield into a long, sharp coral ridge honeycombed with interlocking caves that were perfect for defense. Thus far they had thrown back all of the U.S. infantry attacks and were holding out with about five hundred ragged soldiers, all that remained of the original force.

From his vantage point on Owi, Lindbergh could clearly see the brownish coral ridge where the Japanese were dug in, rising out of the green jungle on Biak Island, and hear the distant boom and crash of artillery and see flashes of explosions. One day from his cliff Lindbergh watched the final assault on the Japanese caves. It was preceded by a tremendous air strike of thousand-pound bombs from eight B-24s, flying low, as there was no antiaircraft fire. Lindbergh could actually see the bombs being released, causing tremendous explosions. Then the artillery began its bombardment in preparation for the infantry attack.

The attack, however, proved unnecessary; the infantry had moved in and occupied the area barely firing a shot. They found Japanese and parts of Japanese, and the ones still alive were too dazed from the bombs to do anything but lie or sit placidly on the ground. Two days later Lindbergh and several other officers went over to the Japanese airfield on Biak, which had become the new base of operations for the 475th Fighter Group, and drove a jeep to the site of the Japanese caves.

They came first to a pass clogged with dead Japanese soldiers and marines, "sprawled about in the gruesome positions only mangled bodies can take," Lindbergh said. Some were merely fragments of bodies and severed heads and limbs. There were unmistakable signs that the American infantry had been prospecting for gold teeth. All over the ridgeline it was the same, torn and battered human bodies, some single, many heaped in piles. They came across a deep pit crammed with dead bodies and, to Lindbergh's horror, topped off with garbage from the American soldiers' encampment, an indignity he found utterly repugnant.

They located an entrance to the caves and descended into the pit on a rickety thirty-foot Japanese ladder. Using his Abercrombie & Fitch flashlight, Lindbergh threw a beam on the dripping walls and the floor, littered with ammunition, food crates, rifles and machine guns, and souring bags of rice; in each of the caves' many offshoots and tunnels lay dead and stinking bodies and, in some of them, charred bones and skulls where the flamethrowers had done their grisly work. At the entrance to one cave was the headless body of a Japanese soldier in an upright position, roped to a pole, it was said, by his comrades for trying to surrender to the Americans. It was as gruesome a tableau as could be taken in on a single afternoon, and when they could stand it no longer Lindbergh and his companions drove away in their jeep to a nearby spring—close enough that it had probably been used by the Japanese in the caves, he said—where they stripped down and tried to wash away the stench and the recollection of the horrors they had seen.

In the morning the 475th, with Lindbergh leading a section, flew cover for a wave of four B-25s in a strike on the Japanese base at Halmahera Island, about five hundred miles farther northwest. Some of the squadron ran into enemy airplanes and shot several of them down. McGuire's kill temporarily made him the theater's leading ace. As an added attraction they had to fly over an erupting volcano that filled their cockpits with sulphurous fumes and in places visibility dropped to zero because of the volcanic ash.

Friday, July 28, seemed to shape up as another routine day. After breakfast, Lindbergh and the other pilots arrived at the airstrip on Biak at dawn and took off shortly afterward; their destination: Japanese airstrips on the large island of Ceram in the Moluccas, reported to have strong fighter forces.

A storm nearly forced the group commander to call off the mission. They had climbed to 18,000 feet but still could not top it out. They nevertheless pressed on, a flight of eighteen twin-engine P-38s. As they approached the Japanese airstrips the weather cleared, but when they dropped down to 10,000 feet no enemy planes could be seen on the runways. The Japanese were very good at hiding planes or flying them away if necessary when American fighters appeared.

They continued on to secondary targets but nothing seemed worth shooting at. They then turned east to return toward Biak when suddenly the radios came alive with the sounds of a dogfight.

"There he is now. Go in and get him!"

"Can't somebody shoot him down?"

"Goddamn, I'm out of ammunition!"

Neither Lindbergh nor any others of the 475th were able to see the action and Colonel MacDonald radioed asking the location of the fight. Two Mitsubishi Sonias, two-man fighter reconnaissance planes, it seemed, were returning from an air rescue mission for one of their downed pilots when they came to the attention of American pilots of the 49th Fighter Group (code word "Captive" squadron), who were flying above, and a melee ensued. One of the Mitsubishis was piloted by the veteran pilot Captain Saburo Shimada, and the other by the highly experienced Sergeant Saneyoshi Yokogi. For all of their vaunted prowess, the American aviators were finding themselves outflown by the skillful Japanese fliers.[14]

"The son of a bitch is making monkeys out of us!" blared the radio.

"I'm out of ammunition, too."[15]

Two of the 49th's pilots at last engaged one of the Mitsubishis and a lengthy burst from behind put Sergeant Yokogi on a long, smoking death glide into the sea. That left Captain Shimada, who for nearly thirty minutes had successfully fought off the entire Captive Squadron, had run several of them out of ammunition, and during this aerial dogfight had drawn them back toward the Japanese base and its antiaircraft guns at Amahi aerodrome.

Meanwhile, MacDonald's group was "frantically searching for the fight." As they banked around a great pulsing thunderhead immediately ahead they saw the puffs of flak and smoke of 20 millimeter cannon fire that revealed the aerial battle. MacDonald led the dive, releasing his drop tanks and firing a short burst that spattered the Zero but did not seem to hurt it. Shimada was trapped, and knew it, but he decided to fight it out anyway. He jerked his plane left in a violent banking dive that caught MacDonald's fliers off guard. Two of the 475th thought they had him dead to rights, but just as they were about to press the triggers, by ferocious maneuvering Shimada masterfully vanished from their gun sights. Then along came Lindbergh.

The Japanese plane was just coming out of its wrenching turn, its mottled green camouflage contrasting with the bright red Rising Sun insignia, when Shimada came face-to-face with the Lone Eagle, flying at him head-on at a combined speed of 500 miles per hour. Colonel MacDonald could only watch as the wing edges of the Zero lit up "like so many acetylene torches" as Shimada fired at Lindbergh. Lindbergh himself "instinctively sighted on the Mitsubishi's radial engine and pressed the buttons." His P-38 shuddered at the recoil for at least six seconds as the two planes closed in on a no-win collision course. Bits of Shimada's propeller flew off, he was hit badly, but he appeared determined to simply slam his plane into Lindbergh's.

At almost the last possible moment Lindbergh yanked up on the stick with all his might. Shimada also pulled up, "trying for a crash," but Lindbergh averted him by a matter of feet—maybe even inches. He was close enough to be shuddered by the air shock as he shot past the Zero, which, as had its erstwhile companion, rolled into a long, smoking death spiral and splattered into the ocean below.

Lindbergh's wingman Lieutenant Joseph E. "Fishkiller" Miller (so named for erroneously dropping bombs into the ocean, causing thousands of stunned fish to surface) had also taken a run at the stricken Japanese plane but, as he declared afterward, "I was there. The old man got a Sonia fair and square . . . I blew some pieces off the wing, but it was Mr. Lindbergh's victory." Congratulations were in order when Lindbergh and the 475th returned to base.

A few days later Lindbergh almost flew his final mission when the 475th, using his fuel economy measures, ventured all the way north to the Palau Islands, looking for a fight. They found one that quickly turned into a melee, leaving Lindbergh with a Zero on his tail, a situation "that could not have been worse," according to Colonel MacDonald. The Japanese plane was faster and appeared larger and larger in Lindbergh's rearview mirror, as he hunched low in his seat, trying to squeeze all of himself behind the armor plating in back of it, waiting for the bullets to slam home. Colonel MacDonald watched in horror as the Zero's tracers flickered out, embracing Lindbergh's P-38, and yelled out, "Break right! Break right!" Lindbergh responded by putting his plane in a ferociously tight right turn that brought the dogfight directly in the line of sight of MacDonald's section, which saved the Lone Eagle's bacon by shooting the Zero to pieces.

Word of Lindbergh's close encounter spread. When they returned Colonel MacDonald was summoned to higher headquarters where he was reprimanded and grounded for two months. Everyone assumed it was because he had allowed the Lone Eagle to get in harm's way, but that wasn't it. It seems that bomber command had been requesting fighter cover over Palau from the 475th (a mission that the fighter pilots loathed as boring), and MacDonald had been turning them down on grounds that the distance was too great. Now they had flagrantly disproved their own argument by flying all the way up there and back—using Lindbergh's fuel-saving techniques—to engage in dogfights. General Kenney, however, modified MacDonald's punishment by granting him the same two months as leave to go back to the States to his wife and newborn son, whom the colonel had never seen.

For Lindbergh, there were dogfights yet to come, some ending in tragedy but most with the Americans wildly victorious. He had become especially fast friends with twenty-three-year-old Tommy McGuire (the two were also roommates) who would remain the second leading Pacific war ace. Five months later McGuire was killed during a dogfight over the Philippines, but he was posthumously awarded the Medal of Honor for distinguished valor in his flying career.

In early August 1944, Lindbergh concluded his tour of the Second World War in the Pacific with fifty combat missions to his credit, a Zero kill, and enough information to draw informed conclusions about the contrast between single-engine versus twin-engine fighter planes. In the process he had immeasurably helped MacArthur's slow crawl northward from New Guinea to the Philippines by giving his fighters—and thus his bombers—some three hundred more miles of range in a watery wasteland where three hundred miles could be an eternity.

CHARLES LINDBERGH HAD MADE an uneasy peace with his conflicted reasoning and emotions about the war. He still felt he'd been right in supporting the America First Committee, and as time went on his original fears began to manifest themselves as Stalin's totalitarian Soviet Union continued to absorb nation after eastern European nation into the great maw of communism. He had been wrong about England, however, and consequently the fate of western Europe, which he freely admitted. England had been the bulwark that saved them. Against Lindbergh's predictions of defeat, she had defended herself triumphantly against the onslaught of Göring's Luftwaffe in the Battle of Britain (which left 544 of her fliers and 24,000 British citizens dead) and became for a time the lone outpost of Western Civilization from which the Allies launched the fight against Nazism and then the strain to contain communism.

As for himself, when word got out to the public about Lindbergh's exploits in the Pacific, there was a kind of general softening among the American people who rejoiced that their hero was indeed genuine. This was expressly reinforced when *Collier's,* one of the most widely read and respected magazines of its day, carried a two-part series in early 1946 by Colonel MacDonald titled "Lindbergh in Battle." MacDonald described in glowing terms all of the Lone Eagle's contributions to the war effort, including the fact that he flew as a volunteer on more combat missions than regular army fighter pilots were required to do. Roosevelt was dead, and no one seemed anxious to take up the old animosities. Indeed, Lindbergh's services were once more embraced by the military. It wasn't a complete vindication, especially by the eastern press, but it was a strong beginning.*

For Lindbergh, the war had been a breathtaking revelation. For nearly two decades he had stood out—along with Rickenbacker—as the foremost proponent of the notion that the airplane, and all the applied science that went with it, was a tremendous force for good in civilization. What Lindbergh had seen with his own eyes in the war now convinced him that it might not be so anymore, that airplanes had become monumental engines of destruction including, along with the atomic bomb, the possible annihilation of life on the planet. Use of the airplane in expanding "civilization" to all parts of the earth also brought with it a more subtle kind of destruction, which Lindbergh had noticed with the miserable inhabitants of the Solomon Islands and New Guinea, who now disrupted their own simple civilizations with so-called cargo cults. These quasi-religious rites, which lasted into the 1980s, fixated natives on the anticipated return of the dominant culture's airplanes, which had brought gifts of trinkets but departed forever after the war ended.

It wasn't simply the airplane but science itself, Lindbergh concluded, that had taken such gigantic leaps in recent years, and as a result, it universally threatened civilization as well as aided it. He began to call for a stepping back of sorts, a retrenchment to old values. With the advances of science he saw moral perspective being lost. Science and technology practically took on the role of religion, so that man was actually worshipping at the altar of science, a fallacy, if not a heresy, that could lead to the undoing of the American spirit. Lindbergh expressed these thoughts in a splendid speech while accepting the Wright Brothers Memorial Trophy at the Washington Aero Club in January 1946. Titling his speech "Honoring

---

* The exceptions to the general forgiveness of Lindbergh's prewar positions included many people of Jewish descent who have carried notions of his betrayal with them throughout the years. It is understandable, since it was their people undergoing the suffering at the hands of the Nazis, and they gave little credence to his warning that there would be worse suffering under the communists—a point that was at least debatable until the Holocaust.

the Wright Brothers," he took as his theme "the way in which science was divorcing man from his old sense of independence and moral values."[16]

Of the Wright brothers, Lindbergh said, "It is customary and proper to recognize their contribution to scientific progress. But I believe it is equally important to emphasize the qualities in their pioneering life and the character in man that such a life produced. The Wright brothers balanced success with modesty, science, and simplicity. At Kitty Hawk their intellects and senses worked in mutual support. They represented man in balance, and from that balance came wings to lift a world."

What Lindbergh was getting at was the notion that technology had overstepped its bounds, and not just in skewing the sense of balance in man's progress. It was rapidly making a mess of the world around him. The once pristine rivers and creeks near industrial plants were polluted almost beyond recognition, great heaps of scrap and discards lay everywhere, huge tanks of fuel oil blotted the horizon, smokestacks belched out odoriferous if not poisonous fumes on a twenty-four-hour basis, and so forth.

That Lindbergh had the vision to absorb and process all this was remarkable because there existed at the time no organized environmental movement. There were or had been a number of conservationists from time to time, notably Teddy Roosevelt, John Muir, and later Rachel Carson, but "environmentalism" as such was a concept that had not yet been developed. Lindbergh began to embrace the fundamental ideas of conservation, however. In time he became one of the most enthusiastic environmentalists on earth and, as with most passions in his life, one of the most formidable as well.

The war had forced Lindbergh into awkward contradictions. On the one hand he loathed the brutality of it, yet he willingly participated in the killing. He came to see the relentless march of technology as a negative, even a danger, but he was unwilling to give up his concept of flight. The war unquestionably transformed Lindbergh, whipsawed him in major ways. Afterward, his outlook and behavior became increasingly esoteric, introspective, eccentric, and sometimes frankly weird. Even though his war service had rehabilitated him in the eyes of most of the American public, the remainder of Lindbergh's life must have seemed at times like a puzzle, perhaps even to himself.

CHAPTER 14

★ ★ ★ ★ ★

MASTERS OF THE SKY

Jimmy Doolittle nearly didn't make it to Gibraltar, where he was to command the newly formed Twelfth Air Force for the invasion of North Africa. Early in the morning of November 5, 1942, just six and a half months after his historic raid on Japan, Doolittle secretly boarded one of six stripped-down B-17 bombers at a remote base on England's south Channel coast for the eight-hour flight to the Mediterranean "Rock," where temporary headquarters would be located until the invasion was successfully in progress. Passengers on the other planes included General Dwight D. Eisenhower, the overall commander of the operation—which was code-named Torch—as well as Generals Mark Clark, Carl "Tooey" Spaatz, and other high-ranking American and British officers.

Even though German fighters often patrolled the air routes toward their destination, both of the waist guns were removed from the bombers in order to have extra room for passengers and equipment. They retained only three of the six machine-gun positions on each plane and carried no trained gunners. It was a risk but they lived in risky times.

After receiving his Medal of Honor and being made a brigadier general, Doolittle was selected by Hap Arnold and George Marshall as chief of the Twelfth Air Force, which had been activated only two months earlier. Eisenhower, however, had made it plain from the outset he didn't want Doolittle, in all likelihood because he was a reservist and not a regular (West Point) officer. His famous raid on Japan notwithstanding, Doolittle was known mainly as an airplane-racing hotshot.

After the Allies decided it would be impractical and risky to attempt an invasion of France across the English Channel in 1943, Torch was conceived to attack the Axis in its "soft underbelly," as well as to relieve pressure on the Soviet Union, which was being overrun by Nazi armies. The vast areas involved in the North African operation made Doolittle's job doubly difficult, but strong Allied airpower was vital to the success of the plan. To make things even dicier, most of Morocco and all of Algeria and Tunisia, where the main Allied invasion was to take place, were controlled by military forces of the Vichy French, who maintained an uneasy collaboration with the occupying Germans. Their reaction to the arrival of American and British forces remained an open question.

The first sign of trouble occurred at takeoff from Hurn aerodrome. Five of the B-17s were in line on the run-up strip when the plane Doolittle rode in began taxiing toward them. Suddenly the pilot, John Summers, screamed at the copilot, Thomas Lohr—both of them mere twenty-two-year-old lieutenants—"We've lost hydraulic pressure! Hit the wobble pump!" The big four-engine bomber continued to lumber toward the row of B-17s containing the other Twelfth Air Force staff officers. Since all the planes were fully loaded with gasoline, Doolittle realized, there was likely to be an enormous explosion if a collision occurred. Lohr was furiously working the emergency pump to put fluid in the brake cylinders while the other planes sat innocently on the runway, "like birds on a wire," unaware that there was big trouble coasting toward them. Just as it seemed a crash was unavoidable Summers, still yelling "Pump! Pump!," stomped the left brake, which grabbed the tarmac and spun the plane off the runway into the mud, saving the lives of practically the entire Torch command and staff.

The other B-17s took off without a hitch, although the one containing the major general in charge of logistics never made it to Gibraltar. It simply disappeared and was never heard from again. After a day spent repairing and servicing Doolittle's plane, the B-17 took off next morning, heading out over the Atlantic to avoid enemy air patrols. They were about halfway to their destination when, as luck would have it, the pilot glimpsed four German Ju 88s, heavily armed twin-engine fighter-bombers, which had gone out that morning from Biarritz to prey on Allied shipping.

The Junkers immediately turned toward the lone B-17 and broke into pairs. For some tense minutes they respectfully flew on either side of it just out of range, trying to size up the ship's defenses. They had been in the theater long enough to know that a fully armed B-17 was not called a Flying Fortress for nothing. While Doolittle went back to the empty waist gun positions for a better look at the intruders, Torch's chief of staff, General Lyman Lemnitzer, "began to fiddle with the gun in the radio compartment." Presently Lemnitzer, never one to miss an opportunity, for better or worse, let off a blast at the Germans from the twin .50-caliber machine guns.

The sight of flaring tracers provoked the Junkers, which immediately peeled off and lined up to attack. They were armed with four 20 millimeter machine guns firing forward and one or two 20 mm in the rear. The Germans must have concluded that the Americans were manning all guns, however, because they chose not to attack from behind—a preferred angle—but raced around to get ahead and make close, head-on passes, where only the nose gun could get at them. Meantime, Summers dove down on the deck at wave-top level and "firewalled" the throttles, hoping to outrun the Germans and keep them from getting under him. The Americans' situation was clearly desperate—a lone half-armed B-17 with no trained machine gunners aboard, hundreds of miles out in the Atlantic, and set upon by four of the Luftwaffe's most dangerous attack planes.

As the Ju 88s dived and fired, Summers threw the B-17 into a skid, which spoiled the Germans' aim, but they lined up again for another pass. Doolittle watched helplessly through a porthole as Summers turned straight into the oncoming 88s, as if to deliberately bring on a collision. This caused the Germans to sheer off prematurely, but they ripped past blazing away with machine guns and 20 millimeter cannons. Still, the B-17 miraculously seemed to escape hits until, with shocking suddenness, the windshield shattered from a direct strike by one of the 20 mm tracers, which "looked like flaming footballs," hurling glass into the faces of the pilot and copilot before ripping through Lohr's arm and ricocheting around the cockpit, striking the instrument panel and scorching Lohr's scarf in his lap.

Summers and Lohr were temporarily blinded by the flying shards of glass and Lohr, badly injured and bleeding profusely from his wound, staggered from his seat toward the rear of the plane. Summers screamed for Doolittle, who had never flown a B-17, and Jimmy scrambled into

Lohr's place in the copilot's seat. General Lemnitzer was still blasting away with his machine guns but stopped long enough to help Lohr. Meantime, the number three propeller on the plane "began to run away," caused apparently by damage to its governor sometime during the attack. This put them in immediate risk of its tearing loose and chopping into their own fuselage, "like a giant power saw." If it did, Doolittle said, "it could cut the plane in half." While Summers struggled to keep the B-17 from plunging into the sea, Doolittle tried to figure out how to feather the third engine prop. And there were still the German fighters to contend with.

The 88s continued their attacks from head-on, but apparently on their next pass General Lemnitzer hit one of them, and mercifully the third engine prop slowed down somewhat on its own, indicating to Doolittle that the rpm governor was not entirely out of action. Then, without so much as a howdy do, the four German fighters, one belching smoke, broke off the battle and headed for the coast. After the war, German records showed the Ju 88s had been low on gas from their patrol and nearly ran out of fuel on their way back to Biarritz. Using the B-17's first aid kit officers managed to stanch the flow of blood from Lohr's arm and the plane made it to the Rock of Gibraltar without further incident.

The North African invasion was a success, but not without serious casualties, many of them inflicted by the Vichy French, and the going from there on, with General George S. Patton commanding the ground troops, was painfully and bloodily slow. Doolittle and Patton, however, got on famously; "Old Blood and Guts" was most appreciative of the support his men received from the Twelfth Air Force.

The German reaction to the landings was to conduct ferocious bombing and tank attacks against the Allies as they moved eastward toward Tunisia and the Egyptian desert. These included frequent attacks on Doolittle's airfields, and in one of them a German bomb killed his faithful crew chief Paul Leonard, who had consoled him on the Chinese hillside amid the wreckage of his plane.

While in Gibraltar, Doolittle first learned from one of Roosevelt's radio addresses on the armed forces radio that three of his Tokyo raiders who had been captured had been executed by the Japanese. The president called it "barbarous." He also learned that the carrier *Hornet* had been sunk in the Battle of the Santa Cruz Islands. His own boys were grown up now; the oldest, James, was a combat pilot in the South Pacific, while John was in his first year at West Point. During this time, Jimmy wrote home once a week to Joe, who was busy christening ships for the navy and raising funds for servicemen, but his letters were mostly confined to small talk for security reasons.

Doolittle turned out to be excellent in high command, though the largest unit he had previously commanded was the raid on Japan. Now he led an air force of fifteen thousand men—one thousand of them officers—which would grow to twice that size before the year was out. Three weeks after the landings he was promoted to major general. He was very much a hands-on leader, who made a point of showing up at a combat squadron right before a bombing mission and climbing aboard one of the planes. It not only gave the fliers confidence to have the commanding general along on a mission, but it gave Doolittle firsthand knowledge of the problems they were experiencing. It also gave Ike Eisenhower fits, because as an air force commander Doolittle knew about Ultra, the high-priority top secret interception and decoding of German secret messages, and if he were shot down and captured he might be forced to reveal his knowledge of this vital source of intelligence.

One of the best illustrations of Doolittle's leadership strategy came when Jimmy got word that many crews of the B-26 Marauder were rebelling against flying the twin-engine medium bomber, mainly due to its aerodynamic characteristics and high landing speeds. There were so many fatal accidents the B-26 had become known as a killer plane, or "widowmaker," but Doolittle was determined to show the men that the aircraft should be "respected but not feared."

He took his personal B-26 around to the various B-26 combat units and had the men assembled beforehand beside the runway. While they looked on, he would perform a perfect no-bounce landing, taxi up, feather the props, and climb out along with his crew chief, who was wearing coveralls. That in itself told the fliers Doolittle was serious, for regulations required both a pilot and copilot fly the B-26. Then he would select one of the assembled number to go for a plane ride with him while the others watched from the ground.

At one of the B-26 units Doolittle selected as his demonstration partner Major Paul W. Tibbets, who would go on in 1945 to pilot the

Enola Gay when it dropped the first atomic bomb over Japan. Doolittle informed Tibbets, "It's just another airplane. Let's start it up and play with it." Then, as Tibbets recounted in his memoirs, they began circling the field at 6,000 feet when Doolittle abruptly cut one of the engines and flew the plane all over the sky in full view of the startled pilots below. "Suddenly, he put the plane into a dive," Tibbets remembered, "built up excess speed and put it into a perfect loop—all with one engine dead." When they got to the bottom of the loop, Tibbets said, Doolittle restarted the engine and they made a low pass over the field, banked, and performed a perfectly smooth landing. "It was an important start," Tibbets remembered, "in convincing [the pilots and operations people] that the B-26 was just another airplane."[1]

On the battleground, the British under Bernard Montgomery drove Rommel's German army westward out of Egypt in a pincers maneuver into the waiting arms of Patton, who was thrusting his army eastward out of Tunisia. The Twelfth Air Force was a critical part of this, as Doolittle noted in a confidential memo to his commanders: "We have had losses, but the enemy has paid a price of more than two-to-one for every airplane we have lost."

In April 1943, on the anniversary of the famous raid on Japan, Doolittle convened the first reunion of the raiders when a dozen of his fliers now with the Twelfth Air Force met in a battered farmhouse in North Africa. There, in the middle of the battle, using army-issue coffee cups filled with brandy, they drank their first toast to one another, a tradition they have continued at reunions every year since.

In the 1960s each man acquired a sterling silver goblet of his own to drink the toast with. The goblets have the owner's name engraved on two sides, one side to be seen with the cup standing straight up and the other so it is seen upside down. When one of their number passes away, his goblet is turned over—his name always readable—and placed in a display case at the U.S. Air Force Academy, guarded by two cadets.

A bottle of brandy corked in 1896, the year of Doolittle's birth, also stays in the case. By tradition, when only two raiders remain, these men will uncork the brandy, drink a last toast, return their cups to the case, and the tradition will be ended.

In November of 2013 the final toast of the Doolittle raiders will be made at the National Museum of the U.S. Air Force in Dayton, Ohio. It will have been the raiders' seventy-first reunion.

IN MAY 1943, the battle of North Africa ended with the surrender of 250,000 Axis troops, the last of Rommel's army, whose troopships had been so decimated by Doolittle's fighter-bombers that German and Italian fighting units were unable to escape their fate. Shortly afterward Doolittle received a "Dear Jimmy" letter from Eisenhower, sending him personal congratulations from Roosevelt on a job well done, accompanied by a generous spraying of words such as "superb," "magnificent," etc. The way was now clear for an invasion of Italy as well as a new air force for Jimmy Doolittle.

Late that year Eisenhower decided to split the air duties in the Mediterranean theater. When the Allies landed in Sicily in November the Twelfth Air Force was assigned to perform "tactical" or close support for the U.S. Army, which was marching north through Italy. Meanwhile, a new Fifteenth Air Force, commanded by Doolittle, became responsible for the long-range bombing of targets in southern Germany and other strategic areas.

It was around then that Doolittle paid a visit to his friend George Patton, with whom he had become close during the battles in North Africa and who had gotten himself in hot water with Eisenhower by slapping a soldier who had complained that he "just couldn't take it" at the front. The incident, which had occurred some months earlier, had been revealed by the popular columnist Drew Pearson in his radio broadcast, and newspapers in the United States were demanding Patton's resignation. Staving off calls for a court-martial, Eisenhower reprimanded Patton severely and ordered him to apologize to his entire army, unit by unit. It was one of the most humiliating punishments ever inflicted on a senior U.S. Army commander, and Doolittle felt that "Georgie" might need a little bucking up.

He flew over to Palermo, Sicily, one day, where Patton was in temporary exile as a sort of potted plant for various ceremonial occasions. Doolittle identified himself to the control tower and requested permission to pay his respects to the general. When he landed, Doolittle found Patton waiting for him on the runway in his jeep, with the three-star flags of a lieutenant general adorning the hood, wearing his polished helmet and famous ivory-handled revolvers. Patton, his face beaming like a harvest moon, rushed to Doolittle as soon as he climbed down from the plane, threw his arms around him, and broke into tears exclaiming, "Jimmy, I'm glad to see you. I didn't think anyone would ever call on a mean old son of a bitch like me!"

A STRATEGY CONFERENCE IN CAIRO in late 1943 between Roosevelt and Churchill produced, among other things, orders for Doolittle to report on January 5, 1944, to Supreme Allied Headquarters at Bushy Park, about a dozen miles from London, as the new commander of the Eighth Air Force. It was the choicest plum, as well as the most difficult job of all, for not only did the Eighth have the strategic mission of daily, daytime bombing of Germany, with all of its horrifying casualties (battle deaths would run into five figures); it would also assume the tactical mission of supporting the coming invasion of Normandy in the spring of 1944.

The reason the Eighth was able to stage precision daylight raids over Germany lay in the fact that the B-17s had fighter cover. At the beginning of the war there were few Allied fighters that had the range to escort the big bombers past the coast of France, but over time with drop tanks and other devices long-range fighter cover increased to Berlin itself and even farther eastward. Still, there was something Doolittle found awry when he took over. Although the fighters had cut down on casualties during the B-17 raids they had yet to clear the skies of German fighters, which remained a dangerous threat to American troops as well as to aircraft. In addition, the Germans had found a way to arm their attack ships with rockets and other weapons that outranged the B-17 defenses.

Doolittle had been at Bushy Park less than a week when he walked into the headquarters of the Eighth's Fighter Command and noticed a sign above the desk of the commander, General William E. Kepner, that read:

THE FIRST DUTY OF THE EIGHTH AIR FORCE FIGHTERS
IS TO BRING THE BOMBERS BACK ALIVE.

"Who dreamed that up?" Doolittle asked Kepner.

"It was here when we arrived" was the answer.

"Take the sign down. That statement is no longer in effect," Doolittle told the startled Kepner. "Put up a new sign," he continued, reading:

THE FIRST DUTY OF THE EIGHTH AIR FORCE FIGHTERS
IS TO DESTROY GERMAN FIGHTERS.

Kepner looked at Doolittle uncomprehendingly for a moment, then choked up; tears had come to his eyes. For two years he had been begging permission for his fighters to pursue the enemy and was repeatedly turned down. As a fighter pilot like Doolittle, Kepner understood that both the fighters and their pilots were designed for aggressive and offensive action, but much to the consternation of Kepner and his aviators they had been kept on the defensive as escorts. Doolittle told them now to go after the German fighters and shoot them down before they even got near the bombers. And if the Germans refused to rise up after the bombers, then he told them to seek out and destroy them on their flying fields.

It was an entirely new concept in modern aerial warfare, and as far as Doolittle was concerned it "was the most important and far-reaching military decision I made during the war."

At this time Doolittle had more than five thousand combat planes under his command, including twenty-five heavy bomber groups and fifteen fighter groups. (He would soon have twice that number.) Among the 250,000 men of the Eighth were the actors Clark Gable and Van Heflin, who served in public relations, and Jimmy Stewart, who was a bomber pilot. Besides the Germans, Doolittle's greatest enemy was the weather. He had begun to send out huge attack flights of six hundred planes or more deep into Germany, and the fickle European winter weather gave him fits. Weather forecasting was inexact, to say the least, and there was trouble and danger on both ends. If the target was closed in, there was danger of dropping bombs on innocent civilians and also exposing the planes and crews to unnecessary peril from German fighters and flak. As well, if the typical pea soup weather closed in on the bases back in England before the bombers returned, the crews, who lacked solid instrument training, were in extreme danger of crashing. Doolittle solved part of the problem by sending relays of fighters out ahead of the bombers to check visibility at the targets, but the problem of weather closing in on home base on return was never satisfactorily solved.

Nevertheless, the raids conducted by the Eighth Air Force were spectacularly successful and helped bring the war to an early end. Hermann Göring himself said he knew the war was lost for Germany when he saw the American bombers and their P-51 escorts over the capital city of Berlin. This time Eisenhower personally barred Doolittle from going on big raids, because he knew about not only Ultra,* the secret code-breaking project, but also the invasion plans.

By D-day on the beaches of Normandy there were scarcely any Luftwaffe planes left to intercept the Allied invasion force. Someone on Eisenhower's staff gave Doolittle the mission of low-level saturation bombing by B-17s to clear the way just ahead of the invasion troops as they moved inland from Normandy. It was a bad idea; the B-17 crews were not trained for low-altitude bombing, and about sixty of the twenty-five hundred planes dropped their loads short, killing a hundred U.S. soldiers as well as an army lieutenant general, and wounding five hundred more. Eisenhower's chief of staff blamed Doolittle, who responded that close air support was "not a feasible mission" for the Eighth Air Force. But Eisenhower disagreed, and so the low-level bombing continued, with predictable results. Even with these horrid "friendly fire" casualties, Ike and General Omar Bradley, chief U.S. commander on the ground in France, nevertheless praised Doolittle and the Eighth, saying that the close air-support bombing was what allowed the Allies to break out of Saint-Lô and other points of German resistance.

After Eisenhower moved his headquarters to France Doolittle, who had been promoted to lieutenant general, became the highest-ranking American officer in England. On Christmas Eve, 1944, when the Germans had a considerable part of the U.S. Army on the defensive and the 101st Airborne Division surrounded in Bastogne in the Battle of the Bulge, it was fighters and bombers of the Eighth Air Force that allowed them to break out and retake the offensive. But because of his exalted

---

* He knew as well about Magic, the American project that broke the Japanese naval code.

rank, Doolittle now found himself increasingly in the company of such luminaries as Winston Churchill and the king and queen of England.

When the Germans finally surrendered in May 1945 Doolittle toted up the butcher's bill. The Eighth Air Force had dropped nearly a million tons of bombs, mostly on Nazi Germany, and shot down or destroyed 18,512 enemy aircraft. This, however, came with the price of 43,742 bomber and fighter pilots and crewmen killed, and 4,456 bombers lost. Just when Doolittle thought he'd be headed back to the States, orders came to pack up the Eighth Air Force headquarters and head for the Pacific where, from Okinawa, Doolittle would command the new B-29 bombers in the ongoing attack on Japan. They barely got started when the atomic bombs were dropped on Japan.

At Kadena Air Base, Okinawa, he lived in a tent and rode in a jeep, a substantial comedown from the fashionable London town house and chauffeur-driven Cadillac he'd enjoyed in England. On July 16, 1945, the Eighth Air Force, Pacific, was established. That same day at Los Alamos, New Mexico, the world's first nuclear bomb was exploded. The B-29s had just begun to arrive for the Eighth Air Force when, on August 6, the *Enola Gay* dropped a nuclear device over Hiroshima, and three days later another bomb destroyed Nagasaki. Six days after that Japan surrendered. Doolittle was among those attending the surrender ceremonies on September 2 aboard the battleship *Missouri* in Tokyo Bay.

He returned home to his beloved Joe. They planned to build a home on Monterey Bay, but the army was not yet finished with Doolittle. His presence was desired on all sorts of commissions, boards, and committees, the most important of which, to him, was a panel that outlined the creation of an air force separate from the army, which at last became reality with the National Security Act of 1947. After that, Doolittle resigned from the service and accepted a senior vice presidency and board membership with Shell Oil, which meant living in New York, but Joe was used to the migrant life.

Doolittle watched with dismay the Soviet military buildup of the 1940s and '50s and the takeover of eastern Europe, the Berlin blockade, and the Korean War, which he abhorred on the grounds that the U.S. government had settled for a draw instead of outright victory. He continued to make news by his contributions to the improvement of

flight. In April 1958, while attending a meeting of air force officers in
Puerto Rico, he was shattered by the news that his son and namesake
James Jr.—Jim—had taken his life. Jim had been a major in the air force
and was a veteran combat pilot in the Pacific during World War II and
in Korea. There was no note, and no definite insight as to why he had
committed suicide, only the suggestion that he was despondent "about
his situation in life." It was a blow from which Jimmy would never
fully recover.

Doolittle retired from Shell in 1967, at the age of seventy, but instead
of remaining idle, which he could have comfortably done, he accepted
membership on the boards of several other aviation corporations on the
theory that early retirement leads to the grave. He and Joe bought the
first home they had ever owned, close to the ocean in Santa Monica. He
had long since quit flying but found time now to indulge in his favorite
sports—hunting and fishing—which he had enjoyed since his childhood
in Alaska. He shot birds and fly-fished for trout all over the country and
hunted big game in Africa and Alaska.

In 1978 he and Joe moved into a fashionable retirement community in
Carmel and Jimmy began to resign from his commissions. During these
years many awards of the "lifetime achievement" type came his way;
he was especially pleased at one of these events attended by President
Ronald Reagan, Bob Hope, Charlton Heston, and other luminaries.
Hope's wife, Dolores, said of Joe: "As we know . . . [Jimmy] spent forty-
five years in the air. Joe Doolittle spent forty-five years waiting for him
to land. At military bases, at civilian airports—and sometimes at the end
of a runway that didn't exist until he landed."

In November of 1988 Joe had a stroke and on Christmas Eve she
passed away. Before she died Joe donated her priceless damask tablecloth
with its five hundred–plus embroidered signatures of famous people
they had met to the Smithsonian Institution, where it may be seen
in the Air and Space Museum. She was buried in Arlington National
Cemetery, near Washington, D.C. Jimmy joined her there five years
later, in the autumn of 1993, at the age of ninety-six. After the services
and formal honors a lone fifty-year-old Mitchell B-25 bomber flew
over the grave site, while Jimmy's great-grandson played taps, flawlessly
by all accounts.

NO SOONER HAD EDDIE RICKENBACKER recuperated from his Pacific ordeal than the secretary of war called upon him again for a secret mission. An internecine battle had developed within the Roosevelt administration between the War Department, on the one hand, and the State Department and Roosevelt on the other. At issue was whether the Soviets were making proper use of all the Lend-Lease materials being sent them, in particular heavy shipments of combat aircraft, which might otherwise have gone to American units.* Admiral William Standley, the U.S. ambassador to Moscow, had publicly condemned the Soviet government for being secretive about its use of American Lend-Lease aid, which caused a serious diplomatic brouhaha that caught the attention of Rickenbacker's old friend Secretary of War Henry Stimson. Roosevelt had made it plain he didn't want any pressuring of the Soviets about Lend-Lease for fear that Stalin might become angry and make a separate peace with Hitler. Roosevelt and the State Department rejected all of Stimson's overtures concerning the issue.

That is how matters stood in early April 1943, when Stimson summoned Rickenbacker to Washington and gave him another carte blanche letter ordering any American official anywhere, military or otherwise, to provide Rickenbacker with whatever assistance he needed for any purpose whatever, by order of the United States secretary of war. In fact what Stimson wished was for Rickenbacker to go to Moscow and find out just what in hell the Soviets were doing with all of the stuff coming out of American factories that was being convoyed to them across the Atlantic by the millions of tons and billions of dollars.

Stimson was sure that neither the White House nor the State Department would approve Rickenbacker's mission—not the least because Eddie had been entirely outspoken regarding the Roosevelt administration, and not always positively, in particular of its handling of the war in the Pacific and Roosevelt's involvement with organized labor. Stimson therefore decided to disguise the mission as a goodwill and

---

* Unlike the arrangement with England in which the British traded U.S. war aid in exchange for long-term leases of British military bases around the world, with the Soviets there was U.S.-lend but no corresponding leases or repayment.

fact-finding tour, starting in Casablanca and Algiers, where the Americans were battling the Germans for North Africa. From there, under secret cover, he would travel to and report on the situation at Cairo, at Tehran in British-held Iran, India, China, and, last, Moscow, with a clandestinely stamped passport validating a Rickenbacker visit to the Soviet Union that was secretly arranged at the State Department by Eddie's old friend Edward R. Stettinius, now head of the Lend-Lease program, whom Eddie had known through his association with the Rockefellers.

On April 26 Rickenbacker left Washington for Miami in an army C-54 transport and the first leg of his trip, which would carry him to South America, then across the Atlantic. He was armed with an array of gifts that Adelaide had assembled for important people, paramount among them nylon stockings, cosmetics, cigarettes, and liquor. Cruising for fifteen hundred miles above the vast and empty Sahara desert from Senegal to Morocco, Eddie ventured that if given the choice of spending twenty-four days on the Pacific or twenty-four days on the desert, he would choose the ocean any day.

At each base he visited he would perform his old routine, pepping up the troops, making them feel important, asking what was wrong. He was flying to as many as six groups a day, delivering a forty-five-minute talk to each. At Algiers he met with Eisenhower. Later that evening, while Eddie was having dinner with Jimmy Doolittle, the Germans staged an air raid. The two of them stepped onto the balcony of Doolittle's hotel room to watch the fireworks from U.S. antiaircraft guns. Eddie was fascinated by the terrific artillery show but Doolittle, ever conscious of the calculated risk, soon observed that "all of this stuff they're shooting up there has got to come down" and went back inside. Sure enough next morning Eddie found a twisted hunk of shrapnel on the balcony right near where he'd been standing.

At the behest of Eisenhower, Rickenbacker took on the highly disagreeable task of telling pilots of the Twelfth Air Force, who had been promised they could go home after flying twenty-five combat missions, that such assurances were no longer "operable," due to the demands of the war. It was a terrible position to put Rickenbacker in because the news was both shocking and dreadful, but he was chosen for it, and accepted the challenge, because he was one of the world's most respected airmen. Almost anyone else probably would have been driven from the microphone.

The 94th Aero Pursuit Squadron, Eddie's old outfit from World War I, was stationed in North Africa. Before he left the states, Eddie had a New York jeweler make up gold and enameled "Hat in the Ring" pins, and he handed them out when he visited the squadron's base.

After finally landing in Moscow Rickenbacker soon noticed two men he took to be members of the "secret police" that were shadowing him. Everything in the Soviet Union, he found, was difficult. There were mountains of bureaucratic red tape; secretive, sometimes nonsensical delays; and a sinister, unpleasant air to just about everything. Eddie was prepared to loathe the Soviet Union and everything it stood for, and at first it did not disappoint. Upon meeting Admiral Standley, the ambassador, Rickenbacker said that he wished to see the Russian front, as many Soviet air bases as possible, and Stalin, in that order. Standley thought he was joking, and said so in his diary.[2]

In the meantime word of the famous flier's presence in Moscow got around to the Soviet military and everyone began to clamor for Eddie's attention. This provided Rickenbacker the opportunity to demonstrate his fabled capacity to hold his liquor—in this case vodka—which, as a bourbon drinker, he detested and called "liquid fire." Eddie's capacity to drink Russians into insensibility soon gave him a mythical prestige among the Soviets. One of his admirers was Marshal Georgy Zhukov, who had engineered the defeat of the Germans at Stalingrad.[3] To everyone's astonishment, Zhukov gave Eddie permission to visit any Soviet fighting front or military base he wanted.

First Rickenbacker was taken to the headquarters of the Moscow air defenses deep underground and was startled when the Soviet commander rushed up in a bear hug, crying "Ah, Eddie!" Turned out this officer was the pilot of a plane that had flown from Moscow to California in 1937, and Rickenbacker had entertained him in royal style when he came through New York. When Eddie asked why the Germans were bombing targets five hundred miles inside Russia but not Moscow, the young colonel handed him a stopwatch and picked up the telephone. "I will show you. When I telephone, you push," he said. Eddie pushed the stopwatch and they rushed up to an observation post where the sky was empty. "Suddenly they began to appear," Rickenbacker said, "American P-39s." In thirty-nine seconds, Eddie counted more than a hundred fighter planes. He had his answer.

True to his word, Zhukov's blessing soon had Eddie flying over fields of Russian and Lend-Lease aircraft at the fighting front so well camouflaged they could be discovered only by flying at treetop level. Upon landing he found that all of these aircraft were maintained in fine fighting condition and had accumulated a first-rate battle record against the Germans. So far as he could tell, the Lend-Lease was working in that regard. Rickenbacker also ascertained from Russian aviators that the quality of the German pilots was deteriorating. Either they were sending their best fliers back to Berlin as a result of the round-the-clock bombing by the Eighth Air Force or they were simply running out of good pilot material. In any case, it was a valuable piece of information for Stimson, George Marshall, and Hap Arnold. It certainly wasn't the sort of military intelligence that was coming from the Soviets through regular channels.

In the following weeks Rickenbacker visited the various Russian combat fronts, including the Kursk front, where he was present when the Germans launched their third unsuccessful attack with thousands of tanks. Though the battle was five miles away it sounded like the end of the world. The ground was shaking violently, the entire sky was lit up, and the guns increased to a continuous roar. Rickenbacker was thoroughly impressed by the fortitude and sense of confidence of the Soviet army commanders and their determination not only to defend Russian territory but to "tear [the German army] to shreds." In his report to Stimson Rickenbacker emphasized that nothing he had seen indicated that the Russians would cave in and sign a separate peace with Germany as they had in 1917 during the First World War.

Back in Moscow, Eddie was given a Lend-Lease C-47, a personal pilot and interpreter, and an escort of five Yak fighters. When he protested to the Russian air force general that he didn't think a fighter escort was necessary, the answer was, "If something should happen to you, what do you think would happen to me?" Eddie had the kind of personality, backed up by his well-known flying and racing record, that made people want to take him into their confidence. This, coupled with the copious amounts of vodka that the Soviet officers consumed, made for interesting and enlightening conversations. When Eddie once asked a group of high-ranking Russian officers why they were being so frank in discussing with him what surely must have been secret technical details, he was told, "There are two kinds of foreigners we entertain. One kind is those we must. The other is those we like."

In the meantime, Rickenbacker learned something about Russian communism, including, to his surprise, that work was performed on "the incentive plan"—the higher the quality and quantity of the product, the more pay the worker received, or other emoluments such as better food and housing. "What kind of Communism is *that?*" Rickenbacker demanded. It sounded more like capitalism to him. Also he learned that only those who worked received ration cards and housing. People who, for one reason or another, were unable to perform either begged or starved.

By mid-July Rickenbacker departed after having spent nearly two months in the Soviet Union. Stopping briefly in London, he stayed, as always, at the Savoy, where Winston Churchill sent a car to bring him to Chequers, the country residence of Great Britain's prime ministers, for a briefing. Afterward Eddie returned to the United States by the circle route that Lindbergh had pioneered in 1927, arriving over the Long Island Sound. Below him he noted the hundreds of sailboats and thousands of beachgoers enjoying a Saturday afternoon, while halfway around the world millions of Russians were fighting for their lives.

Initially, the visit to Russia softened Rickenbacker's harsh opinion of communism, and he published a well-received book about his experiences, with the somewhat grandiose title *World Mission.* In it, he theorized that when the war ended Russia, China, and the United States would emerge as world leaders, while the British and French empires crumbled. Eddie was impressed by the Russian people and considered them friendly to the United States. He had not met Stalin, but he did meet his chief deputy Vyacheslav Molotov (of "cocktail" fame), but in the end he had badly misjudged the intentions of the Soviet regime. Likewise, his experience in China had discounted the rise and takeover of Maoist communism. He said that the Russians had shed the old Bolshevik version of Marxism, and they were no longer concerned with taking over other nations and might even emerge from the war as "the greatest democracy in the world." None of this occurred, of course, but at the time his views were reassuring.*

In 1946 Eddie's mother, Elizabeth, died in Los Angeles at the age of eighty-three. That same year his friend Damon Runyon passed away from throat cancer. Eddie had promised to scatter his ashes by plane over lower Manhattan, a pledge he kept even though it was against the law.

In the meantime, Rickenbacker returned to his Eastern Air Lines offices in Rockefeller Center and all of the critical decisions that needed making— purchasing of new planes, training of pilots, new air routes, maintenance, dealing with government regulation, passenger comfort, safety, and the like.†

Commercial airline safety after World War II remained questionable at best. The war had advanced aviation considerably, but there were still terrible issues with the large passenger planes. Wings fell off at an alarming rate, there were midair collisions, crashes on takeoffs and landings, bodies falling from the sky, all gruesomely recorded by photographers and splattered across the pages of newspapers and magazines. The science of metal fatigue had not yet overtaken the forces of thousands of horsepower, pressurized cabins, and the strain of flying at hundreds of miles per hour.

Eddie was justly proud, however, that Eastern was the only airline that had been maintained at a healthy profit and without government subsidy throughout the war and on into the decade of the 1950s. *Time* magazine featured Eddie on its cover in 1950 as a "captain of industry," and like Doolittle he began to gather all sorts of honors and salutations from everything from American Legion branches to Rotary Clubs. He hobnobbed with other captains of industry, as well as movie stars, politicians, and sports figures, and he had his own table at New York's 21 Club.

---

* Later, when both the Soviets and the Chinese began acting aggressively toward the United States and other democracies, Rickenbacker admitted he'd been wrong and resumed his abiding hatred of communism.

† One bane for Rickenbacker was the question of stewards versus stewardesses. He preferred the men because, he said, the women soon marry, have children, and quit. However, since flying catered largely to businessmen, who preferred stewardesses, by the 1950s all of the airlines used ("the girls") women.

He and Adelaide had grown somewhat apart, mainly because Eddie was constantly traveling. As their boys, David and Bill, moved out, married, and began families of their own, Eddie and Adelaide began an almost nomadic existence, living in hotel apartments all over New York's Upper East Side. At times they occupied suites at the Carlyle, Park Lane, Stanhope, Dorset, Regency, and the Waldorf Astoria. Eddie also bought a 2,700-acre ranch in Texas, complete with an imposing hacienda, but after eight years he donated the entire spread to the Boy Scouts because he said he wasn't using it enough.[4]

In 1959, at the age of seventy, and with Eastern still showing considerable profits, Eddie stepped down as president, though he remained chairman of the board of directors. Thus began a period of the airline's decline, as it slipped into unprofitability because of union strikes, inflation, rising labor costs, and increased competition and regulations from the Civil Aeronautics Board. Physically, Eddie's health was remarkable (during the New York City blackout of 1965 he walked up twenty-one flights of stairs to his apartment at the Regency on Park Avenue), considering that for much of his life he smoked several packs of cigarettes a day and drank copious amounts of bourbon.* His friends were now dying away at an alarming rate and one day, without even a vow, he simply stopped drinking and smoking because "it no longer did anything for him."[5]

Neither did New York, so he moved to Florida. He and Adelaide had for some time maintained a large home in Coral Gables but sold it for a private villa in the old Key Biscayne Hotel, which was located on the ocean just down the Rickenbacker Causeway from Coral Gables. It was a little island paradise with a golf course, pool, broad lawns, and palm trees swaying in the ocean breezes. In October 1972, only weeks after celebrating his fiftieth wedding anniversary, Eddie suffered a major stroke, which required a dangerous operation. He survived it, however, as well as kidney damage, but he had lost the ability to talk. This latter he quickly regained with the aid of a speech therapist at a nursing home.

The following summer he told Adelaide he wanted to go to Switzerland and see where his parents had been born. She agreed to go,

---

* It has been said that his drinking was partially a cause of his leaving Eastern.

too, because there was also hope Swiss doctors could find some relief for her fading eyesight. In Zurich, before they could get into the countryside, Eddie suffered a period of irregular breathing. The doctors diagnosed pneumonia. Three days later he was dead. At eighty-two he had used up the lives of a dozen cats but couldn't escape what he always referred to as "the old man with the knife on the stick."

His body was cremated and even though as a Medal of Honor recipient he could have been buried at Arlington he had chosen to be laid to rest in Columbus, Ohio, beside his parents. General Jimmy Doolittle gave the eulogy at the funeral service, praising Eddie for his "courage, humanity, patriotism, and integrity."

"I have known him for over half a century," Doolittle said, "and I cannot conceive of his 'warping a fact,' " adding that "he believed he was his brother's keeper."

After the interment, four sleek jet fighters from the 94th Aero came out of the clouds, and as they reached the cemetery the lead ship zoomed straight up and out of sight in the missing leader formation. At the reception afterward, family and friends remarked on it, agreeing, "Captain Eddie would have liked that."

THROUGHOUT THE FINAL YEAR of the war Lindbergh continued working with United Aircraft as a test pilot. He likewise retained his status as a military technician, and less than two weeks after Germany surrendered in May of 1945 he was once more pressed into duty in concert with the U.S. Navy to study German advances in rocketry and jet propulsion. On May 17 he arrived in Mannheim, which had been wrecked so badly by Allied bombing that it reminded Lindbergh of a Dalí painting.

For security's sake he was dressed like a GI, complete with boots and overseas cap, and for protection he carried a .38 automatic in a shoulder holster.* In Munich he found more of the same, so that "you felt it would take a century to rebuild and reorganize." Everywhere, there were

---

* Even after the unconditional surrender there were reports of sniping and German "werewolves"—bitter Nazis who vowed sabotage even after losing the war.

hungry or starving Germans—men, women, and children—but Allied regulations forbade "fraternization," which included handing out food, cigarettes, or candy. Lindbergh thought that was not only cruel but stupid and frequently broke the rules.

In a military jeep Lindbergh visited Berghof, in Berchtesgaden, Hitler's mountain retreat in the Bavarian Alps. The house had been bombed to rubble, the kitchen floor blanketed with shards of broken china, and there was the distinctly unpleasant odor of dead bodies. He had dinner with officers of the occupying U.S. Army at one of Göring's houses on a lake.* He even drank some of Göring's Rhine wine, which he found had "an exceptionally fine flavor."

He located the redoubtable professor Willy Messerschmitt, designer of the famous German Messerschmitt warplanes, living in a hovel. Messerschmitt had developed the world's first jet engine, and the appearance of German jet fighters in combat late in the war had seriously alarmed the Allies because of their speed and agility. Both Doolittle and Rickenbacker, in fact, had gone into great detail on them in their reports. Messerschmitt told Lindbergh that the Me 262 twin-engine jet had been ready for production in 1938 but Hitler wasn't interested. He prophesied that in the future travel time for passenger jets between Europe and the United States would be one to two hours. Lindbergh asked if Messerschmitt was interested in working in America. He was.

Likewise, the head of German jet and rocket development, Dr. Helmut Schelp, was living in a nondescript single-story house near Munich, surrounded by an American rifle platoon bristling with automatic weapons. A team of Russians, it seemed, had moved in next door to Schelp and it was feared they intended to kidnap him into their territory, as they had been doing with other top German scientists. Lindbergh tried to persuade Schelp to come to America also, but he was frightened because his wife and child were in Dresden, which was within the Russian zone.

Lindbergh located a BMW factory that had been manufacturing jet engines and arranged for a number of them to be shipped to the United

---

* Göring was a prisoner and committed suicide by cyanide in order to escape the hangman after his conviction for war crimes by the Allied court.

States. While he was there a man came up and said that as the Allied armies neared he had been given the plans and drawings for numerous jet engines and told to destroy them. Instead he had buried them in the woods. This man was put in Lindbergh's jeep and driven to the forest where they soon dug up a treasure trove of secret German engine plans.

Lindbergh drove through the Harz Mountains, notorious for harboring former SS snipers, to Nordhausen where the Germans made the V-2 rockets that had so traumatized London. In the process he stumbled on a Nazi death camp known as Dora. There he saw the furnaces and a vast pit of ashes and charred human bones. One of the former inmates told him they killed "twenty-five thousand in a year and a half." A rotting body of a man, left lying on a stretcher beside the ovens by Germans fleeing the Russian onslaught, testified to the gravity of the inmate's claim.

During his stay in Germany, which was before the Russians could occupy all of the German territory to which they were entitled under the surrender agreement, Lindbergh helped arrange for dozens of German rocket and jet propulsion scientists and their families to evacuate to the American side and later to the United States, where they brought their expertise in the fields of jet passenger travel, ballistic missiles, and, eventually, the moon rocket. Wherever the Soviets had consolidated their occupation, they machine-gunned anyone trying to cross into American territory. The riverbanks on the Russia side were littered with bodies, including that of a little girl, age about seven, according to the U.S. Navy commander in charge of the occupation.[6]

For years after the war Charles was haunted by the death and destruction he had seen, the dead, mutilated corpses of Japanese soldiers, the rubble of so many historic German cities, the Nazi concentration camp with its grisly furnaces and pit of bones. He regularly prayed for the soul of the Zero pilot he had killed. At Nordhausen in the enormous whitewashed catacombs that the Germans had carved into the Harz, he had seen the V-2 rockets, nearly five stories tall, that had been launched at England by the thousands with enough explosives to shatter a city block. "Who would imagine finding this demon of sheer space hiding in a mountain like a giant grub?" he asked afterward, reflecting that Nazism had been "a strange mixture of blindness and vision, patriotism and hatred, ignorance and knowledge."

In Lindbergh's life, flight had meant freedom, progress, a step toward the human good, but the war had changed that for him. In 1947 he flew over Hiroshima, still flat, prostrated, tens of thousands of people incinerated simply by the push of a button. He shuddered to think there was a reverse side of science, of flight, that was a pit of dark horror and could be used to wipe out mankind itself. "That is why I have turned my attention from technological progress to life, from the civilized to the wild," he declared.[7]

Ever restless, Lindbergh traveled the world, often raising money for environmental organizations. He was especially enthralled by East Africa and the teeming plains of Mount Kilimanjaro, spent time in the gloomy jungles of Borneo, and also returned to investigate New Guinea and its primitive tribal culture. This did not mean, however, that he had completely given up on aviation. He became a consultant to W. Stuart Symington, secretary of the new air force, and worked with the Strategic Air Command, as well as serving on a top secret committee examining America's vast arsenal of weapons.

He returned to writing and in 1948 published *Of Flight and Life,* with Charles Scribner's Sons, which became an immediate best seller, surprising since he had once been so reviled by a large segment of the population. It was a quixotic little book based on edgy experiences in his life—the faulty oxygen gauge in the P-47 over Willow Run that nearly killed him; the Japanese Zero that got on his tail in the Pacific; the ruins he had seen in Germany after the war; Nazism, he said, "was scientific truth, unbalanced by the truths of religion. The German scientists had partaken of a fruit from which death had surely followed."

Like Jimmy Doolittle and Eddie Rickenbacker, during this period an array of honors was flung Lindbergh's way—the prestigious Wright Brothers Memorial Trophy, the Daniel Guggenheim Medal, and an interview that put him on the cover of *Newsweek,* revealing his war record. By now it was twenty-five years since the historic Paris flight. The administration not only restored his military rank but, upon the recommendation of President Dwight D. Eisenhower, he was made a general.

In 1953 *The Spirit of St. Louis,* Lindbergh's own story of the 1927 flight, was published by Scribner and became at once a massive best seller, with favorable reviews everywhere. It was serialized in the *Saturday Evening Post* for $100,000 and bought for the movies by Billy Wilder's production company for $200,000 and 10 percent of the first gross dollar—an almost unheard of Hollywood concession—and made into a major motion picture starring Jimmy Stewart as Charles. To top it off, he was awarded the Pulitzer Prize that year.

The following year Charles's mother, Evangeline, passed away at the age of seventy-eight. Ever proud of her son, she had lived out her life as a high school chemistry teacher in Detroit. Three months later Anne's mother, Elizabeth "Betty" Morrow, died at eighty-one. Both women had left a positive and lasting impression on their children.

The resurrection of all of this publicity, however, had an adverse effect on Anne. Charles was habitually gone much if not most of the year, and too often Anne found herself on crying jags. A successful author in her own right, she was once more completely overshadowed by her husband. "The boom days are here again," she told her diary upon the publication of *The Spirit of St. Louis.* "The Great Man—the Great Epic—the Great Author, etc. etc. I am living in the aura of 1929 again. Only I am different."

Whether there was a tinge of jealousy there, or merely frustration, something drove Anne into psychoanalysis, and the same thing doubtless drove her into an affair with her psychiatrist Dr. Dana W. Atchley, whose own marriage was crumbling. Lindbergh apparently never knew about this assignation and after a while Anne ended it, recommitting herself to Charles and a life she had come to hate.

They did not as much fight, it seems, as simply grow apart. He went his way and she went hers, except on those frequent formal occasions such as weddings, funerals, and White House dinners—for a variety of presidents both Democrat and Republican—where they were expected to arrive as man and wife. They had long since gotten rid of the place at Illiec, and Charles built a chalet for Anne in Switzerland, while he kept a modest house on the island of Maui, in Hawaii, which he called home.

All the while Lindbergh brooded whether "the fascinating life I've led, taking part in man's conquest of air and space," had not instead unleashed some Frankenstein monster upon the world. There was an "overemphasis on science," he said, "that weakens the human character, and upsets life's balance." He went into the Rift Valley in Kenya and lived with a nomadic Maasai tribe to try and discover what kind of culture clash aviation had brought to these people. He became an officer with the newly formed World Wildlife Fund, which had begun publishing an "endangered list" of animals subject to extinction because of human intrusions. He flew around the world half a dozen times a year, visiting exotic places and gathering information for reports on imperiled species, and he became a conservation icon after he declared, "I would rather have birds than airplanes."[8]

Lindbergh called the Vietnam War "a bad battlefield, badly chosen," but as a loyal military man and staunch anticommunist he refused to condemn it.[9] When in 1967 his son Scott declared he was giving up his American citizenship to avoid the draft, Lindbergh lambasted him as ungrateful and irresponsible and threatened to cut him off financially.

In 1969 Lindbergh was asked by the astronaut Neil Armstrong, whom he and Anne had met at a dinner in the Lyndon Johnson White House, to be his guest of honor for the launching of Apollo 11, the moon shot. Immediately after, however, Lindbergh journeyed to the remotest part of the Philippines in order to study a tribe of cavemen who had just been discovered. The contrast could not have been greater. Lindbergh seemed increasingly swayed toward primitive, esoteric, even mystical cultures; sometimes he was known to wade Long Island Sound perfectly nude except for mud he'd smeared on his privates.

In 1972 he was diagnosed with lymphoma, a dangerous form of blood cancer, and underwent radiation that seemed to put the disease into remission. He continued working with the World Wildlife Fund, soliciting big donations from the many wealthy friends he had made along the way. In 1974 the cancer returned and he was treated with chemotherapy in New York. It was too late this time, however, and the condition was diagnosed as fatal. Lindbergh said he wanted to "go home," to Maui. The doctors thought he was much too sick and would die on the way, but they at last relented and he was put aboard a plane on a stretcher and flown west.

He lingered for a month, surrounded by family and friends, and conferred constantly with Anne and the children about his funeral service and burial. He'd acquired a plot of land nearby, overlooking the sea, and he said he wanted his coffin to be built of native wood, constructed locally, rough sawn, and rectangular. The pallbearers would be local workers and the mourners confined to people he had made friends with on the island. He went into minute detail on how the inside of the coffin was to be lined. For a headstone he ordered a slab of granite that would contain his name, dates of birth and death, and a verse from the 139th Psalm, the one that begins, "If I take the wings of the morning . . ."

He wanted a short burial service with a Hawaiian hymn and prayer from the Navajo, as well as readings from Saint Augustine, Gandhi, and Isaiah. He died on August 26, a Monday, and the services were carried out as ordered.[10] To the last, as usual, Charles Lindbergh was in control. It was a fitting irony that one of the most celebrated Americans of the twentieth century would pass from the scene "in the utmost simplicity," as the *New York Times* noted, "far from the crowds that had hailed and repelled him in his lifetime."

ANNE LIVED ON TO THE RIPE AGE OF NINETY-FOUR, publishing a series of well-received books of her diaries and letters, covering the years from 1922 to 1986, and collecting numerous honorary degrees from colleges and universities, before succumbing to a stroke in 2001.

Charles had always been a man of many surprises, but perhaps none was more astounding than the revelation, three years after Anne had passed away, that between 1957 and 1967 he had fathered seven children by three different women in Germany. He supported these secret families until his death—one woman was a Prussian socialite, another a Bavarian hat maker, and the other was a sister to the hat maker who later took up residence in Switzerland. Considering the aura of sanctity that had surrounded Lindbergh almost like a cloud, the disclosure left people stunned and amazed. Word of the matter leaked out from the hat maker's niece, who had seen some letters Lindbergh had written, and naturally the media descended upon Lindbergh's American children for an explanation. There wasn't any, really, except from his youngest daughter, Reeve, who was as shocked as everyone else until she considered that "the arrangement made a certain kind of sense. No one woman could possibly have lived with him all the time."

Lindbergh was a frustrating man in many ways, but as he became older he apparently became obdurate to the extent that an atmosphere of tension invaded the household when he arrived, and departed with him when he left. Reeve Lindbergh put it this way: "I remember my father as a deeply intelligent and incredibly energetic man, a man of warmth and humor and charm and a kind of old-fashioned shy courtesy that I always attributed to his Midwestern upbringing." But, she went on, "I also remember my father as the most infuriatingly impossible human being I have ever known . . . when he was home his very presence often crowded and startled everyone else in the family, even the dog."[11]

That seems more or less what John Marquand had meant when he said of Lindbergh, "You've got to remember that all heroes are horses' asses." Marquand might have added, however—though it probably wasn't necessary—that being a horse's ass, or "infuriatingly impossible," for that matter, does not detract from the deeds of heroism themselves. In Lindbergh's case—the splendid Paris flight, his contributions to aviation, his service in World War II—the heroism was authentic.

I don't know why it is these days that this dirty linen has to be aired in books about otherwise decent and interesting people, but the public seems to demand it. On that account, in fairness, it becomes in order to take up the private lives of Jimmy Doolittle and Eddie Rickenbacker. A story about Doolittle having a fling has surfaced in a couple of books, including one by his granddaughter. The woman in question was a "New York model," who in 1940 or thereabouts threatened Doolittle with blackmail if he didn't buy her a fur coat. The versions vary in detail but both suggest that Doolittle interceded with Joe and confessed the affair, promising not to repeat it. For her part, Joe wrote a simple note to the woman in question that said, "Well, he never bought *me* a fur coat. I don't know how *you* could possibly expect one."[12]

As for Rickenbacker, during taped interviews in connection with his autobiography, the subject of extramarital affairs arose and was just as quickly put down with characteristic Rickenbacker taciturnity.

"I never had the time," he said. Nobody's disputed him yet.[13]

THE LIVES OF RICKENBACKER, LINDBERGH, AND DOOLITTLE give weight to the question: where do we find such men? Theirs, in fact, is the almost perfect American story; a tale straight from Horatio Alger but without the fabled gift of money to help things along. These men did it all themselves: they set the standards, assumed the risks, and flew like shooting stars across the arc of American history. They were raised in an age of horsecarts and buggies and lived to see men fly to the moon, and they could claim a part of that for themselves, because they were the pioneers. They were also the warriors, in the most dignified sense of the word—tough, smart, smooth, fair, patriotic, and fearless, because they managed to overcome their fears for the greater good.

When the terrible danger approached in the 1940s, these First World War–era aviators might have simply sat it out comfortably in their middle age and no one would have blamed them. Instead all three marched up and prepared to lay down their lives for their country.

They became heroes first when the nation needed heroes. Eddie Rickenbacker, in the most pitiless days of World War I while more than fifty thousand American doughboys died on the battlefields of France, emerged as the Ace of Aces, America's answer to the inimitable Red Baron, the German fighter pilot Manfred von Richthofen.

In the midst of the languid 1920s, when America had slipped back into isolationism and wallowed in indifference, Charles Lindbergh turned the light of the world upon the United States with a long-chance gamble from which few believed he would return.

And Jimmy Doolittle, in the horrible crisis months of World War II, came soaring out of the skies to jolt the Japanese empire to its bones, bolstering Allied spirits and confidence everywhere, and shaking loose a fabulous trove of military secrets that helped the Allies read the enemy's codes.

In their time, the three of them probably knew more about flying than all the collective knowledge in aviation history. They had graduated from cloth-and-wood flying machines in the dawn of human flight to steel and aluminum behemoths with thousands of horsepower and terrific firepower; they were truly among the first to "slip the surly bonds of earth and touch the face of God." They were giants who ruled the air. In their time few could have matched them, and years after they have died their dust still sparkles in the lore that binds the national trust.

Notes

★ ★ ★ ★ ★

2: The King of Dirt

1 Sources for Rickenbacker's air action are taken from Rickenbacker's *Fighting the Flying Circus* and *Rickenbacker: An Autobiography* and from transcriptions of taped interviews by Booton Herndon.

2 Details of Rickenbacker's childhood are taken from the Herndon transcripts; *Rickenbacker*; Finis Farr, *Rickenbacker's Luck: An American Life*; W. David Lewis, *Eddie Rickenbacker: An American Hero in the Twentieth Century*; and the Isabel Leighton transcripts.

3 Lewis, *Eddie Rickenbacker*.

4 For Rickenbacker's early career in the automotive business I relied principally on the transcripts from Herndon; a fifty-page transcript of an interview with Rickenbacker by an "unidentified interviewer," which is contained in the Rickenbacker Papers at Auburn University, Alabama; Rickenbacker's own published autobiography; and Lewis's *Eddie Rickenbacker*.

5 Details of Rickenbacker's racing career were gleaned from the Herndon transcripts; in two lengthy "unidentified interviewer" transcripts (Reel No. 4, side 2 and Reel No. 5, side 1) contained in the Rickenbacker Papers; Farr, *Rickenbacker's Luck*; *New York Times*, August 24, 1914; and published materials of the Sioux City (Iowa) Public Museum.

6 Hans Christian Adamson, *Eddie Rickenbacker*.

7 The varying details of Rickenbacker's epiphany are found in the Herndon transcripts; the "unidentified interviewer" transcripts; the Rickenbacker autobiography; Adamson, *Eddie Rickenbacker*; and Farr, *Rickenbacker's Luck*.

8 These details of Rickenbacker's personal life are included in Adamson's *Eddie Rickenbacker*.

9 Eddie's encounters with Glenn Martin and T. F. Dodd are chronicled in the Herndon transcripts, and by Adamson, Farr, and Lewis.

3: The Man with the Outside Loop

1 Details of Doolittle's youth and army life were guided principally by his autobiography, *I Could Never Be So Lucky Again*, which I cite as a general source rather than clutter the notes with *ibids* and *op cits*.

2 Quentin Reynolds, *The Amazing Mr. Doolittle*.

3 Sources for Mitchell and his famous court-martial are derived from the autobiographies of Doolittle and Rickenbacker and from Rebecca Maksel, "The Billy Mitchell Court-Martial," *Air and Space* (July 2009).

4 Reynolds, *The Amazing Mr. Doolittle*.

5 Information on Harry Guggenheim and the Guggenheim funds comes from the U.S. Centennial of Flight Commission.

4: Can Those Be Stars?

1 Lindbergh's flight to Paris is taken principally from his autobiographical *Spirit of St. Louis* and an earlier account by him published right after the flight, called *We*.

2 Lindbergh, *Lindbergh Looks Back: A Boyhood Reminiscence*. For the facts surrounding Lindbergh's youth and early flying experiences I relied on this and on earlier biographies by Ross, Mosley, Gill, Giblin, and Berg as well as Lindbergh's own passages in his *Autobiography of Values* and *Of Flight and Life*.

3 Various of the Lindbergh biographies and *Autobiography of Values*.

5: Air Combat Is Not Sport, It Is Scientific Murder

1 The original story of Rickenbacker's good-luck charms is included in *Eddie Rickenbacker* by Hans Christian Adamson.

2 Sources for the spy episode include Booton Herndon and the Herndon transcripts; Adamson, *Eddie Rickenbacker*; W. David Lewis, *Eddie Rickenbacker: An American Hero in the Twentieth Century*; Rickenbacker's autobiography; and the typewritten version of a story by *Los Angeles Times* auto racing writer Al G. Waddell, "Shadowed

by Scotland Yard," published in *Radco Automotive Review* in September 1929. Each of these versions diverges from the other in some fashion; I tried to make the best sense of it as I could.

3 Adamson, *Eddie Rickenbacker.*

4 The British agent is sourced in Herndon's transcripts; Rickenbacker's autobiography; Adamson, *Eddie Rickenbacker;* and H. Paul Jeffers, *Ace of Aces: The Life of Capt. Eddie Rickenbacker..*

5 Gunnery school details come from Herndon's transcripts and Rickenbacker himself.

6 Quentin Reynolds, *They Fought for the Sky.*

7 Hat in the Ring emblem creation comes from Rickenbacker's autobiography.

8 Kenneth Sydney Davis, *The Hero: Charles A. Lindbergh, the Man and the Legend.*

9 Rickenbacker's first combat patrol is documented in the Herndon tapes; Rickenbacker's autobiography; Davis; and Rickenbacker's *Fighting the Flying Circus.* Understandably, over time stories differ—stories even get better, as is their wont. I have tried here, where there are differences, to present the most likely scenario.

10 Rickenbacker's autobiography.

11 Lufbery's crash from ibid.

12 The account of the shooting down of Hall is taken from the Herndon transcripts; Rickenbacker's *Fighting the Flying Circus;* Rickenbacker's autobiography; Davis; and Finis Farr, *Rickenbacker's Luck.*

13 Rickenbacker, *Fighting the Flying Circus.*

14 Reynolds, *They Fought for the Sky.*

15 Rickenbacker and the Spad from Rickenbacker, *Fighting the Flying Circus.*

16 History of the 93rd's insignia by H. H. Wynne, *Cross & Cockade* (Spring 1960).

6: New York to Paris

1 A. Scott Berg, *Lindbergh.*

2 Ibid.

3 Ibid.

4 Lindbergh, *We, The Spirit of St. Louis.*

5 Lindbergh's dealings with the St. Louis business community and the airplane makers are detailed in his two autobiographies *We* and *The Spirit of St. Louis;* Berg, *Lindbergh;* and Walter Ross, *The Last Hero.*

6 The story of the building of the *Spirit of St. Louis* and its subsequent flight across the Atlantic is contained in Lindbergh's *The Spirit of St. Louis* and *We.*

7 The details of Lindbergh's acquisition of the *Spirit of St. Louis* and outfitting for his flight are contained in his autobiographical *The Spirit of St. Louis.*

8 The building and testing of the *Spirit* is contained in Lindbergh's autobiography and *The Spirit of St. Louis;* Berg, *Lindbergh;* and Ross, *The Last Hero.* Lindbergh's self-image is contained in his autobiographical *Of Flight and Life.*

9 New England's plentiful stones and rocks and boulders are the remains of the last ice age, debris that was pushed forward by the great glacier and known as a terminal moraine.

7: Man's Greatest Enemy in the Air

1 The source for this section, unless otherwise noted, is Doolittle's autobiography, *I Could Never Be So Lucky Again.*

2 Quentin Reynolds, *The Amazing Mr. Doolittle.*

3 Ibid.

4 Ibid.

5 Ibid.

6 Lowell Thomas and Edward Jablonski, *Doolittle.*

7 Ibid.

8 Dik Alan Daso, *Doolittle: Aerospace Visionary.*

9 Ibid.

10 Charles Lindbergh, *Autobiography of Values.*

11 W. David Lewis, *Eddie Rickenbacker: An American Hero in the Twentieth Century.*

12 A. Scott Berg, *Lindbergh.*

13 Doolittle, *I Could Never Be So Lucky Again.*

8: I Was Saved for Some Good Purpose

1 W. David Lewis, *Eddie Rickenbacker: An American Hero in the Twentieth Century.*

2 Ibid.

3 Ibid.

4 Finis Farr, *Rickenbacker's Luck.*

5 Lewis, *Eddie Rickenbacker.*

6 Quoted in ibid.

7 Farr, *Rickenbacker's Luck.*

8 Lewis, *Eddie Rickenbacker.*

9 H. Paul Jeffers, *Ace of Aces: The Life of Capt. Eddie Rickenbacker.*

10 Lewis, *Eddie Rickenbacker.*

11 Ibid.

12 Jeffers, *Ace of Aces.*

13 Lewis, *Eddie Rickenbacker.*

14 Ibid.

15 Cited from *Motor Age* (1923) in ibid.

16 Farr, *Rickenbacker's Luck.*

17 Dominic A. Pisano, "The Crash that Killed Knute Rockne," *Air and Space/Smithsonian* 6 (December 1991).

18 Quoted in *Smithsonian* (April 2013).

19 Ibid.

20 Ibid.

21 *New York Times,* June 26, 1941; Rickenbacker's autobiography; Lewis, *Eddie Rickenbacker.*

9: An Inspiration in a Grubby World

1 Leonard Mosley, *Lindbergh.*

2 *New York Times,* May 23, 1927.

3 Mosley, *Lindbergh.*

4 A. Scott Berg, *Lindbergh.*

5 Charles A. Lindbergh and Fitzhugh Green, *We.*

6 Ibid.

7 Mosley, *Lindbergh.*

8 Unpublished material from the diaries of Harold Nicolson, quoted in Mosley, *Lindbergh.*

9 Berg, *Lindbergh.*

10 Mosley, *Lindbergh.*

11 Betty Rogers, *Will Rogers* (University of Oklahoma Press, reprint [1941]).

12 Quoted in John Ward, *The Meaning of Lindbergh's Flight.*

13 All quotes here from ibid.

14 Berg, *Lindbergh.*

15 Ibid.

16 Charles Lindbergh, *The Spirit of St. Louis,* appendix.

17 Mosley, *Lindbergh.*

18 Ibid.

19 Ibid.

20 Ibid.

21 Berg, *Lindbergh.*

22 Ibid.

23 Anne Morrow Lindbergh, *Bring Me a Unicorn.*

24 Ibid.

25 Berg, *Lindbergh.*

26 Ibid; also Mosley, *Lindbergh.*

27 Anne Morrow Lindbergh, *Unicorn.*

28 Ibid.

29 Ibid.

30 Anne Morrow Lindbergh, *Hour of Gold, Hour of Lead.*

31 Ibid.

32 Ibid.

33 Ibid.; Berg, *Lindbergh;* Mosley, *Lindbergh.*

34 Berg, *Lindbergh.*

35 Ibid.

36 Anne Morrow Lindbergh, *Hour of Gold.*

37 George Waller, *Kidnap* (Dial Press, 1961); Berg, *Lindbergh;* Mosley, *Lindbergh;* and Anne Morrow Lindbergh, *Hour of Gold.*

38 Anne Morrow Lindbergh, *Hour of Gold.*

39 Walter S. Ross, *The Last Hero;* Berg, *Lindbergh;* Anne Morrow Lindbergh, *Hour of Gold.*

40 Mosley, *Lindbergh.*

10: His Halo Turned into a Noose

1 William Hoffman, The Doric Column, University of Minnesota, November 1998.

2 Susan Hertog, *Anne Morrow Lindbergh.*

3 Ibid; A. Scott Berg, *Lindbergh;* Edna Ferber, *New York Times,* January 28, 1935.

4 The account of threats is from Lindbergh's *Autobiography of Values.*

5 Berg, *Lindbergh.*

6 Lindbergh, *Autobiography of Values.*

7 The gist of the Lindberghs' trip to Germany is from *Autobiography of Values.*

8 Ibid.

9 Berg, *Lindbergh.*

10 Ibid.

11 Lindbergh, *Autobiography of Values.*

12 Ibid.

13 *Air Intelligence Activities,* Office of the Military Attaché, American Embassy, Berlin, German, August 1935–April 1939.

14 Max Wallace, *The American Axis;* Berg, *Lindbergh.*

15 Berg, *Lindbergh.*

16 Anne Morrow Lindbergh, *War Within and Without.*

17 Berg, *Lindbergh;* James P. Duffy, *Lindbergh vs. Roosevelt.*

18 Ibid.

19 Lindbergh, *War Within and Without.*

20 Duffy, *Lindbergh vs. Roosevelt.*

21 Leonard Mosley, *Lindbergh.*

11: The Raid

1 Quentin Reynolds, *The Amazing Mr. Doolittle.*
2 Duane Schultz, *The Doolittle Raid.*
3 Reynolds, *The Amazing Mr. Doolittle.*
4 Craig Nelson, *The First Heroes.*
5 Doolittle recounts this in *I Could Never Be So Lucky Again.*
6 Schultz, *Doolittle Raid.*
7 Lowell Thomas and Edward Jablonski, *Doolittle.*
8 Ted W. Lawson, *Thirty Seconds Over Tokyo;* transcript of interview with Edgar McElroy, Pacific Aviation Museum, Ford Island, Oahu, Hawaii, April 2011.
9 Joseph C. Grew, *Ten Years in Japan;* Schultz, *Doolittle Raid.*
10 Schultz, *Doolittle Raid.*
11 Ibid.
12 Lawson, *Thirty Seconds Over Tokyo.*
13 Edgar McElroy interview.
14 The official Web site of the Doolittle Raiders, www.doolittleraider.com.
15 Nelson, *The First Heroes.*
16 Lt. Col. Robert G. Emmens, *Guests of the Kremlin* (New York, 1949).
17 Thomas and Jablonski, *Doolittle.*
18 Schultz, *Doolittle Raid.*
19 Thomas and Jablonski, *Doolittle.*
20 Winston Groom, *1942* (New York, 2004).
21 David Kahn, *The Codebreakers* (New York, 1967).

12: We Were Slowly Rotting Away

1 Rickenbacker, *Rickenbacker.*
2 *New York Times* obituary, September 12, 1968.
3 W. David Lewis, *Eddie Rickenbacker: An American Hero in the Twentieth Century.*
4 Lewis, *Eddie Rickenbacker;* Finis Farr, *Rickenbacker's Luck.*
5 Hans Christian Adamson, *Eddie Rickenbacker.*
6 Lewis, *Eddie Rickenbacker;* interview with John Bartek; Booton Herndon transcripts, Special Collections and Archives, Auburn University.
7 James C. Whittaker, *We Thought We Heard the Angels Sing;* Adamson, *Eddie Rickenbacker.*
8 Adamson, *Eddie Rickenbacker;* Rickenbacker, *Seven Came Through.*
9 Rickenbacker, *Seven Came Through.*
10 Ibid; Booton Herndon transcripts.
11 Whittaker, *Angels Sing.*

12 Lewis, *Eddie Rickenbacker;* interview with Rickenbacker's son William.
13 Lewis, *Eddie Rickenbacker.*
14 Adamson, *Eddie Rickenbacker;* Booton Herndon transcripts.
15 Lewis conversation with William Rickenbacker.
16 Ibid.

13: The Lone Eagle Goes to War

1 Max Wallace, *The American Axis.*
2 A. Scott Berg, *Lindbergh.*
3 Charles Lindbergh, *The Wartime Journals of Charles A. Lindbergh.*
4 Anne Morrow Lindbergh, *War Within and Without.*
5 Lindbergh, *Of Flight and Life.*
6 Berg, *Lindbergh.*
7 Ibid.
8 Stephen Birmingham, *The Late John Marquand* (Philadelphia, 1972).
9 Charles MacDonald, "Lindbergh in Battle," *Collier's* (February 16, 1946).
10 Ibid.
11 http://www.charleslindbergh.com (*Lightning Strikes,* Ronald Yoshino).
12 MacDonald, "Lindbergh in Battle."
13 Ibid.
14 Yoshino, *Lightning Strikes.*
15 Lindbergh, *Wartime Journals.*
16 Leonard Mosley, *Lindbergh.*

14: Masters of the Sky

1 Paul W. Tibbets, *The Tibbets Story* (New York, 1978).
2 W. David Lewis, *Eddie Rickenbacker: An American Hero in the Twentieth Century.*
3 Ibid.
4 Ibid.
5 Finis Farr, *Rickenbacker's Luck.*
6 Charles Lindbergh, *The Wartime Journals of Charles A. Lindbergh.*
7 Lindbergh, *Autobiography of Values.*
8 A. Scott Berg, *Lindbergh.*
9 *Esquire* magazine (March 1971), cited in Berg, *Lindbergh.*
10 Berg, *Lindbergh.*
11 Reeve Lindbergh, *Forward from Here.*
12 Lowell Thomas and Edward Jablonski, *Doolittle;* Jonna Doolittle Hoppes, *Calculated Risk.*
13 Rickenbacker interview with Kincaid.

Notes on Sources and Acknowledgments

ALL THREE SUBJECTS OF THIS BOOK are no longer living so I felt fortunate that each in his lifetime had written an autobiography. It is often said that autobiographies are skewed to be self-serving, which is probably true, but a similar argument could be made about anything the subject says to an interviewer. I consulted a great many sources in the process of writing this book, which are listed in the bibliography.

In Rickenbacker's case I owe a debt of gratitude to Dwayne Cox, head of Special Collections and Archives at Auburn University, who was kind enough to provide me access to several thousand pages of Rickenbacker interviews over the years. These cover practically every aspect of his life, from his early racing days to World War I, the Rickenbacker Motor Company fiasco, Eastern Air Lines, his horrible airplane crack-up in Atlanta, and of course his ordeal in the Pacific. These papers constitute the basis for his 1967 autobiography *Rickenbacker,* written in collaboration with Booten Herndon. They were also central to the most comprehensive biography of Rickenbacker, written by the late W. David Lewis, history professor at Auburn University, and published in 2005. A 1979 biography of Rickenbacker by Finis Farr was also useful. On the Pacific ordeal, James C. Whittaker's account *We Thought We Heard the Angels Sing,* published in 1943, provides an interesting contrast to Rickenbacker's *Seven Came Through,* issued the same year.

Two years before his death in 1993, Jimmy Doolittle published an exhaustive autobiography, *I Could Never Be So Lucky Again,* in collaboration with the retired air force colonel Carroll V. Glines, who had previously written five books on the Doolittle raid and Doolittle himself. There is also a useful 1976 biography, called simply *Doolittle,* by the well-known broadcaster Lowell Thomas, a friend of Doolittle's, coauthored by Edward Jablonski. A fine little gem is *Doolittle: Aerospace Visionary* published in 2003 by Dik Alan

Daso. The raid itself has been covered extensively, most recently by Craig Nelson in *The First Heroes,* published in 2002, and by Duane Schultz in *The Doolittle Raid,* from 1988. Another very good read is the famous first-person account *Thirty Seconds Over Tokyo* by raider pilot Ted Lawson.

Unlike Doolittle and Rickenbacker, Charles Lindbergh did not collaborate with anyone but his editor on his autobiography and many other books. He was an amazingly facile writer, perceptive, sensitive, and incredibly observant. *The Spirit of St. Louis,* his almost stream-of-consciousness account of the 1927 Atlantic crossing, published in 1953, is riveting. As well, his *Wartime Journals* makes fascinating reading for anyone interested in the workings of Lindbergh's complicated mind. Here he gives a good account of his service in the Pacific flying U.S. fighter aircraft against the Japanese. Filling in the Lindbergh story were his books *We* (1927), *Of Flight and Life* (1948), *Lindbergh Looks Back: A Boyhood Reminiscence* (1972), and his *Autobiography of Values* (1976). Also highly literate, insightful, and useful to this story were the diaries of Anne Morrow Lindbergh covering the period from their meeting and marriage, in 1929, and ending five volumes later in 1986.

I have relied heavily on these various autobiographies, biographies, journals, interviews, and more to construct the narrative of this story but have chosen not to footnote every usage, which would clutter the notations in the individual chapters with a blizzard of *ibids*. Instead, I have annotated important direct quotes and also events that seemed so extraordinary they begged to be sourced. Fortunately there are many such events emanating from the extraordinary characters in this tale.

The Internet today provides a wealth of information if you are sufficiently versed in separating the wheat from the chaff. Back issues of many periodicals and newspapers, notably the *New York Times,* are available online for a fee and proved immensely helpful in framing the stories of these men.

I owe a deep debt of gratitude to my late literary agent Theron Raines, who died as this book was being finished. He read every word, as I wrote, up to his death. In the thirty-five years I was with him, Theron was a guide, inspiration, mentor, and friend. I shall miss him terribly. Theron's son Keith, who took over from his father, has been a comfort and a friend through it all.

My editor at National Geographic Books, Lisa Thomas, has been a whirlwind of editing, encouragement, and support and deserves a colossal note of thanks, as well as an all-expenses-paid two-month vacation wherever she wants to go. Line editor Andrew Michael Carlson proved himself again to be positively brilliant with the pencil, and Don Kennison, my copy editor of many years, has saved me from myself more times than I care to mention. I owe a deep debt of gratitude to stellar aviators Adam Shaw and John L. Marty, who read the manuscript and set me straight on the finer points of flying. As usual, my faithful executive assistant Dr. Wren Murphy once more organized a huge research project with skill, enthusiasm, and graciousness. Last but never least, my wife, Anne-Clinton Groom, deserves at least a Distinguished Flying Cross (with Oak Leaf Clusters) for putting up with me all these years.

WINSTON GROOM
Point Clear, Alabama, April 2013

BIBLIOGRAPHY

Adamson, Hans Christian. *Eddie Rickenbacker.* New York: Macmillan, 1946.

"American Squadron Is Flying Near Toul." *New York Times,* May 26, 1918.

Berg, A. Scott. *Lindbergh.* New York: G. P. Putnam's Sons, 1998.

Birmingham, Stephen. *The Late John Marquand: A Biography.* New York: Lippincott, 1972.

Burke, Kathleen. "Up and Away." *Smithsonian* 44, no. 1, April 2013.

Chang, Iris. *The Rape of Nanking: The Forgotten Holocaust of World War II.* New York: Penguin Books, 1977.

Chun, Clayton K. S. *The Doolittle Raid 1942: America's First Strike Back at Japan.* Oxford: Osprey, 2006.

Cole, Wayne S. *Charles A. Lindbergh and the Battle Against American Intervention in World War II.* New York: Harcourt Brace Jovanovich, 1974.

Consodine, Bob. Interviews of Rickenbacker: "Rick's Life." "Bob Consodine Story." "First Flight with Martin." "Talking Engine." "A. G. Waddel." "Scotland Yard." "War Service." Transcripts, 1965, Special Collections and Archives, Auburn University.

Copp, DeWitt S. *Forged in Fire: Strategy and Decisions in the Airwar Over Europe 1940–1945.* Garden City, NY: Doubleday, 1982.

Daso, Dik Alan. *Doolittle: Aerospace Visionary.* Washington, DC: Potomac Books, 2003.

Davis, Kenneth Sydney. *The Hero: Charles A. Lindbergh, the Man and the Legend.* London: Longmans, Green, 1950.

D'Olive, Charles R. History of 93rd Aero Squadron Insignia, at http://freepages.military.rootsweb.ancestry.com.

Doolittle, General James H., with Carroll V. Glines. *I Could Never Be So Lucky Again.* New York: Bantam Books, 1991.

Drury, David. World War I Flying Ace Raoul Lufbery, at http://connecticuthistory.org/world-war-i-flying-ace-raoul-lufbery.

Duffy, James P. *Lindbergh vs. Roosevelt: The Rivalry that Divided America.* Washington, DC: Regnery, 2010.

"Eddie Rickenbacker." *Life,* January 25, 1943.

Farr, Finis. *Rickenbacker's Luck: An American Life.* Boston: Houghton Mifflin, 1979.

First Pursuit Group History, May through July 1918, at http://acepilots.com/wwi/us.

Fisher, Jim. *The Lindbergh Case.* New Brunswick: Rutgers University Press, 1987.

"Flying Tank Defeats Ace." *New York Times,* May 21, 1918.

Franks, Norman. *American Aces of World War 1.* Oxford: Osprey, 2001.

Friedman, David M. *The Immortalists: Charles Lindbergh, Dr. Alexis Carrel, and Their Daring Quest to Live Forever.* New York: HarperCollins, 2007.

Gardner, Lloyd C. *The Case That Never Dies: The Lindbergh Kidnapping.* New Brunswick: Rutgers University Press, 2004.

Giblin, James Cross. *Charles A. Lindbergh: A Human Hero.* New York: Clarion, 1977.

Gill, Brendan. *Lindbergh Alone: May 21, 1927.* New York: Harcourt, Brace, 1977.

Glines, Carroll V. *Jimmy Doolittle: Daredevil Aviator and Scientist.* New York: Macmillan, 1972.

———. *The Doolittle Raid: America's Daring First Strike Against Japan.* Atglen, PA: Schiffer Military/Aviation History, 1991.

Grew, Joseph C. *Ten Years in Japan.* New York: Simon & Schuster, 1944.

Guttman, Jon. *USAS 1st Pursuit Group.* Oxford: Osprey, 2008.

Herndon, Booton. Rickenbacker interview transcripts: "Auto Racing." "Racing Death." "Atlanta Crash." "Indy Speedway Eastern Air Lines." "Fight with Roosevelt." "Fighter Pilot World War I." "Mission to China, Mideast, Russia." "Travel Home from Russia." "Criticism of B-17." "Mission to Russia." "British Plane." "Comet." "Britain World War II." "Moscow Trip." "Letters Re: Pacific Crash and Commendation." "Pacific Mission Crash." "Report to Stimson." "After World War II, 1930s." "Children, Ranch." "Glenn Martin." "Mrs. Rickenbacker's Diary." "Trip Around the World." "View on U.S. Government." "1962 Prediction of Things to Come." "Views on Big Government." "Communism." "Trips to North Africa, India, China." (Conducted 1965–1966.)

Hertog, Susan. *Anne Morrow Lindbergh: Her Life.* New York: Doubleday, 1999.

Highstone, Herbert H. "In Terms of Reliability, Nicolson Lies Lower Than Frank Harris." Review of Harold Nicolson, *Diaries and Letters,* at Amazon.com.

Hixon, Walter L. *Charles A. Lindbergh: Lone Eagle.* New York: Pearson Longman, 2007.

Hoppes, Jonna Doolittle. *Calculated Risk: The Extraordinary Life of Jimmy Doolittle—Aviation Pioneer and World War II Hero.* Santa Monica, CA: Santa Monica Press, 2005.

Jeffers, H. Paul. *Ace of Aces: The Life of Capt. Eddie Rickenbacker.* New York: Ballantine Books, 2003.

Kessner, Thomas. *The Flight of the Century: Charles Lindbergh and the Rise of American Aviation.* New York: Oxford Univeristy Press, 2010.

Kreis, John F., ed. *Piercing the Fog: Intelligence and Army Air Forces Operations in World War II.* Honolulu, Hawaii: University Press of the Pacific, 2004.

Larson, Bruce L. *Lindbergh of Minnesota: A Political Biography.* New York: Harcourt, Brace, 1971.

Larson, Erik. *In the Garden of Beasts: Love, Terror and an American Family in Hitler's Berlin.* New York: Crown, 2011.

Lawson, Captain Ted W. (edited by Robert Considine). *Thirty Seconds Over Tokyo.* New York: Random House, 1943.

Leighton, Isabel. Rickenbacker interview transcripts: "Love Affairs." "Auto Racing." "Views on Race." "Atlanta Crash." "Stops Flying." "Leadership." "Courtship, Marriage." "Germany, Udet." "Loss at Sea."

Lewis, W. David. *Eddie Rickenbacker: An American Hero in the Twentieth Century.* Baltimore: Johns Hopkins University Press, 2005.

Lindbergh, Anne Morrow. *Bring Me a Unicorn: Diaries and Letters of Anne Morrow Lindbergh, 1922–1928.* New York: Harcourt Brace Jovanovich, 1971.

————. *Hour of Gold, Hour of Lead: Diaries and Letters, 1929–1932*. New York: Harcourt Brace Jovanovich, 1973.

————. *Locked Rooms and Open Doors: Diaries and Letters, 1933–1935*. New York: Harcourt Brace Jovanovich, 1974.

————. *Flower and the Nettle: Diaries and Letters of Anne Morrow Lindbergh, 1936–1939*. New York: Harcourt Brace Jovanovich, 1976.

————. *War Within and Without: Diaries and Letters, 1939–1944*. New York: Harcourt Brace Jovanovich, 1980.

————. *Against Wind and Tide: Letters and Journals, 1947–1986*. New York: Pantheon Books, 2012.

Lindbergh, Charles A. *We, N-X-211*. New York: G. P. Putnam's Sons, 1927.

————. *Of Flight and Life*. New York: Scribner, 1948.

————. *Spirit of St. Louis*. New York: Scribner, 1953.

————. *The Wartime Journals of Charles A. Lindbergh*. New York: Harcourt Brace Jovanovich, 1970.

————. *Autobiography of Values*. New York: Harcourt Brace Jovanovich, 1976.

————. *Lindbergh Looks Back: A Boyhood Reminiscence*. St. Paul: Minnesota Historical Society Press, 1972, 2002.

Lindbergh, Reeve. *Forward from Here: Leaving Middle Age—and Other Unexpected Adventures*. New York: Simon & Schuster, 2008.

Lund, Lt. Col. Earle, USAF. The Battle of Britain: A German Perspective, at http://www.ibiblio.org/hyperwar/ETO/BOB/BoB-German/Bob.

MacDonald, Col. Charles. "Lindbergh in Battle." *Collier's*. February 16, 23, 1946.

Mason, John T., Jr., ed. *The Pacific War Remembered: An Oral History Collection*. Annapolis: Naval Institute Press, 1986.

McElroy, Edgar. Account of Doolittle Raid off the Hornet, 1942, at http://www.doolittleraider.com/raiders/mcelroy.htm.

Milton, Joyce. *Loss of Eden: A Biography of Charles and Anne Morrow Lindbergh*. New York: HarperCollins, 1993.

Mosley, Leonard. *Lindbergh: A Biography*. New York: Dover, 1976.

Nelson, Craig. *The First Heroes: The Extraordinary Story of the Doolittle Raid—America's First World War II Victory*. New York: Penguin, 2002.

Nicolson, Harold George, Sir. *Diaries and Letters*, ed. Nigel Nicolson. New York: Atheneum, 1966.

Reynolds, Quentin. *The Amazing Mr. Doolittle: A Biography of Jimmy Doolittle*. New York: Arno Press, 1952.

————. *They Fought for the Sky*. New York: Holt, Rinehart & Winston, 1957.

Richthofen, Manfred von. *The Red Fighter Pilot: The Autobiography of the Red Baron*. St. Petersburg, FL: Red and Black Publisher, 2007.

Rickenbacker, Edward V. *Seven Came Through: Rickenbacker's Full Story*. New York: Doubleday, 1943.

————. *Fighting the Flying Circus*. New York: Doubleday, 1965.

————. *Rickenbacker: An Autobiography*. New Jersey: Prentice Hall, 1967.

Ross, Walter S. *The Last Hero: Charles A. Lindbergh*. New York: Harper and Row, 1964.

Salisbury, Harrison Evans. *A Journey for Our Times: A Memoir*. New York: Harper and Row, 1983.

Schultz, Duane. *The Doolittle Raid*. New York: St. Martin's Press, 1988.

Serling, Robert J. *From the Captain to the Colonel: An Informal History of Eastern Air Lines.* New York: Dial Press, 1980.

Smith, Truman. *Berlin Alert: The Memoirs and Reports of Truman Smith,* ed., Robert Hesson. Stanford: Hoover Institution Press, 1984.

Thomas, Lowell, and Edward Jablonski. *Doolittle: A Biography.* New York: DeCapo Press, 1976.

Tuchman, Barbara W. *Stilwell and the American Experience in China, 1911–45.* New York: Grove Press, 1970.

"The Vivid Air." *Over the Front Review,* Winter 2007, at http://thevividair.blogspot .com/2008/03/review-over-the-front-winter.

Wallace, Max. *The American Axis: Henry Ford, Charles Lindbergh and the Rise of the Third Reich.* New York: St. Martin's Press, 2003.

Ward, John W. "The Meaning of Lindbergh's Flight." *American Quarterly* 20, no. 1, Spring 1958.

Watson, C. Hoyt. *Deshazer.* Coquitlam, B.C., Canada: Galaxy Communications, 1998.

Whittaker, Lt. James C. *We Thought We Heard the Angels Sing: The Complete Epic Story of the Ordeal and Rescue of Those Who Were with Eddie Rickenbacker on the Plane Lost in the Pacific.* New York: E. P. Dutton, 1943.

Wolk, Herman S. *Cataclysm: General Hap Arnold and the Defeat of Japan.* Denton, TX: University of North Texas Press, 2010.

Yoshino, Ronald. *Lightning Strikes: The 475th Fighter Group in the Pacific War, 1943–1945.* Manhattan, KS: Sunflower University Press, 1988.

Zorn, Robert. *Cemetery John: The Undiscovered Mastermind of the Lindbergh Kidnapping.* New York: Overlook Press, 2012.

Illustrations Credits

INDEX

Maps by Carl Mehler and Gregory Ugiansky, National Geographic.

Map Sources

General sources
Ballard, Robert D. *Graveyards of the Pacific: From Pearl Harbor to Bikini Atoll*. Washington, D.C.: National
Geographic, 2001.
Theater of War in the Pacific Ocean. Washington, D.C.: National Geographic, 1942.

Doolittle Raid
USS Enterprise CV-6 the Most Decorated Ship of the Second World War. Action Report (Serial 008)-18 April, 1942.
Available online at www.cv6.org/ship/logs/action19420418-88.htm.
USS Enterprise, Track from 1200 April 13 – 0800 April 21, 1942.
General Doolittle's Report on Japanese Raid April 18, 1942. Available online at www.ibiblio.org/hyperwar/AAF/rep/
Doolittle/Report.html.